The Right of States to Regulate in International Investment Law

International Arbitration Law Library

VOLUME 50

Editors

Professor Julian D.M. Lew QC has been involved with international arbitration for more than forty years as counsel, as arbitrator and as an academic. He is the founder and has been the Head of the School of International Arbitration, Centre for Commercial Law Studies, Queen Mary University of London since its creation in 1985. He is now an independent international arbitrator at 20 Essex Street, London.

Stavros Brekoulakis is Professor at Queen Mary University of London and an associate member of 3 Verulam Buildings (Gray's Inn). He is a leading academic in international arbitration and has led, or been involved in, several projects with ICCA, ICC Commission and ILA. He also acts as an independent arbitrator and has been appointed as chairman, sole arbitrator, co-arbitrator and emergency arbitrator under the rules of all the major arbitration rules.

Introduction

Since its first volume published in 1993, this authoritative practitioner-oriented series has published in-depth and analytical works on niche aspects of international arbitration, authored by specialists in the field.

Objective

This authoritative and established series covering in-depth analyses of niche areas appeals to both practitioners and academics. The series includes specific monographs and PhD dissertations of high quality, which are practical and cover issues not fully explored in general texts.

Frequency

A volume is published whenever an interesting topic presents itself.

The titles published in this series are listed at the end of this volume.

The Right of States to Regulate in International Investment Law

The Search for Balance Between Public Interest and Fair and Equitable Treatment

Yulia Levashova

Wolters Kluwer

Published by:
Kluwer Law International B.V.
PO Box 316
2400 AH Alphen aan den Rijn
The Netherlands
E-mail: international-sales@wolterskluwer.com
Website: lrus.wolterskluwer.com

Sold and distributed in North, Central and South America by:
Wolters Kluwer Legal & Regulatory U.S.
7201 McKinney Circle
Frederick, MD 21704
United States of America
Email: customer.service@wolterskluwer.com

Sold and distributed in all other countries by:
Air Business Subscriptions
Rockwood House
Haywards Heath
West Sussex
RH16 3DH
United Kingdom
Email: international-customerservice@wolterskluwer.com

ISBN 978-94-035-0931-0

e-Book: ISBN 978-94-035-1015-6
web-PDF: ISBN 978-94-035-1063-7

Table of Contents

Acknowledgements xi

CHAPTER 1
Introduction 1
§1.01 The Fair and Equitable Treatment and the State's Right to Regulate in Context 1
§1.02 The State of Art on the FET and the State's Right to Regulate in Legal Literature 6
[A] FET as an Embodiment of (i) The Concept of Justice and (ii) The Rule of Law 8
[B] FET Standard: The Case Law Approach 9
[C] Studies on the Right to Regulate in International Investment Law 11
[D] A Synthesis of the Literature in the Context of This Book 12
§1.03 Methodology 16

CHAPTER 2
International Investment Agreements and the Right to Regulate: An Introduction 19
§2.01 Introduction 19
§2.02 International Investment Agreements 19
§2.03 The Right to Regulate 24
[A] The Legal Basis of the Right to Regulate 25
[B] The Right to Regulate in IIAs 26
[C] The Right to Regulate in FET Investment Cases 34
[D] The Right to Regulate in Academic Literature 37
[E] Elements of the Right to Regulate 40
§2.04 Summary of the Chapter and the Interim Conclusions 44

CHAPTER 3
The Fair and Equitable Treatment Standard in International Investment Agreements 45
§3.01 Introduction 45
§3.02 Introduction of the FET Standard in International Law 45
§3.03 Categories of FET Standard Provisions in IIAs 48
[A] IIAs in Which the FET Standard Is Formulated as an Unqualified Treaty Standard 51
[B] IIAs in Which the FET Standard Provisions Include a Reference to a Norm of Unwritten International Law 52
[C] IIAs in Which the FET Standard Provision Is Qualified with Additional Content 59
[D] IIAs in Which the Preamble Provides a Reference to the FET Standard 64
[E] IIAs' Additional Agreement of the Parties on the Interpretation of the FET Standard 66
§3.04 Summary of the Chapter and Interim Conclusions 71

CHAPTER 4
Investment Jurisprudence on the FET Standard and the Right to Regulate: A General Overview 73
§4.01 Introduction 73
§4.02 The Interpretation of the FET Standard under the General Rule of Treaty Interpretation 75
[A] Ordinary Meaning of the Treaty 78
[B] Context of the Treaty 78
[C] Object and Purpose of the Treaty 81
[D] Subsequent Agreement and Subsequent Practice 84
§4.03 Supplementary and Subsidiary Means of Interpretation of the FET Standard 87
[A] The Preparatory Work of the Treaty and the Circumstances of Its Conclusion 87
[B] Previous Decisions of Investment Tribunals 89
[C] Reliance on Scholarly Writings 91
[D] Reliance on National Law 94
[E] Summary: The Interpretation and Application of the FET Standard 96
§4.04 General Principles of Law: The Role of Proportionality and Reasonableness 98
[A] Proportionality and Reasonableness 99
[B] Deference and the Margin of Appreciation 102
§4.05 Summary of the Chapter and Interim Conclusions 104

CHAPTER 5
Introduction to the Legal Conditions on the Right to Regulate Identified by Tribunals 107

CHAPTER 6
The State's Right to Regulate and the Legitimate Expectations of the Investor 113

§6.01 Introduction 113
§6.02 Early References to Legitimate Expectations in FET Investment Decisions 116
§6.03 Specific Representations Made by the Host State 123
[A] Introduction 123
[B] The Competence of the State Authority 124
[C] The Legal Force of the Specific Representations: (i) Their Legal Form, (ii) Their Content and (iii) Their Wording 126
[D] The Designation of the Investor in the State's Representations 132
[E] Specific Representations Arising from Contractual Commitments 134
[F] Summary: Defining Specific Representations 138
§6.04 The Nature and Impact of a Change to a General Regulatory Framework 140
[A] Introduction 140
[B] Claims Based on the Expectation of the Stability of a General Regulatory Framework 140
[C] The Level of the Impact on Investments Due to the Transformation of a General Regulatory Framework 143
[D] The Manner of the Transformation of a General Regulatory Framework by a Host State 144
[E] Summary: Expectations Concerning the Stability of a General Regulatory Framework 151
§6.05 The Factor of Special Economic and Sociopolitical Circumstances in a Host State 152
[A] Introduction 152
[B] Economic and Financial Crisis in a Host State 154
[C] The Sociopolitical and Economic Transition of Former Socialist Countries 157
[D] The Economic Challenge of an Electricity Tariff Deficit in the Renewable Energy Sector 158
[E] Summary: The Economic and Socio-political Circumstances in a Host State 162
§6.06 Investor's Conduct 162
[A] Introduction 162
[B] Due Diligence and Risk Assessment 163
§6.07 Summary of the Chapter and Interim Conclusions 166

CHAPTER 7
Conditions for a State to Lawfully Exercise Its Right to Regulate 173
§7.01 Introduction 173
§7.02 The Objective of the State's Measure 174
[A] Introduction 174
[B] The Legitimacy of the State's Objectives 174
[C] Protection of the Environment, Human Rights and Public Health 180
[D] The Illegitimacy of State Objectives 195
§7.03 Summary: The Host State's Objectives 200
§7.04 Assessment of the State's Measure 204
[A] The Principles of Reasonableness, Proportionality and the Prohibition of Arbitrariness in the Assessment of a State's Measure 205
[1] The Relationship Between a State's Measure and Its Objective 207
[2] The Possibility of Employing Alternative Measures in Achieving an Objective 210
[3] Loss Suffered by an Investor as a Consequence of a State's Measure 211
[B] The Principle of Non-discrimination in the Assessment of a State's Measure 212
[C] The Principle of Transparency in the Assessment of a State's Measure 215
[D] Summary: The Assessment of the State's Measure 218
§7.05 The Legality of the State's Measure under National Law 220
[A] Tribunals' Assessment of the Legality of a State's Measure under National Law 220
[B] Restrictive Assessment of National Law Violations in the Evaluation of the FET Standard 221
[C] Criteria for a Violation of the FET Standard by Breaching National Law 224
[D] Summary: The Legality of a State's Conduct under National Law 230
§7.06 Summary of the Chapter and Interim Conclusions 231

CHAPTER 8
Towards a More Balanced Approach 237
§8.01 Introduction 237
§8.02 The Right to Regulate in International Investment Law 238
§8.03 The IIAs' FET Standard Provisions in Connection with the Right to Regulate 240

§8.04 The Development and Interpretation of the FET Standard by International Arbitral Tribunals 243
§8.05 The Legal Conditions under Which States May Regulate in the Public Interest 246
[A] Introduction 246
[B] Conditions Focusing on the Legitimacy of an Investor's Expectations 246
[C] Conditions Focusing on the Lawfulness of the State's Measure 251
§8.06 The Reflection of FET Jurisprudence in the New Generation of IIAs 255
[A] Introduction 255
[B] The Extent of Codification of FET Investment Jurisprudence in the New Generation of IIAs 256
[C] The Balance Between the State's Right to Regulate and Investor Protection under the FET Standard in Recent IIAs and Investment Jurisprudence 268

ANNEX A
Selected Bilateral Investment Treaties 277

ANNEX B
Regional Treaties 281

ANNEX C
Categories of the IIAs' FET Standard Formulations 283

ANNEX D
Investment Cases 287

Index 291

Acknowledgements

This book is based on my doctoral thesis and the result of a challenging journey that started with a spark of interest in the field of international investment law during my early legal studies, which only deepened and strengthened over the years of research in this fascinating field. This book has been completed because of the input, support and guidance of many people.

I would like to express my gratitude to Professor Ige Dekker and Professor Tineke Lambooy LLM for their supervision and guidance. I would also like to thank Professor Stephan Schill, Professor Cedric Ryngaert, Professor Marleen van Rijswick, Professor Seline Trevisanut and Dr James Harrison for examining my doctoral dissertation and providing valuable comments.

I am grateful to my colleagues at Nyenrode Business University and Utrecht University who always encouraged and supported me throughout the writing of this book.

My gratitude also goes to Anna Ledvinka for her excellent editing work.

Most of all, my eternal gratitude goes to my family without whom I would not be able to complete this book. Thank you to my parents who have never doubted me and provided me with the unconditional love, support, help and encouragement through my entire life. I am grateful to my grandmother who is a true inspiration to me and my husband and two lovely daughters who brought light and perspective into my life while I was working on this book.

CHAPTER 1
Introduction

§1.01 THE FAIR AND EQUITABLE TREATMENT AND THE STATE'S RIGHT TO REGULATE IN CONTEXT

One of the most important pillars of investment protection under international law is the understanding that a foreign investor investing in a host state should be treated fairly and equitably.[1] The importance of this notion is supported by the inclusion of the fair and equitable treatment (FET) standard in virtually all current International Investment Agreements (IIAs), as well as its invocation in the vast majority of investment disputes.[2] The United Nations Conference on Trade and Development (UNCTAD) indicates in the World Investment Report of 2016 that in the investor-state cases filed in 2015, 'tribunals most frequently found breaches of the fair and equitable treatment provision ...'.[3] This implies that the host state's conduct, under an applicable

1. R. Klager, 'Revisiting Treatment Standards – Fair and Equitable Treatment in Light of Sustainable Development', in S. Hindelang, M. Krajewski (eds) *Shifting Paradigms in International Investment Law* (Oxford University Press, 2016) 65.
2. S. Schill, 'Fair and Equitable Treatment, the Rule of Law, and Comparative Public Law', in S. Schill (ed.) *International Investment Law and Comparative Public Law* (Oxford University Press, 2010) 151. Schill states that the FET standard features in 2,600 BITs and numerous regional and multilateral agreements; C. Henckels, Proportionality and Deference in Investor-State Arbitration (Cambridge University Press, 2015) 70. With reference being made to numerous scholars, Henckles indicates that the FET standard appears in most investment treaties and is the most frequently employed and most successfully argued standard. For more details on the FET standard in investment agreements, *see*: Chapter 3, which provides an analysis of FET standard provisions in IIAs.
3. UNCTAD, 'World Investment Report 2016' (2016) 107 http://unctad.org/en/PublicationsLibrary/wir2016_en.pdf accessed on 1 June 2018. *See also* A. Reinisch, Standards of Investment Protection (Oxford University Press, 2008) 2. According to Reinisch, 'investor claims involving breaches of FET standards have taken the pivotal position once occupied by claims for expropriation with approximately 62% of successful awards since 2006'.

IIA, was often found to be unfair and inequitable towards the foreign investor and its investments.[4]

A variety of FET standard provisions exist in international treaties.[5] A distinction is made between FET standard provisions that include a reference to the minimum standard of treatment (MST) of aliens under customary international law and unqualified FET standard clauses.[6] As will be demonstrated later in this study, in most IIAs the FET standard has been concisely formulated, simply requiring states to provide 'FET' to foreign investments.[7] As emphasised by Schreuer and Dolzer, from the early inception of the FET standard in IIAs, the purpose of this clause was to 'fill gaps that may be left by the more specific standards, in order to obtain the level of investor protection intended by the treaties'.[8]

In interpreting these openly formulated FET standard clauses, investment tribunals were faced with the task of defining the meaning and scope of the standard. This involved determining what conduct would give rise to responsibility and liability under the FET standard. In several investment decisions, especially in the early period of the decisions on the FET standard (approximately between 2000 and 2005), tribunals established a broad scope of a host state's obligations under the FET standard.[9] This included, e.g., the host state's obligation to act with full 'transparency' towards an investor,[10] to respect the 'legitimate expectations of the investor'[11] or to provide a

4. The structure and the content of IIAs is explained in Chapter 2, section §2.02.
5. *See* Chapter 3 for an overview and explanation of the different FET formulations found in IIAs.
6. The difference between the two formulations is explained in further detail in Chapter 2, section §2.02.
7. *See* Chapter 3. This finding is based on the research carried out in this study. It is also consistent with other sources. For example, according to the UNCTAD Mapping Project that includes 1,959 IIAs, 1,498 IIAs contain an unqualified FET standard provision; *see* UNCTAD 'IIA Mapping Project 2016' (2016) http://investmentpolicyhub.unctad.org/IIA/mappedContent#iiaInner Menu accessed on 1 June 2018.
8. R. Dolzer, C. Schreuer, Principles of International Investment Law (Oxford University Press, 2008) 122. *See also* T. Weiler, The Interpretation of International Investment Law: Equality, Discrimination and Minimum Standards of Treatment in Historical Context (Brill, 2013) 289. In discussing the US practice, e.g., Weiler observed that the FET standard has the potential of being a 'catch-all provision' from the very beginning.
9. M. Paparinskis, The International Minimum Standard and Fair and Equitable Treatment (Oxford University Press, 2013) 112. *See also* Sonarajah, who observed that 'the law on the fair and equitable standard is of recent vintage, created largely through interpretations placed on the phrase by arbitrators who favoured expansion.' M. Sonarajah, 'Fair and Equitable Treatment: Conserving Relevance', in M. Sonarajah (ed.) *Resistance and Change in the International Law on Foreign Investments* (Cambridge University Press, 2015) 247.
10. *Tecmed v. Mexico*, ICSID Case No. ARB(AF)/00/2 Award (29 May 2003) para. 167; Paparinskis has noted that in the *Tecmed* decision, 'the tribunal elaborated exacting requirements of legitimate expectations and transparency, flowing from fair and equitable treatment, without any obvious source.' M. Paparinskis, 'Good Faith and Fair and Equitable Treatment in International Investment Law', in A. Mitchell and others (eds) *Good Faith and International Economic Law* (Oxford University Press, 2015) 144.
11. Examples where the tribunal relied primarily on the breach of legitimate expectations in the assessment of the FET standard include *Eureko BV v. Republic of Poland* [2005] UNCITRAL Arbitration, IIC 98, Partial Award (19 August 2005) para. 235; *Azurix Corp. v. The Argentine Republic*, ICSID Case No. ARB/01/12 Award (14 July 2006); *CMS Gas Transmission Co. v. The Argentine Republic*, ICSID Case No. ARB/01/8 Award (12 May 2005) paras 274-276; *LG&E*

'stable and predictable legal and business framework'.[12] As Klager observed, the FET standard is like a 'black box full of surprises', the scope of its obligation being difficult to predict.[13]

The broad interpretation of the FET standard, as derived from several investment decisions, has led to concerns by states and international organisations that a broad interpretation of this provision has the potential to 'considerably constrain the state's sovereignty'.[14] These concerns have intensified further, particularly as a result of FET claims in which investors have challenged a variety of state decisions in publicly sensitive areas, e.g. renewable energy,[15] waste management,[16] public health issues[17] and access to water.[18] In this regard, tribunals have often been criticised for attaching insufficient weight in their assessment of the FET standard to a state's right to regulate.[19] The academic and policy discourse on the application of the FET standard

Energy Corp., LG&E Capital Corp. & LG&E International v. The Argentine Republic, ICSID Case No. ARB/02/1 Decision on Liability (3 October 2006); and others.

12. *Occidental v. Ecuador,* LCIA Case No. UN3467 Final Award (1 July 2004) para. 183. The tribunal stated that '[t]he stability of legal and business framework is thus an essential element of fair and equitable treatment.' *PSEG v. Turkey,* ICSID Case No. ARB/02/5 Award (19 January 2007) para. 253. The tribunal also asserted that '[t]he aggregate of the situations explained raise the question of the need to ensure a stable and predictable business environment for investors to operate in, as required not only by the Treaty but also by the Turkish Constitution as noted above.' *LG&E Energy Corp., LG&E Capital Corp. & LG&E International v. The Argentine Republic,* ICSID Case No. ARB/02/1 Decision on Liability (3 October 2006) para. 131. The tribunal concluded that the FET standard consists of 'the host State's consistent and transparent behavior, free of ambiguity that involves the obligation to grant and maintain a stable and predictable legal framework necessary to fulfill the justified expectations of the foreign investor'.
13. R. Klager, (2016) 67.
14. *Ibid.* This concern has been also expressed by the UNCTAD and the OECD. These organisations have published several research papers related to the right to regulate and the FET standard that were primarily based on the input of the Member States of these organisations. *See,* e.g., UNCTAD, 'Fair and Equitable Treatment: UNCTAD Series on IIAs II: A Sequel' (2012) xiiv http://unctad.org/en/Docs/unctaddiaeia2011d5_en.pdf accessed on 1 June 2018. The report states that the 'wide application of the FET obligation has revealed its protective value for foreign investors, but also exposed a number of uncertainties and risks.' *See also*: OECD, 'Addressing the Balance of Interests in Investment Treaties' (2017) Working Papers on International Investment (2017) 2017/03, 5 http://www.oecd-ilibrary.org/finance-and-investment/addressing-the-balance-of-interests-in-investment-treaties_0a62034b-en accessed on 1 June 2018. The report provides that 'FET has leapt to prominence in the last 15 years as the principal ground for liability at issue in many if not most of investment treaty arbitration claims. It also appears to be the substantive treaty provisions most often cited in debates about the impact of investment treaties on the right to regulate.'
15. *Charanne Construction v. Spain,* SCC Case No. 062/2012 Award (21 January 2016); *Eiser Infrastructure Limited and Energia Solar Luxembourg v. Spain,* ICSID Case No. ARB/13/36 Award (4 May 2017); *Isolux Netherlands BV v. Spain,* SCC Case V2013/153 Award (17 July 2016).
16. *Tecmed v. Mexico,* ICSID Case No. ARB(AF)/00/2 Award (29 May 2003); *Waste Management v. Mexico* (Case II), ICSID Case No. ARB(AF)/00/3 Award (30 April 2004).
17. *Philip Morris v. Uruguay,* ICSID Case No. ARB/10/7 Award (8 July 2016); *Apotex v. US,* ICSID Case No. ARB(AF)/12/1 Award (25 August 2014).
18. *Biwater Gauff (Tanzania) Ltd. v. United Republic of Tanzania,* ICSID Case No. ARB/05/22 Award (24 July 2008); *Suez and Interagua v. ArgentinaSuez, Sociedad General de Aguas de Barcelona, S.A.* and *Interagua Servicios Integrales de Agua, S.A. v. Argentine Republic* and *AWG v. Argentina,* ICSID Case No. ARB/03/17, Decision on Liability (30 July 2010).
19. K. Miles, The Origins of International Investment Law (Cambridge University Press, 2013) 168-172.

and the state's right to regulate has featured primarily in relation to certain elements attributed by the tribunals to the FET standard. These include (i) the legitimate expectations of investors and (ii) the obligation to provide a stable legal and business framework for investments.[20] The underlying conflict in this regard lies between an investor's expectation of a stable legal and business environment, which is essential for the planning of investments, and the legal power of host states to regulate in the public interest, particularly in the light of changing social, economic and political circumstances.[21] The Argentinian economic crisis that led to the devaluation of Argentinian currency and the creation of a wave of investment cases constitutes an example of such a sudden economic change.[22] Similarly, in a few investment cases, the preparation for the accession of several Eastern European states to the European Union (EU) resulted in a change of legislation in various sectors, adversely affecting investors and leading to several investment claims.[23]

This book addresses the balance between the host state's right to regulate and the investor's right to obtain the FET standard under an applicable IIA. In this book, the right to regulate is understood as a concept of international law that has its legal basis in the international legal principle of state sovereignty. This right is not absolute and can be limited by, e.g., the obligation to afford FET under an applicable IIA. The right to regulate is further explained in Chapter 2, which outlines several elements which are pertinent to this right.

Today, in the process of negotiating the new generation of investment agreements,[24] the issue of the right to regulate in the context of investment law is high on the

---

20. M. Paparinskis, (2013) 259; P. Muchlinski, '"Caveat Investor"? The Relevance of the Conduct of the Investor under the Fair and Equitable Treatment Standard' [2006] 55(3) *Cambridge International and Comparative Journal of International Law*, 527-558; M. Sonarajah, 'Fair and Equitable Treatment: Conserving Relevance', in M. Sonarajah (ed.) *Resistance and Change in the International Law on Foreign Investments* (Cambridge University Press, 2015) 246-299.
21. M. Valenti, 'The Protection of General Interests of Host States in the Application of the Fair and Equitable Treatment Standard', in G. Sacerdoti and others (eds) *General Interests of Host States in International Investment Law* (Cambridge University Press, 2014) 41.
22. *LG&E Energy Corp., LG&E Capital Corp. & LG&E International v. The Argentine Republic,* ICSID Case No. ARB/02/1 Decision on Liability (3 October 2006); *CMS Gas Transmission Co. v. The Argentine Republic,* ICSID Case No. ARB/01/8 Award (12 May 2005); *BG Group v. Argentina,* Final Award (24 December 2007); *Continental Casualty v. Argentina,* ICSID Case No. ARB/03/9 Award (5 September 2008); *AWG v. Argentina* [2010] UNCITRAL Arbitration, Decision on Liability (30 July 2010); and others.
23. *Ioan Micula v. Romania,* ICSID Case No. ARB/05/20 Final Award (11 December 2013); *Mr. Franck Charles Arif v. Republic of Moldova,* ICSID Case No. ARB/11/23 Award (8 April 2013); *Electrabel v. Hungary,* ICSID Case No. ARB/07/1 Decision on Jurisdiction, Applicable Law and Liability (30 November 2012) and *Electrabel v. Hungary,* ICSID Case No. ARB/07/1 Final Award (25 November 2015); *AES Summit v. Hungary,* ICSID Case No. ARB/07/22 Award (23 September 2010).
24. New generation of IIAs are those concluded after 2010. *See*: UNCTAD, Issue Note: Phase 2 of IIA Reform: modernising the existing stock of old generation treaties (6 June 2017) http://investmentpolicyhub.unctad.org/Publications/Details/173. For an example of the new generation of IIAs, *see*: the Draft Investment Chapter of the Transatlantic Investment and Partnership Agreement between EU and the US available at http://trade.ec.europa.eu/doclib/docs/2015/november/tradoc_153955.pdf. Both websites accessed on 1 June 2018.

political agenda of states.[25] The need to ensure that 'policy space' is preserved in the context of the FET standard has been articulated by negotiators and contracting states within the framework of several of the most recent agreements.[26] However, striking the right balance between the interests of host states and investors in these new treaty formulations has proved to be challenging.[27]

The complexities surrounding the FET standard are the result of (i) the plurality of legal regimes contained in thousands of IIAs, most of which have the open formulation of the FET standard and (ii) the diverse interpretations of the FET standard provided by multiple tribunals, most of them making decisions on the basis of different legal regimes.[28] The difficulty, which derives from this dynamic, is the lack of clarity regarding the legal conditions that apply to a host state's right to regulate, and as regards the application of the FET standard provisions in IIAs. As will be further outlined in the study, some states and arbitral tribunals have attempted – in FET cases – to clarify the scope of the FET standard in order to balance the FET obligation by providing sufficient policy space for host states to regulate and for investors to obtain protection under the FET standard.[29] This book aims to contribute to the effort in clarifying the legal conditions which apply to the right to regulate through analysing IIAs, the investment jurisprudence on the FET standard and the relevant literature. Therefore, the ultimate goal of this book is to analyse: how can a host state's right to regulate concerning the protection of a public interest be balanced against a host state's obligation to provide FET under international investment law?

25. *See* European Commission, Communication, 'Towards a Comprehensive European International Investment Policy', COM(2010) 343 Final (7 July 2010). The right to regulate has been placed as one of the main objectives of the EU in the negotiation of new types of investment and trade agreements. The communication provides that 'investment policy will continue to allow the Union, and the Member States to adopt and enforce measures necessary to pursue public policy objectives' and that 'principles and objectives of the European Union's external action more generally, including the promotion of the rule of law, human rights and sustainable development' (Article 205 TFEU and Article 21 TEU) (p. 9). Also *see*: European Commission, Communication, 'Trade for All: Towards a More Responsible Trade and Investment Policy', COM(2015) 497 Final (14 October 2015). The Communication emphasises 'promoting a new approach to investment'. And stating 'while boosting investment is at the heart of the Commission's economic priorities, investment protection and arbitration have triggered a heated debate about fairness and the need to preserve the right of public authorities to regulate both in the EU and in partner countries ...' (p. 14).
26. For EU agreements that have been already concluded, or currently in a semi-final state or under negotiation, the FET standard provision has been formulated as an exhaustive list of host state obligations. In the context of the Comprehensive Economic and Trade Agreement between Canada and the EU (CETA), the European Commission has explained this approach as an attempt to have a defined concept of FET that expresses precisely what this standard of treatment consists of, 'without leaving unwelcome discretion to the Members of the Tribunal'. European Commission, 'Investment Provisions in the EU-Canada Free Trade Agreement (CETA)' (Press Release, 3 December 2013) 2. http://trade.ec.europa.eu/doclib/docs/2013/november/tradoc_151918.pdf accessed on 1 June 2018.
27. *See* Chapter 3 in which recent FET standard provisions are evaluated and Chapter 8 in which some of the new formulations in recent treaties and their implications for the right to regulate are assessed.
28. *See* Chapter 4, section §4.01 for a further explanation of the complexities of the FET standard.
29. *See* Chapter 3, section §3.03[C] for examples of the new generation of IIAs' FET standard formulations and Chapters 6 and 7, where the case law on the FET standard is analysed from the perspective of the right to regulate.

§1.02 THE STATE OF ART ON THE FET AND THE STATE'S RIGHT TO REGULATE IN LEGAL LITERATURE

Legal research on the FET standard has been driven by the objective to conceptualise its content and application. There is consensus in the legal literature that the FET standard exhibits a lack of clarity in its meaning and scope.[30]

Being framed in most IIAs as simply an obligation to provide 'FET', this standard of protection has been labelled, among other characterisations, as 'generic and vague',[31] having a 'ubiquitous presence in investment arbitration',[32] and possessing a 'lack of clarity in its normative content'.[33] The absence of a definition of the FET standard in treaties has resulted in a broad range of different FET standard interpretations rendered by investment tribunals.[34] Hence, the ambiguity regarding the meaning of the FET standard has generated uncertainty with regard to the scope and limitations of the state's regulatory power directed at public welfare.[35]

In light of these developments, scholarship on the FET standard has emerged with the common objective to explain the application and interpretation of the FET standard in view of the growing jurisprudence. Two mainstream approaches in the analysis of the FET standard can be distinguished:

(1) One stream of literature has attempted to clarify the content and scope of the FET standard by developing a conceptual framework on the basis of legal doctrine.[36] A prominent example of this approach is the identification of the FET standard as an expression of the 'rule of law'.[37] Another example of this

30. R. Klager, Fair and Equitable Treatment in International Investment Law (Cambridge University Press, 2011) p. 4; S. Schill, (2010) 151; A. Diehl, The Core Standard of International Investment Protection: Fair and Equitable Treatment (Kluwer Law International, 2012) xxiv; P.J. Rodriguez, 'International Contractualism Revisited: Non-pecuniary Remedies under the Fair and Equitable Treatment Standard' [2018] 18 *Chicago Journal of International Law*, p. 675. 'At the center of the controversy is the fair and equitable treatment (FET) standard. A vaguely written phrase appearing in nearly every bilateral investment agreement currently in force, this standard has puzzled commentators and tribunals for years.'
31. *Mamidoil v. Albania*, ICSID Case No. ARB/11/24 Award (30 March 2015) para. 599.
32. R. Dolzer, 'Fair and Equitable Treatment: A Key Standard in Investment Treaties' [2005] 39 *International Lawyer*, 87.
33. S. Schill, (2010) 151.
34. A. Newcombe, L. Paradell, Law and Practice of Investment Treaties: Standards of Treatment (Kluwer Law International, 2009) 263.
35. L. Wandahl Mouyal, International Investment Law and the Right to Regulate: A Human Rights Perspective (Routledge, 2016) 16.
36. *See* S. Schill, who has conceptualised the FET standard as an embodiment of the rule of law; S. Schill, (2010). *See also* R. Klager who argues that the FET standard is the embodiment of justice; R. Klager, (2011). Other theories include the FET standard as representing the concept of good faith; *see* T.J. Grierson-Weiler, I. Laird, 'Standards of Treatment', in P. Muchilinski and others (eds) *The Oxford Handbook of International Investment Law* (Oxford University Press, 2008) 272; *see also* the discussion on this topic in M. Paparinskis, (2015) 143.
37. S. Schill, (2010) 154; *See also* K.J. Vandevelde, 'A Unified Theory of Fair and Equitable Treatment' [2010] 48 *International Law and Politics*, 52. Vandevelde also conceptualises the FET standard as a rule of law concept. He articulates four principles, namely 'reasonableness, consistency (or security), nondiscrimination, and transparency' which constitute the core component of the rule of law and an expression of the FET standard.

approach is the scholarly work that defines the FET standard as an 'embodiment of justice within the system of international investment law'.[38] In both conceptualisations of the FET standard, several recurring elements in investment jurisprudence on the FET standard (e.g., legitimate expectations)[39] have been identified. Furthermore, these elements are analysed within the broader theoretical framework reflected in a theory of justice and the concept of the rule of law. Later in this Chapter, a more detailed explanation of these approaches is provided.

(2) The second stream of literature does not focus on developing a theory for the analysis of the FET standard but is based on the premise that the 'reasoning of each arbitral decision is specific to the factual matrix before the tribunal.'[40] As such, it is understood that the content of FET standard can be attained through the identification of certain FET standard elements and a comparison of the decisions on each element.[41] For example, Valenti asserts that the 'appropriate methodology to deal with the standard consists then in distinguishing different fact-specific situations to which it applies and intensifying the ensuing obligations.'[42]

Despite the different approaches towards the FET standard adopted in the aforementioned studies, the question that has been raised in the literature directly as well as indirectly, and which is particularly pertinent for this book, is the scope of the FET standard vis-à-vis a state's right to regulate.[43] The question has been formulated by Klager, who queries the extent to which 'fair and equitable treatment should enable arbitral tribunals to review sovereign acts of host states interfering with the business of foreign investors'.[44] Valenti has conveyed this enquiry in terms of host state obligations, by posing the question: 'when exactly is the host state's conduct towards the foreign investor to be considered unfair and inequitable?'[45] Scholars representing the aforementioned streams of literature have attempted to provide answers to these enquiries. The arguments of both these approaches are the subject of the discussion in the following section.

---

38. R. Klager, (2011) 153.
39. Legitimate expectations became a term of art used by investment tribunals and in the literature. *See* Chapter 6 discussing the legitimate expectations of the investor.
40. J. Bonnitcha, Substantive Protection under Investment Treaties: A Legal and Economic Analysis (Cambridge University Press, 2014) 166; Also *see*: R. Dolzer, 'Fair and Equitable Treatment: Today's Contours' [2014] 12(1) *Santa Clara Journal of International Law*, 15. Dolzer argues that the arbitral tribunals have succeeded in clarifying the content of the FET standard via 'groups and clusters of sub-groups with more defined contours'; M. Valenti, (2014) 33; C. Schreuer, 'Fair and Equitable Treatment in Arbitral Practice' [2005] 6(3) *The Journal of World Investment and Trade*, 357-386.
41. J. Bonnitcha, (2014) 167.
42. M. Valenti, (2014) 33.
43. *Ibid.*, p. 26. Valenti observes that 'a "debate" about the scope of the standard has therefore evolved at different levels, namely at the level of arbitral tribunals which apply the FET that led to jurisprudence that was not always consistent; at the level of scholarship; and at the level of states which support a specific position while negotiating the IIAs.'
44. R. Klager, (2011) p. 4.
45. M. Valenti, (2014) 35.

[A] FET as an Embodiment of (i) The Concept of Justice and (ii) The Rule of Law

(i) The literature provides a general conceptual framework for understanding the FET standard; it does not, however, clarify the scope of the right to regulate in the context of the FET standard. Klager, in classifying the FET standard as a concept of justice, refers to six competing substantive principles or objectives applied in investment cases. The principles identified by Klager are sovereignty, legitimate expectations, non-discrimination, sustainable development, fair procedure and transparency.[46] He argues that a certain level of coherence has to be found between the arguments derived from these competitive principles or objectives in order for the decision of a tribunal on the FET standard to be legitimate. The sovereignty principle constitutes a counterbalancing factor against the interests of foreign investors. The regulatory space of states has limitations and, as such, the 'allocation of the specific weight of sovereignty in relation to other principles involves a balancing act by arbitrators.'[47] Klager argues that in performing this balancing exercise, 'tribunals [should] display the criteria for the specific weight allocation in the most transparent way possible.'[48] There is limited attention in the study for the criteria that should be provided by tribunals that would allow for different interests to be properly weighed against each other.

(ii) In a similar vein, Schill identifies seven clusters generated from the FET standard as an embodiment of the rule of law found in major domestic legal systems, namely stability, predictability and consistency, legality, the protection of legitimate expectations, administrative due process and an absence of the denial of justice, protection against arbitrariness and discrimination, transparency and reasonableness and proportionality. In the context of investment law, he argues that the identified clusters are 'expressions of the broader concept of the rule of law found in major legal systems' that frequently appear in investment decisions.[49] Schill claims that the FET standard should be considered as a 'public law concept with quasi-constitutional ramifications that conditions the conduct of states *vis-à-vis* foreign investors'.[50] He also proposes the use of a comparative public law method. This method is based on the premise that the challenges of investment arbitration are not new. For example, the 'legitimate expectations' doctrine has not just appeared in international investment law; it is also known in other fields of international, European and domestic legal systems. As such, by comparing the arising issues and obtaining inspiration

46. R. Klager, (2011) 154-256.
47. *Ibid.*, 164.
48. *Ibid.*
49. M. Jacob, S. Schill, 'Fair and Equitable Treatment: Content, Practice, Method', in M. Bungenberg and others (eds) *International Investment Law: A Handbook* (Beck/Hart, 2015) 719.
50. M. Jacob, S. Schill, (2015) 761.

from other, more developed legal subjects, clarification and a better understanding of the public law concepts can be attained.[51] In this way, tribunals can achieve a better balance between the interests of host states and foreign investors. But, as noted by several commentators, the transplantation of the rule of law concept into investment law generates a range of new questions, e.g. the choice of comparative legal systems and the criteria for selecting unified elements among the different perceptions of the rule of law concept.[52]

[B] FET Standard: The Case Law Approach

The literature that conceptualises the FET standard on the basis of the case law has proposed several criteria that impose conditions on the state's right to regulate. For example, Dolzer, on the basis of arbitral jurisprudence, has unfolded the FET standard by presenting a series of casuistic subgroups that impose conditions on the state's regulatory conduct. These include:

> (1) good faith in the conduct of a party; (2) consistency of conduct; (3) transparency of rules; (4) recognition of the scope and purpose of laws; (5) due process; (6) prohibition of harassment; (7) a reasonable degree of stability and predictability of a legal system; and, in particular (8) recognition of the legitimate expectations on the part of the investor.[53]

Valenti defined the content of the FET standard through a group of 'elements'. According to Valenti, these elements derived from arbitral decisions in which tribunals applying the FET provisions in concrete cases 'progressively clarified the constitutive elements of the standard'.[54] These elements are: (1) 'the stability, consistency, predictability and transparency of the regulatory framework;'[55] (2) 'protection of the foreign investor's legitimate expectations;'[56] and (3) 'procedural fairness and due process'.[57]

Both Dolzer and Valenti observe that the emerged subcategories can be developed into an adequate tool for arbitrators to assist them in their interpretation of the FET standard in investment cases.[58] As Dolzer asserts, the current trend is that the FET standard is applied by tribunals on the basis of subcategories 'amenable to objective

51. S. Schill, (2010) 154.
52. For an analytical review of this theory, *see* R. Klager, Fair and Equitable Treatment in International Investment Law (Cambridge University Press, 2013) 125-127; J. Bonnitcha, (2014) 145; M. Sonarajah, 'Fair and Equitable Treatment: Conserving Relevance', in M. Sonarajah (ed.) *Resistance and Change in the International Law on Foreign Investments* (Cambridge University Press, 2015) 295.
53. R. Dolzer, [2014] 15.
54. M. Valenti, (2014) 33.
55. *Ibid.*, 39.
56. *Ibid.*, 48.
57. *Ibid.*, 52.
58. *Ibid.*, 55.

criteria tied to objective conduct on the part of the host state', rather than on subjective arguments on behalf of an investor.[59]

More elaborately, Bonnitcha uses a 'taxonomy' of FET standard elements to understand the interpretation of the FET standard rendered by tribunals. Within his taxonomy, decisions are differentiated into categories as follows: (1) decisions that deal with the investor's legitimate expectations; (2) decisions that review the state's conduct on procedural grounds; and (3) decisions that review the state's conduct on substantive grounds.[60] Each of these elements has the capacity to operate as a 'quasi-independent liability rule'.[61] On the basis of an analysis of the case law, Bonnitcha identifies various interpretations of the FET standard. These interpretations constitute disparate levels of protection for investors and fall under the three aforementioned categories of decisions. For example, under the decisions that review the investor's legitimate expectations, the four interpretations of legitimate expectations detected in investment jurisprudence by Bonnitcha are:

(1) The legal rights approach, in which legitimate expectations can only be based on the legal rights vested in the investor;
(2) The representations approach, in which legitimate expectations can be based on clear and specific unilateral statements made by the host state;
(3) The stability approach, in which legitimate expectations can be based on general regulations in force at the time the investment is made;
(4) The business plan approach, in which legitimate expectations can be based on an investor's business plan, if the host state knew of these plans.[62]

After revealing the different interpretations which are pertinent to each element of the FET standard (e.g., legitimate expectations), Bonnitcha compares and applies them to the theoretical framework he has developed. This framework is based on an evaluation of the consequences of various levels of protection deriving from the interpretations of each element of the FET standard. Each interpretation is assessed on the basis of the 'effect on efficiency; the distribution of economic costs and benefits; flows of FDI into host states; the realisation of human rights and environmental conservation in host states; and respect for the rule of law host states'.[63] In conducting this analysis, Bonnitcha attempts to answer the question as to the desirable level of investment protection. For example, in decisions evaluating the legitimate expectations of the investor, the legal rights approach, which only protects the specific legal rights of the investor, has been chosen as the most suitable. Bonnitcha has concluded that this approach can potentially ensure economic efficiency; a fair distribution of income according to the theories of distributive justice; and a better achievement of human rights protection and the conservation of the environment.[64]

59. R. Dolzer, (2014) 32.
60. J. Bonnitcha, (2014) e-book, Chapter 4.1, 4-5.
61. *Ibid.*, Chapter 4.1, 5.
62. J. Bonnitcha, 'Fair and Equitable Treatment', in J. Bonnitcha (ed.), *Substantive Protection under Investment Treaties: A Legal and Economic Analysis* (Cambridge University Press, 2015), e-book, Chapter: 4.5.5, pp. 115-116.
63. *Ibid.*, Chapter: 6.2, p. 4.
64. *Ibid.*, Chapter: 6.3.4, p. 37.

[C] Studies on the Right to Regulate in International Investment Law

In addition to the literature on the FET standard, several scholars have attempted to explain the meaning and application of the right to regulate in international investment law, which is the central concept of this study. Two studies on the right to regulate conducted by Titi[65] and Mouyal[66] have attempted to conceptualise the application of the right to regulate in international investment law.

Both studies indicate a rise in the importance of the right to regulate in the context of international investment law. However, there is a principal difference between the two approaches. Titi addresses the right to regulate as a relevant juridical concept that constitutes an exception to the obligation to protect investments. In this vein, Titi defines the right to regulate as:

> The legal right exceptionally permitting the host state to regulate in derogation of international commitments it has undertaken by means of an investment agreement without incurring a duty to compensate.[67]

Moyual, however, discusses the right to regulate from a human rights perspective. Accordingly, she defines the right to regulate as an:

> [A]ffirmation of the sovereign right for states to choose their political, social and economic priorities – within certain limits – through the adoption of legislation and administrative practices without violating international rules protecting foreign investments.[68]

The definition and the elements pertinent to the right to regulate outlined in these two studies are discussed in detail in Chapter 2. What is relevant for this book is how these studies address the right to regulate in relation to FET. In both studies, the FET standard is not the main subject of the research. Instead, the FET standard is only discussed briefly as an example of one of the standards of investment protection. Focusing on the expropriation standard as a case study, Mouyal mentions that the FET standard is 'rooted in customary international law'.[69] She further provides that investment tribunals usually evaluate the FET with reference to '(1) legitimate expectations and (2) due process',[70] but she does not elaborate on this qualification.

Titi addresses the FET standard in relation to the right to regulate in her analysis of IIAs and FET case law by observing that most FET standard provisions do not include exceptions for a specific public interest.[71] By referring to some cases on the FET standard, Titi concluded that in the course of the development of the FET standard jurisprudence, arbitral tribunals have interpreted the FET standard by breaking it into

65. A. Titi, Right to Regulate in International Investment Law (Nomos, 2014).
66. L. Wandahl Mouyal, (2016); A. Titi, (2014).
67. A. Titi, (2014) 33.
68. L. Wandahl Mouyal, (2016) 8.
69. *Ibid.*, 41.
70. *Ibid.*
71. A. Titi, (2014) 147.

several elements. These are the 'protection of legitimate expectations, non-discrimination, fair procedure and proportionality'.[72] She asserts that, through the development of these elements, the idea of a balancing test that allows the tribunal to take into account the legitimate interests of the host state has been embedded in investment practice.[73] She underlines that the FET standard by its 'very nature requires a balancing of interests'.[74] Consequently, in assessing the FET standard, a tribunal that 'completely ignores the legitimate interests of a host state will hardly appear to be fair and equitable'.[75] Titi does not focus on the issue of balancing as such. She even reports that the balancing that tribunals can accumulate in their examination of the FET standard is beyond the scope of her study.[76] The subject of balancing of the state's right to regulate and the protection of a foreign investor under the FET standard is the principal topic, which is assessed in this dissertation.

[D] A Synthesis of the Literature in the Context of This Book

There are several observations that can be made on the basis of the legal literature concerning the relationship between the FET standard contained in IIAs and the right to regulate. Scholars have acknowledged the pivotal role of the sub-elements of the FET standard that are primarily expressed in the obligations of states towards investors. This reflects the contemporary content of this standard. Among the scholarship addressed in this Chapter, there is consensus that the balancing and weighing of interests should be performed in the assessment of the FET standard. In this regard, the boundaries of the state's right to regulate have been expressed in a list of principles or objectives to which the state should adhere in its actions towards foreign investors, e.g. according to the rule of law or the concept of justice. On the basis of investment cases, a number of authors have identified several limitations to the state's right to regulate or, alternatively, desirable levels of investment protection under the FET standard.

Recent literature on the right to regulate focusing on international investment law have provided some insight into how the right to regulate has been applied in IIAs, general international law and investment jurisprudence.[77] However, there is still a need for a systematic analysis for the application of a host state's right to regulate in the specific context of exercising such a right, while the host state has also committed itself

72. *Ibid.*, 145.
73. *Ibid.*
74. A. Titi, (2014) 277.
75. *Ibid.*
76. *Ibid.*, 275.
77. A. Titi, (2014); L. Wandahl Mouyal, (2016); V. Korzun, 'The Right to Regulate in Investor-State Arbitration: Slicing and Dicing Regulatory Carve-Outs' [2017] 50(2) *Vanderbilt Journal of Transnational Law*, pp. 355-414; D. Gaukrodger, 'The Balance Between Investor Protection and the Right to Regulate in Investment Treaties: A Scoping Paper', (2017) OECD Working Papers on International Investment 2017/02, OECD Publishing, Paris; A. Pellet, 'Police Powers or the State's Right to Regulate', in M. Kinnear, G. Fischer et al. (eds) *Building International Investment Law – The First 50 Years of ICSID* (Kluwer Law International, 2016); V. Kube, E.U. Petersmann, 'Human Rights Law in International Investment Arbitration', in A. Gattini et al. (eds) *General Principles of Law and International Investment Arbitration* (Brill/Nijhoff, 2018).

to comply with the FET standard under the IIA. This combination of assessing the state's right to regulate and the FET standard in a selected number of IIAs and cases has not been fully addressed in those works.[78]

To explore this theme in more depth, in this book a selection has been made of eighty-nine IIAs concluded by Organisation for Economic Co-operation and Development (OECD) Member States, as well by Russia and China, and the corresponding case law. Other case law, which seemed particularly relevant for assessing this subject, has been added to the selection; hence, in total, sixty-six cases have been examined for the analysis in this study.

This book investigates how the right of states to regulate can be exercised in the public interest while also being balanced against the obligation to provide FET. The analysis in this book departs from the notion that the state's right to regulate has its legal basis in the international legal principle of state sovereignty.[79] The contribution of the present work lies in the identification of the elements by which the right to regulate is characterised in relation to the FET standard. The identified elements that are pertinent to the state's right to regulate and that have emerged from the analysis of the selected treaties, cases and literature are explained in section §2.03[E] of Chapter 2.[80] It is proposed that these elements constitute a useful framework for an examination of investment decisions on the FET standard and the right to regulate, which takes place in Chapters 6 and 7.

This book provides a valuable categorisation and systematisation of a number of IIAs and investment cases concerning the question of under which conditions a host state can exercise its right to regulate while also being bound to respect the FET standard.

First, various categories of the FET standard provisions emerged from the analysis of the selected IIAs and are subsequently analysed from the perspective of the state's right to regulate.[81] This analysis of all selected IIAs contributes to the already existing knowledge on the FET standard and provides a further assessment of this standard in connection with the right to regulate.

Second, the cases selected for this study concern – among other things – the application of the state's right to regulate in an assessment of the FET standard by arbitral tribunals. Hence, the core of this book comprises an analysis of cases in which

78. A. Titi, (2014); L. Wandahl Mouyal, (2016).
79. S. Besson, 'Sovereignty, International Law and Democracy' [2011] 22(2) *European Journal of International Law*, 376. 'State sovereignty is often understood in international law as a competence, immunity, or power, and in particular as the power to make autonomous choices (so-called sovereign autonomy).'
80. In section §2.03[E] of Chapter 2, it will be explained that the identified elements that are pertinent to the right to regulate are characterised by the following: (1) it is limited by the international obligations under general international law and international treaties, such as the FET obligation towards foreign investors under an IIA; (2) it has to be balanced against the rights and obligations of investors; (3) it can usually be specified by contracting states in IIAs through the inclusion of the public interest or legitimate policy objectives; (4) its exercise can entail different consequences, which are usually related to liability under an IIA, and/or the obligation to pay compensation in the case of a violation of treaty obligations, e.g. the obligation to provide fair and equitable treatment to an investor.
81. *See*: Section §3.03 of Chapter 3.

a state's measure is motivated by a public interest which falls within its right to regulate, while at the same time the same measure might possibly violate the state's obligations pursuant to the FET standard.[82] These cases are categorised in accordance with various tests, which tribunals employ in order to decide on the legitimacy of an investor's expectations and the lawfulness of a disputed state's measure, in judging an alleged violation of the FET standard. The analysis of these decisions helps to clarify how the state's right to regulate can be conceptualised in connection with the FET standard.

Third, in this book the results of the analyses of the IIAs and the case law are combined in order to identify the legal conditions for a state to regulate while providing FET to investors under international investment law. By distilling such concrete conditions from the case law and treaty provisions, and by examining how the investment jurisprudence in FET cases has been reflected in the new generation of IIAs with regard to the FET standard and the state's right to regulate, this study can contribute to practise by offering solutions for testing the lawfulness of a host state's application of its right to regulate in the context of an applicable FET standard, as well as for drafting provisions on this topic in new IIAs.

Fourth, another important aspect of this book lies in the analysis that has been conducted of the recent EU policy developments concerning the drafting of FET standard provisions in the new generation of IIAs. Specifically, the new generation of IIAs, e.g., Comprehensive Economic Trade Agreement (CETA), Transatlantic Investment and Partnership Agreement (TTIP) and the EU-Singapore Free Trade Agreement (FTA) are evaluated in view of the question of how they deal with the tension between the application of the FET standard and the state's right to regulate. These relatively new IIAs contain specific language that attempts to clarify the scope of the state's right to regulate. Recently, several scholars have also researched these new IIAs and published articles on this topic.[83] As explained above, the objective of this book is to analyse the new generation of IIAs from the perspective of the balancing question concerning the state's right to regulate and the investor's right to receive the FET standard.

Hence, the questions that are addressed in this study concern: (1) to what extent is FET jurisprudence and the right to regulate reflected in the new generation of IIAs and (2) has the direction of the balance shifted in these new IIAs in comparison to FET

82. *See*: Chapter 6 where the state's right to regulate and the legitimate expectations of the investor are discussed and Chapter 7 that analyses the conditions for a state to lawfully exercise its right to regulate.
83. A. Reinisch, 'The Likely Content of Future EU Investment Agreements', in M. Bungenberg et al. (eds) *International Investment Law: A Handbook* (Hart Publishing, 2015); A. Giodesen, et al., 'A Waiver for Europe? CETA's Trade in Services, and Investment Protection Provisions and Their Legal-Political Implications on Regulatory Competence', in G. Adinolfi et al. (eds) *International Economic Law: Contemporary Issues* (Springer, 2017) pp. 41-57; S. Schill, H.L. Bray, 'The Brave New (American) World of International Investment Law: Substantive Investment Protection Standards in Mega-Regionals', in T. Rensmann (ed.) *Mega-Regional Trade Agreements* (Springer, 2017); E. De Brabandere, 'States' Reassertion of Control over International Investment Law – (Re)Defining "Fair and Equitable Treatment" and "Indirect Expropriation"', in A. Kulick (ed.) *States' Reassertion of Control over International Investment Agreements and International Investment Treaty Dispute Settlement* (Cambridge University Press, 2016).

decisions. The answers to these questions are provided in section §8.06 of Chapter 8. The comparison is conducted between the new generation of IIAs and the most relevant case law on this point. The result of this comparison indicates the extent of the codification of the FET jurisprudence in the new IIAs. Based on the findings from this comparison, this study assesses whether, and if so, in which direction, the new generation of IIAs and the investment jurisprudence on the FET standard have shifted the balance between the state's right to regulate and the FET standard. In addition, this book contributes to the existing research and provides practical guidelines because it identifies gaps in the new type of formulations of the FET standard in terms of creating a balance between a host state's right to regulate and the protection of the rights of investors under the FET standard.[84] To this end, suggestions are provided for treaty drafters regarding formulations of the FET standard that can contribute to achieving such a balance.[85]

To conclude this section, the understanding of how states' regulatory conduct exercised in the public interest can be evaluated against the interests of investors under FET provisions is limited. It should be kept in mind that the international legal investment system has not been created to 'promote uniformity or consistency of either rule-making or rule-interpretation'.[86] The FET obligation, interpreted by tribunals in various ways, has developed as an open standard with several evolving components, such as the prohibition of arbitrariness.[87] At present, through recent IIAs and case law, the content of the FET standard tends to acquire uniform characteristics.[88] A number of tribunals and commentators[89] have stressed the importance of predictability and consistency in the assessment of the FET standard as being instrumental to the legitimacy of the system.[90] Consequently, a benchmark that will provide indications regarding the conditions applicable to exercising the right to regulate in the context of the FET standard appears to be necessary. In this book, an attempt is made to identify the conditions and limitations of the right to regulate vis-à-vis the obligation to observe the FET standard. However, the complexity of FET claims that include a web of state conduct sometimes performed over a long period of time does not allow for a simplification of the FET standard and the right to regulate. It is, however, possible to

84. The reference is made to: (1) the principles of reasonableness and proportionality and (2) two criteria often discussed in the context of assessing whether an investor's expectations were legitimate, namely the special circumstances in a host state and the investor's conduct.
85. *See* these suggestions in section §8.06[C] of Chapter 8.
86. R. Dolzer, [2014] 15.
87. *See* Chapter 4, section §4.03[B] for an elaboration on the sub-elements of the FET standard.
88. *See* the preliminary conclusions of Chapter 3 on the FET standard formulations and Chapters 6 and 7 that analyse the conditions which apply to the right to regulate.
89. *See* A. Bjorklund, 'Investment Treaty Arbitral Decisions as Jurisprudence Constante' (2008) UC Davis Legal Studies Research Paper 158, 265. The author noted that 'the informal and dispersed regime of investment treaty arbitrations is not well suited to developing a system of formal precedent. Eventually, however, an accretion of decisions will likely develop a *jurisprudence constante* – a "persisting jurisprudence" that secures unification and stability of judicial activity'.
90. *See Burlington Resources Inc. v. Republic of Ecuador*, ICSID Case No. ARB/08/5 Decision on Jurisdiction (2 June 2010) para. 100. The Tribunal in this case asserted its ambition 'to contribute to the harmonious development of investment law and thereby to meet the legitimate expectations of the community of States and investors towards the certainty of law'.

reveal certain common patterns in the tribunals' assessment of state conduct in investment decisions. Furthermore, the development of new FET standard provisions that include some clarifications of the host state's conditions to regulate in the public interest through a list of state obligations is also taken into consideration.

§1.03 METHODOLOGY

The present book utilises an inductive method in evaluating investment decisions on the FET standard.[91] Similar patterns that can be revealed in the argumentation of investment tribunals are instrumental in identifying common features in the assessment of the conditions which apply to the right to regulate. A close examination of recent FET cases and the new generation of FET standard treaty provisions suggests an increased convergence in articulating the conditions which are applicable to the state's right to regulate under the FET standard. As such, the goal is to capture these emerging trends in order to further contribute to the understanding of how a state's right to regulate can be balanced against the rights of investors to obtain FET. Building upon the doctrinal research that has investigated FET standard provisions and cases, this book outlines solutions that are already in existence, i.e. are covered by a number of treaties and cases. Following such an appraisal, the last chapter of this study reflects on how the FET standard provisions and the right to regulate are balanced in treaties and jurisprudence.

The main question of this book is: how can the host state's right to regulate concerning the protection of a public interest be balanced against the host state's obligation to provide FET under international investment law? In order to answer this question, initially, the book describes the key features of IIAs and defines the right to regulate. The basis of this analysis is a review of the secondary literature. It then proceeds to discern the current state of affairs towards the right to regulate in the assessment of the FET standard. In order to do so, the book adopts a two-tier approach. First, the FET standard provisions in selected IIAs are examined. Second, selected FET investment cases are analysed. The selected treaties are included in the tables in the Annexes contained at the end of this publication. The aim of the treaty and jurisprudence analysis as well as the rationale for selecting certain IIAs and FET cases are further explained in this section.

The IIAs and investment jurisprudence are the main sources of this book. In the first phase of this research, a survey of the selected IIAs most of which are Bilateral Investment Treaties (BITs) was conducted in order to clarify how the FET standard is formulated in treaties. The selection of BITs is limited to the treaties between eight states that are members of the OECD, as well as two other large economies: China and Russia, and ten developing or post-transition countries (host states) (*see* Annex A for an overview of the selected treaties).[92] The survey also includes nine regional treaties

91. J. Bonnitcha, (2014) e-book, Chapter 4.1, 4. *See also* G. Schawerzenberger, The Inductive Approach to International Law (Stevens & Sons, 1965).
92. Annex A can be found at the end of the study.

(*see* Annex B).[93] The goal of the survey was not to cover all existing IIAs, of which on 2018 there are 3,322,[94] but to present a representative sample of different BITs and the most significant and recent regional agreements in order to analyse the variety of formulations of the FET standard that presently exist. The categories of IIAs' FET standard provisions are analysed and presented in Chapter 3 (*see* Annex C).[95] The treaties of eight OECD Member States and two additional states, China and Russia, have been selected on the basis of Foreign Direct Investment (FDI) volumes, namely Australia, Canada, Russia, China, Japan, the US, the UK, Germany, the Netherlands and France. These states are the world's leading economic powers.[96] Most of these selected OECD states have concluded a large number of BITs,[97] and investors from these countries often act as the claimants in investor-state arbitration proceedings.[98]

The selection of host states was based on two criteria. First, the study included the main capital-importing economies. Latin American host states selected for this survey represent the key capital-importing countries, which became the leading respondent states in investment arbitration proceedings (including, e.g., Ecuador, Mexico, Argentina). Colombia, a growing economy, is an interesting example that has only recently engaged in the treaty negotiating process and has introduced a more elaborate approach towards the drafting of the FET standard. Ukraine and the Czech Republic are Eastern European countries that became major capital-importing countries and frequent respondent states in investment arbitration. Two major developing economies, namely Egypt and India, have actively negotiated BITs and are among those states that have concluded the largest number of treaties. Trinidad and Tobago was selected as a representative country of small island states. Second, treaties from states from different parts of the world were selected in order to avoid any geographical bias.

The analysis of the treaties focuses specifically on the new generation of investment agreements (e.g., recent EU agreements). These treaties have introduced innovative approaches to the FET standard with the intention of accommodating regulatory flexibility so as to accept states' policies adopted in the public interest.

The second phase involves an analysis of selected investment cases involving FET claims. The goal of this part of the analysis is to identify the conditions that apply

---

93. Annex B can be found at the end of the study.
94. UNCTAD, 'World Investment Report 2018' (2018) xii http://unctad.org/en/PublicationsLibrary/wir2018_en.pdf accessed on 1 June 2018.
95. Annex C can be found at the end of the study.
96. To exemplify this, OECD research for 2014 has indicated that the US, Russia, China and Japan are the four largest outflow investors, the investments of which account for half of the global outflows.
97. *See*, e.g., the Netherlands (95 BITs), Germany (135 BITs), China (129 BITs) and France (102 BITs).
98. *See*, e.g., the UNCTAD World Investment Report 2015, on the latest trends on FDI based on the regions; UNCTAD, 'World Investment Report 2015' (2015) http://unctad.org/en/PublicationsLibrary/wir2015_en.pdf accessed on 1 June 2018.

to the right to regulate and which are present in the tribunals' assessment of the FET standard.

Sixty-six cases have been analysed for this study (*see* Annex D).[99] During the initial process of selection, the decisions in the cases concerned were based on the selected IIAs. Consequently, the selected IIA has been an applicable treaty in the elected decision. As the study progressed, additional decisions have been included in this study based on the relevance of the specific arbitral awards. The relevance of these awards has been determined on the basis of the review of the literature and the review of the ICSID database and other investment databases, where the claims have been outlined. Several decisions that included relevant aspects of an assessment of the right to regulate (a concept elaborated upon in Chapter 2) were selected. Only concluded decisions, e.g. final arbitral awards, partial awards with rulings on the FET standard, and decisions on liability were selected.

In the course of analysis, on the basis of the specific sub-elements pertinent to the FET standard - which are analysed by tribunals interchangeably - the study identifies several prominent, but not exhaustive, criteria that have been present in the majority of cases and which serve as factors in the assessment of regulatory conduct. Taking into account the complexity of the analysis of the FET standard, the identified elements do not always constitute the threshold for a state's regulatory measures under the FET standard. They merely provide guidance regarding the assessment of the right to regulate in the context of the FET obligation. These conditions are differentiated on the basis of an analysis of arbitral decisions, in combination with case commentaries and secondary literature on investor-state arbitration.

The final part of this book analyses how the investment jurisprudence in FET cases has been reflected in the new generation of IIAs. The conditions, which are applicable to a lawful exercise of the right to regulate, identified in this study, are compared to the relevant provisions in several of the newest investment agreements. Observations are provided on how the FET standard and the state's right to regulate are balanced in the new generation of IIAs.

99. The research on the main body of case law has been closed on 31 August of 2016. However, several more recent cases that were particularly relevant for this study have been added to the analysis. Annex D can be found at the end of the study.

CHAPTER 2

International Investment Agreements and the Right to Regulate: An Introduction

§2.01 INTRODUCTION

This Chapter introduces and explains two concepts that play a central role in the research carried out in this book. The legal basis for the rights and obligations of investors and host states are laid down in IIAs. As such, section §2.02 will provide a brief overview of the general content and structure of IIAs. The main part of this Chapter elaborates on the right to regulate in international investment law in section §2.03. The application of this concept in IIAs, investment cases and literature is explained. At the end of this section, the key elements of the right to regulate, and which are pertinent to this book, are identified. Section §2.04 summarises the main conclusions of this Chapter.

§2.02 INTERNATIONAL INVESTMENT AGREEMENTS

IIAs constitute the most important source of international investment law in which the rights and obligations of host states and investors are laid down.[100] There are several different types of IIAs. First, on the multilateral and regional levels, IIAs consist of FTAs and Economic Partnership Agreements. These types of agreements contain either investment chapters or investment provisions. Which states will become parties to these treaties depend on the geographical region or sector in which cooperation in trade and investment is being sought. To exemplify this, the Energy Charter Treaty (ECT) is

100. R. Dolzer, C. Schreuer, (2008) 76.

a multilateral treaty that is applicable to the energy sector.[101] This treaty includes investment protection rules for investors in the energy sector.[102]

Second, IIAs can also be in the form of Bilateral Investment Treaties (BITs). These are concluded between states on a bilateral level. BITs are the most commonly encountered type of IIA and make up the majority of IIAs analysed in the present book. A general overview of the development of BITs, their structure and their content is provided below.

According to the UNCTAD World Investment Report of 2016, there are currently 3,304 IIAs, of which there are 2,946 BITs.[103] The first BIT was signed between Pakistan and Germany in 1959.[104] The number of BITs experienced significant growth, particularly between the early 1990s and the early 2000s.[105] For example, around 200 BITs were concluded in 1996 during a one-year period, in comparison to only 165 BITs having been signed in the entire period between 1959 and 1979.[106] Since 2010, there has been a noticeable decline in treaty making, evidenced by the aforementioned UNCTAD report. For example, in 2017, a total of eighteen IIAs were concluded, of which nine were BITs.[107]

Despite the growing preference of states to conclude regional treaties, BITs still account for the largest network of IIAs.[108] They differ from country to country and from treaty to treaty. However, a general structure is discernable in most BITs.[109] It includes the following provisions:

(1) Commonly, a BIT begins with the goals of the treaty formulated in the preamble. These goals have been formulated primarily to encourage and to

101. Energy Charter Treaty [1994] 2080 UNTS 95 (updated 15 January 2016) http://www.energycharter.org/process/energy-charter-treaty-1994/energy-charter-treaty/ accessed on 12 June 2018.
102. Energy Charter Treaty [1994] 2080 UNTS (updated 15 January 2016). At present, the Member States of the European Union and another fifty-one states have ratified the ECT. *See also* on the Energy Charter Treaty: R. Dolzer, C. Schreuer, 2nd edn., (2012) 77.
103. UNCTAD 'World Investment Report 2016' (2016) 101 http://unctad.org/en/PublicationsLibrary/wir2016_en.pdf accessed on 12 June 2018.
104. Germany-Pakistan BIT (signed in 1959, entered into force 1962). This BIT has been replaced by the 2009 Germany-Pakistan BIT (2009). For the original text *see* http://investmentpolicyhub.unctad.org/IIA/treaty/1732 accessed on 12 June 2018.
105. *See* 'Table of IIAs Trends Concluded Between 1980-2015' in UNCTAD, 'World Investment Report 2016' (2016) 101 http://unctad.org/en/PublicationsLibrary/wir2016_en.pdf accessed on 12 June 2018.
106. *See* UNCTAD, 'Figure 1: Growth of the Number of BITs, 1959-1999' in UNCTAD, 'Bilateral Investment Treaties, 1959-1999' (2000) 1 http://unctad.org/en/docs/poiteiiad2.en.pdf accessed on 12 June 2018.
107. UNCTAD 'World Investment Report 2018' (2018) 88 http://unctad.org/en/PublicationsLibrary/wir2018_en.pdf accessed on 12 June 2018.
108. UNCTAD, 'World Investment Report 2012: Towards a New Generation of Investment Policies' (2012) 84 http://unctad.org/en/PublicationsLibrary/wir2012_embargoed_en.pdf accessed on 12 June 2018 which states that there is a 'gradual shift towards regional treaty making, where a single regional treaty takes the place of a multitude of bilateral pacts and where regional blocs (instead of their individual members) negotiate with third States'.
109. J. Bonnitcha, (2014), e-book, Chapter 1.1, 4.

promote investment, as well as to create favourable conditions for investment. In more recent BITs there is a tendency to include non-economic statements in the preambles, such as those concerning sustainable development.[110] A further elaboration of the role of the preamble with regard to the interpretation of the FET standard is addressed in Chapter 4, sections §4.02[B]-§4.02[C].

(2) The treaty usually follows with its scope of application being regulated, including the definitions of an 'investor' and 'investments'. These definitions are essential in order to understand who qualifies as an investor and what amounts to an investment under the specific BIT. BITs also often contain provisions regulating the admission of investments and the 'right of establishment'.[111] The provisions that regulate the right of admission provide a set of rules for the investor's entry into a host state.[112] The right of establishment, however, specifies certain requirements regarding an investor's activity for the duration of the investment.[113]

(3) The operative part of BITs includes key substantive investment protection clauses that usually contain provisions on (a) direct and indirect expropriation; (b) FET; (c) full protection and security; (d) discriminatory and arbitrary treatment; (e) protection on the basis of the Most Favoured Nation (MFN) and National Treatment (NT) standards; and (g) free transfer of payments.

(4) In terms of the procedural rights of investors, a predominant part of BITs provides for the possibility of dispute settlement mechanisms.[114] Most BITs offer the foreign investor the possibility to seek recourse against the host state through an investor-state dispute settlement system (ISDS).[115] The most well-known ISDS system is established by the Convention on the Settlement of Investment Disputes between States and Nationals of other States (ICSID Convention), created under the auspices of the World Bank, which entered into force in 1966. This Convention provides an institutional and procedural framework for the settlement of investment disputes through arbitration and

110. From the UNCTAD database of IIAs, it follows that of 1,959 IIAs, 54 include a reference to sustainable development; *see* UNCTAD 'IIA Mapping Project 2016' (2016) http://investmentpolicyhub.unctad.org/IIA/mappedContent#iiaInnerMenu accessed on 12 June 2018.

111. I. Gomez-Palacio, P. Muchlinski, 'Admission and Establishment', in P. Muchilinski et al. (eds) *The Oxford Handbook of International Investment Law* (Oxford University Press, 2008) 229.

112. For example, many IIAs provide that investments will be admitted according to the law of the host state. *See* Article 2 of the Russia-Egypt BIT (2000), which states that '(1) Each Contracting Party shall encourage the investors of the other Contracting Party to make capital investments on its territory and shall permit such capital investments in conformity with its legislation.' For the text of the treaty *see* http://investmentpolicyhub.unctad.org/Download/TreatyFile/1105 accessed on 15 January 2017.

113. I. Gomez-Palacio, P. Muchlinski, (2008) 230.

114. A. Reinisch, L. Malintoppi, 'Methods of Dispute Resolution', in P. Muchilinski and others (eds) *The Oxford Handbook of International Investment Law* (Oxford University Press, 2008) 692-693.

115. S. Franck, 'Development and Outcomes of Investment Treaty Arbitration' [2009] 50(2) *Harvard International Law Journal*, 442. Note that the host state cannot initiate arbitration proceedings against an investor.

conciliation between foreign investors and host states.[116] The ICSID Convention does not contain substantive rules on international investment.[117] Currently, 153 contracting states have ratified the ICSID Convention. Whether the parties can make use of the possibilities offered in the ICSID Convention depends on whether this dispute settlement instrument is provided in IIAs and/or the investment contract between the host state and the investor.[118]

ICSID is not the only framework for the international settlement of investment disputes. With regard to plural arbitration forums, there are substantial variations in the choices provided by BITs to settle disputes between foreign investors and host states.[119] A large number of BITs offer investors the choice as to which arbitration regime to use. Most BITs permit *inter alia* arbitration before the World Bank's ICSID.[120] This has been the most common forum to settle investment disputes.[121] The ICSID offers the parties detailed procedural rules, institutional support and secretarial assistance. Other institutional arbitration forums include the Permanent Court of Arbitration (PCA), the International Court of Arbitration of the International Chamber of Commerce and the Stockholm Chamber of Commerce, which are all well-known institutions under which state-investor arbitration proceedings are administered. Investors also have the option of referring to ad hoc arbitration, where parties have more flexibility, and can, e.g., select the applicable arbitration rules. For these purposes, parties frequently employ the United Nations Commission for International Trade Law (UNCITRAL) procedural rules.[122]

---

116. C. Schreuer, et al., The ICSID Convention: A Commentary (2nd edn., Cambridge University Press, 2009) xi.
117. R. Dolzer, C. Schreuer, 2nd edn., (2012) 75.
118. There are several ways to consent to arbitration. Consent may be given, first, in the form of a direct agreement between an investor and a host state, which is a frequent practice in investment contracts. Second, consent may be provided for in a clause under national law, stipulating that investment arbitration is the preferred option for dispute settlement. Third, consent may be included in the provision of a BIT. Consent to an arbitration procedure can be found in the texts of many BIT arbitration clauses. *See* R. Dolzer and C. Schreuer, (2008) 352. Consent to submit arbitration to the ICSID is provided for in the texts of most German, French and UK BITs. For example, Article 8 of the UK-Albania BIT provides that '(I) Each Contracting Party hereby consents to submit to the International Centre for the Settlement of Investment Disputes (hereinafter referred to as "the Centre") for settlement by conciliation or arbitration under the Convention on the Settlement of Investment Disputes between States and Nationals of Other States ....' UK-Albania BIT (entry into force in 1994), http://investmentpolicyhub.unctad.org/Download/TreatyFile/38 accessed on 12 June 2018.
119. For an overview of the different options *see* J. Pohl, et al., 'Dispute Settlement Provisions in International Investment Agreements: A Large Sample Survey' (2012) OECD Working Papers on International Investment Law 2012/02, https://www.oecd.org/investment/investment-policy/WP-2012_2.pdf accessed on 12 June 2018.
120. T. Eilmansberger, 'Bilateral Investment Treaties and EU Law' [2009] 46 *Common Market Law Review*, 386.
121. UNCTAD 'Figure 1: Known ISDS Cases, 1987–2015' in UNCTAD 'Investor-State Dispute Settlement: Review of Developments in 2015' (2016) 2 http://investmentpolicyhub.unctad.org/Publications/Details/144 accessed on 12 June 2018.
122. United Nations Commission on International Trade Law (UNCITRAL) Arbitration Rules (1976) that were revised in 2010. With the adoption of the UNCITRAL Rules on Transparency for Treaty-Based Investor-State Arbitration in 2013, a new Article 1, paragraph 4 was added to the

Overall, it should be noted that the ISDS has become a popular mechanism for the settlement of investment disputes. As of summer 2018, the number of publicly known investment claims had reached 855. For 2017, according to the World Investment Report, sixty-five new investment cases were registered.[123] At present, claims are being increasingly filed against Western, developed states that have become both capital exporters and capital importers. In 2018, Croatia, India and Spain were the most frequent respondent state in investment proceedings.[124]

The underlying ambition of the World Bank mechanism was to create an independent, depoliticised and effective dispute resolution system for states and investors.[125] To some extent, this ambition has been realised. At the same time, the ISDS has attracted some criticism for not representing the interests of host states and foreign investors in a balanced way.[126] Attempts have been made to reform the ISDS, by including an independent investment court system or an appeal procedure, for example. These improvements have been proposed in the context of new agreements, such as those negotiated between the EU.[127] The need to reform the ISDS derives from a common critique that the ISDS tends to focus on the interests of investors and that it lacks transparency and legitimacy.[128] It is argued that the latter is reflected in, among

text of the Arbitration Rules (as revised in 2010) to incorporate the Rules on Transparency for arbitration. *See* http://www.uncitral.org/uncitral/en/uncitral_texts/arbitration/2010Arbitration_rules.html accessed on 21 March 2017.

123. UNCTAD 'World Investment Report 2018' (2018) xiii http://unctad.org/en/PublicationsLibrary/wir2018_en.pdf accessed on 12 June 2018.
124. UNCTAD 'Table: Most Frequent Respondent States, Total as of End of 2017' in UNCTAD, UNCTAD 'World Investment Report 2018' (2018) 92 http://unctad.org/en/PublicationsLibrary/wir2018_en.pdfs accessed on 12 June 2018.
125. J. Kalicki, A. Joubin-Bret, Reshaping the Investor-State Dispute Settlement System (Brill/Nijhof, 2015) 1.
126. G. Van Harten, 'Investment Treaty Arbitration and Public Law' Chapter 5: The Transformation of International Law (Oxford University Press, 2007) 95-120. This study is the first comprehensive analysis of the investment treaty arbitration system, where the problematic areas of ISDS have been highlighted.
127. European Commission, 'Investment in TTIP and Beyond: The Path for Reform: Enhancing the Right to Regulate and Moving from Current Ad Hoc Arbitration Towards an Investment Court' (2015) European Commission Concept Paper http://trade.ec.europa.eu/doclib/docs/2015/may/tradoc_153408.PDF accessed on 12 June 2018.
128. European Parliament, Director General for External Policies, 'The Investment Chapters of the EU's International Trade and Investment Agreements in a Comparative Perspective' (2015) http://www.europarl.europa.eu/RegData/etudes/STUD/2015/534998/EXPO_STU(2015)534998_EN.pdf; European Parliament, 'Investor-State Dispute Settlement (ISDS) Provisions in the EU's International Investment Agreements' Volume 2: Studies (2014) http://www.europarl.europa.eu/RegData/etudes/STUD/2014/534979/EXPO_STU(2014)534979_EN.pdf; *see also*: UNCTAD, 'Reform of Investor-State Dispute Settlement: In Search of a Roadmap' (2012) UNCTAD Issues Note, 3. The report states that the main concern in ISDS is the lack of 'legitimacy and transparency'. In terms of the lack of legitimacy, '[i]n many cases foreign investors have used ISDS claims to challenge measures adopted by States in the public interest .... Questions have been raised whether three individuals, appointed on an ad hoc basis, can be seen by the public at large as having sufficient legitimacy to assess the validity of States' acts, particularly if the dispute involves sensitive public policy issues'. With regard to transparency, the report states, 'even though the transparency of the system has improved since the early 2000s, ISDS proceedings can still be kept fully confidential – if both disputing parties so wish – even in cases where the dispute involves matters of public interest.' http://unctad.org/en/PublicationsLibrary/webdiaepcb2013d4_en.pdf. All websites accessed on 10 May 2018.

other things, the procedural aspects of the ISDS, such as the procedure for the choice of arbitrators.[129] Also, the role and collection of scientific evidence in some investment disputes has been questioned as well.[130] The ISDS has also been criticised on substantive grounds. For example, some question whether and to what extent tribunals should have the authority to review the sovereign decisions of host states directed at public welfare.[131] Whether these claims are well grounded in the context of the arbitral tribunals assessing the FET standard will be considered in Chapters 4-7, in which the FET investment cases are analysed. As for this Chapter, the following section will proceed with an introduction to the right to regulate as it relates to the FET standard.

§2.03 THE RIGHT TO REGULATE

The right to regulate has become a relevant concept in the context of international investment law. Some recent investment agreements,[132] arbitral decisions[133] and policy documents[134] refer to the right to regulate. Two monographs have attempted to clarify and conceptualise this concept.[135] Consequently, the goal of this section is to

129. On the independence and impartiality of arbitrators in ISDS, *see*: L. Malintoppi, 'Independence, Impartiality and Duty of Disclosure of Arbitrators', in P. Muchilinski and others (eds) *The Oxford Handbook of International Investment Law* (Oxford University Press, 2008) 792-815.
130. J. Harrison, 'Addressing the Procedural Challenges of Environmental Litigation in the Context of Investor-State Arbitration', in Y. Levashova, et al. (eds) *Bridging the Gap Between International Investment Law and the Environment* (Eleven Legal Publishing, 2015) 109.
131. *See*: UNCTAD, 'Reform of Investor-State Dispute Settlement: In Search of a Roadmap' (2012) UNCTAD Issues Note, 3 http://unctad.org/en/PublicationsLibrary/webdiaepcb2013d4_en.pdf accessed on 12 June 2018.
132. *See*, e.g., the CETA, 30 October 2016 http://trade.ec.europa.eu/doclib/docs/2014/september/tradoc_152806.pdf accessed on 15 June 2018. *See also* Chapter 8, Articles 13*bis* of the Draft EU-Vietnam FTA (2016) http://trade.ec.europa.eu/doclib/docs/2016/february/tradoc_154210.pdf accessed on 15 June 2018.
133. *See Saluka v. Czech Republic* [2006] Permanent Court of Arbitration, IIC 210, Partial Award (17 March 2006) para. 305. In this award, the tribunal referred to the 'host state's legitimate right subsequently to regulate domestic matters in [the] public interest'. In *Parkerings v. Lithuania*, ICSID Case No. ARB/05/8 Award (11 September 2007) para. 324, the tribunal made a reference to the state's 'undeniable right and privilege to exercise its sovereign legislative power'. In *AWG v. Argentina*, UNCITRAL Arbitration, Decision on Liability (30 July 2010), para. 236, the tribunal referred to the 'reasonable right to regulate'.
134. D. Gaukrodger, 'The Balance Between Investor Protection and the Right to Regulate in Investment Treaties: A Scoping Paper' (2017), OECD Working Papers on International Investment, 2017/02, OECD Publishing, Paris https://www.oecd-ilibrary.org/docserver/82786801-en.pdf?expires = 1529508425&id = id&accname = guest&checksum = 9EE4C53FA8B55C7493FA89A5A14AFAB8; OECD, '"Indirect Expropriation" and the "Right to Regulate"' (2004) OECD Working Paper on International Investment Law 2004/04 https://www.oecd.org/daf/inv/investment-policy/WP-2004_4.pdf. Also *see*: the policy documents of the EU on the negotiation of EU agreements, such as between Canada and the EU or the EU and the US contain 'right to regulate' terminology in all its documents and in the draft investment chapters. *See*, e.g., European Commission, 'Investment in TTIP and Beyond: The Path for Reform: Enhancing the Right to Regulate and Moving from Current Ad Hoc Arbitration Towards an Investment Court' [2015] European Commission Concept Paper http://trade.ec.europa.eu/doclib/docs/2015/may/tradoc_153408.PDF; European Commission, 'CETA: EU and Canada agree on new approach on investment in trade agreement' (Press Release, 29 February 2016) http://europa.eu/rapid/press-release_IP-16-399_en.htm. All websites accessed on 12 June 2018.
135. L. Wandahl Mouyal, (2016); A. Titi, (2014).

clarify the meaning of the right to regulate. Such a clarification is necessary as the right to regulate constitutes a central concept in this book that is assessed within the framework of IIAs' FET standard provisions and investment cases on the FET standard.

To clarify how the right to regulate is addressed in international investment law, this section will first briefly explain what the legal basis of the right to regulate consists of. Second, this Chapter will review how the concept of the right to regulate has been addressed and defined in IIAs, investment decisions on the FET standard and academic literature. Third, on the basis of such an analysis, several elements of the right to regulate will be outlined and explained.

[A] The Legal Basis of the Right to Regulate

The right to regulate has a thorough legal basis in the international legal principle of state sovereignty. Sovereignty is a fundamental notion in international law[136] that comprises multiple elements and plays a role in relation to concepts such as the 'sovereign equality of states', 'domestic jurisdiction' and 'permanent sovereignty over natural resources'.[137] Within international law, sovereignty has internal and external dimensions.[138] The right to regulate is an expression of internal sovereignty. This right includes the state's right to 'prescribe the laws that set the boundaries of the public order of the state' on its territory.[139] The right also protects the public interest of the state's citizens that, e.g., includes the protection of public health and safety. The notion of public interest has a growing importance in the context of the internal sovereignty of the state.[140] Within the restrictions laid down by international law, the state is free to choose its methods for achieving its regulatory objectives.[141]

136. Besson has summarised the concept by stating that 'state sovereignty is often understood in international law as a competence, immunity, or power, and in particular as the power to make autonomous choices (so-called sovereign autonomy).' S. Besson, [2011] 373-387.
137. *See* J.H. Jackson, 'Sovereignty: Outdated Concept or New Approaches', in W. Shan, P. Simons, et al. (eds) *Redefining Sovereignty in International Economic Law* (Hart Publishing, 2008) 4. He underlines that the 'concept of equality of nations is linked to sovereignty concepts because sovereignty has fostered the idea that there is no higher power than the nation-state, so its "sovereignty" negates the idea that there is a higher power, whether foreign or international (unless consented by the nation-state).' Regarding the concept of 'permanent sovereignty over natural resources' that stemmed from the general notion of sovereignty, *see* N. Schrijver, Sovereignty over Natural Resources (Cambridge University Press, 2007).
138. I. Brownlie, Principles of Public International Law (4th edn., Oxford University Press, 1990; 5th edn., Oxford University Press, 1998; 7th edn., Oxford University Press, 2008); J. Crawford, Brownlie's Principles of Public International Law (8th edn., Oxford University Press, 2012); R. Brand, 'External Sovereignty and International Law' [1995] 18 *Fordham Journal of International Law*, 1685.
139. C. Staker, 'The Scope of Sovereignty', in M. De Evans (ed.) *International Law* (Oxford University Press, 2014) 316.
140. L. Wandahl Mouyal, (2016) 99. *See also* M. Shaw, International Law (Cambridge University Press, 2008) 55, who has argued that the responsibility of the state towards its citizens in providing public welfare has increased.
141. L. Wandahl Mouyal, (2016) 32.

In the context of investment law, the steady growth in investment treaties and arbitration cases has resulted in limitations being placed on state sovereignty.[142] Consequently, a number of sovereignty issues have surfaced. Disputes in the area of the environment and public health have instigated a discussion on the extent to which investment agreements are able to limit a state's internal sovereignty. The right to regulate that has acquired prominence in the context of investment law is perceived to be better suited as an expression referring to the regulatory aspects of (internal) sovereignty.

[B] The Right to Regulate in IIAs

The term 'right to regulate' has only just come to the forefront in recent IIAs. This section provides examples of the ways in which states have, directly or indirectly, referred to the right to regulate in the provisions of IIAs, with a specific focus being placed on FET standard provisions.

Even though the appearance of the 'right to regulate' in the investment context is relatively recent, the provisions that deal with the regulatory autonomy of states already featured in the first IIAs.[143] The concept of the right to regulate has been implicitly specified through general and specific exceptions (such as those relating to public morals and health, e.g.),[144] preambular statements, specific provisions regulating particular public interests such as the environment[145] or labour[146] and through exceptions in the context of substantive provisions such as expropriation or FET.[147]

---

142. J. Karl, 'International Investment Arbitration: A Threat to State Sovereignty', in W. Shan and others (eds) *Redefining Sovereignty in International Economic Law* (Hart Publishing, 2008) 230.
143. For example, the general provision on the right to regulate has appeared in the Multilateral Agreement on Investment's (MAI) negotiating text. Article 3 of the MAI entitled 'Affirmation of Right to Regulate' provides that '[a] Contracting Party may adopt, maintain, or enforce any measure that it considers appropriate to ensure that investment activity is undertaken in a manner sensitive to health, safety or environmental concerns provided that such measures are consistent with this agreement.' *See* OECD, 'Multilateral Agreement on Investment' [1995] Annex, para. 3, 143 http://www.oecd.org/investment/internationalinvestmentagreements/multilateralagreementoninvestment.htm accessed on 10 June 2018.
144. A. Newcombe, General Exceptions in International Investment Agreements: Paper Prepared for the BIICL Eighth Annual WTO Conference (London, 2008) http://www.biicl.org/files/3866_andrew_newcombe.pdf accessed on 15 June 2018.
145. *See* K. Gordon, J. Pohl, 'Environmental Concerns in International Investment Agreements: A Survey' (2011) OECD Working Papers on International Investment 2011/01, 14, Part X on the 'Right to Regulate – Reserving Policy Space for Environmental Regulation' https://www.oecd.org/daf/inv/investment-policy/WP-2011_1.pdf accessed on 7 January 2017. The survey presents multiple examples of IIAs that have incorporated the provision including the protection of environmental concerns.
146. V. Prislan, R. Zandvliet, 'Labor Provisions in International Investment Agreements: Prospects for Sustainable Development', in A. Bjorklund (ed.) *Yearbook of International Investment Law and Policy 2012/2013* (Oxford University Press, 2014) pp. 377-411.
147. A. Titi, (2014) 180-186. In the context of expropriation, *see* the example of the US Model BIT (2012) 'Annex B (4)(b): Expropriation' where the exceptions to indirect expropriation are provided. *See*: US Model BIT (2012) https://ustr.gov/sites/default/files/BIT%20text%20for%20ACIEP%20Meeting.pdf; Article 3(d) of the Colombia-Model BIT (2008) where the exceptions

Indirect references to the right to regulate in the provisions of IIAs can be illustrated by several examples.

Frequently, the right to regulate has featured indirectly as an exception to a specific regulatory concern or a group of concerns, with the intention of excluding such concern(s) from the scope of the particular provision or the entire treaty.[148] For example, Article 10 of the Canada-Peru BIT (2006) states that:

> [N]othing in this Agreement shall be construed to prevent a Party from adopting or enforcing measures (a) to protect human, animal or plant life or health; (b) to ensure compliance with laws and regulations that are not inconsistent with the provisions of this Agreement; or (c) for the conservation of living or non-living exhaustible natural resources.[149]

Even though this type of provision does not refer to the right to regulate, by inserting such a general exception clause, the intention of the contracting states was to 'enhance regulatory flexibility, by allowing host states to regulate foreign investment without incurring international liability for their actions'.[150] Titi, in her study on the right to regulate, has noted that the exceptions contained in IIAs that are either specific or general constitute the most common tool for states to safeguard their right to regulate.[151] Such exception clauses can be found in older IIAs as well as in more recent treaties.[152] UNCTAD's Investment Policy Framework for Sustainable Development (IPFSD) has asserted that the growing number of recent IIAs 'reaffirm the State's right to regulate by introducing general exceptions'.[153] The reason for this, according to UNCTAD, is that 'exceptions allow for the measures, otherwise prohibited by the agreement, to be taken under specified circumstances'.[154] By means of inserting general exceptions, states attempt to preserve regulatory flexibility in designated policy areas.

---

to fair and equitable treatment are provided. Colombia-Model BIT (2008) http://investmentpolicyhub.unctad.org/Download/TreatyFile/2821. Websites accessed on 18 June 2018.

148. These types of provisions are usually modelled on Article XX of the General Agreement on Tariffs and Trade (GATT) that are also referred to as general exceptions. These types of exceptions include a list of public interest concerns, which the contracting parties incorporate into their agreements in order to be exempted from liability in adopting this type of public interest measure; *see*: A. Titi, (2014) 206.
149. Canada-Peru BIT, Article 10 (2006) http://investmentpolicyhub.unctad.org/Download/TreatyFile/626 accessed on 15 June 2018.
150. L. Sabanogullari, The Merits and Limitations of General Exception Clauses in Contemporary Investment Treaty Practice (Investment Treaty News, 21 May 2015) https://www.iisd.org/itn/2015/05/21/the-merits-and-limitations-of-general-exception-clauses-in-contemporary-investment-treaty-practice/ accessed on 15 June 2018.
151. A. Titi, (2014) 300.
152. The UNCTAD IIA Mapping Project states that 1,958 IIAs, 98 included general public policy exceptions (e.g., cultural heritage, public order, health). Most of these IIAs were concluded after 2000. *See* UNCTAD 'IIA Mapping Project 2016' (2016) http://investmentpolicyhub.unctad.org/IIA/mappedContent#iiaInnerMenu accessed on 12 January 2017.
153. UNCTAD, 'Investment Policy Framework for Sustainable Development (IPFSD)' (2015) 103 http://unctad.org/en/Pages/DIAE/International%20Investment%20Agreements%20(IIA)/IIA-IPFSD.aspx accessed on 2 February 2018.
154. *Ibid.*

However, the inclusion of exceptions to FET standard provisions is extremely rare.[155] One example has been identified in the Columbia Model BIT of 2008.[156] It includes an exception for a state's regulatory measures in the context of the FET standard. Consequently, Article 4(d) of this Model BIT states that:

> [F]air and equitable treatment shall not be construed as to prevent a Contracting Party from exercising its regulatory powers in a transparent and non-discriminatory manner and in accordance with due process.[157]

This provision makes an explicit reference to the exercise of regulatory powers, which, in this context, has a meaning that is identical to the right to regulate. No specific public interests are mentioned where the state has the right to regulate. However, this provision stipulates that the state has the right to regulate subject to the condition that its actions are carried out in a 'transparent and non-discriminatory manner and in accordance with due process'.[158] A comparable formulation of an exception to a state's regulatory measures can often be found in indirect expropriation clauses, for example. In an increasing number of IIAs, the legitimate measure taken in the public interest is exempted from liability under an indirect expropriation clause. For example, Annex B(4)(b) of the United States (US) Model BIT of 2012 provides that 'except in rare circumstances, non-discriminatory regulatory actions by a Party that are designed and applied to protect legitimate public welfare objectives, such as public health, safety, and the environment, do not constitute indirect expropriations.'[159] In contrast to Article 4(d) of the Colombia-Model BIT, this provision provides examples of public interest, which are exempted from liability under an indirect expropriation clause if they are applied in a non-discriminatory manner. To strengthen this regulatory flexibility, a general reference to the concept of the right to regulate is sometimes incorporated through a reference to the protection of a specific public interest in the operative part of the treaty. Commonly, these public interests, incorporated in some IIAs, include the protection of health and the environment and the protection of labour standards.[160] Several recent agreements also include provisions on corporate social responsibility (CSR).[161] For example, the CSR provision has been included in Article 16 of the Benin-Canada BIT that provides that:

155. A. Titi, (2014) 300. For other investment protection standards such as MFN clauses and indirect expropriation clauses, the exceptions are more common (pp. 126 and 151).
156. The Colombia-Model BIT, Article 3(d) (2008) http://investmentpolicyhub.unctad.org/Download/TreatyFile/2821 accessed on 12 June 2018.
157. The Colombia-Model BIT, Article 3(d) (2008).
158. *Ibid.*
159. Annex B (Expropriation) of the US Model BIT (2012) para. 4 (b) https://ustr.gov/sites/default/files/BIT%20text%20for%20ACIEP%20Meeting.pdf accessed on 1 April 2017.
160. The UNCTAD IIAs Mapping Project underlines categories of additional provisions, next to typical provisions found in IIAs. Consequently, the most common reference in the additional provisions found in the survey of the 1,958 IIAs includes either separate clauses on or references in other provisions to health, environment and labour standard provisions. *See* UNCTAD 'IIA Mapping Project 2016' (2016) http://investmentpolicyhub.unctad.org/IIA/mappedContent#iiaInnerMenu accessed on 12 January 2017.
161. The UNCTAD IIAs Mapping Project states that 1,958 IIAs, 28 included Corporate Social Responsibility provisions. Most of these IIAs were concluded after 2000. *See* UNCTAD 'IIA

> Contracting Party should encourage enterprises operating within its territory or subject to its jurisdiction to voluntarily incorporate internationally recognized standards of corporate social responsibility in their practices and internal policies, such as statements of principle that have been endorsed or are supported by the Contracting Parties. These principles address issues such as labour, the environment, human rights, community relations and anti-corruption.[162]

The CSR provision in IIAs, as exemplified in the Benin-Canada BIT, imposes an obligation on contracting states to promote responsible business conduct for companies operating within the territory or under the jurisdiction of one of the contracting states.[163] The incorporation of CSR standards suggests the increasing role of the responsibilities of foreign investors in international investment law. This type of provision does not impose direct obligations on foreign investors; however, it does recognise the role of companies in furthering labour, human rights and environmental issues.[164] The increasing role of investor conduct can be observed in an assessment of the FET standard by investment tribunals. In the tribunals' assessments of the legitimate expectations of investors under the FET standard, reference is frequently made to the investor's proper due diligence as one of the elements that should be taken into account in the overall evaluation of the legitimate expectations of the investor.[165]

To exemplify how the protection of the environment is incorporated into the operative part of the treaty, the BIT between the US and Uruguay (2005) serves as an appropriate illustration. Article 12 of the Investment and Environment section of the US-Uruguay BIT provides that:

> 1. The Parties recognize that it is inappropriate to encourage investment by weakening or reducing the protections afforded in domestic environmental laws. ....
> 2. Nothing in this Treaty shall be construed to prevent a Party from adopting, maintaining, or enforcing any measure otherwise consistent with this Treaty that it considers appropriate to ensure that investment activity in its territory is undertaken in a manner sensitive to environmental concerns.[166]

This type of provision is formulated as a positive obligation for the host state not to lower environmental standards.[167] It also reaffirms that the state has the right to adopt measures in a 'manner sensitive to environmental concerns'. However, these measures have to be consistent with the obligations under the treaty. From such a

Mapping Project 2016' (2016) http://investmentpolicyhub.unctad.org/IIA/mappedContent#iiaInnerMenu accessed on 12 January 2017.

162. Benin-Canada BIT, Article 16 (2013) http://investmentpolicyhub.unctad.org/Download/TreatyFile/438 accessed on 29 May 2017.
163. R. Peels et al., ILO Research Paper, 'Corporate Social Responsibility in International Trade and Investment Agreements: Implication for States, Business and Workers,' ILO Research Paper No. 13, April 2016, p. 15 http://www.ilo.org/wcmsp5/groups/public/---dgreports/---inst/documents/publication/wcms_476193.pdf accessed on 27 May 2018.
164. R. Peels et al., (2016) p. 15.
165. *See*: Chapter 6.
166. US-Uruguay BIT (2005) http://investmentpolicyhub.unctad.org/IIA/country/225/treaty/3069 accessed on 2 January 2017.
167. A. Titi, (2014), 104. Titi defines positive language concerning regulatory interest as language that 'does not create legally enforceable rights and obligations'.

formulation it follows that the state regulating in the field of the protection of the environment will not be exempted from the obligations under the treaty. Therefore, this provision, though placing importance on environmental issues that might be taken into consideration by tribunals, is not likely to be a solid legal ground for exempting the state from liability under the FET standard and other substantive obligations under the IIA concerned.[168]

A direct reference to the right to regulate has been incorporated in the South African Development Community (SADC) Model Bilateral Investment Treaty Template of 2012. The document provides a template for new BITs that are to be negotiated by the Member States of the SADC. Article 20.1 of the SADC Model BIT, entitled a 'State's Right to Regulate', provides that:

> In accordance with customary international law and other general principles of international law, the Host State has the right to take regulatory or other measures to ensure that development in its territory is consistent with the goals and principles of sustainable development, and with other legitimate social and economic policy objectives.[169]

The right to regulate in Article 20.1 is identified in accordance with (1) customary international law and other general principles of international law; (2) the goals and principles of sustainable development; and (3) other legitimate social and economic policy objectives. Article 20.1 emphasises the goals and principles of sustainable development in the context of the right to regulate. The concept of sustainable development occupies a central position in the SADC Model BIT. It is referred to as a 'main objective' of the agreement, with a view to 'encourage and increase investments ... that support the sustainable development of each Party ...'.[170] The intention behind this provision is to stress the link between foreign direct investment and the promotion of sustainable development. This connection was meant to emphasise that the role of foreign direct investment is to 'contribute to the development objectives of each State and the region as a whole, rather than simply being an end in itself'.[171] Article 20.1 also mentions 'legitimate policy and economic policy objectives'. Examples of what this category comprises are not provided. The commentary to Article 20.1 of the SADC Model BIT explains that the goal of this provision is to emphasise that a state's right to regulate should not be compromised in the course of complying with investment obligations.[172] The commentary to this provision also explains that this general

168. J. Vinuales, 'The Environmental Regulations of Foreign Investment Scheme under International Law', in P.-M. Dupuy, J. Vinuales (eds) *Harnessing Foreign Investment to Promote Environmental Protection Incentives and Safeguards* (Cambridge University Press, 2013) 284; A. Romson, Environmental Policy Space & International Investment Law (Studia Juridica Stockholmiensia, 2 September 2015) pp. 303-305.
169. The South African Development Community (SADC) Model BIT Template of 2012 with Commentaries, Article 20.1 http://investmentpolicyhub.unctad.org/Download/TreatyFile/2875 accessed on 12 June 2018.
170. The South African Development Community (SADC) Model BIT Template of 2012 with Commentaries, Article 1, p. 8.
171. *Ibid.*
172. The South African Development Community (SADC) Model BIT Template of 2012 with Commentaries, Article 20.1, p. 40.

provision on the right to regulate should be read in conjunction with more specific investment protection clauses, e.g. FET provisions that provide more clarity on the scope of a state's rights and obligations.[173] As the commentary states, 'all of these provisions are intended to work together.'[174]

Article 20.2 of the SADC Model BIT further elaborates on the right to regulate by stating that:

> Except where the rights of a Host State are expressly stated as an exception to the obligations of this Agreement, a Host State's pursuit of its rights to regulate shall be understood as embodied within a balance of the rights and obligations of Investors and Investments and Host States, as set out in this Agreement.[175]

The host states' right to regulate, according to Article 20.2 of SADC Model BIT, 'shall be understood as embodied within a balance of the rights and obligations of Investors and Investment and Host States'.[176] This indicates that the right to regulate should be balanced against the rights of investors under the treaty. This provision is viewed by the drafters as the 'broader goal' that will ensure that arbitrators will not consider 'investment treaties purely as investor rights'.[177] The commentary to Article 20.2 further emphasises that 'in view of the broad obligations in BITs, it is useful to reaffirm the Host State's right to regulate investments in the public interest'.[178]

The right to regulate has also been incorporated in the texts of new EU (draft) investment agreements.[179] Since the entry into force of the Lisbon Treaty in 2009, the EU has obtained an 'express treaty-making power with regard to foreign direct investment ...'.[180] In formulating the EU approach towards foreign direct investment,

173. *Ibid.*, Article 20, p. 40.
174. *Ibid.*
175. *Ibid.*
176. *Ibid.*
177. *Ibid.*
178. The South African Development Community (SADC) Model BIT Template of 2012 with Commentaries, Article 20.2, p. 40.
179. CETA (signed on 30 October 2016) http://ec.europa.eu/trade/policy/in-focus/ceta/; The EU-Vietnam FTA, draft text (January 2016), Chapter 8: Trade in Services, Investment and E-Commerce, Articles 13*bis* http://trade.ec.europa.eu/doclib/press/index.cfm?id=1437. Both websites accessed on 12 June 2018.
180. A. Reinisch, Essentials of EU Law (2nd edn., Cambridge University Press, 2012) 245. The exclusive competence of the EU in the sphere of the FDI has its legal basis in Article 207 of the Treaty on the Functioning of the European Union (TFEU). *See* 'Consolidated Version of the Treaty on European Union' 2010 O.J. C 83/01; 'Consolidated Version of the Treaty on the Functioning of the European Union' 2008 O.J. C 115/47 http://eur-lex.europa.eu/legal-content/EN/TXT/?uri=celex%3A12012E%2FTXT accessed on 12 June 2018. *See also* the opinion of the Court of Justice of the European Union on the EU-Singapore Free Trade Agreement that decided on the allocation of competences between the EU and its Member States in negotiating the EU-Singapore FTA. In the opinion of the court this is a mixed agreement, where, e.g., the ISDS falls under mixed competence, whereas the foreign direct investment is an exclusive competence of the EU. *See*: The Opinion of the Court of Justice of the European Union Free Trade Agreement between the European Union and the Republic of Singapore, Opinion 2/15, 16 May 2017, http://curia.europa.eu/juris/document/document.jsf?text=&docid=190727&pageIndex=0&doclang=EN&mode=req&dir=&occ=first&part=1&cid=116501 accessed on 29 May 2017.

the state's right to regulate has been referred to in some EU policy documents,[181] the recently signed CETA between the EU and Canada[182] and the Draft EU-Vietnam FTA.[183] In an EU paper on the Investment Chapter in the proposed economic trade agreement between the EU and the US, entitled 'Investment in TTIP and beyond – the path for reform,' the EU Commission has outlined its approach towards foreign direct investment policy.[184] In this paper, the challenge for EU investment policy has been formulated as the necessity to 'ensure that the goal of protecting and encouraging investment does not affect the ability of the EU and its Member States to continue to pursue public policy objectives'.[185] The paper further explains that the new approach towards EU investment policy involves the 'reaffirm[ation] of the right to regulate'.[186] The example used in the aforementioned paper is the CETA, at that time still a provisional text, but it was finally signed on 30 October 2016.[187] In the CETA's operational part of the Investment Chapter, Article 8.9(1) (Investment and regulatory measures) stipulates that:

> (1) For the purpose of this Chapter, the Parties reaffirm their right to regulate within their territories to achieve legitimate policy objectives, such as the protection of public health, safety, the environment or public morals, social or consumer protection or the promotion and protection of cultural diversity.[188]

Article 8.9(1) explicitly refers to the state's right to regulate. The right to regulate extends to legitimate policy objectives exemplified in paragraph 1 of the aforementioned provision. The Joint Interpretative Instrument on the CETA between Canada, the EU and its Member States (hereinafter 'Joint Interpretative Instrument') clarifies some of the provisions of the CETA.[189] The right to regulate is laid down in this document by stating that:

181. European Commission, 'Investment in TTIP and Beyond: The Path for Reform: Enhancing the Right to Regulate and Moving from Current Ad Hoc Arbitration Towards an Investment Court' [2015] European Commission Concept Paper http://trade.ec.europa.eu/doclib/docs/2015/may/tradoc_153408.PDF accessed on 16 February 2017; Council of the European Union, 'Joint Interpretative Instrument on the Comprehensive Economic and Trade Agreement (CETA) between Canada and the European Union and its Member States' 13541/16 (Brussels, 27 October 2016) 3.
182. CETA (signed on 30 October 2016) http://ec.europa.eu/trade/policy/in-focus/ceta/ accessed on 14 June 2018.
183. EU-Vietnam Free Trade Agreement (agreed text as of January 2016) Chapter 8: Trade in Services, Investment and E-Commerce, Articles 13*bis* http://trade.ec.europa.eu/doclib/press/index.cfm?id=1437 accessed on 14 June 2018.
184. European Commission, 'Investment in TTIP and Beyond: The Path for Reform: Enhancing the Right to Regulate and Moving from Current Ad Hoc Arbitration Towards an Investment Court' [2015] European Commission Concept Paper http://trade.ec.europa.eu/doclib/docs/2015/may/tradoc_153408.PDF accessed on 12 June 2018.
185. *Ibid.*, p. 1.
186. *Ibid.*, p. 2.
187. CETA (signed on 30 October 2016) http://ec.europa.eu/trade/policy/in-focus/ceta/ accessed on 12 June 2018.
188. *Ibid.*
189. Further clarification of the legal status of the Joint Interpretative Instrument can be found in Chapter 3 of this book.

> CETA preserves the ability of the European Union and its Member States and Canada to adopt and apply their own laws and regulations that regulate economic activity in the public interest, to achieve legitimate public policy objectives such as the protection and promotion of public health, social services, public education, safety, the environment, public morals, social or consumer protection, privacy and data protection and the promotion and protection of cultural diversity.[190]

The Joint Interpretative Instrument in the aforementioned statement restates the formulation of Article 8.9(1) of the CETA. It specifies that the adopted laws and regulations of a state should be in the 'public interest'. In comparison to the list of legitimate objectives mentioned in Article 8.9(1), the Joint Interpretative Instrument has added 'social services', 'public education' and 'privacy and data protection' as examples of a state's legitimate objectives. This indicates that the list of legitimate objectives in the text of the CETA are merely examples and, as such, the list is not exhaustive.[191]

Article 8.9(2) of the CETA further clarifies that:

> (2) For greater certainty, the mere fact that a Party regulates, including through a modification to its laws, in a manner which negatively affects an investment or interferes with an investor's expectations, including its expectations of profits, does not amount to a breach of an obligation under this Section.[192]

Article 8.9(2) of the CETA is particularly relevant for the current analysis of the principle of FET. This is because Article 8.9(2) of the CETA refers to the expectations of the investor, which is a key element of the FET standard.[193] As will be discussed in more detail in Chapter 6, the frustration of the legitimate expectations of an investor may result in a violation of the FET standard.[194] In several investment decisions on the FET standard, tribunals have broadly interpreted legitimate expectations, focusing primarily on the rights of investors, with limited consideration being given to the state's right to regulate.[195] The formulation adopted in Article 8.9(2) may be read as an attempt by the contracting parties to avoid such a broad interpretation of legitimate expectations in future investment cases. This is supported by the clarification in the Joint Interpretative Instrument, which asserts that: 'CETA clarifies that governments

---

190. Council of the European Union, 'Joint Interpretative Instrument on the Comprehensive Economic and Trade Agreement (CETA) between Canada and the European Union and its Member States' 13541/16 (Brussels, 27 October 2016) 3.
191. U. Kriebaum, 'FET and Expropriation in the Comprehensive Economic Trade Agreement between the European Union and Canada (CETA)' [2016] 13(1) *Transnational Dispute Management*, 24; 'The list of purposes mentioned in the provision is not exhaustive, and the goals mentioned are only examples since the list is proceeded by "such as".'
192. Article 8(9)(2) of the CETA (signed on 30 October 2016) http://ec.europa.eu/trade/policy/in-focus/ceta/ accessed on 15 June 2018.
193. *See* Chapter 6 of this book.
194. J. Bonnitcha, (2015) 40. 'The common understanding of arbitral decisions and commentators is that a breach of legitimate expectations is sufficient to establish liability'.
195. Examples include *CME v. Czech Republic* [2001] UNCITRAL Arbitration, Partial Award (13 September 2001); *Tecmed v. Mexico,* ICSID Case No. ARB(AF)/00/2 Award (29 May 2003); *Occidental v. Ecuador*, LCIA Case No. UN3467 Final Award (1 July 2004); *MTD Equity Sdn. Bhd. and MTD Chile S.A. v. Republic of Chile*, ICSID Case No. ARB/01/7 Award (25 May 2004). This issue is addressed in further details in Chapter 5.

may change their laws, regardless of whether this may negatively affect an investment or investor's expectations of profits.'[196] Whether Article 8.9(2) imposes a limitation on the FET standard vis-à-vis the state's right to regulate should be assessed in combination with Article 8.10 on the FET standard.

On the basis of the survey of treaties undertaken in this section, it can be observed that states rely on different safeguards to preserve the right to regulate in IIAs. In many instances, the reference to the right to regulate is indirect and is made through exception clauses or provisions on specific public interests, e.g. environmental protection. However, recent treaties, e.g. the CETA and the SADC Model BIT, have included a direct reference to the right to regulate. On a general level, the provision on the right to regulate in the CETA and the SADC Model BIT reaffirms that the state has the right to regulate, this right being inherent in state sovereignty. The CETA limits the right to regulate to 'legitimate policy objectives'. Article 8.9(1) includes examples of these objectives, e.g. the environment and public morals. The SADC Model BIT, in similar terms, refers to 'legitimate social and economic policy objectives' with emphasis being placed on the goals and principles of sustainable development. Furthermore, Article 20(2) of the SADC Model BIT states that the state's right to regulate should be taken into account in balancing the rights and obligations of investors and host states.[197] Consequently, the right to regulate is understood as including a variety of goals and interests of states and investors. In Article 8.9(2) of the CETA, a further clarification of the right to regulate is provided, stating that the state's competence to modify its laws will not, per se, incur liability, at least as intended by the contracting parties.

[C] The Right to Regulate in FET Investment Cases

In international investment cases, various tribunals have referred to the right to regulate, especially in examining regulatory conduct in expropriation and FET claims. As Alvik formulated:

> '[The] right to regulate' has increasingly been conceptualized in investment jurisprudence as an inherent power of the state (police powers), which is defined through a distinction between legitimate non-compensable regulation and deprivatory regulation equivalent in effect of expropriation or a breach of, for example, fair and equitable treatment standard in an investment treaty.[198]

196. Council of the European Union, 'Joint Interpretative Instrument on the Comprehensive Economic and Trade Agreement (CETA) between Canada and the European Union and its Member States' 13541/16 (Brussels, 27 October 2016) 5. A similar statement is contained in European Commission, 'Investment Provisions in the EU-Canada Free Trade Agreement (CETA)' (Press Release, 3 December 2013) 2. This document explains that the objective of Article 8.9(2) is to ensure that states have the possibility to change their legislation even if this, in some cases, does impact on an investor's legitimate expectations of profit http://trade.ec.europa.eu/doclib/docs/2013/november/tradoc_151918.pdf accessed on 10 June 2018.
197. The South African Development Community (SADC) Model BIT Template of 2012 with Commentaries, Article 20.2 http://investmentpolicyhub.unctad.org/Download/TreatyFile/2875 accessed on 12 June 2018.
198. I. Alvik, Contracting with Sovereignty: State Contracts and International Arbitration (Hart Publishing, 2011) 261.

As discussed above, since public interest exceptions that are applicable to substantive investment guarantees – e.g., the FET standard – are rare in treaties,[199] tribunals primarily affirm the state's right to regulate as an element of the state's sovereignty.[200] More recently, tribunals have tended to develop specific criteria for what constitutes (un)fair conduct by the state and have taken the public interest into consideration. Bearing in mind the subject of this book, the main focus of this section is on those cases in which the right to regulate plays a role in connection with the FET standard.

With regard to terminology, in stressing the state's right to regulate, tribunals have used several terms. This terminology ranges from 'the right to regulate' or the 'reasonable right to regulate'[201] to an 'undeniable right and privilege to exercise its sovereign legislative power'.[202]

Tribunals have described the elements of the right to regulate in various investment decisions. These elements are highlighted below.

The starting point underlined by several investment tribunals is that the right to regulate is provided by international law and that this right is limited by, *inter alia*, investment obligations. This point has been summarised in *ADC v. Hungary* where the tribunal underlined that:

> [i]t is the Tribunal's understanding of the basic international law principles that while a sovereign State possesses the inherent right to regulate its domestic affairs, the exercise of such right is not unlimited and must have its boundaries. As rightly pointed out by the Claimants, the rule of law, which includes treaty obligations, provides such boundaries. Therefore, when a State enters into a bilateral investment treaty like the one in this case, it becomes bound by it and the investment protection obligations it undertook therein must be honored rather than be ignored by a later argument of the State's right to regulate.[203]

In several other decisions, other elements have been highlighted. These can be divided into three broad categories: (1) A number of tribunals have reaffirmed that states have the right to change and modify their laws as an integral part of their ability to regulate. (2) In a few cases, tribunals have emphasised the importance of a special public interest of the state, e.g. health protection in the context of the right to regulate. (3) An increasing number of tribunals have been more precise in articulating the criteria for the state's conduct to be lawful. Each of these elements will be briefly discussed below:

(1) The state's right to modify its laws has been stressed by tribunals primarily in the context of an assessment of the legitimate expectations of the investor. This right has been accentuated by tribunals as a result of multiple investors'

199. A. Titi, (2014) 144.
200. A reference to the right to regulate in IIAs is also a feature of new investment treaties that have not yet been tested by tribunals.
201. *See* the *AWG v. Argentina*, UNCITRAL Arbitration, Decision on Liability (30 July 2010) para. 236, where the Tribunal acknowledged 'Argentina's reasonable right to regulate'.
202. *Parkerings v. Lithuania*, ICSID Case No. ARB/05/8 Award (11 September 2007) para. 332.
203. *ADC v. Hungary*, ICSID Case No. ARB/03/16 Award (2 October 2006) para. 423.

claims in which they have challenged regulatory amendments made by host states. The reasoning employed by investors was that such alterations have negatively affected their investment and have therefore frustrated the legitimate expectations of the investor. In *Saluka v. Czech Republic*, the tribunal stated that 'no investor may reasonably expect that the circumstances prevailing at the time the investment is made remain totally unchanged.'[204] In a similar vein, the *Parkerings v. Lithuania* tribunal has emphasised that 'it is each State's undeniable right and privilege to exercise its sovereign legislative power. A State has the right to enact, modify or cancel a law at its own discretion ....'[205] In *El Paso v. Argentina*, the tribunal in assessing the FET standard stated that 'the state has to be able to make the reasonable changes called for by the circumstances and cannot be considered to have accepted a freeze on the evolution of its legal system.'[206] Chapter 6, section §6.05 further elaborates and analyses the FET jurisprudence in which tribunals have underlined the state's right to modify its laws.

(2) A few decisions that have dealt with a specific public interest have stressed the state's deference to regulate such an interest. In analysing the state's conduct in regulating the gambling industry, the tribunal in *Thunderbird v. Mexico* stressed that:

> Mexico has in this context a wide regulatory 'space' for regulation; in the regulation of the gambling industry, governments have a particularly wide scope of regulation reflecting national views on public morals. Mexico can permit or prohibit any forms of gambling as far as the NAFTA is concerned. It can change its regulatory policy and it has a wide discretion with respect to how it carries out such policies by regulation and administrative conduct.[207]

In a similar vein, several tribunals have emphasised their concern about public health, thereby affording the state greater deference to regulate such matters.[208] In *Philip Morris v. Uruguay*, the tribunal stated that 'the responsibility for public health measures rests with the government and investment tribunals should pay great deference to governmental judgments of national needs in matters such as the protection of public health.'[209] Chapter 7, section §7.02[C] provides a further analysis of FET cases that have involved specific public interests.

(3) Finally, several tribunals have attempted to articulate the limits of the right to regulate. Considering that this issue constitutes the most important part of

204. *Saluka v. Czech Republic* [2006] Permanent Court of Arbitration, IIC 210, Partial Award (17 March 2006) para. 305.
205. *Parkerings v. Lithuania*, ICSID Case No. ARB/05/8 Award (11 September 2007) para. 332.
206. *El Paso v. Argentina*, ICSID Case No. ARB/03/15 Award (31 October 2011) para. 365.
207. *International Thunderbird Gaming Corp. v. Mexico* [2006] NAFTA-UNCITRAL Arbitration, Award (26 January 2006) para. 127.
208. For other examples, *see Apotex v. US*, ICSID Case No. ARB(AF)/12/1 Award (25 August 2014); and *Chemtura v. Canada* [2010] NAFTA-UNCITRAL Arbitration, Award (2 August 2010).
209. *Philip Morris v. Uruguay*, ICSID Case No. ARB/10/7 Award (8 July 2016) para. 399.

this book (*see* Chapters 7-8), at this stage it is opportune to only briefly mention that several tribunals have underlined that a state in exercising its right to regulate should not be 'unreasonable or inequitable in the exercise of its legislative power'[210] and that its conduct should not 'manifestly violate the requirements of consistency, transparency, even-handedness and non- discrimination'.[211] These criteria are certainly not exhaustive. However, these elements represent the basic conditions, which are applicable to a state's right to regulate as emphasised in investment decisions.

To summarise, tribunals generally refer to the right to regulate in FET cases. Primarily, tribunals have reaffirmed that states have the right to regulate; of course, this right is limited by the obligations of states under IIA provisions. In several decisions, tribunals have further clarified this basic premise by underlining that states have the right to change and modify their laws as part of their ability to regulate. In a number of decisions, tribunals have stressed the importance of a special public interest of the state, e.g. the protection of public health, in the context of the right to regulate. Finally, in a few FET decisions, tribunals have been more precise in articulating the criteria for the state's right to regulate versus the state's obligation to provide investors with FET. A further clarification is provided in Chapters 6-7 of this book.

[D] The Right to Regulate in Academic Literature

In parallel with the developments concerning the right to regulate in investment treaties and cases, scholars have been developing their thoughts on this subject.[212] A few have provided a conceptual framework for the right to regulate in investment law.[213] In this section, two of these studies are examined.

In '*The Right to Regulate in International Investment Law*,' Titi defines the right to regulate as:

> the legal right exceptionally permitting the host state to regulate in derogation of international commitments it has undertaken by means of an investment agreement without incurring a duty to compensate.[214]

---

210. *Parkerings v. Lithuania*, ICSID Case No. ARB/05/8 Award (11 September 2007) para. 332. In similar terms *see AES Summit v. Hungary*, ICSID Case No. ARB/07/22 Award (23 September 2010) para. 10.3.36. The tribunal assessed the state's measures on the basis of whether they were 'reasonable, proportionate and consistent with the public policy expressed by the parliament'.
211. *Saluka v. Czech Republic* [2006] Permanent Court of Arbitration, IIC 210, Partial Award (17 March 2006) para. 303.
212. Several scholars have discussed the right to regulate in international investment law, primarily through the prism of sovereignty, public policies, sustainable development, human rights. *See*, e.g., I. Alvik, (2011); A. Kulick, Global Public Interest in International Investment Law (Cambridge University Press, 2012); M.-C. Cordonier Segger and others, Sustainable Development in World Investment Law (Kluwer Law International, 2011); P.-M. Dupuy, et al., Human Rights in International Investment Law and Arbitration (Oxford University Press, 2010).
213. L. Wandahl Mouyal, (2016); A. Titi, (2014).
214. A. Titi, (2014) 33.

Titi explains that the right to regulate is a legal right that is derived from several sources: (1) conventional law (i.e., the law found in investment treaties), (2) treaty-based exceptions (general exceptions applied to the entire treaty and exceptions to substantive provisions in the respective standards of treatment) and (3) general international law.[215] According to Titi, under the first two categories, states incorporate the right to regulate in IIAs, primarily through the inclusion of specific exceptions to a particular standard of treatment or through a general set of exceptions that are detached from the specific standard of treatment.[216] For the third category, she refers to the right to regulate under customary international law as reflected in the International Law Commission's (ILC's) Articles on State Responsibility.[217] In particular, she analyses customary international law defences that are reflected in the ILC Articles, as well as the practical availability of these defences to host states during investment arbitration.[218] To this end, she investigates the circumstances precluding wrongfulness under Chapter V of the ILC Articles with a focus on the defence of necessity, *jus cogens*, the *clausula rebus sic stantibus* and bribery.[219]

Titi distinguishes different public interest areas. Based on the result of her research, she specifies the interest to be protected in accordance with the right to regulate contained within IIAs. She has distinguished between: (1) 'essential state security' that includes economic security, access to strategic industries, essential interests in preserving political or economic survival and a balance (among others), the preservation of international peace and security and circumstances of extreme emergency; (2) 'public order' that has various meanings in different treaties and can sometimes refer to riots and violence or measures taken to ensure public health and safety;[220] and (3) 'regulations taken in the public interest', understood as the concept that has been used as an 'unqualified collective noun' that refers to general welfare and as a 'collective noun qualified by a list of specific interests or individual interests' (e.g., public health and safety).[221]

Titi's contribution outlines the different applications and implications of the right to regulate through exceptions found in treaties, or in other words, the 'extent to which general international law or arbitral jurisprudence may or not accommodate state

215. *Ibid.*
216. *See* A. Titi, (2014), Chapters VI, VII, IX. *See also* E. De Brabandere 'Book Review: A. Titi, The Right to Regulate in International Investment Law' [2015] 52 (4) *Common Market Law Review*, 1152-1155.
217. Specifically, Titi refers to the ILC Articles that include six circumstances precluding 'wrongfulness'. These include consent, self-defence, countermeasures in respect of an internationally wrongful act, force majeure, distress and necessity. These circumstances are usually only applicable in extreme circumstances. In the context of general international law, Titi also mentions *jus cogens* norms, the international law on bribery and Article 62 of the VCLT on a fundamental change of circumstances. *See* A. Titi, (2014) 236-273.
218. A. Titi, (2014) 235.
219. A. Titi, (2014).
220. Titi explains that in common law systems, public order acquired relevance in the context of street violence and criminal or police laws. In some US treaties, this term has been used in the context of measures taken in accordance with a party's police powers to ensure public health and safety. *See* A. Titi, (2014) 94-99.
221. A. Titi, (2014) 100.

regulatory flexibility'.[222] An important distinction that Titi makes in her monograph is between the explicit right to regulate and the implicit right to regulate. The latter is evaluated on the basis of decisions by arbitral tribunals. Titi investigates whether the arbitral tribunals, in the absence of a specific treaty provision or defences provided by customary international law, have implicitly acknowledged the state's right to regulate. She concludes that the tribunals have not been eager to take into account the state's right to regulate, especially in FET standard and expropriation claims. Hence, she asserts that an 'implicit right to regulate is not borne out in practice and explicit treaty exceptions are necessary where states wish to ensure a modicum of policy space.'[223]

Titi has carried out legal research that is based primarily on an investigation of international treaties and case law. To reiterate, she defines the right to regulate as 'the legal right exceptionally permitting the host state to regulate in derogation of international commitments it has undertaken by means of an investment agreement without incurring a duty to compensate'.[224] This proposed definition effectively captures the current state of affairs in investment law and offers a useful starting point in identifying the elements that are pertinent to the right to regulate. These aspects are discussed further in section §2.03[E].

A different approach has been adopted by Mouyal in her book entitled '*International Investment Law and the Right to Regulate: A Human Rights Perspective*'.[225] Mouyal has defined the right to regulate as an:

> [A]ffirmation of the sovereign right for states to choose their political, social and economic priorities – within certain limits – through the adoption of legislation and administrative practices without violating international rules protecting foreign investments.[226]

Mouyal argues that developments in the human rights legal regime have altered the concept of sovereignty. She argues that this alteration has formed 'an underlying assumption that states can make binding commitments (e.g., by concluding BITs), provided that they can still take measures to comply with international obligations to make certain policy prioritizations (under the duty to regulate)'.[227]

Mouyal indicates that the right to regulate is occasionally transformed into a duty to regulate when the human rights context is at stake. In this regard, she refers to the obligations under the International Covenant on Economic, Social and Cultural Rights (ICESCR). She argues that under this human rights instrument a state has the 'duty to make certain minimum policy prioritizations'.[228] She concludes that the 'humanisation of international law affects the right to regulate in general international law (including

222. *Ibid.*, 28.
223. *Ibid.*, 297.
224. *Ibid.*, 33.
225. L. Wandahl Mouyal, (2016).
226. *Ibid.*, 8.
227. *Ibid.*, 223.
228. *Ibid.*, 158.

investment law) by adding the element of the underlying human rights presumptions'.[229]

Mouyal's definition of the right to regulate includes a broad range of state priorities, e.g. social, economic and political, in the interest of which states have a right to regulate. Such a specification is supported by an analysis of the rights included in the main international human rights conventions (i.e., the ICESCR). The second part of her definition provides that, by exercising the right to regulate, the state should not be liable under 'international rules protecting foreign investments'. Such formulations adopt a broader position than that of Titi, as Titi only refers to the absence of a duty to compensate as outlined in her definition of the right to regulate. This distinction might be relevant as according to, e.g., the *Biwater v. Tanzania* tribunal, liability can be established without a duty to pay compensation.[230]

Both studies indicate a rise in the importance of the right to regulate in the context of investment law. However, there is a principal difference between the two approaches. Titi addresses the right to regulate as a relevant juridical concept that constitutes an exception to the obligation to protect investments. In discussing the right to regulate from a human rights perspective, Moyual, however, argues that the right to regulate can take priority over the investment obligations of states.

[E] Elements of the Right to Regulate

The right to regulate has become a recognised legal concept in international investment law. It can be characterised by several elements. Some of these elements can be identified according to the example of several IIAs, which in some provisions specify the components that are pertinent to the right to regulate. Another source of elements which are pertinent in comprehending the scope of the right to regulate are the decisions of arbitral tribunals. In the context of the FET standard, recent arbitral decisions have provided more clarity on the status and role of the right to regulate and have provided an exposition of the dimensions and the extent of this right vis-à-vis the state's obligation to provide FET. Lastly, academic writings constitute an additional source, where the right to regulate in the context of investment law has been analysed.[231] Following from such an overview, the following elements of the right to regulate can be identified:

229. *Ibid.*, 223.
230. *Biwater v. Tanzania*, ICSID Case No. ARB/05/22 Final Award (24 July 2008) para. 806. In this case, the arbitral tribunal found violations of BIT provisions, including the FET standard. It did not, however, award any damages to the investor, because the company had failed to show 'compensable monetary damages or loss in this case'.
231. A. Titi, (2014); L. Wandahl Mouyal, (2016); L. Markert, 'The Crucial Question of Future Investment Treaties: Balancing Investors' Rights and Regulatory Interests of Host States', in M. Bungenberg and others (eds) *European Yearbook of International Economic Law* (2011) Springer, 147.

(1) First, the right to regulate is limited by a state's obligations under international law, such as the obligation to provide FET under an IIA.[232] The issue in this regard is the extent of the constraint placed on the state's right to regulate in the context of an FET standard obligation. In this book, it is argued that the right to regulate is limited by certain conditions which apply to the state's right to regulate vis-à-vis the obligation to afford FET. This assumption will be further explored in Chapters 4-7 on the FET jurisprudence in relation to the right to regulate.

(2) Second, as emphasised in Article 20(2) of the SADC Model BIT, the right to regulate is an integral part in balancing the rights and obligations of investors and the investments of host states.[233] The right to regulate has two dimensions. First, from the perspective of investors, in some cases where the state exercises its regulatory authority, e.g. through the enactment or amendment of legislation, this may undermine the stability of the investment climate and generate adverse effects for investment. Consequently, as may be argued by an investor, the state's measures constitute unfair treatment and are hence in violation of the FET standard. Second, from the perspective of the state, however, in addition to fulfilling its obligations under the applicable IIA, the state has a prerogative to ensure public welfare for its population through the exercise of its regulatory authority. As such, a state's exercise of its right to regulate in the public interest may interfere with the right of the investor to obtain FET. However, as will be explained in the next paragraph, the inclusion of a specific public interest in IIAs through an exception to a treaty or to a specific standard of treatment might allow for a derogation from the obligations under an IIA, even if it has an adverse impact on investments.

(3) Third, the right to regulate might be specified by the inclusion of the 'public interest' and/or 'legitimate policy objectives' in IIAs. The public interest usually denotes a state's regulation taken in the interest of the 'welfare of the general public'.[234] For example, the public interest might be differentiated on the basis of 'legitimate public welfare objectives and include the preservation of life, health, the environment, and social standards as well as the promotion of sustainable development and social and ecological progress of the host state'.[235]

Consequently, in some IIAs, contracting states tend to specify what is referred to when reference is made to the public interest.[236] The CETA and

232. As the tribunal in *ADC v. Hungary* underlined: 'the exercise of [the right to regulate] is not unlimited and must have its boundaries.' *ADC v. Hungary*, ICSID Case No. ARB/03/16 Award (2 October 2006) para. 423.
233. The South African Development Community (SADC) Model BIT Template of 2012 with Commentaries, Article 20.2 http://investmentpolicyhub.unctad.org/Download/TreatyFile/2875 accessed on 12 June 2018.
234. Random House, Random House Webster's Unabridged Dictionary (2nd edn., Random House Books, 2014) 151.
235. *Ibid.*
236. P.J. Martinez-Fraga, C. Ryan Reetz, Public Purpose in International Law: Rethinking Regulatory Sovereignty in the Global Era (Cambridge University Press, 2015) 134. The authors explain

SADC Model BITs provide that a state has the right to regulate in order to ensure 'legitimate policy (and economic) objectives'.[237] To be more specific, in the CETA examples of a state's legitimate objectives are included. These include the protection of health, cultural diversity, public morals and consumer protection, among others.[238] In order to specify particular public interests, in a number of IIAs states have inserted exceptions for particular – or a group of particular – public interests that contracting parties have intended to omit from the scope of investment protection.[239] Certain public interests, such as the protection of the environment and health, labour standards and CSR are public areas that have frequently appeared in recent treaties.

Titi, on the basis of treaty research, has also outlined interests that states tend to protect in accordance with the right to regulate. For regulation in the public interest, she has noted that in the new generation of treaties, provisions often include language that allows for a derogation from IIA obligations, where this is essential to protect 'human, animal, or plant life or health, the protection of national treasures of artistic, historic or archaeological value, the environment, conservation of exhaustible natural resources and compliance with laws not inconsistent with the IIA'.[240]

The legitimacy of the objectives underlying a state's regulations is assessed according to the presence of the public interest. Chapter 7 analyses examples of such assessments. On the basis of further research into investment treaties and investment cases, it may be possible to more extensively clarify the notion of public interest, which is pertinent to an analysis of the FET standard.

(4) Another element that is applicable to the right to regulate includes the consequences which result from exercising this right, namely in which circumstances a state, when exercising its right to regulate, is or is not liable towards an investor or does not have an obligation to pay compensation.

Whether a state is liable under the FET standard depends on a variety of factors that tribunals have to consider in their assessment. Primarily, the text of a treaty as a

---

that the presence of a 'public interest' in the definition of the right to regulate both 'limits the right to regulate and also serves as that right's normative foundation'.

237. A. Titi, (2014) 99; L. Markert, (2011) 150.

238. Article 8.9(1) of the CETA (signed on 30 October 2016) http://ec.europa.eu/trade/policy/in-focus/ceta/ accessed on 15 May 2018.

239. These types of provisions are drafted along the lines of the general exception clauses found in Article XX of the GATT. The wording that can be found in several IIAs is very comparable to Article XX of GATT, providing that 'nothing in this Agreement shall be construed to prevent the adoption or enforcement by any contracting party of measures: (a) necessary to protect public morals; (b) necessary to protect human, animal or plant life or health; ...'. The General Agreement on Tariffs and Trade (GATT) (1947) https://www.wto.org/english/res_e/booksp_e/gatt_ai_e/art20_e.pdf accessed on 12 June 2018. For example, a similar clause can be found in the Canada-Model FIPA (2004), http://www.italaw.com/documents/Canadian2004-FIPA-model-en.pdf accessed on 12 June 2018.

240. A. Titi, (2014) 100.

source of the FET obligation provides initial guidance. For example, CETA includes a closed list of state obligations, thereby indicating that only by breaching these obligations (e.g., manifest arbitrariness, targeted discrimination on manifestly wrongful grounds) might the state's conduct give rise to a violation of the FET standard.[241] Furthermore, by taking into account the complexity of FET claims in assessing liability under the FET standard, a range of factors have to be taken into account by tribunals. These factors include an evaluation of the state's objectives in undertaking a certain measure, the degree of interference with investment and the effect on investment, as well as the availability of alternative regulatory tools to achieve the same result, among other things. These factors are elaborated upon in Chapter 7 that analyses investment case law.

Further, the right to regulate relating to the consequences of this right concerns the obligation to pay compensation in the case of a breach of the agreement and/or contract. As the UNCTAD report on FET standard provides, 'the question of measuring compensation for breaches of the FET obligation has not yet received much attention from arbitral tribunals.'[242] There is no clear distinction under the FET standard as to what constitutes compensable state conduct and what qualifies as a state's exercise of a legitimate regulatory action that does not require compensation.[243]

Titi underlines in her monograph that the right to regulate is the ability to regulate that exempts the state from an obligation to pay compensation. She exemplifies that a 'successfully invoked treaty exception is deprived of its meaning, where a subsisting requirement to compensate exists ...'.[244] In this case, where the exception clauses or other types of clauses regulating the public interest are absent in IIAs, other parameters may be considered. For example, several commentators underline that a state's right to regulate should be taken into account in estimating the issue of compensation in accordance with the principle of proportionality.[245] One advocated model is that less compensation should be paid by the state if the regulatory measure is intensely motivated by a public interest and has a lesser effect on investment.[246] In contrast, the amount of damages increases if the regulation is, to a lesser extent, motived by the promotion of a public interest and has caused significant damage to the investment. This model requires further clarity and gives rise to additional questions such as specifying the criteria in assessing the state's measure and how to determine the impact that this measure may or may not have on the promotion of public welfare.

241. Article 8.10(2) of the CETA (signed on 30 October 2016) http://ec.europa.eu/trade/policy/in-focus/ceta/ accessed on 16 May 2018.
242. UNCTAD, 'Fair and Equitable Treatment: UNCTAD Series on International Investment Agreements II' (New York, 2012) xvi.
243. *Ibid.*, 15. Also *see*: I. Tudor, The Fair and Equitable Treatment in the International Law of Foreign Investment (Oxford University Press, 2008), 207.
244. A. Titi, (2014) 34-35.
245. *Ibid.*, 35. *See also* I. Tudor, (2008) 215-228. L. Markert, [2011] 166. In terms of compensation, the author proposes to look for a solution 'in accordance with the principle of proportionality'. Tudor makes the argument that the balancing of investor and state conduct should be performed at the stage of calculating the compensation which is due. She states that the factual situations that tribunals may take into account in calculating compensation are the conduct of the investor and the exceptional situation of the host state.
246. L. Markert, [2011] 166.

§2.04 SUMMARY OF THE CHAPTER AND THE INTERIM CONCLUSIONS

In this Chapter, two concepts of this book have been outlined. At the outset, the general structure and content of IIAs have been explained. The IIA constitutes the legal basis where the rights and obligations of states and investors are laid down. Therefore, in unravelling the meaning of the FET standard, the formulation in the applicable IIA is a primary source for such a determination.

IIAs, most of which are BITs, have experienced a rapid growth, particularly between the early 1990s and the early 2000s. From 2010 onwards, regional IIAs started replacing BITs, thereby accounting for a general decline in BITs. In terms of the content of IIAs, they mostly contain a set of comparable provisions. The procedural guarantees outlined in most IIAs include the direct recourse of foreign investors to ISDS under several options for arbitral forums, usually provided for in IIAs. Currently, the ISDS has attracted a reasonable amount of criticism that is commonly expressed in questioning the legitimacy of the investment arbitration system in reviewing the host state's regulatory conduct. Consequently, the issue of balancing the state's right to regulate while ensuring the protection of the investor and the investment under IIAs has been a topical subject in the general discussion of investment agreements.

In the second section of this Chapter, the right to regulate has been placed in the context of this book. Originating in the international legal principle of state sovereignty, the right to regulate has become a relevant concept in international investment law. This right to regulate as an expression referring to the regulatory aspects of (internal) sovereignty accounts for the protection of citizens' public interest undertaken by states. In the words of Titi, the right to regulate in international investment law refers to 'the legal right exceptionally permitting the host state to regulate in derogation of international commitments it has undertaken by means of an investment agreement without incurring a duty to compensate'.[247] The right to regulate has been directly and indirectly referred to in the texts of IIAs, in the decisions of investment tribunals on the FET standard and in academic writing. Through these sources, several elements can be outlined in relation to the right to regulate: (1) it is limited by the international obligations under general international law and international treaties, such as the FET obligation towards foreign investors under an IIA; (2) it has to be balanced against the rights and obligations of investors; (3) it can usually be specified by contracting states in IIAs through the inclusion of the public interest or legitimate policy objectives; (4) its exercise can entail different consequences, which are usually related to liability under an IIA, and/or the obligation to pay compensation in the case of a violation of treaty obligations, e.g. the obligation to provide FET to an investor.

247. A. Titi, (2014) 33.

CHAPTER 3

The Fair and Equitable Treatment Standard in International Investment Agreements

§3.01 INTRODUCTION

The FET standard provisions in IIAs form the legal basis for the decisions of tribunals on this standard. Therefore, the objective of this Chapter is, first, to identify variations in the normative structure and formulation of the FET standard within the framework of the identified IIAs. In resolving disputes involving this standard, tribunals have to take into account the wording of the FET standard provision in providing their interpretation of this standard.

Second, this Chapter has as its objective to shed light on recent developments in the formulation of FET standard provisions. States have made efforts to formulate the applicable FET standard clauses in a way that will clarify the scope of these provisions and that will ensure regulatory space for host states without incurring liability under the FET standard. The recent innovative language that elaborates on host state obligations incorporated in FET standard provisions is assessed in this Chapter. Before outlining the various categories of IIA FET standard provisions, an introduction to the FET standard in international law is provided in section §3.02.

§3.02 INTRODUCTION OF THE FET STANDARD IN INTERNATIONAL LAW

References to the FET standard appeared in international legal instruments before it was established as one of the key standards of investor protection in IIAs and, more specifically, in BITs.[248] For example, the Havana Charter for the Establishment of an International Trade Organization (1948) – which was widely signed but never entered into force – was the first international agreement in which FET was featured.[249] In Article 11(2) of the Havana Charter entitled: 'Means of Promoting Economic Development and Reconstruction' reference is made to 'just and equitable treatment'. Article 11(2) states that the International Trade Organization may:

> a) make recommendations for and promote bilateral or multilateral agreements on measures designed.
> (i) to assure just and equitable treatment for the enterprise, skills, capital, arts and technology brought from one Member country to another.[250]

This early reference to the FET provided in the Havana Charter has been included by the drafters of the Charter as an attempt by the International Trade Organisation to 'promote arrangements which would facilitate "an equitable distribution" of skills, arts, technology, materials and equipment, with due regard to the needs of all member States'.[251]

A reference to the FET standard was also made in the Abs/Shawcross Draft Convention on Investment Abroad (1959) and the OECD Draft Convention on the Protection of Foreign Property (1967).[252] Both of these instruments have also never entered into force. However, the text of the FET standard that later appeared in many BITs was largely inspired by these two instruments. Article 1 of the OECD Draft Convention, which has as its heading 'Treatment of Foreign Property', provides:

> a) Each Party shall at all times ensure fair and equitable treatment to the property of the nationals of the other Parties. It shall accord within its territory the most constant protection and security to such property and shall not in any way impair

248. OECD, 'Fair and Equitable Treatment in International Investment Law' (2004) OECD Working Papers on International Investment, 2004/03, 5 http://www.oecd.org/daf/inv/investment-policy/WP-2004_3.pdf accessed on 12 June 2018. *See also* R. Dolzer, M. Stevens, Bilateral Investment Treaties (Martinus Nijhoff Publishers, 1995) 58.
249. I. Tudor, (2008) 48.
250. Havana Charter for the Establishment of an International Trade Organization, Article 11(2), [1948] UNCTAD https://www.wto.org/english/docs_e/legal_e/havana_e.pdf accessed on 5 June 2018.
251. *See* OECD 'Study on Fair and Equitable Treatment in International Investment Law' [2004] 3. http://www.oecd.org/daf/inv/investment-policy/WP-2004_3.pdf accessed on 20 January 2017.
252. Alongside the multilateral investment initiatives, reference to fair and equitable treatment started featuring in the US treaties on Friendship, Commerce and Navigation (FCN), the predecessors of the modern BITs. *See*, e.g., the US-Germany BIT (1956); the US- France BIT (1960); the US-Israel BIT (1956); the US-Luxembourg BIT (1962); and the US-Belgium BIT (1961), among others. Some of these treaties include an assurance of 'equitable' treatment, while others make reference to 'fair and equitable treatment'. For example, Article 1 of the US-Germany FCN treaty provides that '(1) Each Party shall at all times accord fair and equitable treatment to the nationals and companies of the other Party, and to their property, enterprises and other interests.' *See* K.J. Vandevelde, 'A Unified Theory of Fair and Equitable Treatment' [2010] 48 *International Law and Politics*, 44; K.J. Vandevelde 'The Bilateral Treaty Program of the United States' [1988] 21 *Cornell International Law Journal*, 201-276.

> the management, maintenance, use, enjoyment or disposal thereof by unreasonable or discriminatory measures.[253]

The OECD Draft Convention's formulation of the FET standard has served as a model in the negotiations on BITs by many of the OECD states, especially in the early period.[254] At present, most BITs and other IIAs have included the FET standard in their texts.[255] According to the survey conducted by Dumberry, in 2014 only 50 BITs of a total of 1,964 did not have an FET standard provision in the treaty.[256] However, despite the high degree of uniformity in the general structure of BITs,[257] a large variety of FET standard provision formulations exist in the treaties.

As Vascianne has observed, 'bilateral investment treaties which omit reference to fair and equitable treatment constitute the exception rather than the rule.'[258] Several other studies have observed that there is a large variety of FET standard formulations,[259] and legal scholars have addressed the implications thereof. Tudor, in her monograph on the FET standard, concluded that:

> BITs do not refer to the FET in a uniform manner .... However, the existent differences do not relate to the content of the FET standard but to the various levels of its application (a clear minimum is fixed in the case of the NAFTA, more liberal in the case of certain BITs) and to its relationship with the other dispositions of the treaty.[260]

253. OECD 'Draft Convention on the Protection of Foreign Property' [1967]. http://www.oecd.org/investment/internationalinvestmentagreements/39286571.pdf accessed on 3 May 2018.
254. UNCTAD, 'Fair and Equitable Treatment: UNCTAD Series on IIAs II: A Sequel' (2012) 5 http://unctad.org/en/Docs/unctaddiaeia2011d5_en.pdf accessed on 12 March 2018. The report states that most OECD countries have used this formulation as a basis in their negotiations. *See also*: OECD, 'Fair and Equitable Treatment in International Investment Law' [2004] Working Papers on International Investment, 2003/2004, 5 http://www.oecd.org/daf/inv/investment-policy/WP-2004_3.pdf accessed on 12 June 2018. This study provides that there is an apparent influence of the OECD Draft Convention in the negotiation of the BITs, especially in the early treaties negotiated between developed and developing countries at the beginning of 1960s. '[O]ne of the main features which gained a position of prominence was the reference to "fair and equitable treatment"'.
255. C. Schreuer, (2005) 359. As the survey conducted in this Chapter demonstrates, some states have omitted the FET clause altogether, including, e.g., Japan and Russia.
256. P. Dumberry, The Formation and Identification of Rules of Customary International Law in International Investment Law (Cambridge University Press, 2016) 145.
257. *See* I. Tudor, (2008) 19; K.J. Vandevelde, 'The Political Economy of a Bilateral Investment Treaty' [1998] 92(4), *The American Journal of International Law*, 621-641. Vandevelde observes that especially in the early treaty-making years, the provisions of these treaties were 'remarkably uniform'.
258. S. Vascianne, 'Fair and Equitable Treatment Standard in International Investment Law and Practice' [1999] 70 *British Yearbook on International Law*, 129.
259. I. Tudor, (2008); P. Dumberry, The Formation and Identification of Rules of Customary International Law in International Investment Law (Cambridge University Press, 2016); A. Diehl, (2012); J. Bonnitcha, 'Fair and Equitable Treatment', in J. Bonnitcha (ed.) *Substantive Protection under Investment Treaties: A Legal and Economic Analysis* (Cambridge University Press, 2014).
260. I. Tudor, (2008) 77.

She asserts that the existence of these diverse formulations does not alter the uniformity of the content of the FET standard.[261] Other scholars place more emphasis on the consequences of these variations in the formulations of the FET standard. Dolzer and Schreur have indicated, in this regard, that:

> [F]or all clauses on fair and equitable treatment, generalization about the standard should be treated with caution. ... Variations in this area are quite significant and every type of clause has to be interpreted in accordance with Article 31 of the Vienna Convention on the Law of the Treaties, duly taking into account its context, and as appropriate its history.[262]

Dumberry, similarly, reflects that 'one cannot truly speak of "virtually uniform" practice of States when FET clauses containing different language actually mean different things.'[263]

With the focus on more recent FET standard formulations in IIAs,[264] the following sections assess the legal implications of various FET standard formulations with due regard being paid to the scope of FET standard provisions regarding the state's right to regulate.

§3.03 CATEGORIES OF FET STANDARD PROVISIONS IN IIAs

This section contains the results of the analysis of the FET standard provisions contained in the IIAs selected for this book (all of them were ratified between 1960 and 2016, *see*: Annex A and Annex B at the end of this book). Based on an assessment of the FET standard provisions of the selected IIAs, the following categories have emerged:

(1) IIAs in which the FET standard provision is formulated as an unqualified treaty standard;
(2) IIAs in which the FET standard provision includes a reference to the norm of unwritten international law, e.g.:
    (a) customary international law;

261. A similar position is taken by A. Diehl who notes that 'the differences [in the FET standard formulations] noted above are merely drafting differences and do not touch upon the core of the FET standard.' A. Diehl, (2012) 135.
262. R. Dolzer, C. Schreuer, (2008) 121.
263. P. Dumberry, The Formation and Identification of Rules of Customary International Law in International Investment Law (Cambridge University Press, 2016) 149.
264. EU agreements provide examples of such agreements, including, e.g., new EU agreements that are still being negotiated, such as the Transatlantic Trade and Investment Partnership Agreement between the EU and the US or the CETA. As explained in a 2015 European Commission report, the exhaustive list approach incorporated in recent EU agreements is motivated by 'the lack of clarity [of the FET standard] that has fueled a large number of ISDS claims by investors, some of which have raised concern with regard to the state's right to regulate. In particular, in some cases, the standard has been understood to encompass the protection of the legitimate expectations of investors in a very broad way, including the expectation of a stable general legislative framework'. *See* European Commission, 'Online public consultation on investment protection and investor-to-state dispute settlement (ISDS) in the Transatlantic Trade and Investment Partnership Agreement' (European Commission Consultation, 13 January 2015) 55.

   (b) general international law; and
   (c) principles of international law.
(3) IIAs in which the FET standard provision is qualified with additional content;
(4) IIAs in which the preamble provides a reference to the FET standard;
(5) IIAs with:
   (a) a joint interpretative instrument clarifying the intent of the treaty parties;
   (b) decisions of a treaty organ on the interpretation of the FET standard.

In the present book, the author has examined the text of the FET standard provisions in the selected IIAs and assigned each of them to one of these five categories. Each of the categories will now be elaborated upon.

The first category includes IIAs where the FET standard provisions are formulated as an unqualified treaty standard.[265]

The second category contains IIAs where the FET standard provisions include a reference to a norm of unwritten international law, e.g. to the MST of aliens under customary international law. The FET standard provision linked to the minimum standard requires an examination of customary international law in order to unravel the meaning of the FET standard in question. Where the FET standard is formulated as an unqualified provision, such an examination is not required. Such differences may result in diverse interpretations of the type of regulatory conduct of the state that may breach the FET standard. A further elaboration of how these key FET standard provision categories are applied and interpreted by arbitral tribunals in investment decisions is included in Chapters 4-7.

The third category includes IIAs where FET standard formulations contain additional content that usually includes a specification of certain state obligations under the FET standard. In the past ten years, several states have inserted more elaborate and detailed language into FET standard provisions in order to clarify their scope and content.[266] In respect of the right to regulate, the language of the FET standard provision is especially relevant as it reflects the intentions of the contracting parties regarding the scope of the FET standard obligation vis-à-vis the regulatory autonomy of the host state.

The fourth category includes IIAs in which the preamble provides a reference to the FET standard. Several treaties identified in this survey include references to the FET standard in their preamble, alongside substantive FET guarantees in the text of the treaty. As will be discussed in Chapters 4-6 on FET case law, in a group of cases, tribunals have relied on the preamble in giving normative content to the FET standard. Consequently, special attention is given to the formulation of preambles in which the FET standard is mentioned.

The last, fifth, category, outlines several examples of IIAs, which include:

265. UNCTAD 'Fair and Equitable Treatment: UNCTAD Series on International Investment Agreements II' (New York, 2012) 20-29.
266. UNCTAD, 'Investment Policy Monitor No. 15' (15 March 2016) 1 http://unctad.org/en/pages/publications/Investment-Policy-Monitor.aspx accessed on 5 June 2018. The report makes the observation that 'recent treaties include general exceptions [and] clarify certain IIAs standards (e.g., fair and equitable treatment (FET) and indirect expropriation) ...'.

(a) a joint interpretative instrument clarifying the intent of the treaty parties; and/or
(b) one or more decisions of a treaty organ on the interpretation of the FET standard.

As outlined in a recent OECD paper, the 'role of joint government action in the interpretative process in investor-state dispute settlement (ISDS) is attracting increasing attention from governments and commentators.'[267] Several examples are presented in this section. The Joint Interpretative Instrument that was issued in the CETA between the EU and Canada on 26 October 2016 is one of them.[268] The mechanisms, which provide for a possibility to review FET standard provisions and the possibility to issue binding interpretations of treaty provisions, have also been included in the CETA.[269] These tools fall under decisions of treaty organs on the interpretation of the FET standard. They are also referred to as a 'built-in treaty mechanisms' that allow states to control the interpretation and application of their treaties.[270]

The focus of this book is on the right to regulate in the context of the FET standard. As such, the identified categories of the FET standard are discussed from this perspective. As this Chapter will demonstrate, there is an emerging trend to clarify the meaning of FET standard provisions as provided, e.g., in the third category, through specifying the FET with an additional content, and in the fifth category, through including in an IIA either a joint interpretative instrument or the binding interpretation, both by (the governments of) the parties concerned, on the FET standard. This development is especially noticeable in BITs concluded in the past five years and other recent IIAs, e.g. multilateral and regional economic agreements that include investment-related provisions. The updated information on these categories of IIAs contributes to the already existing knowledge on the FET standard in treaties and provides a further assessment of this standard in connection with the right to regulate.

It should also be noted that the formulations in the selected IIAs sometimes include combinations, e.g. by combining formulations classified as second- and third-category formulations. The examples thereof are not treated as a separate category but are included under the third category that elaborates on the FET standard provision qualified with additional content.

267. D. Gaukrodger, 'The Legal Framework Applicable to Joint Interpretative Agreements of Investment Treaties' (2016) OECD Working Papers on International Investment 2016/01, 5 http://www.oecd-ilibrary.org/docserver/download/5jm3xgt6f29w-en.pdf?expires=1489837619&id=id&accname=guest&checksum=89A4E0138CF5F98B3A0DA534A2AA6DEB accessed on 16 March 2018.
268. Council of the European Union, 'Joint Interpretative Instrument on the Comprehensive Economic and Trade Agreement (CETA) between Canada and the European Union and its Member States' 13541/16 (Brussels, 27 October 2016) http://data.consilium.europa.eu/doc/document/ST-13541-2016-INIT/en/pdf accessed on 26 February 2017.
269. Consolidated text of the CETA (30 October 2016) http://ec.europa.eu/trade/policy/in-focus/ceta/ceta-chapter-by-chapter/ accessed on 12 June 2018.
270. K. Gordon, J. Pohl, 'Investment Treaties over Time: Treaty Practice and Interpretation in a Changing World' (2015) OECD Working Papers on International Investment 2015/02, 26 http://www.oecd.org/investment/investment-policy/WP-2015-02.pdf accessed on 10 March 2017.

The following sections will elaborate further on each of these categories. The specification of categories of the IIAs' FET standard formulations are provided in Annex C.

[A] IIAs in Which the FET Standard Is Formulated as an Unqualified Treaty Standard

In more than half of the selected IIAs, the FET provisions are formulated as unqualified treaty standards. This approach has been employed in most European, Australian, early Chinese and Russian BITs.[271] This category of FET standard clause is usually concisely formulated by stating that 'each contracting party shall at all times ensure fair and equitable treatment to investments'[272] or that they 'shall ensure fair and equitable treatment [to investments] on its territory'.[273] Alternatively, it provides that foreign investments 'shall be accorded fair and equitable treatment'.[274] The literature on the subject has referred to these FET standard provisions as 'self-standing', 'autonomous' or 'unqualified' FET clauses.[275] The provisions are characterised by the minimalist and open language that does not contain any clarification of the content of the FET standard.

Despite the general uniformity among the texts of the formulations classified in this category of self-standing FET clauses, several variations can be identified. For example, in Article 3 of the Russia-Egypt BIT (2000), the provision on the 'capital investment regime' stipulates that each party 'shall provide on its territory a just and equitable regime for capital investment ...'.[276] The same wording, 'just and equitable', is found in a number of French BITs.[277] The linguistic difference in the notion of 'just' in comparison with 'fair' has been tested by one tribunal on the basis of the French formulations in the France-Argentina BIT (1993), concluding that both terms have the

271. This approach is also followed by the EU BITs. *See* the analysis in S. Hjaccesse, 'Securing High Investment Protection for EU Investors: A Review of EU Member States Model BITs' [2012] 9(3) *Transnational Dispute Management* http://www.transnational-dispute-management.com/article.asp?key=1841 accessed on 23 January 2017.
272. *See* Article 4(1) of the Australia-Argentina BIT (1997); Article 3(2) of the Australia-India BIT (2000); Article 4(1) of the Australia-Mexico BIT (2007); Article 4(1) of the Netherlands-India BIT (1996); Article 3(2) of the Germany-India BIT (1998); Article 3(1) of the China-Argentine Republic BIT (1994); Article 3(2) of the China-India BIT (2007); Article 2(2) of the UK-Egypt BIT (1976); Article 2(2) of the UK-Venezuela BIT (1996) for full details of the aforementioned BITs.
273. Article 3(2) of the Australia-Uruguay BIT (2002); Article 3(1) of the Netherlands-Czech Republic BIT (1992); Article 3(1) of the Netherlands-Argentina BIT (1994).
274. Article 3(1) of the Germany-Trinidad and Tobago BIT (2010); Article 3(2) of the China-Trinidad and Tobago BIT (2004); Article 3(1) of the China-Egypt BIT (1996); Article 2(2) of the Ecuador-UK BIT (1995).
275. *See* UNCTAD 'Fair and Equitable Treatment: UNCTAD Series on International Investment Agreements II' (New York, 2012) http://unctad.org/en/Docs/unctaddiaeia2011d5_en.pdf accessed on 12 June 2018; OECD, 'Fair and Equitable Treatment in International Investment Law' [2004] Working Papers on International Investment, 2003/2004 https://www.oecd.org/daf/inv/investment-policy/WP-2004_3.pdf accessed on 12 June 2018.
276. Article 3(1) of the Russia-Egypt BIT (2000). The same formulation was also used in the Russia-Japan BIT (2000) and the Russia-South Africa BIT (2000).
277. For example, Article 3 of the France-Argentina BIT (1993).

same meaning.[278] In this regard, Jacob and Schill have observed that tribunals, in most cases, have refrained from putting significant emphasis on 'finer textual variations', as exemplified by the 'just' and 'fair' formulation.[279] Comparable provisions have been interpreted 'rather indiscriminately'.[280] Correspondingly, Alvarez has noted - with regard to unqualified FET clauses - that tribunals 'charged with interpreting FET have not emphasised the textual differences among FET clauses ...'.[281]

The present survey indicates that unqualified FET standard provisions have been the most prevalent choice for the FET standard formulation in IIAs. This is in line with the UNCTAD research conclusions, which include a more representative sample of 1,456 IIAs, among which 1,132 IIAs included unqualified FET standard provisions in their treaties.[282]

[B] IIAs in Which the FET Standard Provisions Include a Reference to a Norm of Unwritten International Law

(a) International minimum standard of the treatment of aliens under customary international law

The international minimum standard of the treatment of aliens under customary international law was developed over a century ago.[283] The standard originated from the international law on state responsibility for injuries to aliens.[284] In its contemporary reading, it has been referred to as a norm of customary international law regulating the treatment of aliens.

The meaning of the international minimum standard has been developed primarily through the work of international claims commissions.[285] Originally, the minimum standard is applied to the treatment of foreigners in general terms, without any reference being made to direct foreign investment. As such, procedural rights in criminal matters have been adjudicated under the international minimum standard, for example.[286] However, the interpretation in the landmark *Neer* case, decided by the US-Mexico Claims Commission in 1926, resulted in the emergence of the international

278. *Suez, Sociedad General de Aguas de Barcelona, S.A. and Vivendi Universal, S.A. v. Argentine Republic*, ICSID Case No. ARB/03/19 Decision on Liability (30 July 2010) para. 183.
279. M. Jacob, S. Schill, (2015) 705.
280. *Ibid.*
281. J. Alvarez, The Public International Law Regime governing International Investment (Brill/Nijhoff, 2011) 205.
282. UNCTAD, 'IIA Mapping Project, 2013-2014' http://investmentpolicyhub.unctad.org/IIA/mappedContent accessed on 25 August 2016. In this project, which is still ongoing, the goal is to map all IIAs for which texts are available (about 2,700). Over 1,456 IIAs have been mapped so far.
283. *See* I. Tudor, (2008) 19.
284. P. Dumberry, The Fair and Equitable Treatment Standard: A Guide to NAFTA Case Law on Article 1105 (Kluwer Law International, 2014) 14.
285. E.M. Borchard, The Diplomatic Protection of Citizens Abroad or the Law of International Claims (New York: The Banks Law Publishing Company, 1922).
286. R. Dolzer, C. Schreuer, (2008) 14.

minimum standard in the context of the law regulating investment protection. In this case, the US-Mexico Claims Commission clarified that the international minimum standard would be considered to have been violated where the state's conduct 'should amount to an outrage, to bad faith, to willful neglect of duty, or to an insufficiency of governmental action so far short of international standards that every reasonable and impartial man would readily recognize its insufficiency'.[287]

The aforementioned definition implies that a violation of the FET standard is established by a 'relatively base level of conduct such as bad faith or a gross insufficiency of governmental action'.[288] The relevance of this decision in modern times has been contested in academic literature.[289] It is argued, in particular, that the high threshold of a state's unacceptable conduct under the international minimum standard as articulated in the *Neer* decision does not correspond with the modern investment regime of our times.[290] Despite this, the *Neer* standard continues to serve as a reference for investment tribunals as the original expression of the international minimum standard.[291] Presently, in interpreting the international minimum standard, tribunals have identified several 'elements of minimum standard of treatment where state responsibility may arise for mistreatment of foreign investors and investments'.[292]

287. *L. F. H. Neer and P. Neer (USA) v. United Mexican States* [1926] United States-Mexico Claims Commission, Decision (15 October 1926) Reports of International Arbitral Awards, Vol. IV (United Nations, 2006) para. 4, pp. 61 - 62.
288. L.Y. Fortier, 'Expectations of Governments and Investors v. Practice: A View from the Bench ICSID Review' [2009] 24(2) *Foreign Investment Law Journal*, 353.
289. R. Klager, (2013) 53. In discussing the *Neer* case and similar awards of this period that dealt with personal injury, he provides that 'it is therefore difficult to determine whether these awards may serve as universal standards in the field of modern, highly intricate economic regulations.' *See also* J. Paulsson, G. Petrochilos, 'Neer-ly Mislead?' [2007] 22(2) *ICSID Review*, 257. The authors argue that the '*Neer* formula is of limited import ... The majority of modern claims concern administrative or legislative acts, which in the United States-Mexico General Claims Commission's classification are to be regarded as cases of direct responsibility where the alleged injury flows directly from such acts'.
290. *See* Paparinskins who outlines the problematic nature of the *Neer* decision, M. Paparinskis, (2013) 64. *See also* G. Bucheler, Proportionality in Investor-State Arbitration (Oxford University Press, 2015) 185.
291. *Saluka v. Czech Republic* [2006] Permanent Court of Arbitration, IIC 210, Partial Award (17 March 2006) para. 295; *Azurix Corp. v. The Argentine Republic*, ICSID Case No. ARB/01/12 Award (14 July 2006) para. 365; *Siemens A.G. v. The Argentine Republic*, ICSID Case No. ARB/02/8 Award (17 January 2007) para. 293. Despite the widespread reference to the *Neer* case, in interpreting the customary minimum standard, most tribunals, especially under NAFTA, have primarily taken the 'historic-evolutionary approach', underlying the importance of the high threshold set by the *Neer* case, at the same time emphasising the evolutionary character of the minimum standard. R. Dolzer, A. von Walter, 'Fair and Equitable Treatment – Lines of Jurisprudence on Customary Law', in F. Ortino and others (eds) *Investment Treaty Law: Current Issues, Volume II* (British Institute for Comparative Law, 2007) 113. Cases that have accepted the 'historic-evolutionary approach' include *Pope & Talbot Inc. v. The Government of Canada* [2001] UNCITRAL Arbitration, Final Merits Award (10 April 2001); *Mondev International Ltd. v. United States*, ICSID Case No. ARB (AF)/99/2 Award (11 October 2002); *Cargill, Inc. v. United Mexican States*, ICSID Case No. ARB/AF/05/2 Award (18 September 2009); *Merrill & Ring Forestry L.P. v. Canada* [2010] UNCITRAL Award (31 May 2010); *Loewen Group, Inc. and Raymond L. Loewen v. United States*, ICSID Case No. ARB(AF)/98/3 Award (26 June 2003).
292. A. Newcombe, L. Paradell, (2009) 239. This conclusion is also based on the research conducted for Y. Levashova, 'Fair and Equitable Treatment and the Protection of the Environment: Recent

Based on the formulation contained in recent treaties,[293] and in accordance with the case law and the scholarly work on the topic, Dumberry has concluded that 'a large consensus' exists that the international minimum standard is comprised of 'an obligation for host states to prevent the denial of justice in the administration of justice and provide due process; an obligation to prevent arbitrary conduct; and an obligation to provide investors with "full protection and security"'.[294]

From the IIAs analysed in this book, nine BITs and four regional agreements have made reference to the international minimum standard of the treatment of aliens under customary international law. One of the most prominent formulations of the FET standard with a reference to the minimum standard of the treatment of aliens under customary international can be found in the North American Free Trade Agreement (NAFTA) Free Trade Commission (FTC) Notes. The Notes were designed to somewhat clarify the FET standard with a reference to the minimum standard of the treatment of aliens under customary international law and thereby provided that:

1. Article 1105(1) prescribes the customary international law minimum standard of treatment of aliens as the minimum standard of treatment to be afforded to investments of investors of another Party.
2. The concepts of 'fair and equitable treatment' and 'full protection and security' do not require treatment in addition to or beyond that which is required by the customary international law minimum standard of treatment of aliens.
3. A determination that there has been a breach of another provision of the NAFTA, or of a separate international agreement, does not establish that there has been a breach of Article 1105(1).[295]

Trends in Investment Treaties and Investment Cases', in Y. Levashova, et al. (eds) *Bridging the Gap Between International Investment Law and the Environment* (Eleven Legal Publishing, 2015) 79-82. The author indicates the development of the practical elements created by NAFTA tribunals in simplifying its task in interpreting the international minimum standard. *Waste Management II v. Mexico* 2004 is particularly referenced in this context. *Waste Management v. Mexico* (Case II), ICSID Case No. ARB(AF)/00/3 Award (30 April 2004).

293. Article 2(4)(b) of the UK-Colombia BIT (2014) provides that 'b) "Fair and equitable treatment" includes the prohibition against the denial of justice in criminal, civil, or administrative proceedings in accordance with the principle of due process embodied in the main legal systems of the world.' *See* Article 2 of the UK-Colombia BIT (2014); *see also* Article 4 of the Japan-Colombia BIT (2011) 4. *See also* UNCTAD, 'International Investment Agreements Navigator' http://investmentpolicyhub.unctad.org/IIA/CountryBits/175#iiaInnerMenu accessed on 12 June 2018.

294. P. Dumberry, The Formation and Identification of Rules of Customary International Law in International Investment Law (Cambridge University Press, 2016) 108-109. Several decisions have also referred to the protection of legitimate expectations, e.g. *Glamis v. US* [2009] NAFTA, ICSID 48 ILM 1039 Award (8 June 2009) paras 766-767; *William Ralph Clayton, William Richard Clayton, Douglas Clayton, Daniel Clayton and Bilcon of Delaware Inc. v. Government of Canada* [2015] UNCITRAL, NAFTA, PCA Case No. 2009-04 Award on Jurisdiction and Liability (17 March 2015) para. 603.

295. NAFTA, 'Notes of Interpretation of Certain Chapter 11 Provisions' (NAFTA Free Trade Commission, 31 July 2001) http://www.international.gc.ca/trade-agreements-accords-commerciaux/topics-domaines/disp-diff/NAFTA-Interpr.aspx?lang=eng accessed on 12 June 2018.

The FTC Notes emerged as a reaction to three early FET standard awards[296] decided under the NAFTA that held states liable for a breach of the FET standard.[297] In the aftermath of these cases, NAFTA members were alarmed by the fact that these three tribunals had adopted an 'expansive reading of Article 1105'.[298] Consequently, the US, Mexico and Canada took steps to clarify the scope of the FET obligation by issuing a binding Note of Interpretation.[299]

With the exception of the *Pope & Tabot v. Canada* tribunal[300] that argued that the FTC Notes in question were an 'unlawful amendment' to the treaty, subsequent arbitral decisions have accepted the Notes as a valid and binding interpretation of Article 1105 of the NAFTA.[301] As Klager observes, tribunals 'assessing the validity of the FTC Notes were much more reluctant in challenging the note and generally accepted the understanding of Article 1105 of the NAFTA as being reflective of the minimum standard'.[302] Through the adoption of the FTC Notes, contracting states have attempted to restrict the scope of the FET standard, by explicitly linking the FET standard to the minimum standard of the treatment of aliens under customary international law. The competence of the FTC as a treaty organ is further elaborated under section §3.03[E].

Other FTAs and BITs have included in their IIAs FET standard provisions a reference to the minimum standard. The example of such formulation can be found in

---

296. These three decisions brought a number of issues to the surface that were later addressed in the FTC Notes. The tribunals in all three cases attempted to provide clarification to the meaning of the minimum standard under customary international law by (1) offering an expansive interpretation of the minimum standard under customary international law (*Pope & Talbot Inc. v. Canada* [2001] UNCITRAL Arbitration, Award on the Merits, Phase 2 (10 April 2001)); (2) employing a conventional norm, found in trade law, namely the principle of transparency, to establish a violation of the FET standard in the context of the minimum standard (*Metaclad v. Mexico*, ICSID Case No. ARB(AF)97/1 Award (30 August 2000)); or (3) extending the breach of one provision of the NAFTA to a violation of another standard (*S.D. Myers v. Canada* [2000] UNCITRAL Arbitration, Award (1 January 2000)). For a further analysis, *see* Y. Levashova, 'Fair and Equitable Treatment and the Protection of the Environment: Recent Trends in Investment Treaties and Investment Cases', in Y. Levashova, et al. (eds) *Bridging the Gap Between International Investment Law and the Environment* (Eleven Legal Publishing, 2015) 53-86.
297. R. Klager, (2016) 72.
298. G. Kaufmann-Kohler 'Interpretive Powers of the Free Trade Commission and the Rule of Law', in E. Gaillard, F. Bachand (eds) *Fifteen Years of NAFTA Chapter 11 Arbitration* (Juris, 2011) 181.
299. C. Henckels, Proportionality and Deference in Investor-State Arbitration (Cambridge University Press, 2015) 180.
300. *See Pope & Tabot v. Canada* [2002] UNCITRAL Arbitration, Award in Respect of Damages (31 May 2002). After the adoption of the Notes, the *Pope & Talbot v. Canada* tribunal questioned whether it was bound by the FTC Notes. The tribunal argued that the Notes of interpretation were an amendment to the agreement, rather than an interpretation (para. 47). The tribunal asserted that they were an amendment because the interpretation in the Notes did not merely interpret Article 1105 without changing its meaning, but it restricted the meaning of international law referenced in Article 1105 to customary international law, thereby altering the meaning of the provision (paras 43-46). However, the tribunal proceeded with the ruling, explaining that even if the FTC Notes were applied to the present case, the decision would be the same. For an analysis of this issue, *see* R. Klager, (2011) 72-74.
301. R. Klager, (2011) 72-74.
302. R. Klager, (2013) 73. *See also* T. Gazzini, Interpretation of International Investment Treaties (Hart Publishing, 2016) 197. Despite some initial resistance, arbitral tribunals eventually accepted the interpretation under the NAFTA Notes.

Article 3 of the UK-Mexico BIT (2008) on the 'Minimum Standard of Treatment in Accordance with Customary International Law', which states that:

> (1) Investments of investors of each Contracting Party shall at all times be accorded treatment in accordance with customary international law, including fair and equitable treatment and full protection and security, in the territory of the other Contracting Party.
> (2) The Contracting Parties do not intend the obligations in paragraph 1 above in respect of 'fair and equitable treatment' and 'full protection and security' to require treatment in addition to or beyond that which is required by the customary international law minimum standard of treatment of aliens. A determination that there has been a breach of another provision of this Agreement or of a separate international agreement, does not, in and of itself, establish that there has been a breach of the provisions of this Article.[303]

The second paragraph of Article 3 of the UK-Mexico BIT (2008) underlines that the FET standard does not require treatment in addition to or beyond that which is required by the international minimum standard. It also highlights that a breach of another provision does not automatically establish a breach of the FET standard. This type of formulation can be found in other IIAs.[304] The language adopted was inspired by the formulation used in the NAFTA FTC Notes, which a number of countries have transposed into their IIAs.[305]

The present survey demonstrates that the FET standard linked to the minimum standard of the treatment of aliens under customary international law is a formulation that continues to appear in the new generation of IIAs. In fact, according to the UNCTAD report of 2016, more states are inclined to include a reference to the minimum standard of the treatment of aliens into FET standard provisions than in previous years.[306] The countries that have incorporated the FET standard with reference to the aforementioned MST into their treaties include the US BITs,[307] the Canadian Foreign

303. *See* UK-Mexico BIT (2007) http://investmentpolicyhub.unctad.org/IIA/treaty/2545 accessed on 20 January 2017 for full details on the aforementioned BIT.
304. *See also* Article 3 of the Canada-Czech Republic BIT (2012); Article 4 of the Australia-Mexico BIT (2007); Article 3 of the China-Mexico BIT (2008) for full details on the aforementioned BITs. *See also* UNCTAD, 'International Investment Agreements Navigator' http://investmentpolicyhub.unctad.org/IIA/CountryBits/175#iiaInnerMenu accessed on 20 January 2017.
305. UNCTAD 'Fair and Equitable Treatment: UNCTAD Series on International Investment Agreements II' (New York, 2012) 25.
306. In the analysis undertaken by UNCTAD it follows that between 1962 and 2011, only 2% of BITs referred to the minimum standard of treatment under customary international law, whereas 35% of the BITs negotiated between 2012 and 2014 incorporated such a formulation; UNCTAD, 'World Investment Report' (2016) 114 http://unctad.org/en/pages/PublicationWebflyer.aspx?publicationid=1555 accessed on 12 June 2018.
307. *See* the US Model BITs of 2004 and 2012 (for both Models, Article 5 includes provisions on the international minimum standard, which are formulated very similarly to the NAFTA definition). US BITs concluded after 2004 have included the same formulation. *See* US Model BIT (2012) https://ustr.gov/sites/default/files/BIT%20text%20for%20ACIEP%20Meeting.pdf accessed on 12 June 2018 and US Model BIT (2004) http://www.state.gov/documents/organization/117601.pdf accessed on 12 June 2018.

Investment and Protection Agreements (FIPAs),[308] recent Mexican BITs,[309] several Chinese and Japanese BITs,[310] the Oman-US FTA[311] and others.[312] The NAFTA Member States – the US, Canada and Mexico – have followed the formulations of the NAFTA FTC Notes in their bilateral and regional agreements, replicating that the FET standard does not require treatment beyond the minimum standard of the treatment of aliens under customary international law.[313]

By incorporating the minimum standard of the treatment of aliens under customary international law, states are attempting to raise the liability threshold for the state's right to regulate.[314] As has been observed in the UNCTAD report on the FET standard, states that include the FET standard with a reference to the minimum standard in IIAs are motivated by the intention to 'prevent overexpansive interpretations of the FET standard by arbitral tribunals and to further guide them by referring to an example of gross misconduct that would violate the minimum standard of treatment of aliens – denial of justice'.[315] Consequently, some states consider that by incorporating a reference to the international minimum standard to the FET, they could reduce the risk of incurring liability for a violation of the FET standard. This corresponds with the OECD data that indicate that states have 'greater success defending claims under MST [minimum standard of treatment] FET provisions than under FET provisions that are interpreted as being autonomous'.[316]

---

308. Canada's Foreign Investment Protection and Promotion Agreements (FIPAs) (2004) http://www.italaw.com/documents/Canadian2004-FIPA-model-en.pdf accessed on 10 June 2018.
309. Article 4 of the Australia-Mexico BIT (2007); Article 3 of the UK-Mexico BIT (2007); China-Mexico BIT (2009).
310. *See* China-Colombia BIT (2013); China-Mexico BIT (2009) for full details on the aforementioned BITs. The aforementioned BITs can be accessed at http://investmentpolicyhub.unctad.org/IIA/mappedContent#iiaInnerMenu accessed on 12 June 2018.
311. Chapter 10, Article 10.5 of the Oman-US FTA (January 2009) https://ustr.gov/sites/default/files/uploads/agreements/fta/oman/asset_upload_file976_8810.pdf accessed on 11 March 2018.
312. BITs that incorporated this approach were concluded between 2007 and 2015. This observation is consistent with the UNCTAD research that shows that between 2012 and 2014, 48% of IIAs (as opposed to 4% between 1962 and 2011) included the FET standard with a reference to customary international law. *See* UNCTAD, 'Policy Options for IIA Reform: Treaty Examples and Data Supplementary Material to the World Investment Report 2015' Working Draft (last updated on 24 June 2015), 12. http://investmentpolicyhub.unctad.org/Upload/Documents/Policy-options-for-IIA-reform-WIR-2015.pdf accessed on 12 June 2018.
313. UNCTAD 'Fair and Equitable Treatment: UNCTAD Series on International Investment Agreements II' (New York, 2012) 25 http://unctad.org/en/Docs/unctaddiaeia2011d5_en.pdf accessed on 12 June 2018.
314. UNCTAD 'Fair and Equitable Treatment: UNCTAD Series on International Investment Agreements II' (New York, 2012) 13. In this report, it is explained that states provide a reference to the minimum standard of the treatment of aliens under customary international law in an FET standard in order to convey a 'clear message that only the very serious acts of maladministration can be seen as violating the treaty'(p. 13).
315. UNCTAD 'Fair and Equitable Treatment: UNCTAD Series on International Investment Agreements II' (New York, 2012) 28.
316. D. Gaukrodger, 'Addressing the Balance of Interests in Investment Treaties' (2017) OECD Working Papers on International Investment 2017/03 http://dx.doi.org/10.1787/0a62034b-en accessed on 11 March 2017.

(b) The FET standard with a reference to general international law and/or (c) to principles of international law

A total of twenty-one IIAs include FET standard provisions that contain a general reference to international law or principles of international law. For example, Article 1105(1) of the NAFTA provides that '[e]ach Party shall accord to investments of investors of another party treatment in accordance with international law, including fair and equitable treatment and full protection and security.'[317]

The inclusion by states of IIAs with the FET standard formulation 'in accordance with international law' was meant to ensure that the principles of international law would be employed in the interpretation process.[318] In contrast to a more specific reference to the minimum standard, FET standard provisions in IIAs that include a reference to international law are usually formulated more broadly, stating that the FET should be afforded 'in accordance with principles of international law'.[319] With regard to Article 1105 of the NAFTA, tribunals have interpreted the FET standard more precisely, particularly after the adoption of the FTC Notes, with reference being made to the international minimum standard of the treatment of aliens under customary international law. The FTC Notes are further discussed in section §3.03[E][b].

Another formulation of the IIA FET standard provision with a reference to international law reads that the FET afforded to investors should not be 'less than that required by international law'.[320] Such a formulation was adopted in the 'first wave' of the US BITs concluded in the 1980s[321] and provides that the treatment of the investor should 'not be less' than required by international law, without - however - setting limits to the ceiling of such protection.[322]

According to UNCTAD, this FET standard formulation is 'not strictly linked to the stipulations of international law', as in the case of FET formulations that underline that

317. Chapter 11, Article 1105(1) of the NAFTA [1994].
318. UNCTAD, 'Fair and Equitable Treatment: UNCTAD Series on International Investment Agreements II' (New York, 2012) 22.
319. *See* Article 2 of the Canada-Ecuador BIT (1997); Article 2 of the Canada-Trinidad and Tobago BIT (1996); Article II of the Canada-Ukraine BIT (1995); Article 6 of the Japan-Ukraine BIT (2015); Article 4 of the France-Mexico BIT (2000) for full details on the aforementioned BITs.
320. Article 2 of the US-Argentina BIT (1994); Article 2 of the US-Ukraine BIT (1996); Article 3 of the US-Ecuador BIT (1997); Article 2 of the US-Czech Republic BIT (1992).
321. Vandevelde distinguishes between three waves of the US BIT negotiation programme. The first wave started in 1980 and ended in 1986 with the signing of ten US BITs. The second wave began in 1989 and proceeded through 1999 when BIT negotiations were temporarily frozen until the major revision and development of a new Model BIT in 2004 that has marked the third wave of negotiations; K.J. Vandevelde, U.S. Investment Agreements (Oxford University Press, 2009) 30.
322. This approach was adopted by the US during the second wave of BIT negotiations, where such a formulation attempted to get the best of both worlds. On the one hand, by inserting 'plain' fair and equitable treatment language, the formulation attempted to avoid disputes on the existence and content of the minimum standard that might undermine the protection afforded by this standard to US investors abroad, and, on the other hand, the reference to international law aimed to ensure that the treatment of investors was not below the international minimum standard. The content of FET was left undefined, but in the context of these first treaties, the fair and equitable treatment standard has been seen 'to provide the baseline of protection applicable in all situations'. *See* K.J. Vandevelde, (2009) 30.

FET should be afforded *in accordance* with international law.[323] The reference to international law indicates a minimum level of protection to which investors are entitled. The UNCTAD report on the FET standard asserts that in accordance with such a formulation 'the FET obligation cannot go below that floor but, judging from the text alone, it would seem to give more room for interpreting FET as adding to the international law requirements.'[324]

As the survey conducted for this research demonstrates, the reference to international law in general or principles of international law typically appears in BITs negotiated during the 1990s. The BITs of some countries, however, continue to follow this approach, as is the case with French BITs.[325]

[C] IIAs in Which the FET Standard Provision Is Qualified with Additional Content

This section discusses IIAs in which FET standard provisions are qualified with additional content that usually specifies certain host state obligations. Currently, contracting states tend to be more specific regarding the content of the FET standard, mostly by providing examples of unfair and inequitable conduct. The additional content, usually expressed in the form of a list of state obligations in the FET provision of an IIA, is commonly combined with the aforementioned categories of the FET standard formulations (category 2). For example, a list of state obligations can be found in several FET standard provisions that combine a reference to the minimum standard, discussed in category 2, with examples of lists of host state obligations. The next paragraph provides more clarification.

In BITs and regional treaties,[326] of which there are several, that have incorporated a reference to the international minimum standard of the treatment of aliens under customary international law, the obligations of host states are frequently clarified by including a list of unacceptable forms of state conduct, e.g. the obligation not to 'deny justice'.[327] For example, Article 2(4)(b) of the UK-Colombia BIT (2014) provides that

323. UNCTAD 'Fair and Equitable Treatment: UNCTAD Series on International Investment Agreements II' (New York, 2012) 23.
324. *Ibid.*
325. *See* the France-Venezuela BIT (2004); France-Mexico BIT (2000); France-India BIT (2000).
326. Article 5 of the Japan-Uruguay BIT (signed in 2015); Article 4 of the Japan-Colombia BIT (signed in 2011); Article 2 of the China-Colombia BIT (2013); Article 2 of the UK-Colombia BIT (2014); Article 5 of the US-Uruguay BIT (2006); Article 3 of the UK-Mexico BIT (2007). Also *see* the regional treaties that have incorporated the same formulation, including the Trans-Pacific Partnership Agreement; Agreement establishing the ASEAN-Australia-New Zealand Free Trade Area and the CAFTA-DR (Dominican Republic-Central America FTA). *See also* UNCTAD, 'International Investment Agreements Navigator' http://investmentpolicyhub.unctad.org/IIA/CountryBits/175#iiaInnerMenu accessed on 3 February 2017.
327. UNCTAD, 'Policy Options for IIA Reform: Treaty Examples and Data – Supplementary Material to the World Investment Report of 2015' (24 June 2015) 10 http://investmentpolicyhub.unctad.org/Publications/Details/133 accessed on 1 February 2017. This document discussed the options used by states in the last few years. Regarding the FET standard, the document has included the option to clarify the FET standard through an open-ended list of FET obligations, specifying that these obligations can be formulated in a 'positive' as well as in a 'negative' way.

'b) "fair and equitable treatment" includes the prohibition against the denial of justice in criminal, civil, or administrative proceedings in accordance with the principle of due process embodied in the main legal systems of the world.'[328]

In addition to the 'denial of justice', Article 4 of the Japan-Colombia BIT (2011) also mentions the obligation 'to guarantee access to the courts of justice and administrative tribunals' as a part of the FET standard.[329]

The 'denial of justice' features in most of the FET standard provisions. As Yannaca-Small has summarised, the principle of the denial of justice has been employed in three ways.[330] Broadly, it encompasses the entire 'field of State responsibility, and has been applied to all types of wrongful conduct on the part of the State towards aliens'.[331] Narrowly, the principle refers to hindering the access of investors to local courts and the failure of courts to render judicial decisions. Third, the denial of justice is often applied in connection with inadequate 'administration of civil and criminal justice as regards an alien, including denial of access to courts, inadequate procedures, and unjust decisions'.[332] As emphasised by Yannica-Small, and supported by this survey, this latter category is most commonly applied in the context of IIAs. In several treaties, it is expressed in the form of the obligations of states towards an investor, as exemplified by the UK-Colombia BIT (2014) above.

The approach of including a list of a state's obligations in FET standard provisions has also been adopted in the framework of new EU agreements, several of which have been signed but not yet ratified at the time of writing. These include the Comprehensive Economic and Trade Agreement between Canada and the EU (CETA) (signed in 2016),[333] the Transatlantic Investment and Partnership Agreement between EU and the

328. *See* Article 2 of the UK-Colombia BIT (2014) for full details of the aforementioned BITs. *See also* UNCTAD, 'International Investment Agreements Navigator' http://investmentpolicyhub.unctad.org/IIA/CountryBits/175#iiaInnerMenu accessed on 3 February 2017.
329. Article 4 of the Japan-Colombia BIT (2011). *See also* UNCTAD, 'International Investment Agreements Navigator' http://investmentpolicyhub.unctad.org/IIA/CountryBits/175#iiaInnerMenu accessed on 1 February 2017.
330. OECD, 'Fair and Equitable Treatment in International Investment Law' (2004) OECD Working Papers on International Investment, 2003/2004, 28.
331. *Ibid.*
332. OECD, 'Fair and Equitable Treatment in International Investment Law' (2004) OECD Working Papers on International Investment, 2003/2004, 29. The author refers to Ian Brownlie who emphasised that the meaning of the denial of justice is best captured in the Harvard Research Draft on International Law. The research provides that the denial of justice 'exists where there is a denial, unwarranted delay or obstruction of access to courts, gross deficiency in the administration of judicial or remedial process, failure to provide those guarantees which are generally considered indispensable to the proper administration of justice or a manifestly unjust judgment. An error of a national court which does not produce manifest injustice is not a denial of justice'. *See* Article 9 of the '1929 Harvard Research Draft on the Law of State Responsibility' (reporter for responsibility of states, E.M. Borchard) [1929] 23 Supplement to the *American Journal of International Law*, 173.
333. The CETA (signed on 30 October 2016).

included in the list of new European IIA FET standard formulations can be traced back to investment jurisprudence. As Reinisch observed, the list approach to FET, incorporated by CETA, constitutes an example of the 'potential feedback between treaty-makers and investment tribunals'.[346] This point will be further investigated in Chapter 8.

Several agreements have also included statements specifying that the FET standard does not include a stabilisation obligation.[347] These types of clarification provide additional information regarding the scope of the FET standard. For example, several states have included in the FET provision that the FET standard does not preclude the state from changing its legislation or that the FET standard does not encompass a stabilisation obligation.[348] The BIT between France-Colombia (2014) is an example of such statements. Article 4(1) provides that:

> [F]or greater certainty, the obligation to provide fair and equitable treatment includes, inter alia: a) the obligation not to deny justice in civil, criminal or administrative proceedings in accordance with the principle of due process, b) the obligation to act in a transparent, non-discriminatory and non-arbitrary way with respect to investors of the other Contracting Party and their investments.
>
> This treatment should be consistent with the principles of predictability and the consideration of the legitimate expectations of investors. The determination of a violation of other provisions of the Agreement or other international agreements does not imply that this standard has been violated. It should also be understood that the obligation to provide fair and equitable treatment does not include a stabilization clause or prevents its legislation from being changed according to this paragraph.[349]

The France-Colombia BIT (2014) emphasises that the FET standard does not imply a stabilisation clause and that states are not precluded from changing their laws in the context of the FET standard. Useful guidance as to what one of the contracting states implies by this paragraph is the position paper of the French government published in 2015.[350] Although this document is a proposal addressed to the EU Commission, it nevertheless expresses the position of the French authorities in which

346. A. Reinisch, 'The Likely Content of Future EU Investment' (2015) 1894.
347. A stabilisation obligation or a stabilisation clause is sometimes included in investment contracts between an investor and a host state. The stabilisation clause can take different forms. One such form is the so-called freezing clause that implies that the law has remain unchanged, frozen, for the duration of the contract. *See*: A. Shemberg Stabilization Clauses and Human Rights, A research project conducted for IFC and the United Nations Special Representative of the Secretary-General on Business and Human Rights (IFC, 27 May 2009) http://www.ifc.org/wps/wcm/connect/9feb5b00488555eab8c4fa6a6515bb18/Stabilization%2BPaper.pdf?MOD=AJPERES accessed on 10 June 2018.
348. Article 4(2) of the Japan-Colombia BIT, signed in 2011. *See also* UNCTAD, 'International Investment Agreements Navigator' http://investmentpolicyhub.unctad.org/IIA/CountryBits/175#iiaInnerMenu accessed on 2 December 2016; Article 4 of the France-Colombia BIT (2014). Note that this is an unofficial translation by the author.
349. Article 4 of the France-Colombia BIT (2014). Note that this is an unofficial translation by the author.
350. French proposal to the European Commission, 'Towards a new way to settle disputes between states and investors' (2015) 3 http://www.diplomatie.gouv.fr/fr/IMG/pdf/20150530_isds_papier_eng_vf_cle09912d.pdf accessed on 12 September 2018.

it clarifies that the FET standard should not be interpreted in a way that will prevent states from changing or adopting new laws and regulations. This document provides that 'investors cannot expect that laws will remain unchanged and that they cannot rely on the concept of legitimate expectations to challenge a mere change in the law, even if such a change has caused a significant loss or profit.'[351] It further explains that the FET standard and specifically the legitimate expectations of an investor should not be interpreted as a stabilisation clause that would 'undermine the state's right to regulate and to implement legitimate public policies'.[352]

In addition to the paragraph that clarifies that the FET standard is not a stabilisation clause, the FET standard provision in the France-Colombia BIT, i.e. Article 4(1) of this treaty, also provides that the contracting states have an obligation to act in a 'transparent, non-arbitrary and a non-discriminatory manner'. Article 4(1) of France-Colombia BIT also mentions the principle of predictability and the legitimate expectations of the investor.

To summarise this subsection, states have clarified the FET standard in their IIAs by providing additional content to this standard. Generally, these treaties have included a list of state obligations in the FET standard with the intention being to limit an interpretation of the scope of the FET standard that could potentially impinge on their right to regulate.[353] In addition to the list of state obligations, the treaty drafters in several IIAs have included statements specifying that states are not precluded from changing their laws in the context of the FET standard.

[D] IIAs in Which the Preamble Provides a Reference to the FET Standard

This category focuses on IIAs that include a reference to the FET standard in their preamble, in addition to the substantive FET standard provision. The preamble plays an important role in the interpretation of the FET standard by tribunals.[354] This is further addressed in Chapter 4 of this study.[355]

351. French proposal to the European Commission, 'Towards a new way to settle disputes between states and investors' (2015) 3.
352. *Ibid.*
353. European Commission, 'Investment in TTIP and Beyond: The Path for Reform: Enhancing the Right to Regulate and Moving from Current Ad Hoc Arbitration Towards an Investment Court' [2015] European Commission Concept Paper http://trade.ec.europa.eu/doclib/docs/2015/may/tradoc_153408.PDF accessed on 21 January 2017. The Commission expressed its position regarding the FET standard by explaining that '[f]air and equitable treatment is defined through a clear, closed text which defines precisely the content of the standard without leaving unwelcome discretion to arbitrators.' *See also* E. De Brabandere, 'States' Reassertion of Control over International Investment Law – (Re)Defining "Fair and Equitable Treatment" and "Indirect Expropriation"', in A. Kulick (ed.) *States' Reassertion of Control over International Investment Agreements and International Investment Treaty Dispute Settlement* (Cambridge University Press, 2016) 6-8.
354. *See* A. Newcombe, L. Paradell, (2009) 266, who underline the increasing role of the preamble in the FET standard's interpretation.
355. *See* Chapter 4, section §4.02 on the Interpretation of the FET standard under the General Rules of Treaty Interpretation.

Two types of references to the FET standard in the preamble have been detected in the course of the present survey. First, several treaties refer to FET in the preamble, emphasising the desirability of affording the FET standard to investments. Second, in the preambles of a number of IIAs, references to stable frameworks for investments, as well as FET guarantees, are made.

With regard to the first subcategory, the Netherlands-Egypt BIT (1998) constitutes a suitable example. The preamble to this treaty states that '[r]ecognizing that agreement upon the treatment to be accorded to such investments will stimulate the flow of capital and technology and the economic development of the Contracting Parties and that fair and equitable treatment is desirable.'[356]

This type of reference has typically intensified the importance of the FET standard as interpreted by the tribunals.[357] The UNCTAD report asserts that preambles that include the FET standard among the goals of the treaty in combination with an unqualified FET standard provision signals to tribunals that they should concentrate primarily on the investor's rights, rather than adopting a balancing approach in the assessment of the host state's right to regulate vis-à-vis the treatment of investors.[358]

The second subcategory includes a formulation that incorporates a reference to the stability of the legal framework and can best be illustrated by the US-Argentina BIT (1994), which was the applicable treaty in numerous arbitral decisions.[359] The US-Argentina BIT (1994) provides that the parties to the Treaty agree that '[f]air and equitable treatment of investment is desirable in order to maintain a stable framework for investment and maximum effective use of economic resources.'[360]

As will be assessed in the analysis of investment cases in Chapter 6, this type of formulation has contributed to the interpretation of the FET standard as an obligation to provide a stable and predictable legal and business framework for investments.[361]

In interpreting the FET standard, tribunals have relied on the preamble to provide content to the FET standard in the context and the object of the investment treaty. Therefore, even though preambles are not intended to create legal obligations beyond

356. Netherlands-Egypt BIT (1998); the same formulation is employed in the NL-Czech Republic BIT (1991); Netherlands-Ecuador BIT (1999); Netherlands-Argentina BIT (1992); and the Netherlands-Mexico BIT (1998).
357. In interpreting the FET standard, numerous FET tribunals have considered the context and the objective of the treaty, according to Article 31 of the Vienna Convention on the Law of Treaties. To this end, reference to the FET in the preamble in combination with the treaty's objective to promote investments has been interpreted broadly by some tribunals, covering all types of unfair state conduct. For a further elaboration and examples, *see* Chapter 4, sections §4.02[B]-§4.02[C].
358. UNCTAD, 'Fair and Equitable Treatment: UNCTAD Series on International Investment Agreements II' (New York, 2012) 105.
359. *See CMS Gas Transmission Co. v. The Argentine Republic*, ICSID Case No. ARB/01/8 Award (12 May 2005); *Enron v. Argentina*, ICSID Case No. ARB/01/3 Award (22 May 2007). In both cases the US-Argentina BIT was employed and in both cases the tribunals interpreted the FET standard as an obligation to provide a stable framework for investments.
360. The US-Argentina BIT (1994). The same formulation is employed in the US-Czech Republic BIT (1992); the US-Ukraine BIT (1996); and the US-Ecuador BIT (1997).
361. The 'stability and predictability of the legal framework' has emerged as an element of the FET standard, primarily through the interpretation of the preambles by several tribunals, mostly attributed to US BITs. *See* Chapter 6, section §6.04.

the substantive provisions, 'the presence of the FET in the preamble inspires the general tone and philosophy of the treaty.'[362] With regard to the FET standard, which is often defined or formulated in an open manner, the treaty objectives, e.g. the investment protection provided in some treaties' preambles, have led tribunals in some cases to provide broad interpretations of the FET obligation guaranteed to investors.[363] A further elaboration of this issue is provided in Chapter 4, section §4.02.

[E] IIAs' Additional Agreement of the Parties on the Interpretation of the FET Standard

(a) Joint interpretative instrument clarifying the intent of the treaty parties

In order to further clarify the intent of the contracting parties at the time of the conclusion of the treaty, several instruments can be used. 'Joint instruments that are agreed by all parties to the treaty' may include side agreements, protocols and an exchange of letters, among others.[364] An example of a joint instrument is CETA's Joint Interpretative Instrument (Instrument) that has been adopted alongside the CETA.[365] This Instrument has the objective of providing a 'clear' statement by the contracting states regarding their intentions concerning CETA provisions in the 'sense of Article 31 of the Vienna Convention of the Law of the Treaties' (VCLT).[366] This instrument is binding and has to be taken into account by future tribunals in interpreting the provisions of the CETA.[367] It has been noted that the Instrument contains very general statements, which primarily replicate already existing provisions of the CETA.[368] The

362. I. Tudor, (2008) 21.
363. *Ibid.*
364. K. Gordon, J. Pohl, 'Investment Treaties over Time: Treaty Practice and Interpretation in a Changing World' (2015) OECD Working Papers on International Investment 2015/02, 25 http://www.oecd.org/investment/investment-policy/WP-2015-02.pdf accessed on 17 March 2017.
365. Council of the European Union, 'Joint Interpretative Instrument on the Comprehensive Economic and Trade Agreement (CETA) between Canada and the European Union and its Member States' 13541/16 (Brussels, 27 October 2016).
366. Council of the European Union, 'Joint Interpretative Instrument on the Comprehensive Economic and Trade Agreement (CETA) between Canada and the European Union and its Member States' 13541/16 (Brussels, 27 October 2016) preamble (c), 4. *See* Article 31(2)b of the Vienna Convention on the Law of Treaties (with Annexes) (adopted 23 May 1969, entered into force on 27 January 1980) U.N.T.S 311, vol. 1155.
367. Centre for European Policy Studies (CEPS), 'CETA's Signature: 38 Statements, a Joint Interpretative Instrument and an Uncertain Future' (CEPS, Monday 31 October 2016) https://www.ceps.eu/publications/ceta%E2%80%99s-signature-38-statements-joint-interpretative-instrument-and-uncertain-future accessed on 12 June 2018. The paper specifies that the CETA instrument is a 'legally binding document according to Article 31 of VCLT (as confirmed in the Instrument and several statements of the Council) and will need to be taken into account by the Parties and members of the agreement's Investment Tribunals during dispute settlement procedures'.
368. Centre for European Policy Studies (CEPS), 'CETA's Signature: 38 Statements, a Joint Interpretative Instrument and an Uncertain Future' (CEPS, Monday 31 October 2016). The CEPS publication states that none of the elements discussed in the Joint Instrument are 'revolutionary and they were already quite clear from a reading of CETA's text'. The same point is made

content of the Instrument pertinent to the FET standard is addressed in the subsequent paragraphs.

As a starting point, the Instrument specifies that its particular goal is to clarify several CETA provisions that have been the 'object of public debate and concerns'.[369] These themes include the 'impact of CETA on the ability of governments to regulate in the public interest'; the 'provisions on investment protection and dispute resolution'; as well as 'sustainable development, labour rights and environmental protection'.[370]

With regard to the FET standard, the Instrument includes a somewhat general elaboration in §6 on investment protection. It specifies that 'governments may change their laws, regardless of whether this may negatively affect an investment or investor's expectations of profits.'[371] As discussed in Chapter 2, section §2.03[B] on the right to regulate in IIAs, a similar formulation is included in Article 8.9(2) of the CETA that elaborated on investment protection and regulatory measures.

Furthermore, §6 of the Instrument states that the contracting states are 'committed to review regularly the content of the obligation to provide fair and equitable treatment'.[372] This mechanism has been included in the CETA in order to ensure that the FET standard will 'not be interpreted in a broader manner than they [the contracting states] intended'.[373] In the subsequent sentence, the Instrument mentions the possibility for the contracting states to issue binding Notes of Interpretation. The purpose of both of the aforementioned mechanisms is for Canada, the EU and its Member States 'to avoid and correct any misinterpretation of CETA by Tribunals'.[374] The elaboration of the possibility to issue a binding interpretation in the context of CETA is presented in the following paragraph, where the decisions by treaty organs concerning IIAs are discussed.

(b) Decisions of a treaty organ on the interpretation of the FET standard

Under international law, the parties have 'competence to interpret a treaty, but this is subject to the operation of other legal rules'.[375] The treaty may confer competence on

in S. Lestor, 'Interpreting the CETA Joint Interpretative Instrument' (IEL and Policy Blog, 1 November 2016) http://worldtradelaw.typepad.com/ielpblog/2016/11/the-ceta-joint-interpretative-instrument.html accessed on 27 February 2017. In this publication, the author compares the elements provided in the Joint Instrument with the actual provisions of CETA, which in many instances seem to be very similar, thereby adding little to the already existing text of CETA.

369. Council of the European Union, 'Joint Interpretative Instrument on the Comprehensive Economic and Trade Agreement (CETA) between Canada and the European Union and its Member States' 13541/16 (Brussels, 27 October 2016) 3.
370. *Ibid.*
371. Council of the European Union, 'Joint Interpretative Instrument on the Comprehensive Economic and Trade Agreement (CETA) between Canada and the European Union and its Member States' 13541/16 (Brussels, 27 October 2016) 5.
372. *Ibid.*
373. *Ibid.*
374. Council of the European Union, 'Joint Interpretative Instrument on the Comprehensive Economic and Trade Agreement (CETA) between Canada and the European Union and its Member States' 13541/16 (Brussels, 27 October 2016) section 6 (e).
375. J. Crawford, Brownlie's Principles of Public International Law: 8th Edition (Oxford, 2008) 378.

tribunals to interpret the treaty, as has been done in many IIAs which delegate the power to decide on investment disputes between states and investors.[376]

In several IIAs, treaty parties have found it useful to institutionalise their competence to interpret the FET standard through empowering a treaty organ usually composed of the treaty parties' representatives. Article 2001(2) of NAFTA establishing the FTC is an example of a mechanism that institutionalises the decision of a treaty organ on the interpretation of the FET standard. According to Article 2001(2) of the NAFTA, the FTC has the authority to '(a) supervise the implementation of this agreement; (b) oversee its further elaboration; (c) resolve disputes that may arise regarding its interpretation or application'.[377] In 2001, the FTC, the body comprised of 'cabinet-level representatives' of the NAFTA parties, issued the NAFTA FTC Notes of Interpretation on Certain Provisions of Chapter 11.[378]

The issuing of the FTC Notes may give rise to questions regarding the role of states in monitoring the application of core investment protection standards, such as the FET. As explained in section §3.03[B], the legal status of the Notes was questioned by the *Pope & Tabot v. Canada* tribunal when the Notes had already been issued.[379]As Roberts has argued, the issue of the 'legitimacy' of the FTC's interpretation 'represents a specific manifestation of a more systematic (though less discussed) issue about the role states should play in the interpretation of treaties like human rights and investment treaties that create directly enforceable rights for non-state actors'.[380] Roberts discusses the ways as to how an 'interpretative balance of power' can be attained among treaty parties and tribunals in order to 'promote more legitimate and sustainable investment treaty interpretations'.[381] She proposes that a dialogue should be held on interpreting investment treaties between treaty parties and tribunals through 'subsequent agreements and practice of the Vienna Convention.'[382] To this end, the interpretations adopted by treaty parties through subsequent agreements in order to be perceived by tribunals as being persuasive and relevant should be based on a combination of their 'reasonableness' and 'timing'.[383]

The FTC Notes is not a unique instrument, as there are other examples of IIAs and other agreements such as those regulating trade,[384] which contain the embedded

376. A. Roberts, 'Power and Persuasion in Investment Treaty Interpretation: The Dual Role of States' [2010] 104(2) *American Journal of International Law*, 180.
377. Article 2001(2) of the NAFTA.
378. *See* Article 2001 of the NAFTA entitled 'Free Trade Commission'.
379. *See Pope & Tabot v. Canada* [2002] UNCITRAL Arbitration, Award in Respect of Damages (31 May 2002).
380. A. Roberts, 'Power and Persuasion in Investment Treaty Interpretation: The Dual Role of States' [2010] 104(2) *American Journal of International Law*, 181.
381. *Ibid.*
382. A. Roberts, 'Power and Persuasion in Investment Treaty Interpretation: The Dual Role of States' [2010] 104(2) *American Journal of International Law*, 215.
383. A. Roberts, 'Power and Persuasion in Investment Treaty Interpretation: The Dual Role of States' [2010] 104(2) *American Journal of International Law*, 209.
384. *See* Article IX(2) of the WTO Agreement that provides the ultimate decision to adopt an interpretation of the Agreement by a majority of the Member States. Article IX(2) provides: '2. The Ministerial Conference and the General Council shall have the exclusive authority to adopt interpretations of this Agreement and of the Multilateral Trade Agreements. In the case of an interpretation of a Multilateral Trade Agreement in Annex 1, they shall exercise their authority

competence of the contracting parties to issue a binding interpretation of the provisions of an IIA.[385] The FTC Notes is one example of a mechanism to clarify the FET standard that emerged from this research. However, according to the OECD reports, more and more states include in their treaties various tools that may influence the interpretation of the provisions or a specific provision of an IIA.[386] The European Commission has also stated that it is planning to incorporate provisions in new EU agreements to be negotiated that will 'allow states to maintain control over how the investment provisions are being interpreted'.[387] CETA is a freshly signed new type of EU agreement where the latter ambition of the European Commission has been realised. The CETA includes an instrument, which is comparable to the NAFTA Notes, a built-in treaty mechanism that allows the parties to determine particular aspects of treaty interpretation.

Article 8.10(3) of the CETA, which regulates the FET standard, introduces the possibility for the contracting states to review the content of the FET standard at the request of one of the contracting parties to the agreement.[388]

To exemplify, Article 8.10(3) of the CETA provides that:

---

on the basis of a recommendation by the Council overseeing the functioning of that Agreement. The decision to adopt an interpretation shall be taken by a three-fourths majority of the Members.' The Marrakesh Agreement establishing the World Trade Organization, concluded in Marrakesh on 15 April 1994, entered into force (1 January 1995). *See*: https://www.wto.org/english/docs_e/legal_e/04-wto_e.htm#articleIX accessed on 15 June 2018.

385. Article 10.22(3) of the Dominican Republic-Central America FTA (CAFTA-DR), which provides that 'A decision of the Commission declaring its interpretation of a provision of this Agreement under Article 19.1.3(c) (The Free Trade Commission) shall be binding on a tribunal established under this Section, and any decision or award issued by the tribunal must be consistent with that decision.' *See also* Article 832(1) of the Canada-Colombia FTA (15 August 2011) which provides that '[a] Tribunal established under this Section shall decide the issues in dispute in accordance with this Agreement and applicable rules of international law. An interpretation by the Commission of a provision of this Agreement shall be binding on a Tribunal established under this Section, and any award or other ruling under this Section shall be consistent with the interpretation.' *See also* Article 18(2) of the China-Canada BIT (2014) Article 18(2) which states that '[f]urther to consultations under this Article, the Contracting Parties may take any action as they may jointly decide, including making and adopting rules supplementing the applicable arbitral rules under Part C of this Agreement and issuing binding interpretations of this Agreement'.

386. D. Gaukrodger, 'The Legal Framework Applicable to Joint Interpretative Agreements of Investment Treaties' (2016) OECD Working Papers on International Investment 2016/01, 5. This paper states that '[p]rovisions expressly contemplating the subsequent agreement of treaty parties on binding interpretations were initially introduced in NAFTA. Now ... they have recently been included in an increasing range of treaties.' Also *see*: K. Gordon, J. Pohl, 'Investment Treaties over Time: Treaty Practice and Interpretation in a Changing World' (2015) OECD Working Papers on International Investment 2015/02, 25. The report provides that '[G]overnments appear to be providing more extensive guidance on how arbitrations are to be conducted' http://www.oecd.org/investment/investment-policy/WP-2015-02.pdf accessed on 10 June 2018.

387. European Commission, 'Fact Sheet on Investment Protection and Investor-to-State Dispute Settlement in EU Agreements' (Fact Sheet, November 2013) 2.

388. Article 8.10(3) of the CETA (2016). The same mechanism can also be found in the EU-Vietnam FTA in Article 14(3), which provides that 'treatment not listed in paragraph 2 can also constitute a breach of fair and equitable treatment where the Parties have so agreed in accordance with the procedures provided in Article X.6 (Amendments).' *See* the Draft EU-Vietnam FTA 'Agreed texts of January 2016'.

> The Parties shall regularly, or upon request of a Party, review the content of the obligation to provide fair and equitable treatment. The Committee on Services and Investment, established under Article 26.2.1(b) (Specialised committees), may develop recommendations in this regard and submit them to the CETA Joint Committee for decision.[389]

The recommendations for a revision of the content of the FET standard can be developed by the Committee on Services and Investment and then submitted to the CETA Joint Committee for a decision. In accordance with Article 26.1(1), the CETA Joint Committee includes 'representatives of the European Union and representatives of Canada'.[390] The main tasks of the CETA Joint Committee, according to Article 26(4), are to:

> (a) supervise and facilitate the implementation and application of this Agreement and further its general aims;
> (b) supervise the work of all specialised committees and other bodies established under this Agreement ....[391]

Article 8.10(3) of the CETA that provides for a review of the FET standard is closely linked to another provision of the CETA that concerns the possibility to adopt binding interpretations. Article 8.31(3) of CETA states that:

> Where serious concerns arise as regards matters of interpretation that may affect investment, the Committee on Services and Investment may, pursuant to Article 8.44.3(a),[392] recommend to the CETA Joint Committee the adoption of interpretations of this Agreement. An interpretation adopted by the CETA Joint Committee shall be binding on a Tribunal established under this Section. The CETA Joint Committee may decide that an interpretation shall have binding effect from a specific date.[393]

The mechanism envisioned in Article 8.10(3) of the CETA is applicable to a review of the FET standard. Article 8.31(3) provides for the possibility to adopt binding interpretations of the provisions of the Agreement. It means that the Committee on Services and Investment may recommend an interpretation of the FET standard to the CETA Joint Committee. According to Article 8.31(3), the 'CETA Joint Committee may decide that an interpretation shall have binding effect from a specific date.' Some commentators have observed that such specifications may imply that the interpretation of a certain provision may be issued with 'retroactive effect'.[394]

389. Article 8.31(3) of the CETA (2016).
390. Article 26(1) of the CETA (2016).
391. Article 26(4) of the CETA (2016).
392. Article 8.44(3)(a) of the CETA (2016). Article 8.44(3)(a) provides that 'The Committee on Services and Investment may, on agreement of the Parties, and after completion of their respective internal requirements and procedures: (a) recommend to the CETA Joint Committee the adoption of interpretations of this Agreement pursuant to Article 8.31.3'.
393. Article 8.31(3) of the CETA (2016).
394. N. Lavranos, 'How the European Commission and the EU Member States are Reasserting Their Control over Their Investment Treaties and ISDS Rules', in A. Kulick, *European Commission and the EU Member States, Reassertion of Control over the Investment Treaty Regime* (Cambridge University Press, 2016) 313.

In both provisions, two treaty organs - the Committee on Services and Investment and the CETA Joint Committee - composed of representatives of the EU and Canada have the authority to propose a review of the FET standard and to make interpretations of the provisions of the CETA that are subsequently binding on tribunals.

To sum up, the NAFTA and CETA are examples of agreements that have incorporated built-in treaty mechanisms allowing the treaty organs to issue binding interpretations. As indicated by the OECD reports, states are increasingly using different legal means at their disposal; they institutionalise their competence to issue binding interpretations through establishing treaty bodies with the aim of reinforcing their interpretation and development of substantive provisions.[395] The reason for this, as was explained by the contracting states to the CETA[396] (similar to the states parties to the NAFTA), is that states are concerned about 'preserving their freedom to regulate without incurring liability'.[397]

§3.04 SUMMARY OF THE CHAPTER AND INTERIM CONCLUSIONS

The text of IIA FET standard provisions is the legal basis for decisions of arbitrators on FET claims. Based on the assessment of the FET standard provisions of the selected IIAs conducted in this book, the following categories have been identified: (1) FET standard provisions formulated as unqualified treaty standards; (2) IIAs in which the FET standard provision includes a reference to a norm of unwritten international law, e.g. (a) customary international law; (b) general international law and/or (c) principles of international law; (3) IIAs in which the FET standard provision is qualified with additional content; (4) IIAs in which the preamble provides a reference to the FET standard; and (5) IIAs with (a) a joint interpretative instrument clarifying the intent of the parties to the treaty and/or (b) one or more decisions by a treaty organ on the interpretation of the FET standard.

Consistent with the research results of other studies, e.g. UNCTAD that included a large sample of IIAs, the present survey results demonstrate that most IIAs have been concisely formulated as self-standing clauses. There are thirteen IIAs where the FET standard has incorporated a reference to the minimum standard of the treatment of aliens under customary international law. They seem to have followed the NAFTA formulation clarified in the context of the FTC Notes of Interpretation. Furthermore, the states, which were party to twenty-one IIAs, have chosen to include an FET standard

395. D. Gaukrodger, 'The Legal Framework Applicable to Joint Interpretative Agreements of Investment Treaties' (2016) OECD Working Papers on International Investment 2016/01, 5; K. Gordon, J. Pohl, 'Investment Treaties over Time: Treaty Practice and Interpretation in a Changing World' (2015) OECD Working Papers on International Investment 2015/02, 25.
396. L. Jonson, et al., 'International Investment Agreements, 2014: A Review of Trends and New Approaches', in A.K. Bjorklund (ed.) *Yearbook on International Investment Law and Policy 2014-2015* (Oxford University Press, 2016) 20.
397. F. Jadeau, F. Gélinas, 'CETA's Definition of the Fair and Equitable Treatment Standard: Toward a Guided and Constrained Interpretation' [2016] 13(1) *Transnational Dispute Management*, 13.

provision that makes reference to general international law or principles of international law.

This survey demonstrates that new developments in the drafting of the IIA FET standard have taken place. Since recently, a new category of IIA FET standard provisions has seen the light of day, i.e. FET standard provisions which include a list of state obligations or a further clarification of the FET standard. In eleven IIAs in this survey, the states have opted for more elaborate language in the text of the treaty with regard to what amounts to a violation of the FET standard by including either an exhaustive or a non-exhaustive list of a state's unacceptable conduct. European agreements - such as the CETA, the EU-Vietnam FTA, the EU-Singapore FTA, the TTIP - have included a closed list approach, indicating their intention to clarify the FET standard's application on the basis of a number of state obligations. These include, e.g., the obligations to avoid a fundamental breach of due process and manifest arbitrariness. In addition to the inclusion of a list of state obligations under IIA FET standard provisions, several agreements, e.g. the Colombia-France BIT, have also clarified that the FET standard does not preclude the state from being able to change its legislation or that the FET standard does not encompass a stabilisation clause.

There are also several IIAs that include a combination approach between category 2 and 3. The France-Colombia BIT is an example of such a combined approach that includes a reference to international law and a list of host state obligations.

It is noticeable that an increasing number of states have moved towards specifying the FET standard in their IIAs. This trend is supported by the UNCTAD research that shows that a growing number of countries and regions are reviewing their IIAs.[398] This revision includes a clarification of the FET standard provisions in states' IIAs that a group of states have attempted to clarify, alongside other substantive investment protection clauses.[399]

Furthermore, as follows from the above survey, some IIAs have included additional agreements on the interpretation of the FET standard. In EU agreements, NAFTA and several BITs, the treaty parties have found it useful to institutionalise their competence to interpret the FET standard through empowering a treaty organ usually composed of treaty parties' own representatives. These treaty organs can issue an interpretation of the FET standard or, as exemplified by CETA, can review the content of the FET standard.

398. UNCTAD, 'World Investment Report' (2015) 108. The report provides that '[a]t least 50 countries or regions are currently revising or have recently revised their model IIAs. This trend is not limited to a specific group of countries or regions but includes at least 12 African countries, 10 countries from Europe and North America, 8 Latin American countries, 7 Asian countries and 6 economies in transition. In addition, at least 4 regional organizations have reviewed or are reviewing their models.' http://unctad.org/en/pages/PublicationWebflyer.aspx?publicationid=1245 accessed on 10 June 2018.

399. E. De Brabandere, 'States' Reassertion of Control over International Investment Law – (Re)Defining "Fair and Equitable Treatment" and "Indirect Expropriation"', in A. Kulick (ed.) *States' Reassertion of Control over International Investment Agreements and International Investment Treaty Dispute Settlement* (Cambridge University Press, 2016) 8-9.

CHAPTER 4

Investment Jurisprudence on the FET Standard and the Right to Regulate: A General Overview

§4.01 INTRODUCTION

For a long time, the FET standard was not interpreted and applied by investment tribunals. As was so eloquently stated by Schreuer, the 'FET standard has existed as a sleeping beauty for about 50 years tucked away in a number of documents, but was rarely, if ever, kissed awake.'[400] Since the early 2000s, the FET standard has been invoked by investors and applied by tribunals in almost all investment cases.[401]

In understanding the development of FET jurisprudence, several factors are worth outlining.

First, as dealt with in Chapter 3, IIAs, and BITs in particular, include a broad range of different formulations of the FET standard. Chapter 3 provides examples of different IIA FET standard formulations. A predominant number of these FET standard

400. C. Schreuer, 'Fair and Equitable Treatment in Investment Treaty Law: Introduction', in F. Ortino and others (eds) *Investment Treaty Law: Current Issues II* (British Institute of International and Comparative Law, 2007) 92.

401. *See* D. Gaukrodger, 'Addressing the Balance of Interests in Investment Treaties' (2017) OECD Working Papers on International Investment 2017/03, 5, http://dx.doi.org/10.1787/0a62034b-en accessed on 15 June 2018. The report provides that the 'FET has leapt to prominence in the last 15 years as the principal ground of liability at issue in many if not most investment treaty arbitration claims.' *See* UNCTAD 'World Investment Report 2016' (2016) 107. The report provides that 'in the decisions holding the state liable, tribunals most frequently found breaches of the fair and equitable treatment ...'. *See also*: R. Dolzer, C. Schreuer, 1st edn., (2008) 119; they argue that '[i]t is only since 2000, the first significant cases being *Metalclad* and *Maffenzi*, that investment tribunals haven given content to the meaning of the standard and have applied it to a broad range of circumstances.' *See also Metalclad Corporation v. The United Mexican States*, ICSID Case No. ARB(AF)/97/1 Award (30 August 2000) and *Emilio Agustín Maffezini v. The Kingdom of Spain*, ICSID Case No. ARB/97/7 Award (13 November 2000).

provisions that are currently being interpreted and applied by tribunals contain unqualified, open definitions of the FET standard.[402]

Second, due to the openness of the FET standard, many investment tribunals, especially in the early 2000s, were left with the task of providing meaning to the concept of FET under an applicable IIA.[403] In describing this development, Schill has noted:

> Arbitral tribunals emerge as important rule-makers in international investment law. Their function is not restricted to applying pre-existing rules and principles to the facts of a case, but extends to developing the existing principles into more precise rules and standards of conduct.[404]

Tribunals have developed the FET standard by providing various interpretations.[405] In several FET decisions, some tribunals – especially early ones (decided between 2000 and 2005) – focused primarily on the interests of the investor. Other tribunals broadly defined the FET standard, encompassing a wide range of unlawful conduct by the state. Several other decisions have provided more balanced interpretations of the FET standard, taking into account the interests and circumstances of the host state.[406] This Chapter will elaborate on the ways in which tribunals have interpreted this standard.

Third, at the present time, divergences between the tribunals' interpretations of the FET standard are less apparent. In their decisions, tribunals have moved towards defining the FET standard by 'breaking it down ... into several concrete principles'.[407] The most frequently cited principles include: due process and procedural rights, the protection of the legitimate expectations of the investor and the prohibition of arbitrary and discriminatory treatment of the investor. The current analysis of the FET standard in relation to the right to regulate considers several of these principles, including, e.g.,

402. A large number of IIAs with self-standing or unqualified formulations originated in the majority of all IIAs that were negotiated between the 1990s and the 2000s. Therefore, the unqualified FET standard provisions continue to dominate in comparison with other FET standard formulations. The present survey indicates that unqualified FET standard provisions have been the most prevalent choice for the FET standard formulation in IIAs, as this type of formulation has been adopted in forty-six of eighty-nine IIAs. This is in accordance with the UNCTAD research conclusions, which include a more representative sample of 1,456 IIAs, among which 1,132 IIAs included unqualified FET standard provisions in their treaties. *See* UNCTAD, 'IIA Mapping Project, 2013-2014.' This information was obtained on 25 August 2016 http://investmentpolicyhub.unctad.org/IIA/mappedContent accessed on 12 June 2018.
403. As has been indicated in Chapter 3, the phrasing of these autonomous provisions is of a general character that does not define what unfair and inequitable treatment is composed of. *See*: C. Bucheler, Proportionality in Investor-State Arbitration (Oxford University Press, 2015) 182, who has also pointed to the generality of FET provisions.
404. S. Schill, The Multilateralization of International Investment Law (Cambridge University Press, 2009) 275.
405. R. Dolzer, C. Schreuer, 2nd edn., (2012) 163. The example of different interpretations regarding the FET standard is based on the example of certain tribunals, e.g. NAFTA, that interpret the FET standard in accordance with customary international law and other tribunals that interpret the FET standard 'autonomously on the basis of their respective wording'.
406. This convergence between the interpretations of tribunals is especially evident in the early development of legitimate expectations as a key element of the FET standard. This concept is further explained in Chapter 5.
407. T. Gazzini, Interpretation of International Investment Treaties (Hart Publishing, 2016) 98.

the protection of the legitimate expectations of the investor, the prohibition of discriminatory treatment that are analysed in detail in Chapters 6 and 7.

Fourth, with the growth of investment decisions involving the FET standard, the balance between host states' right to regulate and the right of investors has become a key issue entering academic and practical discussions on the FET standard.[408] As has been identified in Chapter 2, the right to regulate has come to the forefront in several IIAs, investment cases on the FET standard and some of the academic literature on the subject. In deciding on a claim concerning a violation of the FET standard, tribunals refer to the state's right to regulate on a recurring basis. In other words, the assessment of the state's right to regulate, on the one hand, is balanced against the investor's right to obtain FET, on the other. What remains unclear in this equation is the conditions that apply to the lawful exercise of the right to regulate vis-à-vis the rights of an investor to obtain FET that will be introduced in Chapter 5 and are further elaborated upon and discussed in Chapters 6 and 7, and the ways in which the FET standard has been interpreted by tribunals will be explained in the following sections.

Section §4.02 will discuss how arbitral tribunals have interpreted IIAs' FET standard in applying the general rules of treaty interpretation laid down in the Vienna Convention on the Law of the Treaties, 1969 (VCLT). The supplementary and subsidiary means of analysing FET standard interpretations that, e.g., include previous decisions and scholarly writings are addressed in section §4.03.

General principles of law that are sometimes invoked by tribunals in their assessment of a state's conduct against the right of an investor under the FET standard are examined in section §4.04. The Chapter is concluded by a summary in section §4.05.

§4.02 THE INTERPRETATION OF THE FET STANDARD UNDER THE GENERAL RULE OF TREATY INTERPRETATION

In interpreting the FET standard under an applicable IIA, tribunals rely primarily on the rules of treaty interpretation contained in the VCLT. The VCLT provides an important framework for the 'fundamental rules of interpretation ... reflecting customary international law'.[409] These rules of interpretation codified in the VCLT have been identified in accordance with three main schools of interpretation. The first school is based on the 'objective approach' that focuses on the 'actual text of the agreement and emphasises the analysis of the words used'.[410] The second school is based on the 'subjective approach' that considers the intentions of the parties to the agreement.[411] The third, theological, approach centres on the 'object and purpose' of the agreement, as the

408. Klager explains this development by the dynamics present in investor-state arbitration, where at first the FET standard was considered nothing more than just a political 'signal' in the text of agreements and over time has 'revealed a potential to reach further in the traditional *domaine reserve* of the host state than any one of the other rules of the treaties'. *See* R. Klager, (2011) 28.
409. M. Shaw, International Law (5th edn., Cambridge University Press, 2003) 839.
410. *Ibid.*
411. M. Evans, International Law (Oxford University Press, 2006) 199.

'most important backcloth against which the meaning of any particular treaty provision should be measured'.[412] All three approaches are reflected in Articles 31-32 of the VCLT.

Article 31 of the VCLT provides that:

> 1. A treaty shall be interpreted in good faith in accordance with the ordinary meaning to be given to the terms of the treaty in their context and in the light of its object and purpose to be given to the terms of the treaty in their context and in the light of its object and purpose.
> 2. The context for the purpose of the interpretation of a treaty shall comprise, in addition to the text, including its preamble and annexes:
>   (a) Any agreement relating to the treaty which was made between all the parties in connexion with the conclusion of the treaty;
>   (b) Any instrument which was made by one or more parties in connexion with the conclusion of the treaty and accepted by the other parties as an instrument related to the treaty.
> 3. There shall be taken into account, together with the context:
>   (a) Any subsequent agreement between the parties regarding the interpretation of the treaty or the application of its provisions;
>   (b) Any subsequent practice in the application of the treaty which establishes the agreement of the parties regarding its interpretation;
>   (c) Any relevant rules of international law applicable in the relations between the parties. 4. A special meaning shall be given to a term if it is established that the parties so intended.[413]

Further, Article 32 of VCLT stipulates that:

> Recourse may be had to supplementary means of interpretation, including the preparatory work of the treaty and the circumstances of its conclusion, in order to confirm the meaning resulting from the application of article 31, or to determine the meaning when the interpretation according to article 31:
>
> (a) Leaves the meaning ambiguous or obscure; or
> (b) Leads to a result which is manifestly absurd or unreasonable.[414]

The general rules of interpretation, as codified in the VCLT, are legally binding on the tribunal interpreting a treaty (as are other rules of international law, for that matter).[415] Tribunals have often expressly relied on the rules of treaty interpretation embedded in the VCLT when interpreting the FET standard under an applicable IIA. The *MTD v. Chile* tribunal stressed the obligation to interpret BIT provisions according to the VCLT. It argued that the tribunal is 'obliged to apply the provisions of the BIT and

412. M. Shaw, International Law (5th edn., Cambridge University Press, 2003) 839.
413. Article 31(1) of the Vienna Convention on the Law of Treaties, 1155 UNTS 331 (23 May 1969) https://treaties.un.org/doc/Publication/UNTS/Volume%201155/volume-1155-I-18232-English.pdf accessed on 12 June 2018.
414. Article 32 of the Vienna Convention on the Law of Treaties, 1155 UNTS 331 (23 May 1969).
415. As Gazzini underlines, the application of the VCLT as being either customary international law or treaty law has not been disputed by tribunals. *See*: T. Gazzini, Interpretation of International Investment Treaties (Hart Publishing, 2016) 6.

interpret them in accordance with the norms of interpretation established by the Vienna Convention on the Law of the Treaties ...'.[416]

The rules of treaty interpretation embedded in the VCLT, specifically Article 31, 'builds on a centennial tradition deeply rooted in public international law and is clearly part of the applicable law when a treaty is applied'.[417] Article 32 of the VCLT provides for a supplementary means of interpretation, which is usually regarded as consisting of secondary, non-mandatory rules in relation to the elements embedded in Article 31.[418] The application of Articles 31 and 32 of the VCLT in the interpretation of the FET standard is addressed below.

In order to provide meaning to the FET standard, tribunals often turn to an examination of this standard on the basis of the main elements of Article 31(1) of the VCLT, which include (1) the *ordinary meaning* of the FET standard, (2) the *context* in which the FET standard is presented in the treaty and (3) *the object and purpose* of the treaty containing the FET standard.[419] These three elements will be discussed in turn. It should be noted that in interpreting the treaty under Article 31(1), the context, the object and the purpose of the treaty are connected in order to reveal or find the ordinary meaning of the terms used in the treaty.[420] As Gardiner explains:

> While the object and purpose of the treaty is a distinct element assisting the interpreter towards giving meaning to the relevant term in a similar way to the assistance provided by the context, a role for the object and purpose of a particular treaty provision (as distinct from the object and purpose of the treaty as a whole) is not singled out in the general rule.[421]

Gardiner further provides that in treaty interpretation, it comes as no surprise that in the 'examination of context, interpreters sometimes look to the object of a particular provision'.[422] As will be demonstrated further in sections §4.02[B] and §4.02[C], in interpreting the FET standard, tribunals consider the context of the FET provision in the treaty as well as the object and purpose of the particular treaty, which are mostly found in the preambular statements of an applicable IIA.

416. *MTD v. Chile*, ICSID Case No. ARB/01/7 Award (25 May 2004) para. 112. The tribunal mentioned that this rule applies if the FET does not contain a reference to customary international law.
417. H. Ascensio, 'Article 31 of the Vienna Convention on the Law of Treaties and International Investment Law' [2016] 31(2) *ICSID Review*, 369.
418. A. Reinisch, 'The Interpretation of International Investment Agreements', in M. Bungenberg and others (eds) *International Investment Law: A Handbook* (Nomos, 2015) 376.
419. For example, the tribunal in *AWG v. Argentina* explained that it was guided by Article 31 of the Vienna Convention. Specifically, it underlined that 'three elements are of particular importance in interpreting the relevant treaty provisions: (1) the ordinary meaning of the term "fair and equitable," (2) the context in which the term "fair and equitable" is used; and (3) the object and purpose of the three BITs.' *See AWG v. Argentina* [2010] UNCITRAL Arbitration, Decision on Liability (30 July 2010) para. 211.
420. R. Gardiner, Treaty Interpretation (2nd edn., Oxford University Press, 2017) 210.
421. *Ibid.*
422. *Ibid.*

[A] Ordinary Meaning of the Treaty

In order to reveal the ordinary meaning of the FET standard, several tribunals have turned to the literal meaning of words 'fair' and 'equitable'. With references being made to a law dictionary, tribunals have defined the FET standard with synonyms such as 'even-handed' and 'just'.[423] As acknowledged by several tribunals, this approach has proved to add little value to a meaningful understanding of the FET standard.[424] For instance, the tribunal in *Crystallex v. Venezuela* summarised that 'the plain meaning of these terms [fair and equitable] ... does not provide much assistance.'[425] The *Saluka v. Czech Republic* tribunal, in similar terms, provided that 'the "ordinary meaning" of the "fair and equitable treatment" standard can only be defined by terms of almost equal vagueness.'[426] Several scholars have concurred with such assessments, pointing out that references to similarly vague terms do not contribute to a clarification of the FET standard's content.[427] Consequently, in attempting to clarify the meaning of the FET standard, most tribunals have turned to the context as well as the object and purpose of the treaty.

[B] Context of the Treaty

In interpreting the FET standard, a number of tribunals have considered the context in which this standard is presented in the applicable IIA. Article 31(2) of the VCLT explains what is meant by the 'context' of a treaty. It provides that '[t]he context for the purpose of the interpretation of a treaty shall comprise, in addition to the text, including

423. For other examples, *see MTD v. Chile*, ICSID Case No. ARB/01/7 Award (25 May 2004) para. 113 ('[i]n their ordinary meaning, the terms "fair" and "equitable" used in Article 3(1) of the BIT mean "just", "even-handed", "unbiased", "legitimate".'); *See Azurix Corp. v. The Argentine Republic*, ICSID Case No. ARB/01/12 Award (14 July 2006) para. 360, where the tribunal described fair and equitable treatment as 'just', 'even-handed', 'unbiased', 'legitimate'; *National Grid plc v. The Argentine Republic* [2008] UNCITRAL Arbitration, Award (3 November 2008) para. 168. ('[i]n their ordinary meaning, the term "fair" means "just," "even-handed," "unbiased," "legitimate," "reasonable." Equitable is defined as "fair" and "just, fair, and right, in consideration of the facts and circumstances of the individual case"').
424. *AWG v. Argentina* [2010] UNCITRAL Arbitration, Decision on Liability (30 July 2010) para. 213. '... Analyzing the ordinary meaning of the terms "fair and equitable treatment" ... to the present dispute yields little additional enlightenment.' *Mamidoil Jetoil Greek Petroleum Products Societe S.A. v. Republic of Albania*, ICSID Case No. ARB/11/24 Award (30 March 2015) paras 604-605.
425. *Crystallex International Corporation v. the Republic of Venezuela*, ICSID Case No. ARB(AF)/11/2 Award (4 April 2016) para. 538.
426. *Saluka v. Czech Republic* [2006] Permanent Court of Arbitration, IIC 210, Partial Award (17 March 2006) para. 297.
427. R. Klager, (2013) 42. *See also* S. Schill who discusses the 'ordinary meaning' of the FET standard and emphasises that 'In particular, the semantics of fair and equitable treatment do not clarify as against which standard 'fairness and equitableness' has to be measured. It could equally refer to notions of equality or substantive justice, or to less grand notions of procedural due process.' S. Schill, 'Fair and Equitable Treatment under Investment Treaties as an Embodiment of the Rule of Law' (2006) New York School of Law International Law Working Papers 2006/06, 6 http://www.iilj.org/wp-content/uploads/2016/08/Schill-Fair-and-Equitable-Treatment-under-Investment-Treaties-as-an-Embodiment-of-the-Rule-of-Law-2006-2.pdf accessed on 12 June 2018.

its preamble and annexes: a) "any agreement relating to the treaty which was made between all the parties in connexion with the conclusion of the treaty" and (b) "any instrument which was made by one or more parties in connection with the conclusion of the treaty and accepted by the other parties as an instrument related to the treaty".'[428] As Gazzini noted, the context may also include the interpretative notes, footnotes, annexes and other instruments belonging to the treaty.[429]

In considering the context of the FET standard provision, tribunals have predominantly referred to the preamble to the applicable IIA. The *Saluka v. Czech Republic* tribunal explained that 'the broader "context" in which the terms of Article 3.1 (fair and equitable treatment) must be seen includes the other provisions of the Treaty.'[430] In this light, the tribunal referred to the preamble to the applicable Netherlands-Czech Republic BIT that mentioned the FET standard[431] and which provided:

> [R]ecognizing that agreement upon the treatment to be accorded to such investments will stimulate the flow of capital and technology and the economic development of the Contracting Parties and that fair and equitable treatment is desirable.[432]

Based on the formulation in the preamble, the tribunal provided that the 'preamble links the "fair and equitable treatment" standard directly to the stimulation of foreign investments and to the economic development of both Contracting Parties.'[433] From this, it may be assumed that in the context of the preamble, where the objectives of the treaty are underlined, the protection of the FET is identified as being an important standard in achieving the aforementioned objectives.

In the *Lemire v. Ukraine* award, the tribunal also made reference to the preamble by interpreting the FET standard in the context of the treaty.[434] The tribunal in this case provided that words in a treaty 'must be interpreted through their context'.[435] For this purpose, the tribunal resorted to the preamble to the BIT, which established that 'fair and equitable treatment of investment is desirable in order to maintain a stable framework for investment ...'.[436] On the basis of this formulation in the preamble, the tribunal concluded that:

---

428. Article 31(2) of the Vienna Convention on the Law of Treaties, 1155 UNTS 331 (23 May 1969) https://treaties.un.org/doc/Publication/UNTS/Volume%201155/volume-1155-I-18232-English.pdf accessed on 12 June 2018.
429. T. Gazzini, Interpretation of International Investment Treaties (Hart Publishing, 2016) 145.
430. *Saluka v. Czech Republic* [2006] Permanent Court of Arbitration, IIC 210, Partial Award (17 March 2006) para. 298.
431. Netherlands-Czech Republic BIT (1991) http://investmentpolicyhub.unctad.org/IIA/mappedContent/treaty/1212 accessed on 2 November 2016.
432. *Saluka v. Czech Republic* [2006] Permanent Court of Arbitration, IIC 210, Partial Award (17 March 2006) para. 298.
433. *Ibid.*
434. *Lemire v. Ukraine*, ICSID Case No. ARB/06/18 Decision on Jurisdiction and Liability (14 January 2010) para. 264.
435. *Ibid.*
436. US-Ukraine BIT (1996) preamble http://investmentpolicyhub.unctad.org/IIA/CountryBits/219 accessed on 12 June 2018.

> The FET standard is thus closely tied to the notion of legitimate expectations – actions or omissions by Ukraine are contrary to the FET standard if they frustrate legitimate and reasonable expectations on which the investor relied at the time when he made an investment.[437]

In its assessment of the context in which the terms of FET were presented in the treaty, the tribunal in *National Grid v. Argentina* took into consideration the applicable UK-Argentina BIT.[438] The first paragraph of Article 2 of the UK-Argentina BIT entitled 'Promotion and Protection of Investment' stipulates that each contracting party should 'encourage and create favourable conditions for investors'.[439] The second paragraph of Article 2 provides that 'investments of investors of each Contracting Party shall at all times be accorded fair and equitable treatment.'[440] The tribunal interpreted that the 'obligation of fair and equitable treatment is placed squarely in the context of an obligation to encourage and create favorable conditions for investors.'[441] This observation led to the conclusion by the tribunal that the state had no intentions to limit FET as found in the MST of aliens under customary international law.[442]

In the aforementioned examples, the context in which the FET standard is interpreted has involved formulations in preambles or other provisions in which the encouragement and promotion of investments in the host state are being emphasised. In this regard, the FET standard has also been interpreted rather broadly, with prime focus being given to the rights of investors.

At the same time, in recent cases, tribunals have not explicitly paid much attention to the context of the applicable treaty in their interpretation of the FET standard.[443] In *Mamidoil v. Albania*, the tribunal indirectly referred to the context of the treaty by outlining the general goals of the IIAs in question. In this way, it provided that the interpretation of the FET standard in the treaty should be balanced by taking into account the rights of states and investors alike. At the outset of its analysis, the tribunal provided that the interpretation must be according to the rules of the VCLT and

437. *Lemire v. Ukraine*, ICSID Case No. ARB/06/18 Decision on Jurisdiction and Liability (14 January 2010) para. 264.
438. *National Grid plc v. The Argentine Republic* [2008] UNCITRAL Arbitration, Award (3 November 2008) para. 170.
439. Article 2 of the UK-Argentina BIT (1993) http://investmentpolicyhub.unctad.org/IIA/country/221/treaty/161 accessed on 12 June 2018.
440. *Ibid.*
441. *National Grid plc v. The Argentine Republic* [2008] UNCITRAL Arbitration, Award (3 November 2008) para. 170.
442. *Ibid.*
443. *Philip Morris v. Uruguay*, ICSID Case No. ARB/10/7 Award (8 July 2016) para. 317. The tribunal did not analyse the context of the treaty; it only recited the general rules of interpretation. Tribunal provided 'As any other treaty provisions, the text of Article 3(2) of the BIT must be interpreted according to the normal canons of treaty interpretation as contained in Articles 31 and 32 of the VCLT.' *See also*: *Flemingo DutyFree Shop Private Limited v. the Republic of Poland*, UNCITRAL (Award, 12 August 2016), para. 530. The tribunal stated that the 'terms "fair" and "equitable treatment" provided in the Treaty require an interpretation which is in accordance with their "ordinary meaning".' It further provided that these 'terms [fair and equitable treatment] have never had a uniform definition is correct in the sense that these terms in their ordinary meaning do not refer to an established body of legal rules which have to be respected'(para. 530). The tribunal proceeded with an analysis of the facts of the case.

should '[start] with the ordinary meaning of the terms of a given treaty, before a tribunal considers their context and the object and purpose of the treaty'.[444] Furthermore, the tribunal stated that 'generally speaking' the goal of investment treaties is to 'stimulat[e] cross-border in order to foster economic relations between the treaty partners and economic development in the partner countries'.[445] In the light of formulating the goals of investment treaties in general, the tribunal, in the paragraphs that followed, stressed the importance of accounting for the interests of both host states and investors in the assessment of the FET standard. To this end, the tribunal pointed to the responsibility of the state to provide 'long-term physical and social infrastructure'[446] which is important for economic development. In order to pursue such a policy, the state has to take a variety of 'social and economic interests into account, so that individual interests can be safely pursued'.[447] By referring to the stimulation of 'economic development in the partner countries' as a goal of the treaty in the context of the FET standard obligation, the tribunal in this case outlined the significance of balancing the rights and obligations of investors in the assessment of the standard.

[C] Object and Purpose of the Treaty

In addition to its context, the treaty should be interpreted in the light of its object and purpose. The object and purpose of the treaty are not identical concepts, however, and are often 'confounded'.[448] The object is referred to as the 'subject matter subjected to the treaty'.[449] The purpose of the treaty refers to the 'aim of the norm'.[450] Additionally, the object of the treaty is deduced from the 'whole of the treaty provisions, whereas purposes are usually found in the preamble'.[451] Under IIAs, the object of the treaty has commonly been referred to as 'investment protection'.[452] The purpose of an IIA may include different aims provided for in the preamble to the IIA. As illustrated by the SADC Model BIT in Chapter 2, the purpose of the treaty may, e.g., include the encouragement of investment that 'support[s] the sustainable development of each Party'.[453]

---

444. *Mamidoil Jetoil Greek Petroleum Products Société S.A. v. Republic of Albania*, ICSID Case No. ARB/11/24 Award (30 March 2015) para. 611.
445. *Ibid.*
446. *Mamidoil Jetoil Greek Petroleum Products Société S.A. v. Republic of Albania*, ICSID Case No. ARB/11/24 Award (30 March 2015) para. 612.
447. *Ibid.*, para. 614.
448. A. Van Aanken, 'Control Mechanisms in International Investment Law', in Z. Douglas, et al. (eds) *The Foundations of International Investment Law: Bringing Theory into Practice* (Oxford University Press, 2014) 429.
449. R. Kolb, The Law of Treaties: An Introduction (Edward Elgar Publishing, 2016) 145.
450. *Ibid.*
451. H. Ascensio, 'Article 31 of the Vienna Convention on the Law of Treaties and International Investment Law' [2016] 31(2) *ICSID Review*, 370.
452. A. Van Aanken, 'Control Mechanisms in International Investment Law', in Z. Douglas, et al. (eds) *The Foundations of International Investment Law: Bringing Theory into Practice* (Oxford University Press, 2014) 429.
453. Article 1 of the South African Development Community BIT (2012) with commentaries.

When searching for the object and purpose of a treaty, investment tribunals have traditionally referred to the preamble.[454] As in most treaties, preambles, especially earlier ones, stipulate the encouragement and protection of investments, and the FET standard has usually been interpreted as an important standard of treatment that is essential in order to attain these goals.

In *AWG v. Argentina*, the tribunal interpreted the goal of 'economic cooperation' found in the Argentina-Spain BIT and the France-Argentina BIT as 'the commitment to give fair and equitable treatment to important economic actors, such as investors, of a Contracting Party with which a State has committed to cooperate'.[455] Furthermore, the tribunal elaborated that:

> [I]t is difficult to see how cooperation in the economic and investment domain could ever take place unless such fair and equitable treatment is accorded by each State to protected investors and investments from the other State.[456]

The tribunal in *Tecmed v. Mexico* also relied on the objectives of the treaty in interpreting the FET standard. The tribunal referred to the BIT's goals that included the 'intensification of economic cooperation for the benefit of both countries' and the 'creation of favourable conditions for investments'.[457] In this light, the tribunal concluded that by including the provision of the FET standard into the BIT:

> [T]he parties intended to strengthen and increase the security and trust of foreign investors that invest in the member state, thus maximizing the use of the economic resources of each Contracting Party by facilitating the economic contributions of their economic operators.[458]

In *MTD v. Chile*, the tribunal interpreted the FET standard as a proactive obligation of the state in light of the objective of the treaty. The tribunal asserted that the objective of the investment treaty was to protect and to stimulate the flow of investments, and therefore, the FET standard should be understood as a 'proactive statement – "to promote," "to create," "to stimulate" – rather than prescriptions for a passive behavior of the State or avoidance of prejudicial conduct to the investors'.[459]

In interpreting the objective of a treaty, several FET investment decisions have relied upon the preamble in finding that the stability of the legal and business framework constitutes an element of the FET standard. For instance, the *Occidental v. Ecuador* tribunal considered the preamble to the US-Ecuador BIT where the purpose of the treaty also included that the FET standard is 'desirable in order to maintain a stable framework for investment …'.[460] The tribunal interpreted the unqualified FET standard

454. R. Dolzer, C. Schreuer, 2nd edn., (2012) 88 who argued that '[t]ribunals have frequently interpreted investment treaties in light of their object and purpose, often by looking at their preambles'.
455. *AWG v. Argentina* [2010] UNCITRAL Arbitration, Decision on Liability (30 July 2010) para. 219.
456. *Ibid.*
457. *Tecmed v. Mexico*, ICSID Case No. ARB(AF)/00/2 Award (29 May 2003) para. 156.
458. *Ibid.*
459. *MTD v. Chile*, ICSID Case No. ARB/01/7 Award (25 May 2004) para. 113.
460. *Occidental v. Ecuador*, LCIA Case No. UN3467, Final Award (1 July 2004) para. 183.

under Article II(3)(a) of the US-Ecuador BIT[461] on the basis of the aforementioned formulation in the preamble, so as to mean that 'the stability of the legal framework is thus an essential element of fair and equitable treatment.'[462]

In its interpretation of the FET standard in the light of the purpose of the treaty, the tribunal in *CMS v. The Argentine Republic* relied on an identical formulation in the preamble as was the case in *Occidental v. Ecuador*. Paragraph 4 of the preamble in the US-Argentine Republic BIT provides that 'agreeing that fair and equitable treatment of investment is desirable in order to maintain a stable framework for investment and maximum effective use of economic resources'.[463] In interpreting the unqualified, open FET standard under Article II(2)(a) of the US-Argentine BIT, the tribunal asserted that '[the] treaty preamble makes it clear, that one principal objective of the protection envisaged is that fair and equitable treatment is desirable to maintain a stable framework for investments and maximum effective use of economic resources.'[464] The *CMS* tribunal thereby concluded that 'there can be no doubt that a stable legal and business environment is an essential element of fair and equitable treatment.'[465]

The aforementioned examples of the interpretation of the FET standard in light of the object and purpose of the treaty have led tribunals to develop broad interpretations of a state's obligations towards an investor under the FET standard. However, several tribunals, including, e.g., the tribunals in *Société Générale v. Dominican Republic, El Paso v. Argentina* and *Continental v. Argentina*, have adopted a more balanced interpretation with regard to the FET standard in interpreting the standard in the light of the treaty's purpose.[466]

The tribunal in *Société Générale v. Dominican Republic* argued for a cautious approach when invoking the preamble in establishing the object and purpose of the treaty. It provided that 'the preamble sets out the general purposes and objectives of the Treaty ... but cannot add substantive requirements to the provisions of the treaty'.[467] The *Continental v. Argentina* tribunal further explained that the requirement of stability does not comprise a 'legal obligation in itself' and that it can neither 'be properly defined as an object of the Treaty'.[468] The tribunal specified that '[i]t is rather a precondition for one of the two basic objects of the Treaty, namely the promotion of the investment flow, rather than being related to its other objective, that of granting

461. Article II(3)(a) of US-Ecuador BIT provides that '[i]nvestment shall at all times be accorded fair and equitable treatment, shall enjoy full protection and security and shall in no case be accorded treatment less favorable than that required by international law'.
462. *Occidental v. Ecuador*, LCIA Case No. UN3467, Final Award (1 July 2004) para. 183.
463. US-Argentina BIT (1994) http://www.italaw.com/sites/default/files/laws/italaw6017%283%29.pdf accessed on 11 June 2018.
464. *CMS Gas Transmission Co. v. The Argentine Republic*, ICSID Case No. ARB/01/8 Award (12 May 2005) para. 274.
465. *Ibid.*
466. *Continental Casualty v. Argentina*, ICSID Case No. ARB/03/9 Award (5 September 2008); *El Paso v. Argentina*, ICSID Case No. ARB/03/15 Award (31 October 2011).
467. *Société Générale v. Dominican Republic*, LCIA Case No. UN 7927 Award on Preliminary Objections on Jurisdiction (19 September 2008) para. 32. Also *see*: T. Gazzini, Interpretation of International Investment Treaties (Hart Publishing, 2016) 158.
468. *Continental Casualty v. Argentina*, ICSID Case No. ARB/03/9 Award (5 September 2008) para. 258.

protection for investments on a reciprocal basis.'[469] In the same vein, the *El Paso* tribunal implied that some tribunals had been short-sighted when extracting the goal of the treaty on the basis of the purpose to maintain 'a stable framework for investment and maximum effective use of economic resources', without 'taking into account the goal that any State has to pursue as well, which is to guarantee to its population maximum effective use of its economic resources'.[470] In a more general manner, the tribunal in *Saluka v. Czech Republic* also warned against focusing on objectives of the treaty that only benefit the interests of investors. It stated that:

> The protection of foreign investments is not the sole aim of the Treaty, but rather a necessary element alongside the overall aim of encouraging foreign investment and extending and intensifying the parties' economic relations. That in turn calls for a balanced approach to the interpretation of the Treaty's substantive provisions for the protection of investments, since an interpretation which exaggerates the protection to be accorded to foreign investments may serve to dissuade host States from admitting foreign investments and so undermine the overall aim of extending and intensifying the parties' mutual economic relations.[471]

To summarise, in interpreting the FET standard in the light of the object and purpose of the applicable IIA, tribunals frequently refer to the preamble to the treaty, where the object and purpose of the IIA are usually stated. Some tribunals have interpreted the FET standard broadly, focusing primarily on the rights of investors, thereby linking the stability of the regulatory framework, as emphasised in the preamble, and the FET standard. Several other decisions have taken a more balanced position, stressing that the 'protection of foreign investments is not the sole aim of the Treaty.'[472] The goals of stability and the effective use of economic resources have to be considered together with the goals pursued by states, e.g. the protection of a public interest.[473]

[D] Subsequent Agreement and Subsequent Practice

Article 31(3) of the VCLT provides that together with the context, account should also be taken of (a) 'any subsequent agreement between the parties regarding the interpretation of the treaty or the application of its provisions' and (b) 'any subsequent practice in the application of the treaty which establishes the agreement of the parties regarding its interpretation'.[474] The 2013 ILC Report provides a definition of subsequent agreement and subsequent practice. It states that:

---

469. *Ibid.*
470. *El Paso v. Argentina*, ICSID Case No. ARB/03/15 Award (31 October 2011) para. 369.
471. *Saluka v. Czech Republic* [2006] Permanent Court of Arbitration, IIC 210, Partial Award (17 March 2006) para. 300.
472. *Ibid.*
473. D. Rosentreter, 'Article 31(3)(c) of the Vienna Convention on the Law of Treaties and the Principles of Systematic Integration in International Investment Law and Arbitration' (Nomos, 2015) 253.
474. Article 31(3)(a) and (b) of the Vienna Convention on the Law of Treaties, 1155 UNTS 331 (23 May 1969).

> '[S]ubsequent agreement' as an authentic means of interpretation under article 31, paragraph 3 (a) is an agreement between the parties, reached after the conclusion of a treaty, regarding the interpretation of the treaty or the application of its provisions [and] a subsequent practice as an authentic means of interpretation under article 31, paragraph 3 (b) consists of conduct in the application of a treaty, after its conclusion, which establishes the agreement of the parties regarding the interpretation of the treaty.[475]

By using the term 'authentic', the ILC Report implies the presence of '"objective evidence" of conduct of the parties which reflects the "common understanding of the parties" as to the meaning of the treaty'.[476]

The distinction between subsequent agreement and subsequent practice is 'not always clear and the jurisprudence of international courts and other adjudicative bodies shows a certain reluctance to assert it'.[477] The ILC Report has shed some light on the differences between subsequent agreement and subsequent practice. In explaining the nature of a subsequent agreement, the ILC Report stated that it should be '"reached" and presupposes a single common act by the parties by which they manifest their common understanding regarding the interpretation of the treaty or the application of its provisions'.[478] However, subsequent practice includes 'all (other) relevant forms of subsequent conduct by the parties to a treaty which contribute to the identification of an agreement, or the "understanding" of the parties regarding the interpretation of the treaty'.[479] The ILC Report further emphasised that there is a likelihood that '"practice" and "agreement" coincide in specific cases and cannot be distinguished.'[480]

Subsequent agreement and subsequent practice have to be taken into account in the interpretation process. At the same time, the ILC Report clarifies that it does not necessarily mean that subsequent agreement or subsequent practice will have 'a conclusive, or legally binding, effect'[481] and will not necessarily 'override all other means of interpretation'.[482] However, if the contracting parties to the treaty so desire, they can conclude a binding subsequent agreement regarding the interpretation of the treaty,[483] particularly where the treaty provides for the adoption of such an agreement. To exemplify this, the ILC Commission refers to Article 1131(2) of NAFTA.[484] Article 1131 of NAFTA has stipulated that an interpretation by the Commission consisting of

475. United Nations General Assembly 'Report of the International Law Commission: Sixty-Fifth Session' (New York, 2013) Supplement No. 10 (A/68/10) 12.
476. *Ibid.*, 21.
477. *Ibid.*, 32.
478. *Ibid.*, 34.
479. *Ibid.*
480. *Ibid.*
481. United Nations General Assembly 'Report of the International Law Commission: Sixty-Fifth Session' (New York, 2013) Supplement No. 10 (A/68/10) 21.
482. *Ibid.*
483. *Ibid.*
484. United Nations General Assembly 'Report of the International Law Commission: Sixty-Fifth Session' (New York, 2013) Supplement No. 10 (A/68/10) 22.

the representatives of the contracting parties will be binding on the tribunal.[485] In the *Bilcon v. Canada* award, the tribunal discussed the FTC Notes[486] in relation to Article 31(3)(a) of the VCLT, in the following terms:

> Article 31(3)(a) of the Vienna Convention on the Law of Treaties calls on treaty interpreters to take into account 'any subsequent agreement between the parties regarding the interpretation of the treaty or the application of its provisions.' Yet NAFTA Article 1131(2) contains a lex specialis, which goes further in providing that '[a]n interpretation by the Commission of a provision of this Agreement shall be binding on a Tribunal established under this Section.' Under the general rule on interpretation set out in the Vienna Convention, a NAFTA tribunal would only need to 'take into account' the subsequent agreement. However, by virtue of NAFTA Article 1131(2), acts of authentic interpretation by the States parties to the Agreement, like the Notes just referred to, are binding and conclusive.[487]

As exemplified by the mechanism laid down in NAFTA Article 1131(2), the treaty 'specifically incorporated rules on subsequent agreements and practice, [which] form part of the treaty's general regulatory framework'.[488] In the words of the ILC Commission, this constitutes a 'special procedure or an agreement regarding the authoritative interpretation of a treaty which the parties consider binding'.[489] This type of procedure may differ from the subsequent practice of the parties under what became Article 31(3)(a) and (b) – which is only to be taken into account, among other means, 'while subsequent agreements and subsequent practice providing the agreement of the parties concerning the interpretation of a treaty, must be conclusive regarding such interpretation when "the parties consider the interpretation to be binding upon them"'.[490]

485. Article 1131(2) NAFTA http://www.sice.oas.org/trade/nafta/chap-111.asp accessed on 31 March 2017. *See also*, e.g., Article 30(3) of the United States-Uruguay BIT (2005) which states that '[a] joint decision of the Parties, each acting through its representative designated for purposes of this Article, declaring their interpretation of a provision of this Treaty shall be binding on a tribunal, and any decision or award issued by a tribunal must be consistent with that joint decision.' *See*: Article 40 of the ASEAN Comprehensive Investment Agreement (2009) which states that '[t]he tribunal shall, on its own account or at the request of a disputing party, request a joint interpretation of any provision of this Agreement that is in issue in a dispute.' *See* the comprehensive overview of treaties with provisions on authoritative interpretations by treaty partners in K. Gordon, J. Pohl, 'Investment Treaties over Time: Treaty Practice and Interpretation in a Changing World' (2015) OECD Working Papers on International Investment 2015/02, 29 http://www.oecd.org/investment/investment-policy/WP-2015-02.pdf accessed on 12 June 2018.
486. For the elaboration on the NAFTA FTC Notes, *see*: Chapter 3, section §3.03[B].
487. *William Ralph Clayton, William Richard Clayton, Douglas Clayton, Daniel Clayton and Bilcon of Delaware Inc. v. Government of Canada* [2015] UNCITRAL Arbitration, PCA Case No. 2009-04 Award on Jurisdiction and Liability (17 March 2015) para. 430.
488. A. Roberts, 'Power and Persuasion in Investment Treaty Interpretation: The Dual Role of States' [2010] 104(2) *American Journal of International Law*, 208.
489. United Nations General Assembly 'Report of the International Law Commission: Sixty-Fifth Session' (New York, 2013) Supplement No. 10 (A/68/10) 22.
490. *Ibid.*, 21.

§4.03 SUPPLEMENTARY AND SUBSIDIARY MEANS OF INTERPRETATION OF THE FET STANDARD

This section provides an overview of the supplementary and subsidiary means of interpretation pertinent to the FET standard under an applicable IIA. In section §4.03[A], the supplementary means of treaty interpretation which include the preparatory work of the treaty and the circumstances of its conclusion under Article 32 of the VCLT are outlined. In section §4.03[B], the reliance on previous decisions in interpreting the FET standard is analysed. The reference to scholarly writing as a subsidiary means of interpretation is described in section §4.03[C]. Finally, section §4.03[D] discusses the national law in the interpretation of the FET standard.

[A] The Preparatory Work of the Treaty and the Circumstances of Its Conclusion

Article 32 of the VCLT provides for recourse to supplementary means of interpretation, including the 'preparatory work of the treaty and the circumstances of its conclusion'.[491] These supplementary means can be invoked if, in the process of interpretation according to Article 31 of VCLT, the meaning remains 'ambiguous or obscure' or the interpretation has led to a 'manifestly absurd or unreasonable' result.[492]

The preparatory work - usually referred as the *travaux préparatoires* - may include various documents issued at the time of the negotiations that led to the conclusion of the agreement. These documents may encompass:

> successive drafts of the treaty; the negotiation records; the minutes of commission and plenary proceedings; the memoranda and statements of governments and their representatives; the diplomatic exchanges ... [and others].[493]

In interpreting the FET standard, tribunals rarely have recourse to the *travaux préparatoires*,[494] the reason being that in the case of BIT arbitrations, the 'negotiating history of BITs is typically not documented.'[495] As for NAFTA tribunals, the negotiating history of Chapter 11 (Investment) of the NAFTA was not accessible to the public until 2006.[496] Even though the role of the *travaux préparatoires* in the interpretation of the FET standard is limited, they may play a more substantial role in the future. For example, the new generation of IIAs negotiated between groups of states, e.g. the CETA or Central American Free Trade Agreement (CAFTA-DR), often contain available

491. Article 32 of the Vienna Convention on the Law of Treaties, 1155 UNTS 331 (23 May 1969).
492. *Ibid.*
493. M. Mbengue, Rules of Interpretation (Article 32 of the Vienna Convention on the Law of Treaties) 389.
494. *See* M. Jacob, S. Schill, (2015) 713 who observed that the FET standard is not usually 'elucidated by *travaux préparatoires*'.
495. C. Schreuer, 'Diversity and Harmonization of Treaty Interpretation in Investment Arbitration', in M. Fitzamurice and others (eds) *Treaty Interpretation and the Vienna Convention on the Law of Treaties: 30 Years On* (Brill/Nijhof, 2010) 138.
496. *Ibid.*

negotiating records that may be useful in the interpretation of the treaty's provisions.[497] Efforts in making the investment procedural rules more transparent have also been undertaken by, e.g., UNCITRAL in adopting the United Nations (UN) Convention on Transparency in Treaty-Based Investor-State Arbitration that may, in the future, improve the availability of negotiating documents.[498]

In addition to the preparatory work of the treaty and the circumstances of its conclusion, Article 32 does not exclude other supplementary means of interpretation.[499] Occasionally, Model BITs have been referred to as possible supplementary means of interpretation.[500]

Many states use a Model BIT as a starting point in the negotiation of their IIAs. The Model BIT outlines the state's intentions regarding its investment protection provisions. The final result, however, will depend on the negotiating efforts of all contracting parties. Model BITs have sometimes been invoked in the interpretation of tribunals. The example is the dissenting opinion in the *AWG v. Argentina* case.[501] The arbitrator relied on the examples of the new US, Canada and Norway Model BITs to interpret the applicable FET standard with the international MST of aliens under customary international law.[502]

Currently, several states have been adopting new Model BITs that include elaborate provisions on investment protection clauses, such as the Indian Model BIT,[503] the Colombian Model IIA[504] and the SADC Model BIT, among others. The SADC Model outlined in Chapter 2, e.g., also includes commentaries that outline the intentions with regard to specific provisions. In order to provide meaning to the FET standard, future tribunals may, on the basis of new IIAs negotiated at least partially on the basis of the SADC Model, have recourse to the text of the Model and its commentaries. This may be particularly so if the meaning of FET has, e.g., not been clarified through interpretation under Article 31 of the VCLT.

497. The Dominican Republic – Central America – United States Free Trade Agreement (CAFTA-DR) http://www.sice.oas.org/TPD/USA_CAFTA/USA_CAFTA_e.ASP; *see also*: Consolidated text of CETA, 28 October 2016 http://ec.europa.eu/trade/policy/in-focus/ceta/ceta-chapter-by-chapter/ All websites were accessed on 12 June 2018.
498. For example, among the efforts for more transparency in investment arbitration, the most notable is the issuance of the UN Convention on Transparency in Treaty-Based Investor-State Arbitration, adopted on 10 December 2014 and opened for signatures as of 17 March 2015. UNCITRAL, 'UN Convention on Transparency in Treaty-Based Investor-State Arbitration' (New York, 2014) http://www.uncitral.org/uncitral/uncitral_texts/arbitration/2014Transparency_Convention.html accessed on 20 June 2018.
499. M. Mbengue, 'Rules of Interpretation (Article 32 of the Vienna Convention on the Law of Treaties) 394.
500. C. Schreuer, (2010) 136.
501. *AWG v. Argentina* [2010] UNCITRAL Arbitration, Separate Opinion of Arbitrator Pedro Nikken (2010) para. 25.
502. *Ibid.*
503. Model Text for the Indian Bilateral Investment Treaty (2015) https://www.mygov.in/sites/default/files/master_image/Model%20Text%20for%20the%20Indian%20Bilateral%20Investment%20Treaty.pdf accessed on 12 June 2018.
504. Colombian Model BIT (2007) http://www.italaw.com/documents/inv_model_bit_colombia.pdf accessed on 12 June 2018.

[B] Previous Decisions of Investment Tribunals

In interpreting the FET standard, tribunals often rely on previous decisions of investment tribunals and scholarly writings.[505] According to international law and in particular Article 38(1)(d) of the International Court of Justice (ICJ) Statute, 'judicial decisions' and the 'teachings of the most highly qualified publicists of the various nations' can be invoked as 'subsidiary means for the determination of the rules of law'.[506] In light of Article 38(1)(d), judicial decisions are not restricted to the decisions of international courts and tribunals and may also 'include the decisions of municipal courts'.[507] The following paragraphs will explain how investment tribunals apply (1) previous decisions of arbitral tribunals, (2) scholarly works and, sometimes, (3) decisions under municipal law.

With regard to reliance on the previous decisions by international courts and tribunals, Shaw explains that 'while the doctrine of precedent as it is known in the common law, whereby the rulings of certain courts must be followed by other courts, does not exist in international law, one still finds that states in disputes and textbook writers quote judgments of the Permanent Court and the International Court of Justice as authoritative decisions.'[508] The ICJ and other international tribunals frequently refer to other rulings in their decisions.[509] Investment tribunals are no exception in this regard and have 'systematically considered and referred to previous decisions of other tribunals'.[510] The case law on the FET standard is an example of this.

The degree of arbitrators' reliance on earlier decisions varies among tribunals. Several tribunals have emphasised the significance of earlier judgments. As the tribunal in the *AWG v. Argentina* decision on liability asserted, '[a]lthough this tribunal is not bound by such prior decisions, they [prior decisions] do constitute "subsidiary means for the determination of the rules of [international] law".'[511]

The tribunal stressed that the goal of international investment law is to establish a predictable and stable legal framework for investments. In light of this, the *AWG* tribunal stressed that unless there are compelling reasons to the contrary, a tribunal

505. O.K. Frauchald, 'The Legal Reasoning of ICSID Tribunals: An Empirical Analysis' [2008] 19(2) *European Journal of International Law*, 335. The statistical study of the legal reasoning of ICSID tribunals supports this statement, by indicating that the most frequent reference in the reasoning of arbitrators is to the earlier awards. The research shows that from ninety-eight decisions, ninety used previous decisions in their interpretative arguments. The study also differentiates how previous decisions have been used. For example, in some cases references are made to a 'test' used by other tribunals; to the reasoning of other tribunals; and to the conclusion of other tribunals.
506. Article 38(1)(d) of the Statute of the International Court of Justice (29 June 1945) http://www.icj-cij.org/documents/?p1 = 4&p2 = 2#CHAPTER_II accessed on 12 June 2018.
507. M. Evans, International Law (2nd edn., Oxford University Press, 2006).
508. M. Shaw, International Law (5th edn., Cambridge University Press, 2003) 103.
509. *Ibid.*, 104.
510. T. Gazzini, Interpretation of International Investment Treaties (Hart Publishing, 2016) 292.
511. *AWG v. Argentina* [2010] UNCITRAL Arbitration, Decision on Liability (30 July 2010) para. 189.

should 'always consider heavily' the previous decisions established in a series of consistent cases.[512]

In the decision on jurisdiction in *Burlington v. Ecuador*, the tribunal underlined that even though it is not bound by prior case law, it has:

> [A] duty to adopt solutions established in a series of consistent cases. It also believes that, subject to the specifics of a given treaty and of the circumstances of the actual case, it has a duty to seek to contribute to the harmonious development of investment law, and thereby to meet the legitimate expectations of the community of States and investors towards the certainty of the rule of law.[513]

In this case, the tribunal indicated the significance of relying on previous decisions. At the same time, it stated that the specifics of an applicable treaty and the circumstances of the case are still of importance. In international investment law, each tribunal is constituted for a specific case and often based on a different treaty. Consequently, tribunals often rely on different IIAs and have to consider the relevance of previous decisions for the purpose of interpreting the case at hand. This point has also been illustrated in *ADC v. Hungary*, where the tribunal provided that:

> It is true that arbitral awards do not constitute binding precedent. It is also true that a number of cases are fact-driven and that the findings in those cases cannot be transposed in and of themselves to other cases. It is further true that a number of cases are based on treaties that differ from the present BIT in certain respects. However, cautious reliance on certain principles developed in a number of those cases, as persuasive authority, may advance the body of law, which in turn may serve predictability in the interest of both investors and host States.[514]

The tribunal stressed that relying on previous decisions should be a cautious exercise. As Gazzini asserted in this regard, the 'persuasiveness of the legal reasoning prior decisions are based upon, may be strengthened by the degree of consistency of prior decisions.'[515]The development of FET jurisprudence is an illustration of this statement. Early FET decisions have been frequently criticised for a lack of consensual interpretation of this standard, even in cases which are alike.[516]

---

512. *Ibid.*
513. *Burlington Resources Inc. v. Republic of Ecuador*, ICSID Case No. ARB/08/5 Decision on Jurisdiction (2 June 2010) para. 100. Note that one arbitrator in the panel disagreed with this reasoning, stating that each case should be decided on its own merits.
514. *ADC v. Hungary*, ICSID Case No. ARB/03/16 Award (2 October 2006) para. 293.
515. T. Gazzini, Interpretation of International Investment Treaties (Hart Publishing, 2016) 297.
516. The illustration of the inconsistency of investment awards in the context of FET claims can be observed in two contradictory decisions on the FET standard based on the same facts. These cases are *CME v. Czech Republic* [2001] UNCITRAL Arbitration, Partial Award (13 September 2001) and *Ronald S. Lauder v. The Czech Republic* [2001] UNCITRAL Arbitration, Final Award (3 September 2001). These two awards resulted in two contrasting decisions regarding liability under the FET standard. Also the tribunal in *Mamidoil v. Albania* has underlined a lack of consistency in case law, stating that '[t]he Tribunal has looked for and found assistance in awards and decisions that the Parties have submitted. However, this assistance is not only limited by the fact that international arbitral tribunals are under no obligation to rely on precedents, but also by the lack of a jurisprudence constante.' *See Mamidoil Jetoil Greek Petroleum Products Societe S.A. v. Republic of Albania*, ICSID Case No. ARB/11/24 Award (30 March 2015) para. 603.

At present, arbitral tribunals have moved towards defining the FET standard through a number of principles. In *Biwater v. Tanzania* the tribunal supported this assumption by stating that:

> [t]he general standard of 'fair and equitable treatment' as set out above comprises a number of different components, which have been elaborated and developed in previous arbitrations in response to specific factual situations.[517]

It then proceeded by articulating these separate components that include the protection of legitimate expectations, good faith, transparency, consistency and non-discrimination.[518]

Other tribunals have followed a similar reasoning, by identifying the meaning of the FET standard through abstracting FET principles from previous decisions. In interpreting the FET standard, the tribunal in *Philip Morris v. Uruguay* held that:

> Based on investment tribunals' decisions, typical fact situations have led a leading commentator to identify the following principles as covered by the FET standard: transparency and the protection of the investor's legitimate expectations; freedom from coercion and harassment; procedural propriety and due process, and good faith.[519]

Furthermore, the tribunal specified that various aspects of state conduct expressed in the principles of the FET standard are 'indicative of the breach of the FET standard'.[520] In the case at hand, the tribunal provided that the 'legitimate expectations' of an investor that he claimed to have had on the basis of general and specific assurances of the Uruguayan government[521] and the 'stability of the Uruguay legal system' were of relevance as components of the FET standard.[522]

[C] Reliance on Scholarly Writings

In light of Article 38(1)(d), the 'teachings of the most highly qualified publicists of the various nations' can be taken into account by arbitrators as a 'subsidiary means for the determination of rules of law'.[523] Arbitral tribunals make use of scholarly writings in interpreting the substantive protection standards under IIAs.[524] As discovered by research conducted by Frauchald, scholarly writings were cited in seventy-three of the

517. *Biwater v. Tanzania*, ICSID Case No. ARB/05/22 Final Award (24 July 2008) para. 602.
518. *Ibid.*
519. *Philip Morris v. Uruguay*, ICSID Case No. ARB/10/7 Award (8 July 2016) para. 320.
520. *Ibid.*, para. 324.
521. *Ibid.*, para. 342.
522. *Ibid.*, para. 324.
523. Article 38(1)(d) of the Statute of the International Court of Justice (29 June 1945).
524. *See* T. Gazzini, Interpretation of International Investment Treaties (Hart Publishing, 2016) 318, who argued that '[e]mpirical evidence shows that investment tribunals have relied on scholarly writings much more heavily and frequently than other international tribunals, including the ICJ and the WTO Appellate Body'.

ninety-eight ICSID decisions concluded between 1998 and 2006.[525] Below, several examples of how these scholarly writings have been used in FET cases are provided.

In *SD Myers v. Canada*, the NAFTA tribunal relied heavily on scholarly writings in extracting the meaning of the FET standard. In this case, the decision of the tribunal that the breach of the FET standard also extends to the violation of the NT clause was based on a scholarly article by Dr Mann, published in 1981, where he discusses the formulation of the FET standard of British BITs.[526] The *SD Myers* decision, where the tribunal found that the breach of the NT provision extended to a breach of the FET standard and came to this conclusion by relying on scholarly work, has been criticised by all three NAFTA Member States. The US in its submission in *Pope & Talbot v. Canada* criticised the tribunal's reliance in *SD Myers v. Canada* on a construction of the terms 'fair and equitable treatment' on the basis of Mann's article.[527] It stated that:

> [T]he drafters of Chapter Eleven specifically excluded Mann's thesis by selecting language in Article 1105(1) that clearly states that fair and equitable treatment to be a subset of customary international law, not an overarching duty that subsumes other instances of substantive protection.[528]

According to the NAFTA parties, the incorrect interpretation of the FET standard in this case, as well as in the two other decisions, resulted in the issuance of a clarification statement under the 2001 FTC Notes of Interpretation, which provide that '[a] determination that there has been a breach of another provision of the NAFTA, or of a separate international agreement, does not establish that there has been a breach of Article 1105(1).'[529]

Another example of reliance on scholarly writings to provide meaning to the FET standard is the decision in *CME v. Czech Republic*.[530] In defining the FET standard, the tribunal in this case relied on an academic study by Professor Vagts, who provided the threshold of acceptable conduct under international law.[531] The tribunal relied on the study by Professor Vagts that explained the 'elements of a code of unfair bargaining

525. O.K. Frauchald, 'The Legal Reasoning of ICSID Tribunals: An Empirical Analysis' [2008] 19(2) *European Journal of International Law*, 322. The researchers have not differentiated between the decisions on different standards of treatment.
526. *SD Myers v. Canada*, UNCITRAL Arbitration Partial Award (13 November 2000) paras 265-266. *See also* S. Murphy, United States Practice in International Law: Volume 1, 1999-2001 (Cambridge University Press, 2002) 237. In this contribution, the author specifically discusses the reference to the Mann quote and its context.
527. U.S. Department of State, 'The Fifth Submission of the US in *Pope & Talbot v. Canada* under Article 1128 of the NAFTA' (1 December 2000) https://www.state.gov/documents/organization/4175.pdf accessed on 23 February 2017. In this submission, the US commented on certain questions of the interpretation of Article 1105 in the *SD Myers v. Canada* case.
528. U.S. Department of State, 'The Fifth Submission of the US in *Pope & Talbot v. Canada* under Article 1128 of the NAFTA' (1 December 2000) para. 7 https://www.state.gov/documents/organization/4175.pdf accessed on 23 February 2017.
529. NAFTA Free Trade Commission, 'North American Free Trade Agreement Notes of Interpretation of Certain Chapter 11 Provisions' (Foreign Trade Information System, 31 July 2001). http://www.sice.oas.org/tpd/nafta/Commission/CH11understanding_e.asp accessed on 1 March 2017.
530. *CME v. Czech Republic* [2001] UNCITRAL Arbitration, Partial Award (13 September 2001).
531. *Ibid.*, para. 611.

practices during investor-government negotiations which, *inter alia*, prohibits a government from the following acts'.[532] He argued that:

> Cancellation of the franchise, permit, or authorization to do business in which the investor relies, except in accordance with its terms; and Regulatory Action without bona fide governmental purpose (or without bona fide timing) designed to make the investor's business unprofitable.[533]

On the basis of this academic source, the tribunal concluded that the 'threshold test of Professor Vagts' is applicable in this case.[534] In this case, the tribunal held that there had been a breach of the FET standard.

In *Biwater v. Tanzania*, the tribunal considered whether the reference to international law in the UK-Tanzania BIT was intended to limit the FET standard to the minimum standard of the treatment of aliens under customary international law as argued by the state. This was one of the decisive arguments on the basis of which the tribunal concluded that the parties intended the FET standard to be an autonomous, unqualified standard contained in the publication of the scholar. The tribunal explained that it 'sees force in the argument that the Contracting States here ought to be taken to have intended the adoption of an autonomous standard, on the basis, as stated by Christoph Schreuer'.[535] The tribunal further outlined the reasoning of the scholar, with which it concurred, by stating that:

> it is inherently implausible that a treaty would use an expression such as 'fair and equitable treatment' to denote a well-known concept such as the 'minimum standard of treatment in customary international law'. If the parties to a treaty want to refer to customary international law, it must be presumed that they will refer to it as such rather than using a different expression.[536]

In assessing the FET standard, tribunals – particularly in the early cases such as *SD Myers* and *CME* – relied on scholarly writings to provide meaning to the FET standard. The guidance providing meaning to the notion of FET had been sought in the academic literature because the FET had not been defined in applicable IIAs and had not been applied by other tribunals beforehand. In relatively recent decisions on the FET standard, decided approximately in the past ten years, tribunals have relied on academic writings, merely as one source out of many, in order to support other sources, such as previous decisions, in determining the content of the applicable FET standard in the particular case.

532. *Ibid.*, para. 526.
533. *Ibid.*
534. *CME v. Czech Republic* [2001] UNCITRAL Arbitration, Partial Award (13 September 2001), para. 611.
535. *Biwater v. Tanzania*, ICSID Case No. ARB/05/22 Award (24 July 2008), para. 591.
536. *Ibid.*

[D] Reliance on National Law

In assessing the FET standard, several tribunals have had recourse to national law as a subsidiary means for the determination of the international rules of law in clarifying the meaning of legitimate expectations under the FET standard. For example, in *Total v. Argentina*, the tribunal reviewed the origins and the use of legitimate expectations in multiple national systems.[537] The tribunal explained that since the concept of legitimate expectations:

> [I]s based on the requirement of good faith, one of the general principles referred to in Article 38 (1) (c) of the Statute of the ICJ as a source of international law, the tribunal believes that a comparative analysis of the protection of legitimate expectations in domestic jurisdictions is justified. While the scope and legal basis of the principle varies, it has been recognized lately both in civil law and in common law jurisdictions within well defined limits.[538]

In *Total v. Argentina*, the tribunal concluded that the legitimate expectations concept has been employed restrictively by national as well as European and international tribunals. In this regard, the tribunal concluded that 'it appears that only exceptionally has the concept of legitimate expectations been the basis of redress when legislative action by a State was at stake.'[539]

In *Toto v. Lebanon*, the tribunal upheld the argument made in *Total* by stating that 'fair and equitable treatment standard of international law does not depend on the perception of the frustrated investor, but should use public international law and comparative domestic public law as a benchmark.'[540] The tribunal analysed the legitimate expectations of an investor based on the state's assurances that it would expropriate land which was necessary for building a road by the company in a timely and consistent manner. In conducting such an assessment, the tribunal underlined that FET has to be interpreted by employing 'public international law and comparative domestic public law as a benchmark'.[541] The tribunal concluded that the state would be liable under the FET standard if it acted 'in a discriminatory or capricious way, or that it did not comply with the applicable international minimum standards'.[542] The tribunal had not found a violation of the FET standard as the investor was not able to provide sufficient evidence that the state had acted in a discriminatory or capricious way or that its conduct fell below the minimum standard of the treatment of aliens under customary international law.[543]

In *Gold Reserve v. Venezuela*, the tribunal – in assessing the legitimate expectations of an investor, based on the state's assurances, which had been relied upon to operate its mining projects – cited both the *Total* and *Toto* tribunals and turned to the comparative public law method. The tribunal provided that:

537. *Total S.A. v. Argentina*, ICSID Case No. ARB/04/01 Decision on Liability (27 December 2010).
538. *Ibid.*, para. 128.
539. *Ibid.*, para. 129.
540. *Toto v. Lebanon*, ICSID Case No. ARB/07/12 Award (7 June 2012) para. 166.
541. *Ibid.*
542. *Toto v. Lebanon*, ICSID Case No. ARB/07/12 Award (7 June 2012) para. 193.
543. *Ibid.*, para. 205.

> With particular regard to the legal sources of one of the standards for respect of the fair and equitable treatment principle, i.e. the protection of 'legitimate expectations', these sources are to be found in the comparative analysis of many domestic legal systems.[544]

The tribunal undertook a comparative survey of the meaning and application of the legitimate expectations concept in multiple legal systems. It identified, e.g., that:

> in German law, protection of legitimate expectations is connected with the principle of Vertraensschutz (protection of trust) a notion which deeply influenced the development of European Union Law, pointing to precise and specific assurances given by the administration. The same notion finds equivalents in other European countries such as France in the concept of confiance légitime. ...[545]

The tribunal also referred to English law, Argentinian law and Venezuelan law that also contain the equivalent of the concept of legitimate expectations in their legal systems.[546] In applying the FET standard to the facts of the case, the tribunal referred to the application of the concept of legitimate expectations in the administrative law of Venezuela. According to Venezuelan law, the conduct of the government has to be 'constant and reiterated to the point of constituting a stable situation and presupposing its "indefinite" repetition over time whenever the same circumstances exist'.[547] The tribunal found that the state had met these conditions by the consistent issuance of necessary certificates by the state's administration. However, the tribunal found Venezuela to be in breach of the FET standard, primarily relying on the fact that the state's conduct was 'driven by political reasons', as will be further elaborated upon in Chapter 7, section §7.02[D].[548]

The cases discussed above, indicate, in the words of Schill, a 'notable move in investment treaty arbitration more generally to interpret IIA standards against the benchmark of comparative public law'.[549] In these cases, the tribunals analysed the legitimate expectations of an investor by comparing the application of this concept in international, European and some domestic legal systems. In *Gold Reserve v. Venezuela*, the tribunal undertook a comparative assessment of the application of the concept of legitimate expectations in different national laws, with a particular focus on Venezuelan administrative law. In the three cases analysed in this section, the tribunals attempted to provide more clarity to the content of the legitimate expectations

544. *Gold Reserve v. Venezuela*, ICSID Case No. ARB(AF)/09/1 Award (22 September 2014) para. 576.
545. *Ibid.*
546. *Ibid.*
547. *Gold Reserve v. Venezuela*, ICSID Case No. ARB(AF)/09/1 Award (22 September 2014) para. 606.
548. *Ibid.*, para. 607. For a further discussion on this case *see*: Chapter 7, section §7.02[D]: The Illegitimacy of State Objectives.
549. S. Schill, 'In Defence of International Investment Law', in M. Bungenberg, et al. (eds) *European Yearbook of International Economic Law 2016* (Springer, 2016) 327.

concept by using comparisons, and in doing so, maybe even paving the 'way towards the recognition of legitimate expectations as a general principle of law'.[550]

[E] Summary: The Interpretation and Application of the FET Standard

The aforementioned sections have discussed the ways in which tribunals have been interpreting the FET standard. Considering that IIAs are governed by international law, tribunals rely on general rules of international treaty interpretation that can be found in Articles 31-32 of the VCLT. The ILC has underlined that the interpretation of a treaty is a 'single combined operation'.[551] Article 31 includes certain mandatory means of interpretation, that is an interpretation of the treaty according to its ordinary meaning, context, its object and purpose and subsequent agreement and practice. Article 32 provides for non-mandatory but supplementary means of interpretation such as those based on the *travaux préparatoires*.

Tribunals, in many cases, have referred to Article 31 of the VCLT, which provides that a treaty shall be interpreted according to its ordinary meaning, its context and in the light of its object and purpose. In analysing the literal wording of 'fair and equitable' in its ordinary meaning, tribunals have usually arrived at an identification of synonyms of these terms. Several tribunals have had recourse to the context of the treaty in interpreting the FET standard by referring to the preamble to the treaty. In a number of cases, the interpretation of the FET standard with consideration being given to the context of the treaty was closely connected with revealing the object and the purpose of the treaty by referring to the preambles to the IIAs in question. Several decisions on the FET standard have provided a broad interpretation of the FET standard by relying on the objectives of the treaty that focused on investor promotion and protection, as reflected in the preamble. Other decisions, concluded more recently, have opted for a more balanced assessment of the object and purpose of the treaty, thereby underlining that investor protection is not the 'sole aim of the Treaty'.[552] For example, in *Mamidoil v. Albania*, the tribunal referred to the stimulation of 'economic development in the partner countries' as a goal of the IIAs in the context of the FET standard obligation.[553] By stressing that investment protection and promotion are not the only objectives of IIAs, the tribunal emphasised the significance of balancing the rights and obligations of investors in the assessment of the standard.

In interpreting the FET standard, tribunals have sometimes had recourse to supplementary and subsidiary means of interpretation. Article 32 of the VCLT provides for recourse to supplementary means of interpretation, including the 'preparatory work

550. N. Monebhurrun, 'Gold Reserve Inc. v. Bolivarian Republic of Venezuela Enshrining Legitimate Expectations as a General Principle of International Law?' [2015] 32(5) *Journal of International Arbitration*, 558-559.
551. United Nations General Assembly 'Report of the International Law Commission: Sixty-Fifth Session' (New York, 2013) Supplement No. 10 (A/68/10) 21.
552. *Saluka v. Czech Republic* [2006] Permanent Court of Arbitration, IIC 210, Partial Award (17 March 2006) para. 300.
553. *Mamidoil Jetoil Greek Petroleum Products Société S.A. v. Republic of Albania*, ICSID Case No. ARB/11/24 Award (30 March 2015) para. 611.

of the treaty and the circumstances of its conclusion'.[554] In interpreting the FET standard, tribunals rarely have recourse to supplementary means of interpretation such as the *travaux préparatoires*.[555] At the same time, in interpreting the FET standard, tribunals often rely on previous decisions of investment tribunals as subsidiary means of interpretation in accordance with Article 38(1)(d) of the ICJ Statute.[556] In contrast to the early FET decisions where tribunals replicated the meaning of the FET standard provided in prior investment decisions, tribunals in the more recent cases have adopted a more balanced approach in referring to early jurisprudence. In several cases, tribunals have emphasised that the reasoning of previous tribunals on the FET standard is important, but the specifics of an applicable treaty and the circumstances of the case should not be disregarded. Another notable trend is the emergence of several FET principles on the basis of prior investment decisions on the FET standard. A number of tribunals have stated that the FET standard consists of the state's obligation to (i) respect the legitimate expectations of an investor;[557] (ii) provide stability and the predictability of a legal framework;[558] (iii) provide due process to investors;[559] and (iv) provide non-discriminatory treatment.[560] A further elaboration of the application of some of these principles by tribunals is discussed in Chapters 5 and 6.

554. Article 32 of the Vienna Convention on the Law of Treaties, 1155 UNTS 331 (23 May 1969).
555. M. Jacob, S. Schill, (2015) 713 who observed that the FET standard is not usually 'elucidated by *travaux préparatoires*'.
556. O.K. Frauchald, 'The Legal Reasoning of ICSID Tribunals: An Empirical Analysis' [2008] 19(2) *European Journal of International Law*, 335. The statistical study of the legal reasoning of ICSID tribunals supports this statement, by indicating that the most frequent reference in the reasoning of arbitrators is to the earlier awards. The research shows that from ninety-eight decisions, ninety used previous decisions in their interpretative arguments. The study also differentiates how previous decisions have been used. For example, in some cases references are made to a 'test' used by other tribunals; to the reasoning of other tribunals; and to the conclusion of other tribunals.
557. *Saluka Investments BV v. Czech Republic* [2006] UNCITRAL Arbitration Partial Award (17 March 2006) para. 348; *Biwater v. Tanzania* [2008] ICSID Case No. ARB/05/22 Award (24 July 2008) para. 602; *Suez, Sociedad General de Aguas de Barcelona S.A. and Vivendi Universal v. Argentina and AWG v. Argentina* [2010] ICSID Case No. ARB/03/19, Decision on liability (30 July 2010) para. 222. Also *see*: I.A. Laird, B. Sabahi, F.G. Sourgens, N.J. Birch, and K. Duggal, 'International Investment Law and Arbitration: 2014 in Review', in A.J. Bjorklund (ed) *Yearbook on International Investment Law and Policy 2013-2014* (Oxford University Press, 2015) 105. The authors reviewing the decisions on the FET standard rendered in 2013 underlined that 'Tribunals in 2013 recognized that the protection of the claimant's legitimate or reasonable expectations is a well-accepted component of the FET standard'.
558. *Occidental v. Ecuador*, LCIA Case No. UN3467 Final Award (1 July 2004) para. 183; *CMS Gas Transmission Co. v. The Argentine Republic*, ICSID Case No. ARB/01/8 Award (12 May 2005) para. 274; *LG&E Energy Corp., LG&E Capital Corp. & LG&E International v. The Argentine Republic*, ICSID Case No. ARB/02/1 Decision on Liability (3 October 2006) in paras 124-125.
559. *Biwater v. Tanzania* [2008] ICSID Case No. ARB/05/22 Award (24 July 2008) para. 602; *Lemire v. Ukraine*, ICSID Case No. ARB/06/18 Decision on Jurisdiction and Liability (14 January 2010) para. 264; *The Loewen Group, Inc. and Raymond L. Loewen v. United States of America* [2003], Case No. ARB(AF)/98/3 Award (26 June 2003) para. 132.
560. *Biwater v. Tanzania* [2008] ICSID Case No. ARB/05/22 Award (24 July 2008) para. 602; *Lemire v. Ukraine*, ICSID Case No. ARB/06/18 Decision on Jurisdiction and Liability (14 January 2010) para. 284.

In several decisions, in interpreting the FET standard, tribunals have referred to scholarly writings, as subsidiary means of treaty interpretation.[561] The early cases that provided some of the first interpretations of the FET standard relied on scholarly work in providing meaning to the FET. At present, with the development of case law on the FET standard, tribunals tend to refer to scholars as just one of the sources in interpreting the standard.

In assessing the FET standard and clarifying the meaning of legitimate expectations, several tribunals have had recourse to national law as a subsidiary means for the determination of international rules of law. In the three cases analysed in this Chapter, tribunals have attempted to provide more clarity to the content of the legitimate expectations concept by using comparisons of multiple legal systems.

§4.04 GENERAL PRINCIPLES OF LAW: THE ROLE OF PROPORTIONALITY AND REASONABLENESS

The 'general principles of law recognised by civilised nations' constitute one of the main sources of public international law, as mentioned in Article 38(1)(c) of the ICJ Statute.[562] To qualify as a general principle of law, the principle 'must be recognised in the majority of the legal systems'.[563] In the course of the decisional process, tribunals can have recourse to general principles of law in the evaluation of a state's conduct. The prevalent view is that these general principles of law, as mentioned in Article 38(1) of the ICJ Statute, originate from domestic legal systems.[564] Some of these general principles have, at least to a certain extent, their own place, significance and meaning in the international legal system.[565] Consequently, it is generally understood that the principle of proportionality, the principle of reasonableness, the principle of deference and the principle of a margin of appreciation can be identified as general principles of law in the sense of Article 38 of the ICJ Statute.[566] These principles are recognised and

561. Article 38(1)(d) of the Statute of the International Court of Justice (29 June 1945).

562. Article 38(1)(c) of the Statute of the International Court of Justice (29 June 1945).

563. M. Herdegen, Principles of International Economic Law (Oxford University Press, 2013) 45.

564. *See* M. Shaw, International Law (5th edn., Cambridge University Press, 2003) 99 who argues that, nevertheless, 'international law did not refer to the municipal law of a particular state, but rather to the rules generally accepted by municipal legal systems ...'. In a similar line of thought, *see* C. Bucheler, *Proportionality in Investor-State Arbitration* (Oxford University Press, 2015) who argues that '[s]cholars and practitioners however agree that the first category of norms ("principles and rules emanating from domestic legal systems") may give rise to rules of international law under certain conditions'.

565. M. Kohen, B. Schramm, 'General Principles of Law', in T. Carry (ed.) *Oxford Bibliographies in International Law* (Oxford University Press, 2013) http://oxfordindex.oup.com/view/10.1093/obo/9780199796953-0063 accessed on 12 June 2018.

566. C. Bucheler, Proportionality in Investor-State Arbitration (Oxford University Press, 2015) 62 who argues that '[p]roportionality is sufficiently prevalent on the domestic level to pass the first step of identifying a general principle of law – a comparative analysis of domestic legal systems'; F. De Vanna, 'The "Doctrine of Principles" in Neo-Constitutional Theories and the Principle of Reasonableness in Action', in L. Pineschi (ed.) *General Principles of Law: The Role of the Judiciary* (Springer International Publishing, 2015) 79-101; C. Henckels, Proportionality and Deference in Investor-State Arbitration (Cambridge University Press, 2015) 19.

employed across various legal systems and applied by some of tribunals in the assessment of the FET standard.

The principles of proportionality and reasonableness will be addressed in section §4.04[A]. The concepts of deference and a margin of appreciation are briefly explained in section §4.04[B].

[A] Proportionality and Reasonableness

Proportionality and reasonableness are usually referred to as methods of review often employed in investment arbitration cases pertinent to an assessment of the FET standard. The method of review in international investment law refers to a 'technique used by adjudicators (such as proportionality analysis) to determine the permissibility of interference with a right of interest ...'.[567]

In an attempt to strike a balance in FET cases, the proportionality test has made a frequent appearance in tribunals' decisions.[568] The function of proportionality in this context is to address the 'relationship between the ends pursued by a specific government action and the means employed to achieve this end'.[569] The principle of proportionality has been reviewed in investment arbitration usually by virtue of a comparative analysis.[570] Henckles researched the application of proportionality in international investment law using a comparative approach and analysing the proportionality in the European Court of Human Rights (ECtHR), the World Trade Organisation (WTO) Appellate Body and the Court of Justice of the European Union (CJEU). Based on the practice of the aforementioned dispute settlement systems, the proportionality test can be distinguished according to several stages identified in the case law of these bodies.[571] Although the international bodies, e.g. the WTO tribunals and the ECtHR, vary in performing the proportionality test, there are several stages that are

567. *Ibid.*, 31.
568. *EDF (Services) Limited v. Romania*, ICSID Case No. ARB/05/13 Award (8 October 2009) para. 293. This is the first decision in which the term 'proportionality' was used as an applicable method referenced in the FET standard's assessment. The tribunal in *Occidental v. Ecuador* was the first tribunal that employed the complete three-stage proportionality test in the FET assessment. *Occidental v. Ecuador*, ICSID Case No. ARB/06/11 Award (5 October 2012). There are many other examples where tribunals use some elements of the proportionality test in the FET evaluation without a direct reference to this concept, including *Saluka v. Czech Republic* [2006]. Permanent Court of Arbitration, IIC 210, Partial Award (17 March 2006); *Parkerings v. Lithuania*, ICSID Case No. ARB/05/8 Award (11 September 2007); and *AES Summit v. Hungary*, ICSID Case No. ARB/07/22 Award (23 September 2010).
569. B. Kingsbury, S. Schill, 'Public Law Concepts to Balance Investors' Rights with State Regulatory Actions in the Public Interest: The Concept of Proportionality', in S. Schill (ed.) *International Investment Law and Comparative Public Law* (Oxford University Press, 2010) 85.
570. C. Henckels, Proportionality and Deference in Investor-State Arbitration (Cambridge University Press, 2015); B. Kingsbury, S. Schill, 'Public Law Concepts to Balance Investors' Rights with State Regulatory Actions in the Public Interest: The Concept of Proportionality', in S. Schill (ed.) *International Investment Law and Comparative Public Law* (Oxford University Press, 2010); C. Bucheler, Proportionality in Investor-State Arbitration (Oxford University Press, 2015).
571. C. Henckels, Proportionality and Deference in Investor-State Arbitration (Cambridge University Press, 2015) 45.

usually associated with this test and have also been followed in decisions by some of FET tribunals, as will be further illustrated in this section.[572]

The first step of proportionality usually involves an evaluation of the suitability of a state's measure to achieve the desired objective.[573] This step is usually identified as an assessment of the legitimacy of a state's objective and the suitability of the measure to achieve this objective. The second step includes an assessment of the necessity of the measure, which involves an evaluation of whether other, less-invasive means to achieve the measure were available.[574] The third step includes a proportionality assessment *stricto sensu*, usually adopted if the measure is found to be suitable and necessary.[575] It involves an analysis of 'whether the effects of a measure are disproportionate or excessive in relation to the interests affected'.[576]

Proportionality has been increasingly used by investment tribunals in the assessment of the FET standard vis-à-vis the state's regulatory conduct.[577] There are several examples of FET decisions where tribunals have referred to proportionality only in general terms. For example, in *El Paso v. Argentina*, the tribunal concluded without

572. B. Kingsbury, S. Schill, 'Public Law Concepts to Balance Investors' Rights with State Regulatory Actions in the Public Interest: The Concept of Proportionality', in S. Schill (ed.) *International Investment Law and Comparative Public Law* (Oxford University Press, 2010) 86. The authors explain that 'as developed in the jurisprudence of various domestic and international courts, proportionality analysis can be described as comprising three sub-elements: (1) the principle of suitability, (2) the principle of necessity, and (3) the principle of proportionality stricto sensu'.
573. The authors followed the triple structure of the proportionality test. C. Henckels, Proportionality and Deference in Investor-State Arbitration (Cambridge University Press, 2015) 48-53; Henckels provides the following division in analysing proportionality: (1) legitimacy of a regulatory objective and suitability between the measure and its objective; (2) necessity; proportionality *stricto sensu*; B. Kingsbury, S. Schill, 'Public Law Concepts to Balance Investors' Rights with State Regulatory Actions in the Public Interest: The Concept of Proportionality', in S. Shill (ed.) *International Investment Law and Comparative Public Law* (Oxford University Press, 2010) 86. Kingsbury and Schill provide the following structure of the proportionality test: (1) suitability for a legitimate government purpose; (2) necessity; and (3) proportionality *stricto sensu*.
574. C. Henckels, Proportionality and Deference in Investor-State Arbitration (Cambridge University Press, 2015) 57; B. Kingsbury, S. Schill, 'Public Law Concepts to Balance Investors' Rights with State Regulatory Actions in the Public Interest: The Concept of Proportionality', in S. Shill (ed) *International Investment Law and Comparative Public Law* (Oxford University Press, 2010) 86-87.
575. C. Henckels, Proportionality and Deference in Investor-State Arbitration (Cambridge University Press, 2015) 106; B. Kingsbury, S. Schill, 'Public Law Concepts to Balance Investors' Rights with State Regulatory Actions in the Public Interest: The Concept of Proportionality', in S. Shill (ed.) *International Investment Law and Comparative Public Law* (Oxford University Press, 2010) 88.
576. M. Andenas, S. Zleptnig, 'Proportionality: WTO Law in Comparative Perspective' [2007] 20(1) *Cambridge Review of International Affairs*, 388.
577. C. Henckels, 'Proportionality and the Standard of Review in Fair and Equitable Treatment Claims: Balancing Stability and Consistency with the Public Interest' (2012) Society of International Economic Law Working Paper No. 2012/27, 1 https://ssrn.com/abstract=209 1474 accessed on 30 March 2017.

further elaboration that 'fair and equitable treatment is a standard entailing reasonableness and proportionality.'[578] In some cases, tribunals have assessed the proportionality of the state's measure towards its objective.[579]

The judgment provided in *Occidental v. Ecuador* constitutes an example of when a tribunal applied all three stages of proportionality in assessing the FET standard. In evaluating the termination of a contract with an investor, the tribunal first evaluated the state's objective in deciding to terminate the contract.[580] Second, by establishing that the state's objectives were legitimate, the tribunal performed a necessity test by analysing whether the same objective could be achieved by different means.[581] Necessity test consequently provided a list of available options.[582] To this end, the tribunal also assessed whether the stated options were available to the state.[583] Third, according to proportionality *stricto sensu*, the tribunal evaluated the degree of negative effects imposed on an investor due to the state's measures against the degree of harm to the state due to the investor's actions.[584] Ultimately, the tribunal concluded that the damage experienced by the investor because of the state's measures was far more serious than the consequences for the state, despite the legitimacy of its objective.[585]

In addition to the proportionality test, the test of reasonableness has also been applied in the context of the FET standard.[586] Similar to proportionality, reasonableness is 'deliberative methodology ... that is based on a "culture of justification" which requires that governments should provide substantive justification for all their actions'.[587] In international investment law, the test of reasonableness is usually undertaken with regard to the assessment of the reasonableness of a state's conduct (*see* Chapter 7, section §7.04 [A]) and/or the reasonableness of an investor's expectations.[588]

For example, in examining the reasonableness of the state's conduct, the tribunal in *AES Summit v. Hungary* stressed that the existence of a rational policy was not sufficient 'to justify all the measures taken by a state in its name ... [t]he measure must be "reasonable"'.[589] The *AES Summit* tribunal examined the 'reasonableness of the act

578. *El Paso v. Argentina*, ICSID Case No. ARB/03/15 Award (31 October 2011) para. 373.
579. *EDF (Services) Limited v. Romania*, ICSID Case No. ARB/05/13 Award (8 October 2009) para. 293. The tribunal stated that '[i]n addition to a legitimate aim in the public interest, there must be "a reasonable relationship of proportionality between the means employed and the aim sought to be realized"; that proportionality would be lacking if the person involved "bears an individual and excessive burden."'
580. *Occidental v. Ecuador*, ICSID Case No. ARB/06/11 Award (5 October 2012) paras 416-420.
581. *Ibid.*, para. 434.
582. *Ibid.*
583. *Occidental v. Ecuador*, ICSID Case No. ARB/06/11 Award (5 October 2012) paras 428-436.
584. *See* the analysis in C. Henckels, Proportionality and Deference in Investor-State Arbitration (Cambridge University Press, 2015) 85 and J. Bonnitcha, (2014) 160-161.
585. *Occidental v. Ecuador*, ICSID Case No. ARB/06/11 Award (5 October 2012) para. 452.
586. V. Vadi, 'Proportionality, Reasonableness and Standards of Review in Investment Treaty Arbitration', in A. Bjorklund (ed.) *Yearbook of International Investment Law and Policy 2013 – 2014* (Oxford University Press, 2015) 211.
587. *Ibid.*, 210.
588. Such an application of reasonableness in investment cases has also been indicated by V. Vadi (p. 210).
589. *AES Summit v. Hungary*, ICSID Case No. ARB/07/22 Award (23 September 2010) para. 10.3.9.

of the state in relation to the policy'.[590] And to this end, it explained reasonableness as an '[a]ppropriate correlation between the state's public policy objective and the measure adopted to achieve it. This has to do with the nature of the measure and the way it is implemented'.[591]

In *Philip Morris v. Uruguay*, the tribunal defined the reasonable measure as the one that addressed the public interest[592] and which should also not be 'arbitrary, grossly unfair, unjust, discriminatory, or disproportionate'.[593] In assessing legitimate expectations, the tribunal in *Saluka v. Czech Republic* underlined that an investor's expectations, 'in order for them to be protected, must rise to the level of legitimacy and reasonableness in light of the circumstances'.[594] The tribunal outlined that in assessing the reasonableness of an investor's expectations, on the one hand, the 'host State's legitimate right subsequently to regulate domestic matters in the public interest must be taken into consideration.'[595] On the other hand, the investor may expect that the state's conduct is 'reasonably justifiable by public policies and that such conduct does not manifestly violate the requirements of consistency, transparency, even-handedness and nondiscrimination'.[596]

[B] Deference and the Margin of Appreciation

The concepts of 'deference' and a 'margin of appreciation' have been referred to by tribunals in indicating the level of intensity of the review of a state's measure. In deciding FET cases, investment tribunals have exercised some restraint in assessing the legitimacy of a state's measure versus the state's obligations under an applicable treaty, e.g., by evaluating the state's objective behind the measure or the conduct of an investor.[597] In exercising such restraint, tribunals usually refer to the concepts of 'deference' and the 'margin of appreciation'. These concepts are explained below.

Deference refers to a tribunal's 'restraint in adjudication, where there is uncertainty as to what the "right" conclusion to an issue should be, by attaching weight to the primary decision-maker's view and refraining from making or from acting on the adjudicator's assessment of the matter'.[598] Deference has played an important role in some of the decisions on the FET standard. For example, in *SD Myers v. Canada*, the tribunal stated that the determination of whether an investor has been treated unfairly 'must be made in the light of the high measure of deference that international law generally extends to the right of domestic authorities to regulate matters within their

590. *Ibid.*, para. 10.3.7.
591. *Ibid.*, paras 10.3.7-10.3.9.
592. *Philip Morris v. Uruguay*, ICSID Case No. ARB/10/7 Award (8 July 2016) para. 409.
593. *Ibid.*, para. 410.
594. *Saluka Investments BV v. Czech Republic* [2006] UNCITRAL Arbitration Partial Award (17 March 2006) para. 304.
595. *Ibid.*, para. 305.
596. *Ibid.*, para. 307.
597. *See* Chapter 6, section §6.02 on the objective of the state's measure.
598. C. Henckels, 'Balancing Investment Protection and Sustainable Development in Investor-State Arbitration: The Role of Deference', in A. Bjorklund (ed.) *Yearbook on International Investment Law & Policy 2012-2013* (Oxford University Press, 2014) 311.

borders'.[599] The tribunal in this case applied a high degree of deference towards the review of the state's regulatory conduct. As Paparinskis explained in his monograph on the international minimum standard, in assessing the regulatory conduct of a state, international law 'defers to the legitimacy of the purpose and means chosen to pursue it as such (unless they are entirely indefensible), but scrutinize formal and procedural safeguards ...'.[600] Such an assumption supports the tribunal's position, as it avoids questioning the substantive nature of the state's decisions. In this way, the tribunal opted for a lenient approach towards the review of the state's regulatory measures.[601]

The 'margin of appreciation' doctrine has developed through the case law of the ECtHR.[602] Investment tribunals have also referred to the margin of appreciation. One example is provided by the tribunal in *Philip Morris v. Uruguay*, which described the margin of appreciation as a 'methodology for scrutiny by international courts of the decisions of national authorities i.e. national governments, national courts and other national actors'.[603] The tribunal in *Philip Morris* referred to the 'margin of appreciation' clarifying that it is 'not limited to the context of the ECHR but "applies equally to claims arising under BITs," at least in contexts such as public health'.[604] It further provided that the 'responsibility for public health measures rests with the government and investment tribunals should pay great deference to governmental judgments of national needs in matters such as the protection of public health.'[605]

To summarise, in this section, the principle of proportionality, the principle of reasonableness, the principle of deference and the principle of the margin of appreciation that have been identified as general principles of law were discussed. Tribunals have applied different methods of review, such as proportionality and reasonableness in conjunction with various standards of review that rely on the doctrines of deference and the margin of appreciation. A discussion on the extent to which tribunals rely on these legal principles in assessing the FET standard and the right to regulate will be provided in Chapters 6 and 7.

599. *S.D. Myers v. Canada* [2000] UNCITRAL Arbitration Award (1 January 2000) para. 263.
600. M. Paparinskis, (2013) 242.
601. S. Schill, 'Deference in Investment Treaty Arbitration: Re-Conceptualizing the Standard of Review through Comparative Public Law' (2012) Society of International Economic Law Working Paper No. 2012/33, 7. In the context of this case, the author explains that 'deference in that understanding is a parameter of the relationship between international and domestic law and protect a state's domestic policy space against control by international law and international tribunals'.
602. *See*: ECHR, *Case of Handyside v. the United Kingdom*, Application No. 5493/72 (Strasbourg, 7 December 1976). In paragraph 47 of the judgment, the tribunal underlined 'the Court has only to ensure that the English courts acted reasonably, in good faith and within the limits of the margin of appreciation left to the Contracting States by Article 10 para. 2 (art. 10-2).' In para. 49 it further explained that 'the domestic margin of appreciation thus goes hand in hand with a European supervision. Such supervision concerns both the aim of the measure challenged and its "necessity"; it covers not only the basic legislation but also the decision applying it, even one given by an independent court'.
603. *Philip Morris v. Uruguay*, ICSID Case No. ARB/10/7 Award (8 July 2016) para. 410.
604. *Ibid.*, para. 399.
605. *Ibid.*

§4.05 SUMMARY OF THE CHAPTER AND INTERIM CONCLUSIONS

This introductory Chapter on FET jurisprudence and the right to regulate is divided into two parts. The first part has provided an overview of the means that arbitral tribunals rely on in their interpretation of the FET standard. The second part introduced the conditions that apply to the exercise of the right to regulate by the host state vis-à-vis the right of an investor to obtain FET.

In summarising the interpretation of the FET standard by tribunals, this Chapter has observed that tribunals have often invoked the general rules of treaty interpretation that are laid down in Article 31 of the VCLT. In interpreting the FET standard, tribunals often attempt to establish the meaning of FET through its ordinary meaning, its context and by determining the object and purpose of the treaty.

As discussed in section §4.02[A], the search for the ordinary meaning of the FET standard has not resulted in a comprehensible identification of what is implied by the FET standard by arbitral tribunals. As stated by the tribunal in *Crystallex v. Venezuela* 'the plain meaning of these terms [fair and equitable] ... does not provide much assistance.'[606]

As has been outlined in sections §4.02[B] and §4.02[C], in interpreting the FET standard, several tribunals have turned to the context, and the object and purpose of the treaty, with particular emphasis being placed on the preamble to an applicable IIA. Several decisions on the FET standard have provided a broad interpretation of the FET standard by relying on one of the objectives of the treaty reflected in the preamble, focusing - in particular - on investor promotion and protection. Referring to such cases, Reinisch underlines that some tribunals have interpreted the preamble in a 'pro-investor' manner, while others have done so in a 'pro-State' manner.[607] He suggests, however, that a 'more useful view is to recognize that effective investment protection is in the long-term interest of host States, and thus avoids prioritising one over the other.'[608] Certain decisions that have been concluded more recently have opted for a more balanced assessment of the context, object and purpose of the treaty, by underlining that investor protection is not the 'sole aim of the Treaty'.[609] For example, in *Mamidoil v. Albania*, the tribunal indicated that the goal of IIAs also includes the stimulation of 'economic development in the partner countries'.[610] It consequently provided that the FET standard should be interpreted in a balanced manner with due regard being given to the state's right to regulate and the investor's right to be treated fairly and equitably.

In interpreting the FET standard, tribunals sometimes have recourse to supplementary means of interpretation as laid down in Article 32 of the VCLT and subsidiary

606. *Crystallex International Corporation v. the Republic of Venezuela*, ICSID Case No. ARB(AF)/11/2 Award (4 April 2016) para. 538.
607. A. Reinisch, 'The Interpretation of International Investment Agreements' (2015) 397.
608. *Ibid.*
609. *Saluka v. Czech Republic* [2006] Permanent Court of Arbitration, IIC 210, Partial Award (17 March 2006) para. 300.
610. *Mamidoil Jetoil Greek Petroleum Products Société S.A. v. Republic of Albania*, ICSID Case No. ARB/11/24 Award (30 March 2015), para. 611.

means of the determination of international law, in particular judicial decisions.[611] In section §4.03[A], the role of supplementary means of interpretation that include the 'preparatory work of the treaty and the circumstances of its conclusion' was discussed.[612]At present, tribunals rarely refer to supplementary means of interpretation such as the *travaux préparatoires* in interpreting the FET standard.[613] However, in the future the role of the *travaux préparatoires* may become more prominent, considering that in several new generation IIAs, negotiation records have become more readily available than was the case in the past.

As demonstrated in section §4.03[B], tribunals often rely on previous decisions of investment tribunals as subsidiary means of interpretation in accordance with Article 38(1)(d) of the ICJ Statute.[614] Although earlier FET decisions have been criticised for a lack of predictability and consistency, a recent series of FET decisions have been developing in a more predictable manner. In most cases, tribunals agree that the FET standard is composed of several principles, such as legitimate expectations, non-discrimination and others.

In section §4.03[C], the role of scholarly writings in the interpretation of the FET standard was assessed. As the case law on the FET standard has evolved, tribunals tend to refer to scholarly writings as just one of the sources in interpreting this standard.

In section §4.04, the 'general principles of law recognised by civilised nations' that constitute one of the main sources of public international law under Article 38(1)(c) of the ICJ Statute were analysed with regard to the interpretation of the FET standard.[615] The principle of proportionality, the principle of reasonableness, the principle of deference and the principle of the margin of appreciation were reviewed. It has been outlined that FET tribunals frequently apply the proportionality or reasonableness tests in assessing the conduct of a host state. In deciding FET cases, investment tribunals have exercised some restraint in assessing the legitimacy of a state's measure, by evaluating the state's objectives versus the state's obligations under an applicable treaty. In exercising such restraint, tribunals usually refer to the concepts of 'deference' and sometimes to the 'margin of appreciation'.

611. Article 38(1)(d) of the Statute of the International Court of Justice (signed on 26 June 1945, entered into force on 24 October 1945) 1055, 33 UNTS 933.
612. Article 32 of the Vienna Convention on the Law of Treaties, 1155 UNTS 331 (23 May 1969).
613. M. Jacob, S. Schill, (2015) 713. The authors observed that the FET standard is not usually 'elucidated by *travaux préparatoires*'.
614. O.K. Frauchald, 'The Legal Reasoning of ICSID Tribunals: An Empirical Analysis' [2008] 19(2) *European Journal of International Law*, 335.
615. Article 38(1)(c) of the Statute of the International Court of Justice (29 June 1945).

CHAPTER 5

Introduction to the Legal Conditions on the Right to Regulate Identified by Tribunals

As demonstrated in the present book the concept of the right to regulate that has a legal basis in the international legal principle of state sovereignty is recognised and referenced by tribunals in FET claims. As discussed in Chapter 2, section §2.03[C], in recent awards, tribunals tend to include an acknowledgement of the right to regulate in the assessment of the FET standard.[616]

Such a reference in FET decisions is frequently made by tribunals, within balancing the rights of an investor with the state's right to regulate, in the evaluation of an investor's legitimate expectations and in the assessment of the contested state's measure. In some cases, the state's right to regulate is underlined at the outset of the assessment of the FET standard, where the general reasoning in the application and interpretation of the standard is outlined,[617] and sometimes the right to regulate might be referred to during the last stage of the FET assessment as a factor in balancing the rights and obligations of the parties to the dispute.[618]

What remains necessary to clarify on the basis of investment jurisprudence is the extent of a states' right to regulate versus an investor's rights in the assessment of the FET standard. As can be observed, in the early decisions of investment tribunals, the right of the investor to obtain FET was a starting point of the analysis. The state's right to regulate was taken into consideration only to a limited extent. The argumentation of

616. *See*: Chapter 2, section §2.03[C] on the right to regulate in FET investment cases. Also *see*: A. Titi, (2014) 276. Titi underlines that 'recent arbitral jurisprudence has tentatively started to reference the state's regulatory interest even when the latter are not encapsulated in black and white treaty language or in confirmed general international law'.
617. *Mamidoil Jetoil Greek Petroleum Products Société S.A. v. Republic of Albania*, ICSID Case No. ARB/11/24 Award (30 March 2015), para. 614; *SD Myers v. Canada*, UNCITRAL case, partial award (13 November 2000), para. 263.
618. *AWG v. Argentina* [2010] UNCITRAL Arbitration, Decision on Liability (30 July 2010) para. 236.

the state in justifying the contested measure taken in the public interest had played an insignificant role when weighed against the right of investors.[619]

At present, it can be observed that FET tribunals have been taking into consideration the state's right to regulate in their decisions, and what the extent of this right is sometimes explained in a number of decisions. For example, in several cases, tribunals have clarified that states have the right to change and modify their laws as a part of their right to regulate. The state's right to regulate tends to play a more prominent role as an integral factor invoked in balancing the state's right to regulate and an investor's right to obtain FET. The landmark decision of *Saluka v. Czech Republic* in 2006 was followed by a substantial number of tribunals. In its assessment of the FET standard, it provided that in evaluating the legitimate expectations of the investor, a 'host state's legitimate right subsequently to regulate domestic matters in the public interest must be taken into consideration as well.'[620] In *Lemire v. Ukraine*, the tribunal stressed the necessity of balancing a state's right to regulate and the rights of investors, by providing that:

> The evaluation of the State's action cannot be performed in the abstract and only with a view of protecting the investor's rights. The Tribunal must also balance other legally relevant interests, and take into consideration a number of countervailing factors, before it can establish that a violation of the FET standard, which merits compensation, has actually occurred:
>
> - the State's sovereign right to pass legislation and to adopt decisions for the protection of its public interests, especially if they do not provoke a disproportionate impact on foreign investors;
> - the legitimate expectations of the investor, at the time he made his investment;
> - the investor's duty to perform an investigation before effecting the investment;
> - the investor's conduct in the host country.[621]

In other words, the balancing of a state's right to regulate versus the investor's right to receive FET has become an integral part of the FET assessment, as provided in *Saluka*, for example. This study attempts to clarify the conditions limiting the state's right to regulate versus the investor's right to FET, or alternatively the limitations on the FET standard versus the state's right to regulate through an assessment of FET jurisprudence.

The survey of the cases on FET claims in this study will illustrate that a number of decisions - especially those concluded since 2006 - have attempted to provide more clarity on the criteria applied in assessing a regulatory measure and have attempted to establish certain indicators regarding the limits of the state's regulatory conduct in the context of the FET standard. As Alvarez has emphasised, arbitral interpretations on the

619. *Tecmed v. Mexico*, ICSID Case No. ARB(AF)/00/2 Award (29 May 2003); *Metalclad v. Mexico*, ICSID Case No. ARB(AF)/97/1 Award (30 August 2000); *Azurix Corp. v. The Argentine Republic*, ICSID Case No. ARB/01/12 Award (14 July 2006).
620. *Saluka v. Czech Republic* [2006] Permanent Court of Arbitration, IIC 210, Partial Award (17 March 2006) para. 305.
621. *Lemire v. Ukraine*, ICSID Case No. ARB/06/18 Decision on Jurisdiction and Liability (14 January 2010) para. 285.

FET standard show 'a clear progression over time towards more exacting standards for host states'.[622] The study has identified several main conditions that may impose certain limitations on the right to regulate and the circumstances under which the exercise of a state's right to regulate may limit the investor's right to be treated fairly and equitably.

The list of these conditions has been identified in this study, based on final and partial investment awards, investment decisions on jurisdiction and decisions on liability by investment tribunals concerning the FET standard. The list of these conditions does not claim to be exhaustive and does not cover the entire landscape of investment decisions involving FET claims. These conditions may, however, indicate whether – in the final stage of the assessment – a regulatory measure balanced against an investor's rights will be in compliance with the FET standard.

On the basis of an analysis of the case law, the identified conditions are divided into four main categories that apply to the exercise of the right to regulate by the host state vis-à-vis the right of an investor to obtain FET. These categories and their explanation are provided below:

(1) The condition concerning the legitimate expectations of the investor;
(2) The condition concerning the legitimacy of the state's objective;
(3) The condition concerning the content of the state's measure;
(4) The condition concerning the legality of the state's measure under national law.

(1) The element of the legitimate expectations of the investor is analysed in Chapter 6. This Chapter seeks to understand the relationship between the legitimate expectations of the investor and the state's right to regulate. A claim seeking to protect legitimate expectations is generally invoked by an investor on the basis of a state's conduct or changes in the regulatory framework of a host state. In this Chapter, the elements invoked by tribunals in reviewing whether an investor's claim seeking to have its legitimate expectations protected based on a state's representations or the general regulatory framework has been analysed. Not always, but in many cases, an assessment of legitimate expectations is performed independently from the evaluation of a state's objectives, the conduct related to the implementation of a state's objectives and the legality of the measure under national law. This condition can consequently be more easily distinguished from other conditions that frequently overlap with each other.

In Chapter 6, an analysis of what type and what are the elements pertinent to the concept of legitimate expectations in relation to a state's right to regulate is discussed. In Chapter 6, four elements have been identified to have a key role in the determination of whether the expectations of an investor can be considered legitimate and thus capable of limiting the state's right to regulate. These elements are: (i) the specific representations made by

622. J. Alvarez, (2011) 210.

the host state to an investor; (ii) the stability of a general regulatory framework; (iii) the economic and sociopolitical circumstances in the host state; and (iv) the investor's conduct, i.e. due diligence and risk assessment. In sections §6.03-§6.06 of Chapter 6, these four elements are explained and evaluated.

The second, third and fourth categories are discussed in Chapter 7, and their content is briefly explained below.

(2) The objective of the state's measure is addressed in Chapter 7. A number of tribunals have reviewed the objective of the state's measure to determine the legality of the state's measure. The assessment of the legitimacy of a state's objective is one of the prominent steps that in some cases may clarify the extent of a state's right to regulate versus the obligation to afford FET. The assessment of the legitimacy of a state's objectives in implementing a certain measure determines, in some cases, whether a further analysis of other factors related to regulatory conduct is necessary for finding liability under the FET standard. The structure of the chapter is the following. In section §7.02 of Chapter 7, the criteria used by a number of tribunals in evaluating a state's objectives are clarified. Section §7.02[C] discusses certain specific policy objectives taken in the public interest. Lastly, the state's objectives that found by arbitral tribunals to be illegitimate will be reviewed in section §7.02[D].

(3) The assessment of the content of the state's measure is examined in section §7.04. This condition is closely related to the second condition, as after establishing the legitimacy of a state's objectives, tribunals will, in many cases, proceed with an assessment of the state's measure under the FET standard according to the general principles of law: (i) reasonableness, proportionality and the prohibition of arbitrariness, (ii) non-discrimination and (iii) transparency.

In assessing the state's measure, tribunals may evaluate how the measure has been implemented and/or, in some cases, how it relates to certain policy objectives. Different tests are employed by tribunals in assessing the state's measure, which are clarified in Chapter 7. Section §7.04[A] elaborates on the application of the principles of reasonableness, proportionality and the prohibition of arbitrariness in an assessment of the state's measure. Section §7.04[B] addresses the principle of non-discrimination. Section §7.04[C] then discusses transparency in adopting a state's regulatory measure.

(4) The legality of the measure under national law is assessed in section §7.05. In a series of cases, tribunals have conditioned the state's right to regulate on the basis of an assessment of the legality of the state's conduct under national law. In several cases, tribunals have identified the conditions under which a state's illegal conduct under national law or an erroneous interpretation or application of national law may constitute a decisive factor in determining liability under the FET standard. The criteria that the tribunals use in determining the extent of their review of a state's decisions may constitute a

condition for the right to regulate that plays a role in the overall assessment of the FET standard.[623] Sections §7.05[A]-§7.05[D] will elaborate on the extent of this condition.

623. *See* the analysis on this issue (the requirement of lawfulness) by J. Bonnitcha, (2014) section 4.6.2 (e-book) pp. 143-146.

CHAPTER 6

The State's Right to Regulate and the Legitimate Expectations of the Investor

§6.01 INTRODUCTION

The subject of this study is an analysis of the tension between the element of protecting the legitimate expectations of an investor, on the one hand, and the notion of the state's right to regulate, on the other. In this Chapter, the protection of an investor's legitimate expectations will be analysed.

Several tribunals have asserted that the protection of legitimate expectations is the primary objective of the FET standard.[624] Currently, assessing the protection of the legitimate expectations of an investor constitutes a central element of the FET standard evaluation in the majority of FET investment cases.[625] In this vein, it is important to note that the investor's legitimate expectations are usually based on (i) a specific

624. *See Biwater v. Tanzania*, ICSID Case No. ARB/05/22 Final Award (24 July 2008) para. 602 where the tribunal stated that '[t]he purpose of the fair and equitable treatment standard is to provide to international investments treatment that does not affect the basic expectations that were taken into account by the foreign investor to make the investment, as long as these expectations are reasonable and legitimate and have been relied upon by the investor to make the investment.' *See also Suez, Sociedad General de Aguas de Barcelona, S.A. and Vivendi Universal, S.A. v. Argentine Republic*, ICSID Case No. ARB/03/19 Decision on Liability (30 July 2010) and *AWG v. Argentina* [2010] UNCITRAL Arbitration, Decision on Liability (30 July 2010) para. 222, in which it was stated that '[i]n an effort to develop an operational method for determining the existence or nonexistence of fair and equitable treatment, arbitral tribunals have increasingly taken into account the legitimate expectations that a host country has created in the investor and the extent to which conduct by the host government subsequent to the investment has frustrated those expectations'.

625. J. Bonnitcha, (2014) 161-162. Bonnitcha summarises the history of the legitimate expectations doctrine in investment law as follows: 'Since 2006, protection of the investor's legitimate expectations has emerged as the most significant element of the FET standard. The doctrine of legitimate expectations has been sufficiently widely accepted that arbitral decisions now spend more time examining the contours of the doctrine than determining whether compliance with the doctrine is an element of FET. This shared recognition of legitimate expectations as an

representation made by the host state to such an investor regarding its investment or (ii) an assumption on the part of the investor that the general regulatory framework relied upon by it at the time the investment was made will remain stable.

Specific representations can be provided to investors in different forms, e.g. in the host state's legislation or through contractual commitments.[626] Usually, a foreign investor's claim of a breach of its legitimate expectations is based on changes or alterations to the original representation(s) made to that investor by the host state. The 'reversal of [representations] made by the host state that have led to legitimate expectations will violate the principle of fair and equitable treatment.'[627]

In the absence of any specific representations by the host state to the investor, the latter can still have legitimate expectations, i.e. based on the expectation of the stability of the general legal framework.[628] Under the concept of legitimate expectations in international investment law, states are required to maintain a certain degree of stability and predictability in their regulatory framework as this is relied upon by investors when making investments.[629] If the host state makes substantial subsequent changes to the legal framework which was effective at the time when the investment was made, and which have resulted in serious financial losses being suffered by the investor, or in an inability on the part of the investor to continue operating its investment, this can be considered by a tribunal to be a breach of the legitimate expectations of the investor.[630]

The state's right to regulate (elaborated in Chapter 2) plays a central role in determining the limits of the protection of the investor's legitimate expectations. Whether the investor makes a claim for the protection of its legitimate expectations on the ground of a reversal of a specific representation made to it by the host state or on the basis of a substantial change to the general regulatory framework, in both situations it will refer to the state's regulatory and/or administrative conduct, e.g. the change which the state has made to the law, or the revocation of the licence.

The tension between the state's right to regulate and the protection of the legitimate expectations of an investor involves 'a state's insistence on its authority to adapt its rules to the public interest and an investor's insistence on a right to rely on a

element of FET is reflected in academic commentary.' *See also* I. Laird and others, 'International Investment Law and Arbitration: 2014 in Review', in A.J. Bjorklund (ed.) *Yearbook on International Investment Law and Policy 2013-2014* (Oxford University Press, 2015) 105. Reviewing the decisions on the FET standard rendered in 2013, the authors emphasised that 'tribunals in 2013 recognized that the protection of the claimant's legitimate or reasonable expectations is a well-accepted component of the FET standard'.

626. *Suez, Sociedad General de Aguas de Barcelona, S.A. and Vivendi Universal, S.A. v. Argentine Republic,* ICSID Case No. ARB/03/19 Decision on Liability (30 July 2010) para. 222. The tribunal explained that 'when an investor undertakes an investment, a host government through its laws, regulations, declared policies, and statements creates in the investor certain expectations about the nature of the treatment that it may anticipate from the host State'.
627. R. Dolzer, C. Schreuer, (2014) 145.
628. R. Klager, (2011) 164.
629. K. Vandevelde, 'A Unified Theory of Fair and Equitable Treatment' [2010] 43 *New York University Journal of International Law and Policy*, p. 66.
630. M. Valenti, (2014) 41.

regime which induced it to invest'.[631] Tribunals have attempted to resolve this tension by striving to reconcile the subjective interests of the investor deriving from its legitimate expectations and the state's right to regulate in the public interest. [632] In order to build a bridge between the two concepts, tribunals follow several paths.

On the one hand, in general, tribunals' assessment of the legitimacy of expectations involves a review of the subjective interests of an investor in relation to the state's conduct. An important consideration in this assessment is the specific nature of a state's representations.[633] The review of the selected cases in this study reveals that in assessing the level of specificity, tribunals review the legal force of the state's representations through their legal form, content and the wording.[634] The investor may reasonably expect that its expectations are legitimate if they are based on specific and unambiguous state representations.[635] In contrast, in situations where an investor claims that its expectations have been frustrated because of changes implemented in the general regulatory framework, tribunals have clarified that such an investor cannot reasonably expect that the state will not amend its laws.[636] Tribunals have thereby generally expressed the view that only serious changes to a regulatory framework – impacting the investor and its investment – may give rise to the protection of its legitimate expectations.

631. J. Paulsson, Can 'Legitimate Expectations' Ever be 'Rights'? *Lex* (Online Publication), 19 April 2016, https://lex.jotwell.com/can-legitimate-expectations-ever-be-rights/ accessed on 1 June 2018.
632. As observed by F. Dupuy and P.-M. Dupuy, who analysed the role of legitimate expectations in the FET standard, 'many arbitrators consider that it [the FET standard] creates a subjective right for each investor to have its expectations to be protected as far as these expectations are legally "legitimate".' This statement reflects the opinion of many international investment lawyers. Nonetheless in this dissertation, the concept of a subjective right is not pivotal in the discussion in this Chapter as the focus is on the question of how the aforementioned tension between the right to regulate and the protection of investors' legitimate expectations is bridged by tribunals. As provided by F. Dupuy and P.-M. Dupuy, the general idea of legitimate expectations, supported in different legal systems, is to provide a 'balance between the individual's private interest and the public interest represented by the state'. F. Dupuy, P.-M. Dupuy, 'What to Expect from Legitimate Expectations? A Critical Appraisal and Look Into the Future of the 'Legitimate Expectations' Doctrine in International Investment Law', in M.A. Raouf, et al. (eds) *Festschrift Ahmed Sadek El- Kosheri: From the Arab World to the Globalization of International Law* (Kluwer, 2015) 276. This is also reflected in investment jurisprudence, *see*: *Saluka Investments BV v. Czech Republic* [2006] UNCITRAL Arbitration Partial Award (17 March 2006) para. 306. The tribunal provided that the review of the FET standard requires a 'weighing of the Claimant's legitimate and reasonable expectations on the one hand and the Respondent's legitimate regulatory interests on the other'. Also *see*: *El Paso v. Argentina*, ICSID Case No. ARB/03/15 Award (31 October 2011) para. 358. The tribunal emphasised that 'legitimate expectations cannot be solely the subjective expectations of the investor ... investor's legitimate expectations must be grounded in reality, experience and context'.
633. T. Wongkaew, 'The Transplantation of Legitimate Expectations in Investment Treaty Arbitration', in P. Lazo et al. *The Role of the State in Investor-State Arbitration* (Brill, 2015), p. 99, 'Reasonableness or legitimacy is also defined by a degree of specificity of commitment'.
634. *See* section §6.03 of the Chapter for this analysis.
635. *Total v. Argentina*, ICSID Case No. ARB/04/01 Decision on Liability (27 December 2010) para. 117; *Duke v. Ecuador*, ICSID Case No. ARB/04/19 Award (18 August 2008) para. 351.
636. *El Paso v. Argentina*, ICSID Case No. ARB/03/15 Award (31 October 2011) para. 374; *Ioan Micula v. Romania*, ICSID Case No. ARB/05/20 Final Award (11 December 2013) para. 673.

On the other hand, in assessing the legitimacy of expectations, tribunals evaluate factors that are independent of the subjective interests of an investor. For example, they take into account certain special circumstances that were relevant to the investment.[637] This means that tribunals may attach importance to the economic and sociopolitical circumstances that influenced the state's measure.[638] Another aspect which impacts the legitimacy of the investor's expectations is the investor's own conduct, such as whether or not it has properly exercised due diligence.[639] The investor's duty to duly consider the laws and regulations, as well as the economic and sociopolitical circumstances in the host state, have been relevant factors for tribunals in deciding whether an investor's expectations can be considered legitimate and therefore protected.[640]

On the basis of the case law analysis conducted in this dissertation, four elements can be identified, the assessment of which are crucial for the determination whether the expectations of an investor can be considered legitimate and thus capable of limiting the state's right to regulate. These are: (i) the specific representations made by the host state to an investor; (ii) the stability of a general regulatory framework; (iii) the economic and sociopolitical circumstances in the host state; and (iv) the investor's conduct, i.e. due diligence and risk assessment.

In the remainder of this Chapter, section §6.02 will first explain how the concept of legitimate expectations was introduced in early FET cases. Next, in sections §6.03-§6.06 the four elements stated above will be elaborated upon by presenting and analysing recent cases. Section §6.07 contains the concluding remarks.

§6.02 EARLY REFERENCES TO LEGITIMATE EXPECTATIONS IN FET INVESTMENT DECISIONS

The legitimate expectations of an investor became a prominent element of the FET standard in the early 2000s. In *CME v. Czech Republic* – one of the early decisions on the FET standard that was delivered in 2001 – the tribunal indirectly referred to legitimate expectations in its decision. A few years later, in the *Tecmed v. Mexico* award of 2003, the tribunal assessed whether legitimate expectations had to lead to the protection of

637. In the words of the *Saluka* decision, the legitimate expectations doctrine does not just protect the subjective expectations of an investor; they 'must rise to the level of legitimacy and reasonableness in the light of circumstances'. *Saluka Investments BV v. Czech Republic* [2006] UNCITRAL Arbitration Partial Award (17 March 2006) para. 304.
638. *Duke Energy v. Ecuador* [2008] ICSID Case No. ARB/04/19 Award (12 August 2008) para. 340.
639. M. Potestà, 'Legitimate Expectations in Investment Treaty Law: Understanding the Roots and the Limits of a Controversial Concept' [2013] 28(1) *ICSID Review*, 119. The author provided that the 'reasonableness requirement inherent in expectations is in turn affected by a further component, which concerns the role played by the investor in the investment operation'.
640. J. Vinuales, 'Investor Diligence in Investment Arbitration: Sources and Arguments' [2017] 32(2) *ICSID Review*, p. 362.

the investor under the FET standard.[641] Since then, this legal concept has developed and evolved in many international investment cases.[642]

Tribunals have taken different approaches in interpreting the element of legitimate expectations as a part of the FET standard. As Roberts summarised:

> Some investment tribunals have recognized the limited nature of this [legitimate expectations] doctrine, while others have tended to overdraw it and related doctrines, treating them as akin to freezing the regulatory framework at the time of investment.[643]

Two basic approaches in applying the legitimate expectations concept can be distinguished. The first approach includes FET cases in which tribunals have widely applied the legitimate expectations concept, focusing primarily on the rights of investors with limited consideration being given to the rights of host states.[644] Such an approach was primarily adopted in early FET cases. In this regard, Sornarajah has observed that 'legitimate expectations ... go through a process of contraction. The first phase of awards of legitimate expectations consisted of the awards in which the concept was given a wide scope.'[645]

The more recent investment decisions, representing the second approach, emphasise that the legitimate expectations of a foreign investor are limited vis-à-vis the state's right to regulate.[646] The latter category of cases is discussed in the sections §6.03-§6.06.

641. M. Sornarajah, Resistance and Change in the International Law on Foreign Investments (Cambridge University Press, 2015) 257. *See*: T. Wongkaew, 'The Transplantation of Legitimate Expectations in Investment Treaty Arbitration: A Critique', in S. Lalani, R. Lazo, *The Role of the State in Investor-State Arbitration* (Brill Nijhoff, 2015) 75.
642. J. Bonnitcha, (2014) 20. The author states that 'since 2006, protection of the investor's legitimate expectations has emerged as the most significant element of the FET standard. The doctrine of legitimate expectations has been sufficiently widely accepted ...'. M. Sornarajah, Resistance and Change in the International Law on Foreign Investments (Cambridge University Press, 2015) 257. *See also* M. Potestà, 'Legitimate Expectations in Investment Treaty Law: Understanding the Roots and the Limits of a Controversial Concept' [2013] 28(1) *ICSID Review*, 88 who stated that '[i]f one observes the awards given by investment treaty tribunals in the last few years, one will hardly find any example where the concept of "legitimate expectations" has not been invoked by the claimant ...'.
643. A. Roberts, 'Power and Persuasion in Investment Treaty Interpretation: The Dual Role of States' [2010] 104(2) *American Journal of International Law*, 215.
644. Examples of such decisions are: *CME v. Czech Republic* [2001] UNCITRAL Arbitration, Partial Award (13 September 2001); *Tecmed v. Mexico*, ICSID Case No. ARB(AF)/00/2 Award (29 May 2003); *Occidental v. Ecuador*, LCIA Case No. UN3467 Final Award (1 July 2004); *MTD v. Chile*, ICSID Case No. ARB/01/7 Award (25 May 2004). In the academic literature, several commentators have observed that, in some cases, legitimate expectations as an element of the FET are interpreted broadly. *See* S. Schill, (2006) International Justice and Law Working Papers 2006/6 (NYU Law School).
645. M. Sornarajah, Resistance and Change in the International Law on Foreign Investments (Cambridge University Press, 2015) 272.
646. *See, e.g.*, *Saluka Investments BV v. Czech Republic* [2006] UNCITRAL Arbitration Partial Award (17 March 2006) para. 306; *Toto v. Lebanon*, ICSID Case No. ARB/07/12 Award (7 June 2012) para. 165. Also *see*: M. Potestà, 'Legitimate Expectations in Investment Treaty Law: Understanding the Roots and the Limits of a Controversial Concept' [2013] 28(1) *ICSID Review*, 100.

The first approach in interpreting legitimate expectations was adopted in *CME v. Czech Republic* and *Tecmed v. Mexico*. In these two cases, a wide interpretation of the concept of the legitimate expectations of the investor was employed as part of the assessment of the FET standard. These early decisions are still important because they introduced certain aspects which are pertinent to the concept of legitimate expectations. In *Tecmed v. Mexico*, the tribunal referred to the notions of consistency, the lack of ambiguity and transparency, i.e. elements that continue to be relevant in the contemporary evaluation of the FET standard by tribunals.[647] The following investment decisions are reviewed in this section: *CME v. Czech Republic* and *Tecmed v. Mexico*.

(i) *CME v. Czech Republic* (2001)

In *CME v. Czech Republic*, the tribunal referred to the notion of legitimate expectations as a stand-alone concept. The case concerned a US citizen who – in 1993 – had invested in a Czech television broadcasting company.[648] The investment was organised through a Dutch company (CME) with a Czech subsidiary (CNTS). CNTS became the exclusive provider of the first private TV channel in the Czech Republic by making an arrangement with a Czech company (CET 21), which obtained a licence from the regulatory authority (Media Council).[649] At first, the state authorities did not object to the aforementioned structure. However, in 1996, the Media Council started investigating the arrangement between CNTS and CET 21. It initiated administrative proceedings against CNTS, alleging that CNTS was an illegal broadcasting TV station that had been operating without a licence.[650] In the same year the amended Media Law entered into force. This law had an adverse impact on the licensing conditions between CET 21 and CNTS.[651] Eventually, CNTS lost its position as the exclusive provider of the private TV channel and was replaced by other service providers.

In this dispute, CME (the investor) argued that it had been treated unfairly and inequitably and that this was in violation of the FET standard laid down in Article 3(1) of the Dutch-Czech BIT.[652] The tribunal concluded that the FET standard had indeed been violated because of an 'evisceration of the arrangements in reliance upon which

The author, in analysing legitimate expectations as a part of the FET standard, observed that currently 'arbitral tribunals have gradually posed limits and qualifications to such recognition [of legitimate expectations]'.

647. *Tecmed v. Mexico*, ICSID Case No. ARB(AF)/00/2 Award (29 May 2003) para. 154.
648. *CME v. Czech Republic* [2001] UNCITRAL Arbitration, Partial Award (13 September 2001) para. 6.
649. *Ibid.*, paras 8-11.
650. *Ibid.*, paras 107-108.
651. *Ibid.*, paras 109, 235.
652. *Ibid.*, para. 155. *See also* Article 3(1) of the Netherlands-Czech Republic BIT (1992): 'Each Contracting Party shall ensure fair and equitable treatment to the investments of investors of the other Contracting Party and shall not impair, by unreasonable or discriminatory measures, the operation, management, maintenance, use, enjoyment or disposal thereof by those investors.' *CME v. Czech Republic* [2001] UNCITRAL Arbitration, Partial Award (13 September 2001) para. 155.

the foreign investor was induced to invest'.[653] The tribunal stated that the approval of the contractual structure between CET 21 and CNTS to provide broadcasting services must be 'regarded as a legally well-founded basis' for the investor to expect that he could operate relying on the same structure.[654] The amendments to the Media Law and the interference by the Media Council, however, had altered the legal regime of CME's investment structure, and therefore, according to the tribunal, the legitimate expectations of the investor had been violated.[655]

The tribunal relied upon the concept of the legitimate expectations of the investor in assessing the violation of the FET standard, but it did not elaborate upon this concept in its decision. However, shortly after the *CME v. Czech Republic* decision, the *Tecmed v. Mexico* (2003) decision was rendered, in which the notion of legitimate expectations was further developed.[656] The *Tecmed* tribunal emphasised that an investor is entitled to have 'basic expectations' that the host state will act in a 'consistent manner, free from ambiguity and totally transparently' when dealing with an investor.[657]

(ii) *Tecmed v. Mexico* (2003)

In *Tecmed v. Mexico*, a Spanish company, Tecmed (the investor),[658] bought 'property, buildings and facilities and other assets' relating to a landfill of hazardous industrial waste, in an auction organised by the Municipality of Hermosillo, in the State of Sonora, Mexico.[659] Tecmed involved its subsidiary Cytar, a company incorporated under Mexican law, in order to operate the landfill. [660]

For managing the landfill, the operating company Cytar had to obtain a licence from the Hazardous Materials, Waste and Activities Division (INE), which was a federal government agency. Every year, the operating company had to request an extension of the licence. Despite being successful in obtaining an extension in 1996 and 1997, in 1998 Cytar was denied a renewal of the licence to operate the hazardous

653. *CME v. Czech Republic* [2001] UNCITRAL Arbitration, Partial Award (13 September 2001) para. 611.
654. *Ibid.*, para. 457.
655. *Ibid.*, paras 157, 166, 611.
656. *See* M. Potestà, 'Legitimate Expectations in Investment Treaty Law: Understanding the Roots and the Limits of a Controversial Concept' [2013] 28(1) *ICSID Review*, 100. The author states that *Tecmed* was the first arbitral tribunal to clearly spell out that fair and equitable treatment encompasses the protection of expectations. *See* C. Schreuer, U. Kriebaum, 'At What Time Must Legitimate Expectations Exist', in T Wälde and others (eds) *A Liber Amicorum: Thomas Wälde – Law Beyond Conventional Thought* (CMP Publishing, 2009) 276 who argued that *Tecmed v. Mexico* was 'one of the leading cases on fair and equitable treatment and an investor's legitimate expectations'.
657. *Tecmed v. Mexico*, ICSID Case No. ARB(AF)/00/2 Award (29 May 2003) para. 154.
658. The claimant referred to as the investor in the text was the parent company of Tecmed in Spain that had two subsidiaries in Mexico: 'Technicas Medioambientales de Mexico, S.A. de C.V. ("Tecmed"), is a company incorporated under Mexican law, and holds over 99% of the shares of such company. Additionally, Tecmed holds over 99% of the shares of CYTRAR, S.A. DE C.V. ("Cytrar"), a company incorporated under Mexican law through which the investment giving rise to the disputes leading to these arbitration proceedings was made.' *Tecmed v. Mexico*, ICSID Case No. ARB(AF)/00/2 Award (29 May 2003) para. 4.
659. *Tecmed v. Mexico*, ICSID Case No. ARB(AF)/00/2 Award (29 May 2003) para. 35.
660. *Ibid.*

landfill.[661] The Mexican government, in denying the renewal of the licence, explained that the site had not been properly maintained and that its further development would have negative effects for the environment and the health of the population.[662] Even though the investor and the Mexican authorities had agreed to relocate the landfill to a new site, this plan was never realised.[663]

In examining the FET standard under Article 4(1) of the Spain-Mexico BIT, the tribunal assessed whether the denial of a renewal of the investor's operating company's licence to operate the landfill had been in violation of the FET standard.[664]

The investor argued that the agreement to relocate to another site could not justify a refusal to extend the permit to operate the old site. The investor argued that the new site for a hazardous landfill should have been opened before the old one was closed.[665] The investor complained that the denial of the permit to operate the old landfill had violated the FET standard as it 'frustrate[d] its justified expectation of the continuity and duration of the investment made and would impair recovery of the invested amounts and the expected rate of return'.[666]

In its assessment, the tribunal asserted that complying with the FET standard included an obligation for the host state to respect the expectations of an investor. The tribunal stated that the contracting parties to the Spain-Mexico BIT had to treat investments in a way that 'does not affect the *basic expectations* that were taken into account by the foreign investor to make the investment'.[667] The tribunal stated that:

> The foreign investor expects the host State to act in a consistent manner, free from ambiguity and totally transparently in its relations with the foreign investor, so that it may know beforehand any and all rules and regulations that will govern its investments, as well as the goals of the relevant policies and administrative practices or directives, to be able to plan its investment and comply with such regulations.[668]

The tribunal elaborated upon a 'consistent manner' as follows: 'i.e. without arbitrarily revoking any pre-existing decisions or permits issued by the State that were

661. Tecmed is a subsidiary that bought a landfill of hazardous industrial waste and afterwards transferred the landfill to Cytrar, a company created by Tecmed to operate the landfill. *Tecmed v. Mexico,* ICSID Case No. ARB(AF)/00/2 Award (29 May 2003) paras 38-39.
662. *Tecmed v. Mexico,* ICSID Case No. ARB(AF)/00/2 Award (29 May 2003) paras 97, 99, 125.
663. *Tecmed v. Mexico,* ICSID Case No. ARB(AF)/00/2 Award (29 May 2003) para. 112: 'When INE considered the renewal of the Permit, the relocation had not taken place and, reportedly, the final relocation site had not been identified …'. Also *see* on the nature of the permit – para. 160. 'The relocation agreement has not been memorialized in an instrument signed by all the parties involved, the evidence submitted leads to the conclusion that there was such an agreement, as evidenced by the joint declaration of SEMARNAP, the Government of the state of Sonora and the Honorable Municipality of Hermosillo to that effect'.
664. Article 4(10) of the Spain-Mexico BIT states that '[e]ach Contracting Party will guarantee in its territory fair and equitable treatment, according to International Law, for the investments made by investors of the other Contracting Party'.
665. *Tecmed v. Mexico,* ICSID Case No. ARB(AF)/00/2 Award (29 May 2003) paras 40-51.
666. *Ibid.,* para. 41.
667. *Ibid.,* para. 154. *See also* J. Bonnitcha, (2014) 50.
668. *Tecmed v. Mexico,* ICSID Case No. ARB(AF)/00/2 Award (29 May 2003) para. 154.

relied upon by the investor to assume its commitments as well as to plan and launch its commercial and business activities ...'.[669]

The tribunal found that Mexico had violated the FET standard because the state's decision not to renew the licence had violated the legitimate expectations of the investor. According to the tribunal, the investor had been assured by the state's authorities that 'the old site for hazardous waste would be available until it would be possible to relocate to a new site.'[670] The tribunal underlined that the authorities did not provide an 'explicit, transparent and clear warning' to the investor that the site would be closed before relocation.[671] The tribunal asserted that Mexico's conduct was 'characterized by its ambiguity and uncertainty which are prejudicial to the investor'.[672]

The tribunal found that the investor's expectations had been frustrated because of the inconsistent and non-transparent conduct of the authorities.[673] It based its judgment on the reasoning that the state's authorities had assured the investor that he could continue his operations on the old landfill site before relocating to a new one,[674] whereas the state's authorities had, in fact, refused to renew the investor's licence to operate the old landfill.[675] The tribunal concluded that the 'contradictory and ambiguous conduct'[676] of the state's authorities in relation to the investor and the lack of transparency in their decision to deny the renewal of the licence to operate the landfill amounted to a violation of the FET standard under Article 4(1) of the Spain-Mexico BIT.[677]

The decision of the *Tecmed* tribunal has often been cited and referred to by subsequent tribunals, specifically with regard to the obligation to protect the legitimate expectations of an investor.[678] The *Tecmed v. Mexico* award has also attracted criticism, due to the unreasonable demands that had been made in relation to the host state. For example, in an UNCTAD study on the FET standard, the decision has been criticised for placing very strict obligations on host states.[679] Citing Douglas, the UNCTAD study on

669. *Ibid.*
670. *Tecmed v. Mexico*, ICSID Case No. ARB(AF)/00/2 Award (29 May 2003) para. 160.
671. *Ibid.*
672. *Tecmed v. Mexico*, ICSID Case No. ARB(AF)/00/2 Award (29 May 2003) para. 172.
673. *Ibid.*, paras 172-174; *see also* J. Bonnitcha, (2014) 99.
674. *Tecmed v. Mexico*, ICSID Case No. ARB(AF)/00/2 Award (29 May 2003) para. 160.
675. *Ibid.*, paras 172-174; *see also* J. Bonnitcha, (2014) 99.
676. *Tecmed v. Mexico*, ICSID Case No. ARB(AF)/00/2 Award (29 May 2003) para. 172.
677. *Ibid.*, para. 174.
678. *See Occidental v. Ecuador*, ICSID Case No. ARB/06/11 Award (5 October 2012); *MTD v. Chile*, ICSID Case No. ARB/01/7 Award (25 May 2004) (the *Tecmed* reasoning was explicitly applied to this case, *see* para. 115); *LG&E Energy Corp., LG&E Capital Corp. & LG&E International v. The Argentine Republic*, ICSID Case No. ARB/02/1 Decision on Liability (3 October 2006); *PSEG v. Turkey*, ICSID Case No. ARB/02/5 Award (19 January 2007); *Duke Energy v. Ecuador*, ICSID Case No.ARB/04/19 Award (18 August 2008); and others. *See also* R. Dolzer, [2014], 14. The author states that *Tecmed* is the most cited award in investment jurisprudence. *See also* L. Reed, S. Consedine, 'Fair and Equitable Treatment: Legitimate Expectations and Transparency', in M. Kinnear, G. Fisher (eds) *Building International Investment Law: The First 50 Years of ICSID* (Kluwer, 2015) 286.
679. UNCTAD 'Fair and Equitable Treatment: UNCTAD Series on International Investment Agreements II' (New York, 2012). In analysing the *Tecmed* decision, the report provides that the 'list is indeed demanding and nearly impossible to achieve' (p. 65).

the FET standard emphasises that '[t]he Tecmed "standard" is actually not a standard at all; it is rather a description of perfect public regulation in a perfect world, to which all states should aspire but very few (if any) will ever attain.'[680]

The *Tecmed* tribunal's one-sided focus on protecting the investor's expectations has often been considered 'the most far-reaching exposition of the principle underlying the developing notion of legitimate expectations.' [681] At the same time, this decision has become important for the development of the concept of legitimate expectations in international investment law because it clarified its content.[682] In the *Tecmed* decision, the tribunal pointed out that stability is important because it impacts the expectations of an investor. The main premise of the tribunal's argumentation was that an investor is entitled to 'expect the host state to act in a consistent manner' in order to plan its investments and to conduct its business in a host state.[683] This stability element has been invoked and further elaborated upon by other tribunals, both as an element of legitimate expectations and as a separate component of the FET standard.[684]

More recent decisions on the FET standard have given consideration to the state's right to regulate in their assessment of an investor's legitimate expectations. In these decisions, the accent has shifted 'from a protection of investors' subjective beliefs to one that is more accommodating of the host state's sovereignty'.[685] In these decisions, tribunals have identified which elements are relevant in assessing the protection of legitimate expectations. As indicated in section §6.01, these elements comprise: (i) the specific representations made by the host state to an investor; (ii) the stability of a

680. Z. Douglas, 'Nothing If Not Critical for Investment Treaty Arbitration: *Occidental, Eureko* and *Methanex*' [2006] 22 *Arbitration International*, pp. 27-51. *See also* M. Sornarajah in *El Paso v. Argentina*, ICSID Case No. ARB/03/15 Award (31 October 2011) – Expert Opinion, 66-67: 'The *Tecmed* standard is a standard that the most neoliberal state will find difficult to fulfil. It is hardly a standard but the wish-list of the foreign investor which the Tecmed tribunal willingly restated.' Also *see*: *MTD v. Chile* the annulment committee decision, *MTD v. Chile*, ICSID Case No. ARB/01/7 Award (25 May 2004) para. 67. The annulment committee pointed to weakness in the *Tecmed* tribunal's reasoning stating that '[The] Tecmed tribunal's reliance on the foreign investor's expectations as the source of the host state's obligations (such as the obligation to compensate for expropriation) is questionable.' This restrictive interpretation of the meaning of the concept of the legitimate expectations by this kind of appeal court differs from what we see in many awards of ordinary tribunals up to 2004. In this study, an exploration of tribunals' awards after 2004 will be made.
681. C. McLachlan and others, International Investment Arbitration: Substantive Principles (Oxford University Press, 2008) 325.
682. M. Valenti, (2014) 39. Valenti noted that although the *Tecmed* decision has been criticised for being pro-investor, the definition of the FET standard provided in *Tecmed* 'already contained all the elements that are now considered firmly rooted in the standard'.
683. *Tecmed v. Mexico*, ICSID Case No. ARB(AF)/00/2 Award (29 May 2003) para. 154.
684. *Occidental v. Ecuador*, ICSID Case No. ARB/06/11 Award (5 October 2012) para. 185. In this award, the tribunal concluded that the 'stability of the legal and business framework is thus as essential element of FET.' para. 183. In para. 185, the tribunal cited the *Tecmed* decision and explained the obligation of stability. L. Reed, S. Consedine, 'Fair and Equitable Treatment: Legitimate Expectations and Transparency', in M. Kinnear, G. Fisher (eds) *Building International Investment Law: The First 50 Years of ICSID* (Kluwer, 2015) 292. In addition to legitimate expectations, the *Tecmed* tribunal endorsed 'consistency, lack of ambiguity, and transparency' which have been reinforced by other tribunals.
685. K. Schefer, 'State Powers and Investor-State Dispute Settlement', in S. Lalani, R. Lazo, *The Role of the State in Investor-State Arbitration* (Brill Nijhoff, 2015) 18.

general regulatory framework; (iii) the economic and sociopolitical circumstances in the host state; and (iv) the investor's conduct. These four elements are discussed in the following sections.

§6.03 SPECIFIC REPRESENTATIONS MADE BY THE HOST STATE

[A] Introduction

Considering the jurisprudence on the FET standard, it has to be pointed out that a large number of tribunals have stressed that an investor's expectations can only be regarded as legitimate if such expectations are based on specific representations made by a host state.[686] As Dolzer and Schreuer have observed:

> Specific representations play a central role in the creation of legitimate expectations. Undertakings and representations made explicitly or implicitly by the host state are the strongest basis for legitimate expectations. A reversal of assurances that have led to legitimate expectations will violate the principle of fair and equitable treatment.[687]

The tribunal in *White Industries v. India* emphasised that only specific representations, albeit vague and general, may give rise to 'reasonable legitimate expectations that are amenable to protection under the fair and equitable treatment standard'.[688] According to the research undertaken in this study, the level of specificity that is required by a tribunal varies from case to case. From the case law it can be deduced that tribunals tend to pose three main questions in order to determine the level of specificity, namely:

(1) Are the representations generated by the competent state authority?
(2) What is the legal force of the specific representations? This depends on: (i) their legal form; (ii) their content; and (iii) the wording of the representations; and
(3) How has the investor been designated in the state's representations?

Finding the answers to these three questions will assist the tribunal in its determination of the relationship between the investor and the host state and in deciding on the main question of whether legitimate expectations were created upon which the investor was allowed to rely in making or maintaining its investment.

In sections §6.03[B]-§6.03[D], it will be analysed how tribunals apply these three questions. To this end, in section §6.03[B], the first question regarding the competence of the acting state authority is assessed. The second question concerning the legal force of any specific representations is evaluated in section §6.03[C]. Section §6.03[D]

686. UNCTAD 'Fair and Equitable Treatment: UNCTAD Series on International Investment Agreements II' (New York, 2012) 68.
687. R. Dolzer, C. Schreuer, 2nd edn., (2012) 371.
688. *White Industries v. India* [2011] UNCITRAL, Final Award (30 November 2011) para. 10.3.17.

elaborates on the third question, namely how the investor is designated in the state's representation. In section §6.03[E], the question of whether tribunals apply the criteria addressed in sections §6.03[B]-§6.03[D] in a cumulative way is discussed.

A special form of specific representations is contractual commitments between a host state and an individual investor. One could say that the aforementioned questions concerning the level of specificity of the state's representations come together in contractual commitments. Nevertheless, for contractual commitments, in order to constitute a specific representation that may justify the protection of the legitimate expectations of an investor under the FET standard, it is not sufficient to comply with the test of specificity addressed below in sections §6.03[B]-§6.03[D]. The reason for this is that contractual breaches, even if they comply with the test of specificity, are usually not protected under the notion of legitimate expectations under an IIA's FET standard. A breach of contractual commitments may, however, lead to an FET standard violation but only if the host state has exercised its sovereign authority in respect of an investor and the non-fulfilment of the contract has been accompanied by other treaty violations.[689] Such additional requirements are explained in section §6.03[F].

[B] The Competence of the State Authority

A number of tribunals have specified that in order to provide protection to an investor concerning a claim based on a state's representations, these representations have to be provided by the competent state authority.

This requirement was underlined in one of the first NAFTA cases on the FET standard, *Metalclad v. Mexico*.[690] In this case, Metalclad (the investor) disputed the state's decision on the management of hazardous waste. The investor was denied a construction permit to operate a hazardous landfill after a lengthy negotiation process with the Mexican government. The investor claimed a breach of the FET standard.[691]

The investor claimed that it had relied on the federal approval of the project, through obtaining a federal construction permit. Mexico asserted that it was only the municipality that had the authority to issue a construction permit.[692] The permit had however been denied by the municipality on environmental grounds.[693] The tribunal ruled that the investor was correct in 'relying on the representations of the federal government'.[694] The tribunal explained that even if Mexico was right in asserting that the municipal construction permit was necessary, the 'federal authority's jurisdiction was controlling and the authority of the municipality only extended to appropriate

689. S. Bandali, 'Understanding FET: The Case for Protecting Contract-Based Legitimate Expectations', in I. Laird and others (eds) *Investment Treaty Arbitration and International Law* (Juris Publishing, 2014) 151.
690. *Metalclad v. Mexico*, ICSID Case No. ARB(AF)/97/1 Award (30 August 2000). For a more detailed discussion of this case, *see* section §7.02 [C].
691. *Metalclad v. Mexico*, ICSID Case No. ARB(AF)/97/1 Award (30 August 2000) para. 1.
692. *Ibid.*, para. 85.
693. *Ibid.*, para. 59.
694. *Ibid.*, para. 87.

construction considerations.'[695] In this case, the tribunal explained that the investor was 'entitled to rely on the representations of federal officials' which made the investor believe that it was 'entitled to continue its construction'.[696] The tribunal upheld the investor's claim that it could legitimately rely on the federal officials' assurance, who represented the state as a formal, competent authority.

The issue of state authority was also addressed in *Crystallex v. Venezuela*. In this case, Crystallex (the investor) had been working for several years to obtain all the necessary permits in order to start the exploitation of a gold mine in Venezuela. After seven years of securing permits and following the administrative procedures, the investor faced severe difficulties in obtaining the environmental permit that was ultimately denied. The tribunal found that general statements by politicians promising that the process would be successful were too general to generate legitimate expectations.[697]

However, a letter from the Ministry of the Environment, in which Crystallex's environmental impact assessment had been approved and that had promised that the 'permit would be handed over once the requisite bond was posted,' satisfied the level of specificity of the legitimate expectations required by the tribunal.[698] The tribunal further explained that even if 'the ... letter was not considered as the formal accreditation of the project, but rather as a mere request for a bond (as Venezuela and its experts contend), the explicit statements contained therein could not be disregarded'.[699] The tribunal specified that this letter had been provided by the 'Administrative Office of Permissions, which is in charge of processing the requests for the relevant permits' within the Ministry of the Environment.[700] The tribunal thereby underlined that the letter had been sent by a state authority, which was competent to represent Venezuela.

In this case, the letter itself did not constitute an approval for the project. However, the fact that the letter had been sent by the designated competent authority in charge of these permits led the tribunal to conclude that the letter had created a protected legitimate expectation on the part of the investor. As one commentator observed, in this case, the tribunal made it clear that 'the state's commitment should be generated by a specific state authority with relevant decision-making power'.[701] The tribunal pointed out that in order to satisfy the requirements for specificity, besides the necessity to have been generated by the competent authority, the state's representation

695. *Ibid.*, para. 86.
696. *Ibid.*
697. *Crystallex v. Venezuela*, ICSID Case No. ARB(AF)/11/2 Award (4 April 2016) para. 553. '[T]he "assurances" on which the Claimant relies are too general and indeterminate to found a claim of legitimate expectations under the Treaty. For example, it is clear that no legitimate expectation as to the issuance of the environmental Permit may be said to arise out of the rather generic statement by the Ministry of Mines in June 2005 that the Permit was "well on track"'.
698. *Crystallex v. Venezuela*, ICSID Case No. ARB(AF)/11/2 Award (4 April 2016) para. 561.
699. *Ibid.*
700. *Crystallex v. Venezuela*, ICSID Case No. ARB(AF)/11/2 Award (4 April 2016) para. 562.
701. S. Dudas, A Sovereign's Broken Promise: the Golden Ticket to a Billion-Dollar Award? (Kluwer Arbitration Blog, 2016) http://kluwerarbitrationblog.com/2016/06/21/a-sovereigns-broken-promise-the-golden-ticket-to-a-billion-dollar-award/ accessed on 12 June 2018.

towards the investor should also be 'sufficiently specific, i.e. it must be precise as to its content and clear as to its form,' and it should be 'addressed to the individual investor'.[702] These two latter elements of specificity have also been developed in other cases. They form the subject matter of the following two subsections.

[C] The Legal Force of the Specific Representations: (i) Their Legal Form, (ii) Their Content and (iii) Their Wording

In evaluating whether the investor's expectations are based on specific representations, tribunals – in a number of decisions – have evaluated the legal force of the state's representations by assessing: (i) the legal form of the specific representations and (ii) their content. Tribunals have also paid attention to (iii) the wording of the representations. Namely, how clearly and precisely the state's authority has expressed the particular promise directed towards the inducement or encouragement of a particular investment. These three aspects are discussed below.

(i) Legal form

The state's representations, claimed by an investor to generate legitimate expectations, can be expressed in a variety of legal forms, i.e. a licence agreement, a law, a letter, a political statement or a combination thereof.

Tribunals have been largely consistent in stating that a state's representations originating from political statements or speeches, unilaterally pronounced by an organ of the state, are not likely to generate legitimate expectations. An example of a case in which the tribunal upheld such a view is *PSEG v. Turkey*. This case was on the feasibility of investing in a power plant in Turkey by a US company PSEG, the North American Coal Corporation and the Turkish company owned by PSEG (together: the investors).[703] The *PSEG* tribunal explained that not all expectations would qualify as legitimate expectations, but only those which 'by definition require a promise of the administration on which the Claimants rely to assert a right that needs to be observed'.[704] The tribunal had not been convinced that general statements by the Turkish government, which attempted to attract investors to invest in the Turkish energy sector, had generated legitimate expectations. No specific representations by the state authority had been made to the investors.[705] Similarly, the tribunal in *El Paso*

702. *Crystallex v. Venezuela*, ICSID Case No. ARB(AF)/11/2 Award (4 April 2016) para. 547.
703. *PSEG v. Turkey*, ICSID Case No. ARB/02/5 Award (19 January 2007) para. 1. The request for arbitration was submitted by multiple claimants: 'PSEG Global Inc. (PSEG), a company incorporated under the laws of New Jersey, United States of America (USA); the North American Coal Corporation ("North American Coal"), a company incorporated under the laws of Delaware, USA; and Konya Ilgn Elektrik Üretim ve Ticaret Limited (the "Project Company"), described in the request for arbitration as a special purpose limited liability company incorporated under the laws of Turkey and wholly owned through several subsidiaries by PSEG (together referred to as the "Claimants")'.
704. *PSEG v. Turkey*, ICSID Case No. ARB/02/5 Award (19 January 2007) para. 241.
705. *Ibid.*, para. 243.

v. Argentina clearly indicated that presidential statements can persuade investors to invest but that it is not possible 'to rely on these proposals to claim legal guarantees'.[706]

This point was addressed in more detail in the *Continental v. Argentina* case. Here, a US company, Continental (the investor), had relied on 'a series of acts and pronouncements by Argentina's authorities that the original currency convertibility regime adopted before the crisis will be maintained'.[707] In particular, the investor relied on general political statements and general legislative acts. The tribunal assessed the different types of 'factors' that were relevant for the claim based on a breach of legitimate expectations.[708] The tribunal stated that the unilateral representations of a state expressed in political statements have 'the least legal value'.[709] Such statements may have had the impact of inducing the investor, but in the absence of any other state representations, they were unable to generate the legitimate expectations protected under the FET standard.[710] The tribunal further elaborated that 'general legislative statements engender reduced expectations.'[711] The conditions under which such statements may give rise to the protection of an investor's legitimate expectations will be discussed in section §6.04, which addresses the issue of investors' expectations referring to the stability of a general regulatory framework.

Further elaboration on the importance of the legal form of a state's representation has been provided in the *Glamis v. United States* award.[712] In this case, a Canadian gold mining company, Glamis (the investor), invested in an area in the Californian desert conservation zone. When the investor was not able to proceed with its project due to procedures and regulations imposed by the state, the investor relied on the general mining legislation in substantiating its claim for the protection of its legitimate expectations.[713] The tribunal in *Glamis v. United States* asserted that only specific representations would generate legitimate expectations, describing such a representation as a 'quasi-contractual relationship between the State and the investor, whereby the State has purposely and specifically induced the investment'.[714] In the same vein, in *Venezuela Holding v. Venezuela*, the tribunal underlined that an investor's legitimate expectations would only be protected if they are based on 'specific formal assurances given by the host state in order to induce investment'.[715] The tribunal explained that

706. *El Paso v. Argentina*, ICSID Case No. ARB/03/15 Award (31 October 2011) para. 395.
707. *Continental Casualty v. Argentina*, ICSID Case No. ARB/03/9 Award (5 September 2008) para. 252.
708. *Ibid.*, para. 260.
709. *Ibid.*, para. 261.
710. *Ibid.* Also *see* the analysis of this case by T. Wongkaew, The Transplantation of Legitimate Expectations in Investment Treaty Arbitration in P. Lazo et al. *The Role of the State in Investor-state Arbitration* (Brill, 2015) 90.
711. *Continental Casualty v. Argentina*, ICSID Case No. ARB/03/9 Award (5 September 2008) para. 261.
712. *Glamis v. US* [2009] NAFTA, ICSID 48 ILM 1039 Award (8 June 2009).
713. *Ibid.*, paras 633-634, 637.
714. *Ibid.*, para. 766.
715. *Venezuela Holdings B.V. et al v. Venezuela*, ICSID Case No. ARB/07/27 Award (9 October 2014) para. 256.

the specific representations should be of a formal and official character, with the specific goal of encouraging investment.[716]

(ii) Content

The other aspect on which the legal force of a state's representation depends is the content of the representation provided by a host state to an investor. The content of the state's representation should include a 'specific inducement for the investment'.[717] In *Glamis v. United States*, the investor relied on the general mining law as the source of its legitimate expectations. The tribunal stated that this general law, relied upon by the investor, did not meet the threshold of the state 'purposely and specifically induc[ing] the investment'.[718] The tribunal concluded that the federal government 'did not make specific commitments to induce the Claimant to persevere with its mining claims'.[719] In evaluating the mining legislation, the tribunal asserted that the government had not guaranteed the approval of its claims, nor 'did it offer the Claimant any benefits to pursuing such claims beyond the customary chance to exploit federal land for possible profit'.[720] The tribunal clarified that the mere disappointment of the investor would not suffice to upset its expectations.

In *Venezuela Holding v. Venezuela*, the tribunal also underlined that the content of the state's representation should be directed at the specific inducement of an investor.[721] In this case, the investor argued that it had relied on the 'Framework of Conditions of the Association Agreement' (the Association Agreement) agreed upon by the investor and the state. It stipulated that the level of oil production would remain at the same level as originally promised by the state. The investor claimed that by enforcing production and export curtailments, the state had breached the legitimate expectations of the investor. The tribunal examined the state's original representations expressed in the Association Agreement concerning the exploitation, upgrading and marketing of extra-heavy crude oil to be produced in the Cerro Negro area of the Orinoco Oil Belt, which had been approved by the Congress of Venezuela on 24 April 1997.[722] According to the Association Agreement, the level of extra-heavy oil production had been set at 120,000 barrels per day.[723]

The tribunal asserted that according to the terms of the Association Agreement, 'the Claimants [investors] could reasonably and legitimately have expected to produce at least 120,000 barrels per day of extra-heavy crude oil and that their production would not be unilaterally reduced at a lower level ...'.[724] The only exception to the

716. In para. 257, the tribunal indicated the formal character of the Association Agreement underlining that it had been approved by the Congress of Venezuela. In para. 258, the tribunal referred to the agreed terms in the Association Agreement on the level of production.
717. *Glamis v. US* [2009] NAFTA, ICSID 48 ILM 1039 Award (8 June 2009) para. 766.
718. *Ibid.*
719. *Glamis v. US* [2009] NAFTA, ICSID 48 ILM 1039 Award (8 June 2009) para. 767.
720. *Ibid.*
721. *Venezuela Holdings B.V. et al v. Venezuela*, ICSID Case No. ARB/07/27 Award (9 October 2014) para. 256.
722. *Ibid.*, para. 257.
723. *Ibid.*, para. 260.
724. *Ibid.*

quantity of the daily oil production set at a minimum of 120,000 barrels was included in condition 13 of the Association Agreement. Condition 13 provided that '[i]f the Parties are required to reduce their production as a result of the international commitments of the Republic of Venezuela, such reduction shall not exceed the reduction percentage generally applicable to the national oil industry as a whole.'[725]

Problems between Venezuela and the investor arose in 2006 when Venezuela imposed production and export curtailments leading to a reduction in the production of oil to below 120,000 barrels per day, contrary to what had been determined and guaranteed by the Association Agreement.[726] In establishing that these measures were not subject to the exception in condition 13, the tribunal ruled that the 'production and export curtailments imposed from November 2006 were incompatible with the Claimant's reasonable and legitimate expectations.'[727] In this case, the terms of the Association Agreement constituted the content of the representation and satisfied the criteria for the protection of legitimate expectations outlined by the tribunal, namely that these expectations had to derive from 'specific formal assurances given by the host state in order to induce investment'.[728]

In *Mamidoil v. Albania*, the tribunal further defined how the content of representations played a role in determining whether they were specific representations. In this case, a Greek company, Mamidoil (the investor), invested in Albania by undertaking the task of constructing and operating an oil terminal in the port of Durrës. In order to do so, Mamidoil entered into a lease contract that stipulated the lease of the land in the Durrës region for twenty years. However, in later years, the Albanian authorities wanted to relocate the project for environmental and socio-economic reasons. In this case, the tribunal assessed whether the lease contract qualified as a specific assurance that the company could use the designated port area for building and operating the oil terminal.[729] The investor claimed that, following the lease contract, it had the right to use the specific port facilities for tankers. The tribunal did not interpret the terms of the lease contract in the same way, however. It agreed that the contract allowed the company to build and operate the oil terminal, but:

> [T]he business plan, in turn, does not mention the use of port facilities for tankers. The wording and meaning of these clauses and text taken together do not allow an interpretation that implicitly includes the right to discharge petroleum vessels in the port.[730]

The tribunal further explained that if the parties were to include the right for the investor to use these specific port facilities, this was to be made 'explicit, as a specific

725. *Venezuela Holdings B.V. et al v. Venezuela*, ICSID Case No. ARB/07/27 Award (9 October 2014) para. 259.
726. *Ibid.*, para. 264.
727. *Ibid.*
728. *Venezuela Holdings B.V. et al v. Venezuela*, ICSID Case No. ARB/07/27 Award (9 October 2014) para. 256.
729. The oil terminal in this case referred to a facility for the storage of oil which the investor wanted to build in the port of Durrës.
730. *Mamidoil Jetoil Greek Petroleum Products Société S.A. v. Republic of Albania*, ICSID Case No. ARB/11/24 Award (30 March 2015) para. 648.

and detailed right and with probable repercussions on the calculation of the rent'.[731] Considering that this specific right had not been included in the contract, and no other specific assurances or representations had been made by the state, the claim by the investor on the basis of the protection of its legitimate expectations based on specific state representations had not been satisfied.

In *Masdar Solar v. Spain*, the tribunal, in assessing the specific nature of the state's representations, had primarily focused on the content of the state's commitment.[732] In this case, the investor[733] had made his investments in three concentrated solar power (CSP) plants in Spain based on the state's special regime for renewable energy established by RD661/2007.[734] This regime provided various benefits for producers of renewable energy, e.g. remuneration that was based upon a feed-in tariff for the lifetime of the investment.[735] The investor's three plants were also registered, initially in the pre-allocation registry, and afterwards in the Registro Administrativo de Instalaciones de Producción en Régimen Especial.[736] As a part of the preregistration process, each plant of the investor received a separate letter (entitled: Resolution) from the Spanish Directorate General for Energy Policy and Mines. In these Resolutions, it was provided that each plant had been registered in the Pre-Allocation Registry for Compensation and was subject to the application of the special economic regime provided by Royal Decree 661/2007.[737]

However, in 2010, and further in 2012, 2013 and 2014, as a result of the tariff deficit and the economic crisis experienced by Spain,[738] the host state dispensed with the special regime through a series of laws and regulations.[739] The investor's financial position had been affected by the abolition of the incentive-based special regime and its replacement by a far less beneficial regulatory framework.[740] To seek compensation in the form of damages, the investor initiated investment proceedings against Spain,

---

731. *Ibid.*
732. *Masdar Solar & Wind Cooperatief U.A. v. Kingdom of Spain*, ICSID Case No. ARB/14/1 Award (16 May 2018).
733. *Masdar Solar & Wind Cooperatief U.A. v. Kingdom of Spain*, ICSID Case No. ARB/14/1 Award (16 May 2018) para. 82. Claimant: 'Masdar, is owned and controlled by Abu Dhabi Future Energy Company ("ADFEC"), which at all material times has owned 99% of the share capital of Claimant,' although the company, Masdar Solar & Wind Cooperatief U.A., had been incorporated in the Netherlands (para. 2).
734. *Masdar Solar & Wind Cooperatief U.A. v. Kingdom of Spain*, ICSID Case No. ARB/14/1 Award (16 May 2018) para. 115.
735. *Ibid.*, para. 84.
736. *Ibid.*, para. 513.
737. *Ibid.*, para. 516. A. Johannesson Linden, F. Kalantzis, E. Maincent, J. Pienkowski, Electricity Tariff Deficit: Temporary or Permanent problem in the EU? In this report, the authors explain that 'Tariff deficits are shortfalls of revenues in the electricity system, which arise when the tariffs for the regulated components of the retail electricity price are set below the corresponding costs borne by the energy companies.' http://ec.europa.eu/economy_finance/publications/economic_paper/2014/ecp534_en.htm accessed on 27 September 2018.
738. *See* Chapter 6, section §6.05[D] for a further analysis and assessment of the special circumstances concerning the Spanish renewable energy cases.
739. *Masdar Solar & Wind Cooperatief U.A. v. Kingdom of Spain*, ICSID Case No. ARB/14/1 Award (16 May 2018) paras 120-136.
740. *Ibid.*, para. 467.

claiming a violation of the FET standard under Article 10(1) of the ECT.[741] The investor claimed that Spain, by introducing the disputed measures, had breached his legitimate expectations, i.e., that the conditions, which were established under the special regime of 2007, would last for the lifetime of his investments.[742]

In assessing the claim concerning the breach of legitimate expectations under the FET standard, the tribunal determined that the Resolutions,[743] provided by the Directorate General for Energy Policy and Mines and addressed to each of the operating companies of the investor in a separate letter, qualified as specific representations.[744] The tribunal stressed that the content of these Resolutions specified that each operating company fell under the regime created by RD661/2007 and that this regime would apply for the 'operational lifetime' of each company.[745] Therefore, the tribunal concluded that the investor could have legitimately expected that the beneficial regime of 2007 would last for the entire time of his operations.[746] The tribunal considered the Resolutions to be a specific inducement for the investment because these representations were formulated in specific terms and addressed individually to each plant owned by the investor.[747]

(iii) Wording

The content of a state's representation is interlinked with the way in which such an assurance is phrased. Several tribunals have emphasised this aspect in deciding on the specific nature of a state's representation.

In *Glamis v. US*, the tribunal underlined that in order for a state's representation to qualify as being specific, it should be formulated as 'the active inducement of a quasi-contractual expectation'.[748] More precisely, the tribunal explained that the language in the legislation of California – referred to by the investor – was too general and did not provide a specific inducement for the investor to conduct mineral exploration and exploitation in the area within the Californian desert conservation zone. Therefore, according to the tribunal, 'the quasi-contractual inducement' that was a 'prerequisite for consideration of a breach of Article 1105(1) of NAFTA based upon repudiated investor expectations' had not been met.[749]

In *Crystallex v. Venezuela*, the wording in the letter sent to Crystallex (the investor) by the Ministry of the Environment constituted one of the key aspects for the tribunal in its considerations on the question whether the state's assurance was

741. *Ibid.*, para. 390. Please note that the investor, in addition to the compensation, also requested 'full restitution to the Claimant by re-establishing the situation which existed prior to Spain's breaches of the ECT' (para. 138).
742. *Masdar Solar & Wind Cooperatief U.A. v. Kingdom of Spain*, ICSID Case No. ARB/14/1 Award (16 May 2018) paras 461, 463-467.
743. *Ibid.*, para. 516.
744. *Ibid.*, para. 520.
745. *Ibid.*
746. *Masdar Solar & Wind Cooperatief U.A. v. Kingdom of Spain*, ICSID Case No. ARB/14/1 Award (16 May 2018) para. 521.
747. *Ibid.*, para. 517.
748. *Glamis v. US* [2009] NAFTA, ICSID 48 ILM 1039 Award (8 June 2009) para. 799.
749. *Ibid.*, para. 767.

sufficiently specific. Crystallex had argued that the letter from the Ministry of the Environment in which Crystallex's environmental impact assessment had been approved, which in turn was a necessary step to obtain the permit to exploit the gold mine in Venezuela, constituted a specific representation. The tribunal agreed with the investor, explaining that the letter contained an explicit promise that the 'permit would be handed over once the requisite bond was posted.'[750] In the view of the tribunal, the words 'handed over' demonstrated the concrete character of the representation.[751]

In *Mamidoil v. Albania*, the tribunal further clarified that the state's representation should be formulated as 'a clear and identifiable commitment, which is attributable to the person who makes the representation, and which is reasonably conveyed to the addressee'.[752]

To sum up the findings in this section §6.03[C], the legal force of a state's representation depends on its legal form, its content and its wording. In terms of the legal form of a state's representation, it should be a specific formal representation that creates a legal claim for an investor. Additionally, the content of a specific representation should be directed at the purposeful encouragement and inducement of the investment. This excludes general statements, such as political speeches or general laws; these do not create a specific right on the part of the investor. Finally, also the wording of a representation is important to consider: it should reinforce its content by including words that convey a clear and identifiable commitment.

Alongside the assessment of the first two requirements relating to the specificity of a state's representation, i.e., that the representation has to be rendered by the competent authority and must have legal force, tribunals also consider how the investor has been designated in the state's representations. This element is addressed in the next section.

[D] The Designation of the Investor in the State's Representations

For the recognition of the legitimate expectations of an investor based on a state's specific representation, some tribunals require that the representation must be directed at a concrete investor.[753] This requirement has been further clarified in the following cases.

The tribunal in *El Paso v. Argentina* emphasised that the level of specificity of a representation should be assessed from the point of view of the addressee.[754] In particular, the specific representation should be:

> *directly made to the investor* – e.g., in the contract or in a letter of intent, or even through a specific promise in a person-to-person business meeting – and not

750. *Crystallex v. Venezuela*, ICSID Case No. ARB(AF)/11/2 Award (4 April 2016) para. 561.
751. *Ibid.*
752. *Mamidoil Jetoil Greek Petroleum Products Société S.A. v. Republic of Albania*, ICSID Case No. ARB/11/24 Award (30 March 2015) para. 643.
753. M. Potestà, 'Legitimate Expectations in Investment Treaty Law: Understanding the Roots and the Limits of a Controversial Concept' [2013] 28(1) *ICSID Review*, 21.
754. *El Paso v. Argentina*, ICSID Case No. ARB/03/15 Award (31 October 2011) para. 375.

> simply general statements in treaties or legislation which, because of their nature of general regulations, can evolve.[755]

The tribunal in *Total v. Argentina* asserted that the clearer a particular investor is defined in the context of a state's representation, the more it will be entitled to rely on that state's representation. Put differently, the 'more specific the declaration to the addressee(s), the more credible the claim that such an addressee (the foreign investor concerned) was entitled to rely on it for the future in a context of reciprocal trust and good faith.'[756]

The tribunal in *Charanne v. Spain* clarified when the state's representation does not qualify as being specifically directed at the investor.[757] In this case, the company Grupo T-Solar Global S.A (T-Solar) claimed that Spain had unlawfully amended the special regime created for the photovoltaic (PV) solar energy sector that led to various losses by the company.[758] T-Solar asserted that in the early 2000s, Spain created a special legal regime in order to promote renewable energy that included various incentives (e.g., benefits and bonuses) for investors in the solar panel sector. However, a few years later, in 2010, Spain adopted a series of measures that negatively impacted the production of electricity generated by solar PV units. The investor's main argument was that Spain had unlawfully undermined the stability of the legal framework on which the investor had relied.[759]

The tribunal underlined that Spain's special regime, aimed at the promotion of renewable energy, had not been directed specifically at the claimant. In particular, the tribunal rejected the argument of the investor that the regulations implemented by Spain and directed at a limited group of investors would qualify as being specific.[760] These laws were not directed at a specific investor, and the invoked regulations therefore '[did] not lose the general nature that characterizes any law or regulation by their specific scope'.[761] The tribunal further warned against qualifying a regulation that involved a group of beneficiaries rather than a particular investor as 'specific'. According to the tribunal, this could 'constitute an excessive limitation on the power of states to regulate the economy in accordance with public interest'.[762]

In *Philip Morris v. Uruguay*, a tobacco company, Philip Morris (the investor), challenged the tobacco control measures introduced by Uruguay as a part of the state's anti-smoking policy.[763] Some measures restricted the investor in including its trademarks on cigarette packages. The investor claimed damages because these new measures had led to a reduction of its return in Uruguay. The tribunal in this case observed that Uruguay had not provided specific representations to the investor that

755. *Ibid*. Emphasis added by the tribunal.
756. *Total v. Argentina*, ICSID Case No. ARB/04/01 Decision on Liability (27 December 2010) para. 121.
757. *Charanne Construction v. Spain*, SCC Case No. 062/2012 Award (21 January 2016).
758. *Ibid*., para. 80.
759. *Ibid*., para. 478.
760. *Ibid*., para. 493.
761. *Ibid*.
762. *Ibid*.
763. This case will be further explained and addressed in Chapter 6, in sections §6.02 and §6.03.

the tobacco policy would not be changed.[764] The tribunal did not agree with the investor that the general legislation concerning the protection of trademarks constituted a specific representation to Philip Morris with regard to its trademarks and the use thereof.[765] It noted that 'provisions of general legislation applicable to a plurality of persons or of a category of persons do not create legitimate expectations.'[766]

[E] Specific Representations Arising from Contractual Commitments

A special form of specific representations is contractual commitments between a host state and an individual investor. Contracts between a host state and an investor are very common in the context of projects involving, e.g., natural resources. Consequently, investors often refer to their contractual arrangements with a state in order to argue that such a state had induced them to make a particular investment.[767] However, as will be explained in this section, for contractual commitments, in order to constitute a specific representation that may give rise to the protection of the legitimate expectations of an investor under the FET standard, it is not sufficient that those commitments comply with the requirements addressed in sections §6.03[B]-§6.03[E]. Ordinary contractual breaches, even if they comply with the test of specificity, are usually not protected by the notion of legitimate expectations under the IIA's FET standard.

Under customary international law, a violation of a contract does not automatically imply a violation of a treaty.[768] The tribunal in *Noble Ventures v. Romania* explained this international rule by providing that it is:

> A well established rule of general international law that in normal circumstances per se a breach of a contract by the State does not give rise to direct international responsibility on the part of the State. This derives from the clear distinction between municipal law on the one hand and international law on the other, two separate legal systems.[769]

Contractual breaches of an agreement between a state and an investor are commonly governed by the law which has been agreed upon by the parties or, in the absence of such an agreement, this has to be determined by the relevant conflict of law rules.[770] Typically, the domestic law of a host state is the law which governs any

764. *Philip Morris v. Uruguay*, ICSID Case No. ARB/10/7 Award (8 July 2016) para. 429.
765. *Ibid.*, para. 431.
766. *Ibid.*, para. 426.
767. S. Bandali, 'Understanding FET: The Case for Protecting Contract-Based Legitimate Expectations', in I. Laird and others (eds) *Investment Treaty Arbitration and International Law* (Juris Publishing, 2014) 154. *See* the examples of investment cases, demonstrating this point: *Continental Casualty v. Argentina*, ICSID Case No. ARB/03/9 Award (5 September 2008) para. 261; *Venezuela Holdings B.V. et al v. Venezuela*, ICSID Case No. ARB/07/27 Award (9 October 2014) para. 256.
768. M. Shaw, International Law (Cambridge, 7th edn., 2014) 51; J. Crawford, Brownlie's Principles of Public International Law (Oxford, 8th edn., 2012) 23-27.
769. *Noble Ventures v. Romania* [2005] ICSID Case No. ARB/01/11 Award (12 October 2005), para. 53.
770. M. Sasson, Substantive Law in Investment Treaty Arbitration: The Unsettled Relationship Between International Law and Municipal Law (2nd edn.), Chapter 6: 'Treaty Versus Contract Claims, and Umbrella Clauses: When a Contract Breach May Become a Treaty Breach' [2017] 21 *International Arbitration Law Library* (Kluwer, 2017) 200.

contractual disputes between that state and an investor. The national courts usually constitute the competent forum for contractual disputes.[771] However, in some investment cases, a breach of a contract that is tied to an investment falls under the jurisdiction of investment tribunals.[772] In these cases, tribunals have sometimes found that the expectations of an investor arising out of the contract may engender legitimate expectations as tested under the FET standard.[773] In the following paragraphs, it will be explored under what conditions a breach of contractual commitments by a host state may give rise to the protection of the legitimate expectations of an investor as an element of the FET standard.

In investment jurisprudence, tribunals usually distinguish between expectations arising from contractual commitments, on the one hand, and legitimate expectations, on the other. The latter are protected as an element of the FET standard under IIAs.[774] As the tribunal in *Impregilo v. Argentina* stressed, 'the existence of legitimate expectations and the existence of contractual rights are two separate issues.'[775] This tribunal clarified that contractual rights should be distinguished from treaty rights, the relevant criterion being 'whether the State or its entities act as holders of sovereign power or as parties to a contract'.[776]

In the decision on the question of jurisdiction in *Joy Mining Machinery v. Egypt*, the tribunal explained the distinction between the state as the body that exercises sovereign power and the state that acts as a commercial party. According to the tribunal, such a distinction lies in an exploration of whether a state has been involved in some form of interference with the operation of the contract.[777] Only if such

771. C. Annacker, 'The Role of Investors' Legitimate Expectations in Defense of Investment Treaty Claims', in A.K. Bjorklund (ed.) *Yearbook on International Investment Law and Policy, 2013-2014* (Oxford University Press, 2015) 234.
772. M. Sasson, Substantive Law in Investment Treaty Arbitration: The Unsettled Relationship Between International Law and Municipal Law (2nd Edn.), Chapter 6: Treaty Versus Contract Claims, and Umbrella Clauses: When a Contract Breach May Become a Treaty Breach' [2017] 21 *International Arbitration Law Library* (Kluwer, 2017) 200.
773. M. Potestà, 'Legitimate Expectations in Investment Treaty Law: Understanding the Roots and the Limits of a Controversial Concept' [2013] 28(1) *ICSID Review*, 103; T. Wongkaew, 'The Transplantation of Legitimate Expectations in Investment Treaty Arbitration', in P. Lazo et al. *The Role of the State in Investor-state Arbitration* (Brill, 2015), 84; S. Bandali, 'Understanding FET: The Case for Protecting Contract-Based Legitimate Expectations', in I. Laird and others (eds) *Investment Treaty Arbitration and International Law* (Juris Publishing, 2014).
774. *Parkerings v. Lithuania*, 2007, para. 344. *Gustav F W Hamester GmbH & Co KG v. Republic of Ghana*, paras 332-335. *Duke v. Ecuador*, ICSID Case No. ARB/04/19 Award 2008, paras 348-361. *Impregilo S.p.A v. Argentina*, ICSID Case No. ARB/07/17 Award (21 June 2011) para. 292.
775. *Impregilo S.p.A v. Argentina*, ICSID Case No. ARB/07/17 Award (21 June 2011) para. 292.
776. *Ibid.*, para. 296. *See also* the other decisions that asserted that it is only where a state exercises its sovereign authority that a breach of contract may also lead to a breach of a treaty provision, such as the FET standard: *Impregilo S.p.A v. Islamic Republic of Pakistan*, ICSID Case No. ARB/03/3 Decision on Jurisdiction (22 April 2005) para. 260. *Bayindir Insaat Turizm Ticaret Ve Sanayi A.S. v. Islamic Republic of Pakistan*, ICSID Case No. ARB/03/29 Award (27 August 2009) para. 377.
777. *Joy Mining Machinery v. Egypt*, ICSID Case No. ARB/03/11 Decision on Jurisdiction (6 August 2004) para. 72. Also *see*: *CMS v. Argentina*, ICSID Case No. ARB/01/8 (12 May 2005), para. 299. The tribunal came to a similar conclusion as in *Joy Mining Machinery*, stating that: 'Purely commercial aspects of a contract might not be protected by the treaty in some situations, but

interference goes beyond a contractual breach, i.e. requiring an 'allegation of a specific violation of treaty rights as the foundation of [tribunal] jurisdiction', can the state be regarded to act in its capacity of sovereign authority.[778] The tribunal in *Joy Mining Machinery v. Egypt* found that the non-release of a bank guarantee - the subject of the investor's claim under the treaty - was a commercial matter and did not qualify as interference by the state. In this case, according to the tribunal, the link between the treaty and the contract was lacking. The tribunal provided that the state not releasing bank guarantees amounted to a commercial dispute that had not 'transformed into an investment or an investment dispute'.[779]

In *Duke Energy v. Ecuador*, the tribunal discussed in which circumstances the state should be regarded as acting in its capacity as a sovereign authority in a contractual situation. The purpose of the discussion was to decide whether the breaches under the so-called PPAs, which had been entered into by the state-owned company and the investors, met the criteria of a violation of the FET standard.[780] The tribunal found that the acts carried out by the state-owned company, including the 'non-payment of interest on late payments' and the 'irregular imposition of contract fines', did not constitute 'the exercise of sovereign power'.[781] These acts by the state-owned company, according to the tribunal, qualified as ordinary contractual breaches between commercial parties and, therefore, did not constitute a violation of the FET standard under the applicable IIA.

Besides the requirement that the state had acted in its capacity as a sovereign authority, the tribunals in some FET decisions required more in order to come to the conclusion that the contractual expectations of an investor had to be protected under the FET standard. They mentioned that for such a conclusion additional violations under the treaty, such as 'discrimination',[782] or 'outright and unjustified repudiation of the transaction'[783] or the denial of justice,[784] are required.[785] For example, in *Parkerings*

the protection is likely to be available when there is significant interference by governments or public agencies with the rights of the investor'.

778. *Joy Mining Machinery v. Egypt*, ICSID Case No. ARB/03/11 Decision on Jurisdiction (6 August 2004) para. 75. The same conclusion has been reached in: *Compañía de Aguas del Aconquija S.A. and Vivendi Universal v. Argentine Republic* (ICSID Case No. ARB/97/3), Decision on application for annulment, (3 July 2002) para. 113.
779. *Joy Mining Machinery v. Egypt*, ICSID Case No. ARB/03/11 Decision on Jurisdiction (6 August 2004) para. 79.
780. In this case, the state-owned company was the *Instituto Ecuatoriano de Electrificación* ('INECEL'), the entity established under the Ministry of Natural Resources and Energy of Ecuador in order 'to carry out the functions of power generation, transmission, and distribution'. *Duke v. Ecuador*, ICSID Case No. ARB/04/19 Award 2008, para. 10.
781. *Duke Energy v. Ecuador*, ICSID Case No. ARB/04/19 Award 2008, para. 348.
782. *Glamis v. US* [2009] NAFTA, ICSID 48 ILM 1039 Award (8 June 2009) para. 620.
783. *Waste Management v. Mexico II* [2004] ICSID Case No. ARB(AF)/00/3 Award (30 April 2004), para. 115. In deciding whether the contractual breach could give rise to a breach of the FET standard, the tribunal stated: 'For present purposes it is sufficient to say that even the persistent non-payment of debts by a municipality is not to be equated with a violation of Article 1105, provided that it does not amount to an outright and unjustified repudiation of the transaction and provided that some remedy is open to the creditor to address the problem'.
784. *Parkerings v. Lithuania*, ICSID Case No. ARB/05/8 Award (11 September 2007) para. 316; *Glamis v. US* [2009] NAFTA, ICSID 48 ILM 1039 Award (8 June 2009) para. 620.
785. M. Potestà, 'Legitimate Expectations in Investment Treaty Law: Understanding the Roots and the Limits of a Controversial Concept' [2013] 28(1) *ICSID Review*, 105; T. Wongkaew, 'The

v. Lithuania, the tribunal discussed under which conditions contractual expectations could be protected under the FET standard. This case concerned an investor's contract to construct and to maintain parking facilities in the historical town of Vilnius. Certain changes to national law, however, prevented the realisation of the investor's project and eventually resulted in the termination of the contract. The investor filed a claim for a breach of the FET standard under the Norway-Lithuania BIT.[786] In analysing whether, under the FET standard, an investor may rely on expectations arising out of a contract with the state, the tribunal stated:

> It is evident that not every hope amounts to an expectation under international law.
>
> The expectation a party to an agreement may have of the regular fulfilment of the obligation by the other party is not necessarily an expectation protected by international law. In other words, contracts involve intrinsic expectations from each party that do not amount to expectations as understood in international law. Indeed, the party whose *contractual expectations* are frustrated should, under specific conditions, seek redress before a national tribunal *[emphasis added.]*[787]

The tribunal found that the investor's expectations that the 'alleged contractual obligation of the Municipality to inform [the investor] of the future modification of the law' were of a contractual nature.[788] The tribunal concluded that 'the acts and omission of the Municipality of Vilnius' could have violated the contract, but this did not mean that 'they are inconsistent with the Treaty.'[789] The same tribunal provided that, in principle, contractual breaches may result in treaty breaches, but only 'under certain limited circumstances, a substantial breach of a contract could constitute a violation of a treaty.'[790]

These limited conditions include the situation in which an investor is denied access to the domestic courts and hence is deprived of its right to 'obtain redress of the injury and to complain about those contractual breaches'.[791] In *Glamis v. US*, the tribunal underlined that a mere breach of contract, 'without something further such as denial of justice or discrimination, normally will not suffice to establish a breach under Article 1105 of NAFTA'.[792] The *Glamis* tribunal did not elaborate any further on this point.

To conclude this section, a mere breach of contractual obligations does not give rise to protection under the FET standard based on the argument of the legitimate

---

Transplantation of Legitimate Expectations in Investment Treaty Arbitration', in P. Lazo et al. *The Role of the State in Investor-State Arbitration* (Brill, 2015), 85.

786. *Parkerings v. Lithuania*, ICSID Case No. ARB/05/8 Award (11 September 2007) para. 316; *Glamis v. US* [2009] NAFTA, ICSID 48 ILM 1039 Award (8 June 2009) paras 195-197.
787. *Ibid.*, para. 344.
788. *Ibid.*, para. 342.
789. *Ibid.*, para. 345.
790. *Ibid.*
791. *Parkerings v. Lithuania*, ICSID Case No. ARB/05/8 Award (11 September 2007) para. 316; *Glamis v. US* [2009] NAFTA, ICSID 48 ILM 1039 Award (8 June 2009) para. 317.
792. *Glamis v. US* [2009] NAFTA, ICSID 48 ILM 1039 Award (8 June 2009) para. 620.

expectations of the investor.[793] In deciding whether a breach of contractual commitments meets the requirements needed for the protection of legitimate expectations under the FET, the relevant criterion is whether the state in its role as a contractual party has acted in its capacity as a sovereign authority or as a commercial party. As pointed out by Wongkaew, 'the element of sovereign power may be conceived as a procedural fulfillment of the rule that only a sovereign State acting with sovereign power can incur international responsibility.'[794] Tribunals generally provide that only if the state acts in a sovereign capacity may a breach of the FET standard be assumed. The question of whether the state has exercised its sovereign capacity depends on whether the state or its organs has exerted some sort of interference with the operation of the contract.[795] Such interference has to extend beyond a contractual breach. The state can be regarded to have acted in its capacity as a sovereign authority if its actions fall under a 'specific violation of treaty rights as the foundation of [tribunal] jurisdiction'. [796] The *Duke v. Ecuador* tribunal explained that actions of the state, such as the 'irregular imposition of contract fines', cannot be considered to amount to 'the exercise of sovereign power', but rather should be seen as ordinary contractual breaches.[797] Even if the requirement that the state has acted in its sovereign capacity in the contractual relationship is fulfilled, some tribunals have nevertheless underlined that the mere breach of the contract will still not suffice for establishing that the legitimate expectations of the investor should be protected under the FET standard. They imply that additional treaty violations, e.g. a denial of justice or discrimination, are required in order to come to a decision that the FET standard has been breached.[798]

[F] Summary: Defining Specific Representations

Most investment tribunals tend to specify that only a host state's specific representations to a certain investor can form the basis for a claim by the investor that it had legitimate expectations.[799] To determine whether the representations qualify as specific, tribunals usually pose three questions:

793. M. Potestà, 'Legitimate Expectations in Investment Treaty Law: Understanding the Roots and the Limits of a Controversial Concept' [2013] 28(1) *ICSID Review*, 101. M. Sasson, 'Treaty Versus Contract Claims, and Umbrella Clauses: When a Contract Breach May Become a Treaty Breach', in M. Sasson *Substantive Law in Investment Treaty Arbitration: The Unsettled Relationship between International Law and Municipal Law* (2nd edn.), International Arbitration Law Library, Volume 21 (Kluwer, 2017) 200.

794. T. Wongkaew, 'The Transplantation of Legitimate Expectations in Investment Treaty Arbitration', in P. Lazo et al. *The Role of the State in Investor-state Arbitration* (Brill, 2015), p. 85.

795. *Joy Mining Machinery v. Egypt*, ICSID Case No. ARB/03/11 Decision on Jurisdiction (6 August 2004) para. 72.

796. *Ibid.*, para. 75. The same conclusion was reached in: *Compañía de Aguas del Aconquija S.A. and Vivendi Universal v. Argentine Republic* (ICSID Case No. ARB/97/3), Decision on application for annulment, (3 July 2002) para. 113.

797. *Duke Energy v. Ecuador*, para. 348.

798. *Glamis v. US* [2009] NAFTA, ICSID 48 ILM 1039 Award (8 June 2009) para. 620.

799. This is also consistent with the UNCTAD report on the FET standard; UNCTAD 'Fair and Equitable Treatment: UNCTAD Series on International Investment Agreements II' (New York, 2012) 68.

(1) Have the representations been made by a competent state authority?
(2) What is the legal force of the specific representations in terms of their legal form, their content and their wording? And:
(3) Has the investor been directly designated in the state's representations?

With regard to the first question, almost half of the tribunals in the examined cases decided that in order to be able to protect the expectations of an investor, the state's representations that have generated the expectations must be provided to the investor by a competent state authority that has relevant decision-making power.[800]

Regarding the second question, most of the tribunals in the examined cases have underlined that only specific state representations warrant the protection of the investor's expectations. This means that such representations must concern a formal commitment aimed at a purposeful and specific inducement of investment.[801] The content and wording expressed in the state's representations have to be 'explicit', 'specific' and to contain 'detailed right[s]' provided to an investor.[802]

Relating the third question, half of the tribunals in the selected cases have been consistent in stating that the state's representations should be directly addressed to the particular investor. [803] It has been emphasised by tribunals that a specific representation reaching out to a group of investors is insufficient in this respect.[804]

In respect of the contracts concluded between a host state and an investor *under the national law* of the host state within the framework of FET disputes, the following observations should be made. In principle, such contractual commitments do not play a role in international investment disputes. However, an investor's expectations arising out of such a private law contract with the host state can become relevant as an element of the state's FET obligation in the situation where the host state – in its role as a contractual party – has exercised its sovereign authority.[805] Any ordinary contractual breaches committed by the host state are unlikely to give rise to the protection of legitimate expectations. This would only be different if the contractual breaches were to involve, e.g., 'some forms of State interference with the operation of the contract'.[806] Some tribunals have also underlined that next to the condition that a state acts in its sovereign capacity as a party to a contract, other treaty violations, such as a violation of due process or discrimination, need to be established to support a decision of the tribunal that a breach of contractual obligations by a host state has also undermined the legitimate expectations of an investor under the FET standard.

800. *Metalclad v. Mexico,* ICSID Case No. ARB(AF)/97/1 Award (30 August 2000) para. 86; *Crystallex v. Venezuela,* ICSID Case No. ARB(AF)/11/2 Award (4 April 2016) paras 561-562. *Total v. Argentina,* ICSID Case No. ARB/04/01 Decision on Liability (27 December 2010) para. 121.
801. *Glamis v. US* [2009] NAFTA, ICSID 48 ILM 1039 Award (8 June 2009) para. 766.
802. *Mamidoil Jetoil Greek Petroleum Products Société S.A. v. Republic of Albania,* ICSID Case No. ARB/11/24 Award (30 March 2015) para. 648.
803. *El Paso v. Argentina,* ICSID Case No. ARB/03/15 Award (31 October 2011) para. 375.
804. *Charanne Construction v. Spain,* SCC Case No. 062/2012 Award (21 January 2016) para. 494.
805. *Impregilo S.p.A v. Argentina,* ICSID Case No. ARB/07/17 Award (21 June 2011) para. 296.
806. *Joy Mining Machinery v. Egypt,* ICSID Case No. ARB/03/11 Decision on Jurisdiction (6 August 2004) para. 72.

§6.04 THE NATURE AND IMPACT OF A CHANGE TO A GENERAL REGULATORY FRAMEWORK

[A] Introduction

In this section, the conditions for the protection of the legitimate expectations of an investor on the basis of the stability of a general regulatory framework will be discussed. In section §6.04[B], the main aspects concerning the possibility to invoke a claim on the basis of a general regulatory framework are outlined. In sections §6.04[C] and §6.04[D], the limitations imposed by tribunals on invoking such a claim are elaborated upon.

[B] Claims Based on the Expectation of the Stability of a General Regulatory Framework

In a number of FET cases, the tribunals have asserted that legitimate expectations can sometimes be invoked on the basis of relying on the stability of a general regulatory framework, which was in place at the time of making the investment. These claims have been justified on the basis that the FET standard incorporates an 'element of stability of the regulatory framework',[807] the underlying argument being that investors, who rely on a legal order at the time of the investment, have a right to expect that this legal order will not be significantly altered in the long term.[808]

The general regulatory framework usually consists of laws, policies and regulations of general application that existed at the time of the investment and that played a central role in the decision of the investor to make its investment in the host state. The moment of making the investment – and therefore also the moment of the formation of legitimate expectations – constitutes an important consideration in a tribunal's assessment of whether legitimate expectations qualify for protection. Tribunals have underlined that an investor may rely on the conditions offered at the time of the investment to claim that its legitimate expectations should be protected.[809] However, in some cases, the investment process takes place in a number of stages. In this regard, Schreuer and Kriebaum have underlined that investment decisions can be spread over the lifetime of the investment. It implies that legitimate expectations can be assessed by

807. M. Potestà, 'Legitimate Expectations in Investment Treaty Law: Understanding the Roots and the Limits of a Controversial Concept' [2013] 28(1) *ICSID Review*, 28.
808. M. Valenti, (2014) 41. This author explains that tribunals 'progressively shaped the notion of stability of the host country legal system, on which the foreign investor is entitled to rely for the purposes of the FET standard'. This is mainly explained by the phrase: '[the] investors' needs [for] stability in order to plan their business at best.' (p. 41). Also *see*: R. Klager, (2011) 186. The author concluded that 'the protection of the investor's expectations as regards the stability of the host state's conduct is, in general, quite well established ...'.
809. *See Saluka Investments BV v. Czech Republic* [2006] UNCITRAL Arbitration Partial Award (17 March 2006); *Duke Energy v. Ecuador*, ICSID Case No.ARB/04/19 Award (18 August 2008); *Azurix Corp. v. The Argentine Republic*, ICSID Case No. ARB/01/12 Award (14 July 2006); and others.

tribunals 'for each stage at which a decisive step is taken towards the creation, expansion, development or reorganization of investment'.[810]

The tribunal in *AES Summit v. Hungary* underlined in its award in 2010 that 'legitimate expectations can only be created at the moment of the investment,' citing the other investment tribunals that previously referred to this rule.[811] At the same time, the *AES Summit* tribunal explained that 'at the time of investment' could be given a fairly wide interpretation.[812] In this case, AES Summit and AES Tisza (the investors)[813] argued that even though their original investment in Hungary was made in 1996, the investors only started to buy shares and had actually made their investment operative in 2001. Therefore, the investors relied on the state's representations regarding the pricing mechanism established not only in 1996 but also in 2001, in which year the investors had entered into a number of Amended Power Purchase Agreements (APPAs) and in which agreements the purchase price control mechanisms had been agreed upon between the investors and Hungary. The investors argued that Hungary had frustrated their legitimate expectations by reintroducing the price control for electricity generators in 2006, thereby abolishing the price mechanism established in the APPA. The tribunal took both 1996 and 2001 into consideration as the relevant moments at which the legitimate expectations had been formed. Regarding the later period of investment, in 2001, the tribunal explained that 'turning to the year 2001, there can also be no question that AES Tisza then and thereafter made an investment in Hungary as the term "investment" is defined in the Treaty.'[814] The determining factor for the tribunal was that, in 2001, the investors had spent around EUR 98 million to finance the project. Furthermore, the investment was established by concluding the 2001 APPA.

In assessing the existence of legitimate expectations that are based on a general regulatory framework at the moment when the investment is made, tribunals have provided that such expectations can only be protected in a limited number of circumstances.[815] These circumstances are discussed further in this section. As a main

810. C. Schreuer, U. Kriebaum, 'At What Time Must Legitimate Expectations Exist', in T Wälde and others (eds) *A Liber Amicorum: Thomas Wälde – Law Beyond Conventional Thought* (CMP Publishing, 2009) 276.
811. *AES Summit v. Hungary*, ICSID Case No. ARB/07/22 Award (23 September 2010) para. 9.3.8.
812. *Ibid.*, para. 9.3.12.
813. *Ibid.*, para. 2.1.1. 'The Claimants [investors] in this arbitration are AES Summit Generation Limited ("AES Summit") and AES-Tisza Erömü Kft. ("AES Tisza")'.
814. *AES Summit v. Hungary*, ICSID Case No. ARB/07/22 Award (23 September 2010) para. 9.3.16.
815. However, there are several exceptions in investment cases where the stability of the general regulatory framework as a part of the FET standard has been interpreted broadly. *See Occidental v. Ecuador*, LCIA Case No. UN3467 Final Award (1 July 2004) para. 183 where the tribunal stated that the 'stability of the legal and business framework is thus an essential element of fair and equitable treatment.' *See also CMS Gas Transmission Co. v. The Argentine Republic*, ICSID Case No. ARB/01/8 Award (12 May 2005) para. 274. The tribunal stated that stability and predictability are essential elements of fair and equitable treatment. A similar conclusion was reached in *LG&E Energy Corp., LG&E Capital Corp. & LG&E International v. The Argentine Republic*, ICSID Case No. ARB/02/1 Decision on Liability (3 October 2006) in paras 124-125. The tribunal underlined that the stability of the legal and business framework is an essential element of fair and equitable treatment. The tribunal in *Enron v. Argentina*, ICSID Case No. ARB/01/3 Award (22 May 2007), referring to the *LG&E* tribunal, concluded in a

standpoint, however, tribunals have provided that a mere change to the regulatory framework does not suffice to conclude that an investor's expectations have been breached. The tribunal in *AES Summit v. Hungary* supported this position by stating that '[a] legal framework is by definition subject to change as it adapts to new circumstances day by day and a state has the sovereign right to exercise its powers which include legislative acts.'[816]

In *Saluka v. Czech Republic*, the tribunal explained its position regarding the claim by the investor that its expectations were not honoured due to a change to the regulatory framework by providing a comment on a statement made by the tribunal in *Occidental v. Ecuador*. The tribunal in *Occidental* had stipulated that the 'stability of the legal and business framework is thus an essential element of fair and equitable treatment.'[817] In response to this statement, the *Saluka* tribunal warned that if these types of statements are taken 'too literally', it could 'impose upon host States obligations which would be inappropriate and unrealistic'.[818] In a similar vein, the UNCTAD study on the FET standard and its application in investment cases provides that a tribunal's reliance on the stability of a regulatory framework as a basis to protect an investor's expectations may potentially prevent any host state from 'introducing any legitimate regulatory change, let alone from undertaking a regulatory reform that may be called for'.[819]

In conclusion, tribunals are, by and large, in agreement that a claim to the effect that an investor's legitimate expectations have been breached, and which is based on the stability of a regulatory framework, can only be successful if there is a severe negative impact on the investor and its investment caused by changes to that regulatory framework. This question concerning the degree of the impact on the investor is elaborated upon in section §6.04[C].

In a number of cases, tribunals have assessed the way in which the transformation of a regulatory framework was conducted. This has been a predominant factor in determining the presence of a violation of the investor's expectations under the FET standard and is outlined in section §6.04[D].

---

similar fashion that 'a key element of fair and equitable treatment is the requirement of a "stable framework for the investment," which has been prescribed by a number of decisions. Indeed, this interpretation has been considered 'an emerging standard of fair and equitable treatment in international law' (*see* para. 260).' In *PSEG v. Turkey*, the tribunal found that the state's breach of the FET standard was based on inconsistent legislative changes that undermined the stability of the legal framework; *see PSEG v. Turkey*, ICSID Case No. ARB/02/5 Award (19 January 2007) paras 253-254.

816. *AES Summit v. Hungary*, ICSID Case No. ARB/07/22 Award (23 September 2010) para. 9.3.29. The significance of regulating to pursue a specific public interest, i.e., the state's goal to combat 'luxury profits' in the public utility sector (which played a role in this case), is discussed in section §7.02 concerning the legitimacy of the state's objectives in exercising its right to regulate.
817. *Occidental v. Ecuador*, LCIA Case No. UN3467 Final Award (1 July 2004) para. 183.
818. *Saluka Investments BV v. Czech Republic* [2006] UNCITRAL Arbitration Partial Award (17 March 2006) para. 304.
819. UNCTAD 'Fair and Equitable Treatment: UNCTAD Series on International Investment Agreements II' (New York, 2012) 67.

[C] The Level of the Impact on Investments Due to the Transformation of a General Regulatory Framework

Several tribunals have assessed the legitimate expectations of an investor in connection with a particular transformation of the general regulatory system, thereby focusing primarily on the severity of the impact on investments resulting from such transformations.

For example, in *Toto v. Lebanon*, the tribunal stated that:

> changes in the regulatory framework would be considered as breaches of the duty to grant full protection and fair and equitable treatment only in case of a drastic or discriminatory change in the essential features of the transaction.[820]

The tribunal concluded that changes to customs duties and taxes, disputed by the investor, were neither discriminatory nor drastic. First, the extra costs related to the increase in the amount of taxes and customs duties were 'small compared to the overall amount of the project'.[821] Second, the same changes were applicable to other investors as well as Lebanese nationals.[822]

Unlike *Toto*, the tribunal in *El Paso v. Argentina* found a breach of the legitimate expectations of the investor on the basis of a transformation of the general regulatory framework. The reason for establishing the breach was the overall negative impact on the investor's investments, resulting from changes to the regulatory system in the energy sector.

The tribunal initially explained that a foreign investor does not have to anticipate that a rule would be changed 'without justification of an economic, social or other nature'.[823] The investor cannot expect that the 'legal framework will remain unchanged in the face of an extremely severe economic crisis' that Argentina had experienced.[824] However, in evaluating all the separate measures that were part of the change to the regulatory framework, the tribunal found a violation of the FET standard on the basis of not fulfilling the legitimate expectations of the investor due to the 'overall cumulative impact of the measures' implemented by Argentina in the electricity, oil and gas sectors.[825] The tribunal explained that although each measure 'in isolation' could be seen as a 'reasonable measure to cope with a difficult economic situation' and would not be considered a violation under the FET standard, a 'combination of all these measures completely altered the overall framework', and had a severe negative impact on the investor's investments.[826] In this regard, the tribunal

820. *Toto v. Lebanon*, ICSID Case No. ARB/07/12 Award (7 June 2012) para. 244.
821. *Ibid.*
822. *Ibid.*
823. *El Paso v. Argentina*, ICSID Case No. ARB/03/15 Award (31 October 2011) para. 372.
824. *Ibid.*, para. 374.
825. *Ibid.*, para. 510. The tribunal made a lengthy analysis of Argentina's measures: (1) For the electricity sector: (a) caps on spot prices (paras 410-416); (b) alterations to capacity payments (paras 417-422); and (2) In the oil and gas sector, e.g. 'pesification' (i.e., the forcible conversion of dollar-denominated bank deposits into pesos; *see* paras 423-449).
826. *El Paso v. Argentina*, ICSID Case No. ARB/03/15 Award (31 October 2011) para. 515.

referred to a 'creeping violation of the FET standard'.[827] The tribunal made a comparison with the notion of 'creeping expropriation', which – according to the case law on expropriation – implies a 'process extending over time and composed of a succession or accumulation of measures which, ... when viewed as a whole' led to the violation of the expropriation standard.[828] The tribunal applied this logic to the FET assessment, concluding that the accumulation of measures taken by Argentina had resulted in a violation of the legitimate expectations of the investor and hence in a breach of the FET standard in this particular case.[829]

[D] The Manner of the Transformation of a General Regulatory Framework by a Host State

As provided in several investment decisions, a claim for the protection of an investor's legitimate expectations that are based on a general regulatory framework may under certain circumstances give rise to a violation of the FET standard. That is the case when the way in which the modification of the legal framework has been conducted has to be qualified as unfair and unreasonable towards the investor. The tribunals referred to below have elaborated upon the specific elements of what constitutes an unfair and unreasonable modification of a regulatory framework.

The tribunal in *Parkerings v. Lithuania* outlined the criteria that need to be fulfilled in order to decide that the change of a general regulatory framework has undermined the legitimate expectations of an investor. In this case, a Norwegian company, Parkerings (the investor), entered into a contract with the Lithuanian authorities to construct and to maintain parking facilities in the historical town of Vilnius. However, certain changes to the applicable national regulations prevented the realisation of the investor's project. The investor argued that these modifications to the general regulatory framework frustrated its expectations as protected by the FET standard.[830] The tribunal noted that an investor 'has a right to a certain stability and predictability of the legal environment of the investment'.[831] This right of an investor is violated if a host state has acted 'unfairly, unreasonably, or inequitably in the exercise of its legislative power'.[832] In this decision, the tribunal found that 'the record does not show that the state acted unfairly, unreasonably or inequitably in the exercise of its legislative power.'[833]

In *Total v. Argentina*, an investor made investments in the Argentinian gas sector. Similar to other Argentinian cases, its investments had been adversely impacted by the emergency measures adopted by Argentina as a response to the economic crisis of 2001-2002 (in section §6.05[B] below, this case will be further elaborated). In assessing the investor's claim which was based on legitimate expectations, the tribunal

827. *Ibid.*, para. 518.
828. *Ibid.*
829. *Ibid.*
830. *Parkerings v. Lithuania*, ICSID Case No. ARB/05/8 Award (11 September 2007) para. 322.
831. *Ibid.*, para. 333. The facts of the case are also discussed in section §6.03[F] of this Chapter.
832. *Parkerings v. Lithuania*, ICSID Case No. ARB/05/8 Award (11 September 2007) para. 337.
833. *Ibid.*

stressed that an investor cannot expect that the general regulatory framework will not be changed during the lifetime of an investment. However, the tribunal also provided that, under certain limited circumstances, an investor's claim based on the expectation of the stability of a general regulatory framework may be successful. The tribunal explained:

> A claim to stability can be based on the inherently prospective nature of the regulation at issue aimed at providing a defined framework for future operations. This is the case for regimes, which are applicable to long-term investments and operations, and/or providing for 'fall backs' or contingent rights in case the relevant framework would be changed in unforeseen circumstances or in case certain listed events materialize.[834]

The tribunal in this case pointed out that in long-term investment projects and operations 'commonly recognized and applied financial and economic principles' that are based on the concepts of 'regulatory fairness' and 'regulatory certainty'.[835] The tribunal opined that the state had the authority to 'fix the tariffs of a public utility'.[836] However, the state had to do this in 'such a way that the concessionaire is able to recover its operations costs, amortize its investments and make a reasonable return over time, as indeed Argentina's gas regime provided'.[837] The tribunal found that Argentina had failed to do so by setting 'prices, which did not remunerate the investment made nor allow reasonable profit to be gained contrary to the principles governing the activities of privately owned generators under Argentina's own legal system'.[838] In this case, the tribunal found that Argentina had breached the FET standard because, in spite of the economic recovery, Argentina had delayed the negotiations with the investor and failed to readjust the gas tariffs for public utilities.[839]

In *PSEG v. Turkey*, a dispute arose with regard to the legislative requirements applicable to the construction of a power plant. Among the measures disputed by the investor were numerous changes to the legislation that resulted in the need to alter the investment plan. The tribunal underlined that 'the circumstances prevailing at the time the investment is made cannot remain totally unchanged.'[840] At the same time, it stressed that 'stability cannot exist in a situation where the law kept changing continuously and endlessly, as did its interpretation and implementation.'[841] The

834. *Total v. Argentina*, ICSID Case No. ARB/04/01 Decision on Liability (27 December 2010) para. 122.
835. *Ibid.*
836. *Ibid.*
837. *Ibid.* The gas regime is a framework that is governed by a number of key principles found in the Gas Law which regulates transportation and distribution operations in the gas sector (para. 49).
838. *Total v. Argentina*, ICSID Case No. ARB/04/01 Decision on Liability (27 December 2010) para. 333.
839. *Ibid.*, paras 174-175. On the decision in this case *see*: R. Dolzer, [2014], 24. According to Dolzer, the *Total* tribunal had not been persuasive regarding why a claim to stability can be based on the prospective nature of the regulation applicable to the gas regime that had succeeded in this case. The question here is how laws of such a prospective nature differ from other laws which existed at the time of the investment. Because the prospective nature of a regulation can be attributed to any legislation (p. 24).
840. *PSEG v. Turkey*, ICSID Case No. ARB/02/5 Award (19 January 2007) para. 255.
841. *Ibid.*, para. 254.

tribunal called this the 'roller-coaster effect' of continuous legislative changes.[842] The accumulation of the unpredictable legislative changes was ultimately the prevalent ground for liability under the FET standard. The tribunal also underlined that besides the continuing changes in the legislation, 'the attitudes and policies of the administration' were changing as well, thereby contributing to the unpredictability and instability that the investments and investors were faced with.[843]

In several cases concerning the renewable energy sector, such as *Charanne v. Spain* (discussed in section §6.03[D]), *Masdar v. Spain* (discussed in section §6.03[C])[844] and also *Isolux v. Spain, Eiser v. Spain, Antin Infrastructure v. Spain* and *Blusun v. Italy* (which will be introduced below), the tribunals decided on claims for the protection of the investors' legitimate expectations based on a modification of a general regulatory framework. In assessing the expectations of the investors and the alleged violations of the FET standard, the tribunals investigated in which way the modification of the pertinent legal framework had taken place. These cases were decided under the ECT. The obligation to provide the FET standard under Article 10(1) of the ECT also includes the creation of 'stable, equitable, favourable and transparent conditions for Investors of other Contracting Parties to make Investments in its Area'.[845] Relying on Article 10(1) of the ECT, the investors in the aforementioned cases argued that the transformation of the regulatory framework had undermined their legitimate expectations with regard to a stable regulatory framework.

Charanne v. Spain, Isolux v. Spain, Eiser v. Spain, Antin Infrastructure v. Spain and *Blusun v. Italy* are cases that are based on a similar factual background and belong to the array of cases in which investors have challenged states' measures altering the subsidies in the renewable energy sector. The brief background to these cases will be explained below. However, there are important factual variations between the cases, which will be highlighted in the subsequent analysis.

In 2007, Spain created a special legal regime in order to promote and encourage the new generation of renewable energy. The special regime was established by legislative acts that included various incentives (e.g., feed-in tariffs, benefits and bonuses) for investors in photovoltaic solar technology and CSP.[846] However, as a

842. *Ibid.*, para. 250. *See* the discussion on the 'roller-coaster effect' in R. Klager, Fair and Equitable Treatment in International Investment Law (Cambridge Press, 2012) 173.
843. *PSEG v. Turkey*, ICSID Case No. ARB/02/5 Award (19 January 2007) para. 254.
844. This case will not be discussed in this section, because the central part of this tribunal's analysis concerned the question of whether a specific representation had been made to the investor. The tribunal's criteria applied in answering this question have been evaluated in section §6.03[C] of this Chapter.
845. Energy Charter Treaty [1994] 2080 UNTS 95 (updated 15 January 2016), Chapter on Investment Promotion and Protection, Article 10(1). Article 10(1) provides: 'Each Contracting Party shall, in accordance with the provisions of this Treaty, encourage and create stable, equitable, favourable and transparent conditions for Investors of other Contracting Parties to make Investments in its Area. Such conditions shall include a commitment to accord at all times to Investments of Investors of other Contracting Parties fair and equitable treatment ...'.
846. The special regime was created primarily by the way of enacting Royal Decree 661/2007, e.g., providing fixed tariffs for producers. *See*: International Energy Agency, Feed-in tariffs for electricity from renewable energy sources (Special regime), https://www.iea.org/policiesandmeasures/pams/spain/name-23929-en.php accessed on 21 September 2018.

result of the tariff deficit, Spain, in 2010, and later in 2012, 2013 and 2014, adopted a series of measures that reduced and ultimately reversed the special regime created for producers in the renewable energy sector.[847] These state reforms led to several claims by foreign investors against Spain under the ECT.[848] Foreign investors contested the 2010 and 2012-2014 state measures arguing that by changing the regulatory framework for renewable energy, Spain had unlawfully undermined the stability of the legal framework relied upon by investors in making their investments.

In *Blusun v. Italy*, the Italian government had also limited the application of incentive-based schemes that were available to renewable energy producers. This was a similar regulatory reform as the one in Spain and will be elaborated below.

Already introduced in section §6.03[D] of this Chapter, the first renewable energy case against Spain was *Charanne v. Spain*. In this decision, the tribunal established that the state had not undermined the legitimate expectations of the investor, because it was concluded that Spain had made no specific representations to the investor.[849] The tribunal asserted that in the absence of a state's specific representation, there 'cannot be a legitimate expectation that existing rules will not be modified'.[850] Nevertheless, the tribunal noted that, exceptionally, a state's transformation of a regulatory framework might be considered to harm the legitimate expectations of an investor, if these changes had been 'capricious or unnecessary' and amounted to a 'sudden and unpredictable elimination of the essential characteristics of the existing framework'.[851] In this case, the tribunal came to the conclusion that the changes to the regulatory framework were limited and did not eliminate its 'essential characteristics'.[852] In *Charanne v. Spain*, the tribunal asserted that if a transformation of a regulatory framework is conducted in a gradual manner, and without eliminating the essential characteristics of the regulatory framework, such a change will not give rise to a valid claim of the protection of the legitimate expectations of the investor under the FET standard. [853]

847. For example, Royal Decree Law 9/2013 cancelled the special regime under Royal Decree 661/2007. It included the elimination of the fixed tariffs and replacing them by a system in which the producers' remuneration was based on 'standard' (but not actual) costs per unit of installed power.
848. *Novenergia II – Energy & Environment (SCA) (Grand Duchy of Luxembourg), SICAR v. The Kingdom of Spain*, SCC Case No. 2015/063 Award (15 February 2018); *Masdar Solar & Wind Cooperatief U.A. v. Kingdom of Spain*, ICSID Case No. ARB/14/1 Award (16 May 2018); *CSP Equity Investment Sarl v. Kingdom of Spain*, SCC Case No. 094/2013, Notice of Arbitration, June 2013; *DCM Energy and others v. Kingdom of Spain*, ICSID Case No. ARB/17/41, Notice of Arbitration 2017; *Aharon Naftali Biram, and others v. Kingdom of Spain*, ICSID Case No. ARB/16/17, Notice of Arbitration 2016; *FREIF Eurowind v. Kingdom of Spain*, SCC Case No. 2017/060, Notice of Arbitration 2017; *Portigon AG v. Kingdom of Spain*, ICSID Case No. ARB/17/15, Notice of Arbitration 2017.
849. *Charanne Construction v. Spain*, SCC Case No. 062/2012 Award (21 January 2016) para. 494. 'Based on the foregoing, the Tribunal concludes that there was no specific commitment by Spain vis-à-vis the Claimants'.
850. *Charanne Construction v. Spain*, SCC Case No. 062/2012 Award (21 January 2016) para. 499.
851. *Ibid.*, para. 517.
852. *Ibid.*, para. 539.
853. *Charanne Construction v. Spain*, SCC Case No. 062/2012 Award (21 January 2016) para. 539. The reasoning in *Charanne v. Spain* also corresponds to the reasoning in the case *Mamidoil v. Albania*. In *Mamidoil v. Albania*, the tribunal observed that Albania had altered its regulatory

In *Eiser v. Spain* and *Antin Infrastructure v. Spain*, contrary to the *Charanne* decision, the tribunals found that the changes introduced by Spain had eliminated the essential characteristics of the pertinent regulatory framework and had therefore violated the FET standard under Article 10(1) of the ECT. In *Eiser v. Spain*,[854] the investors had invested in the construction and operation of three CSP plants.[855] The investors argued that the changes, which had been implemented in the regulatory framework, especially the 2013/2014 measures, had destroyed their investments and were therefore contrary to Article 10(1) of the ECT.[856] These measures included the cancellation of the special regime for the producers of renewable energy.[857] In *Antin Infrastructure v. Spain*, the investors had invested in two operational CSP plants that used natural gas to intensify the capacity of power generation.[858] In the same vein as in Eiser, the investors in *Antin v. Spain* argued that the state's measures, specifically undertaken in 2013, completely transformed the earlier system of incentives for concentrated solar power relied upon by investors and had 'significant harmful effects' on their investments.[859]

In interpreting Article 10(1) of the ECT, both the *Eiser* and *Antin* tribunals referred to the ECT's object and purpose; i.e., the '... obligation to accord fair and equitable treatment necessarily embraces an obligation to provide fundamental stability in the essential characteristics of the legal regime relied upon by investors in making long-term investments.'[860] Following the *Charanne* formulation, the tribunals in *Eiser* and *Antin* asserted that an investor's legitimate expectations, which are based on the stability of a legal framework, are relevant in assessing an alleged violation of the FET standard and that if a host state eliminates the essential characteristics of the pertinent regulatory framework, this can lead to a violation of the FET standard.[861] In this light, the *Eiser* tribunal concluded that the Spanish legislative measures adopted in 2013 and

framework 'in a gradual way', without the 'back and forth of ever-changing and contradictory norms or administrative processes', and that these alterations were motivated 'by a long-term perspective and not by erratic considerations'. *Mamidoil Jetoil Greek Petroleum Products Société S.A. v. Republic of Albania*, ICSID Case No. ARB/11/24 Award (30 March 2015) para. 660 and para. 662.

854. The investors were the UK-based private equity fund Eiser Infrastructure and its subsidiary based in Luxembourg.

855. *Eiser Infrastructure Ltd. and Energia Solar Luxembourg v. Spain*, ICSID Case No. ARB/13/36 Award (4 May 2017) paras 120-123.

856. *Ibid.*, para. 349.

857. *Ibid.*, para. 146.

858. *Antin Infrastructure Services Luxembourg S.à.r.l. and Antin Energia Termosolar B.V. v. Kingdom of Spain*, ICSID Case No. ARB/13/31 Award (15 June 2018) para. 70.

859. *Ibid.*, para. 154.

860. *Eiser Infrastructure Ltd. and Energia Solar Luxembourg v. Spain*, ICSID Case No. ARB/13/36 Award (4 May 2017) para. 382. *Antin Infrastructure Services Luxembourg S.à.r.l. and Antin Energia Termosolar B.V. v. Kingdom of Spain*, ICSID Case No. ARB/13/31 Award (15 June 2018) para. 532. The formulation was almost identical: 'In sum, considering the context, object and purpose of the ECT, the Tribunal concludes that the obligation under Article 10(1) of the ECT to provide FET to protected investments comprises an obligation to afford fundamental stability in the essential characteristics of the legal regime relied upon by the investors in making long-term investments'.

861. *Antin Infrastructure Services Luxembourg S.à.r.l. and Antin Energia Termosolar B.V. v. Kingdom of Spain*, ICSID Case No. ARB/13/31 Award (15 June 2018) para. 556.

2014 altered the regulatory framework in a totally unreasonable manner; the existing framework was replaced by a 'wholly different regulatory approach'.[862] These changes, according to the *Eiser* tribunal, are not compatible with the FET standard. In *Antin*, the tribunal came to a similar conclusion, finding that through the state's 2013 measures, e.g. replacing the feed-in tariff system by a remuneration system, the essential features of the original regime relied upon by the investor had been eradicated.[863] Both the *Eiser* and *Antin* tribunals highlighted that the factual situation in *Charanne v. Spain* was different from the facts presented in these two cases.[864] Both tribunals pointed out that the state's measures adopted in 2010, which were challenged by the investors in *Charanne*, were far less drastic and damaging in comparison to the later reforms disputed by the investors in the *Eiser* and *Antin* cases. Hence, this was the reason for the different outcomes in those three cases, all three judged on the basis of the ECT.

In two other renewable energy cases, i.e., *Blusun v. Italy* and *Isolux v. Spain*, both also decided under the ECT, the tribunals, contrary to the tribunals' conclusions in the *Eiser* and *Antin* awards, concluded that the host states' measures that altered the subsidies' scheme for renewable energy producers did not undermine the stability of the general regulatory framework. In *Blusun v. Italy* and *Isolux v. Spain*, the tribunals concluded that the host states had not violated the FET standard under the ECT. In *Isolux v. Spain*,[865] the investors had disputed the same 2013 measures as in *Eiser v. Spain* and *Antin v. Spain*.[866] However, in *Isolux*, the tribunal established that the investor had decided to invest in October of 2012 when Spain had already adopted the changes in the regulatory framework. Hence, the reforms that followed were foreseeable, and therefore, the investors could not rely on any legitimate expectations arising out of the stability of the regulatory framework.[867] A further discussion of the tribunal's analysis in *Isolux v. Spain* is provided in section §6.06[B] (concerning the topic of due diligence and risk assessment).

In *Blusun v. Italy*, the tribunal used as a yardstick the principle of proportionality in judging the seriousness of the regulatory change. [868] In this case, the investors[869] had

862. *Eiser Infrastructure Ltd. and Energia Solar Luxembourg v. Spain*, ICSID Case No. ARB/13/36 Award (4 May 2017), paras 362 and 365.
863. *Antin Infrastructure Services Luxembourg S.à.r.l. and Antin Energia Termosolar B.V. v. Kingdom of Spain*, ICSID Case No. ARB/13/31 Award (15 June 2018) para. 560.
864. *Eiser Infrastructure Ltd. and Energia Solar Luxembourg v. Spain*, ICSID Case No. ARB/13/36 Award (4 May 2017) para. 367. *Antin Infrastructure Services Luxembourg S.à.r.l. and Antin Energia Termosolar B.V. v. Kingdom of Spain*, ICSID Case No. ARB/13/31 Award (15 June 2018) para. 558.
865. *Isolux Netherlands, BV v. Kingdom of Spain*, SCC Case V2013/153 Award (6 July 2016). The case was decided a few months after the *Charanne* award in July 2016; however, the text was unavailable until June 2017. Please note that this award is in Spanish, and the analysis of this award is based on an unofficial translation by the author.
866. *Isolux Netherlands, BV v. Kingdom of Spain*, SCC Case V2013/153 Award (July 2016) para. 773.
867. *Isolux Netherlands, BV v. Kingdom of Spain*, SCC Case V2013/153 Award (17 July 2016) para. 796.
868. *Blusun S.A., J.-P. Lecorcier AND M. Stein v. Italy*, ICSID Case No. ARB/14/3 Award, 27 December 2016, para. 319.
869. *Ibid.*, para. 2. Blusun is a Belgian company that is owned and controlled by two individuals: a French national, Mr. Lecorcier, and a German national, Mr. Stein. Blusun controlled two Italian

invested in a 120 MW power project in Puglia.[870] This was a large solar project that contained about 120 PV plants that had to be joined to each other and two substations for connection to the national grid.[871] Each plant could generate under 1 MW. Together, all plants would generate a capacity equal to 120 MW. However, the project had never succeeded and eventually failed because of a lack of funding.[872] According to the investors, this was the result of the 'legal insecurity' created by the Italian government through a series of measures that reduced the incentives for renewable energy producers.[873] According to the investors, legislative changes and, in particular, the adoption of the Romani Decree and the Fourth Energy Account had eliminated the state's incentives and thereby contributed to the loss of the project.[874] The Romani Decree and the Fourth Energy Account introduced measures that limited the term of applicability of the feed-in tariffs to PV plants[875] and set additional conditions for the eligibility of PV plants for governmental incentives.[876] The investors argued that the state's disputed measures fundamentally transformed the regulatory framework upon which the investors had relied, and hence they violated Article 10(1) of the ECT.

In assessing the investors' claim of legal instability[877] under Article 10(1) of the ECT, the tribunal asserted that a host state has the regulatory authority to 'change its laws and regulations to adapt to changing needs, including fiscal needs, subject to respect for specific commitments made'.[878] So that, in principle, if a state has not provided any specific representations to an investor, there is 'no obligation to grant subsidies such as feed-in tariffs, or to maintain them unchanged once granted.'[879] Nevertheless, the tribunal noted that a claim regarding legal instability could be successful if the manner in which the changes have been conducted is 'disproportionate to the aim of the legislative amendment and has no due regard to the reasonable reliance interests of recipients who may commit substantial resources on the basis of the earlier regime'.[880] The tribunal found that the changes, which were introduced by the Italian government, were proportionate to the state's objectives and that their

subsidiaries, Eskosol and Societa Interconnessioni Brindisi S.R.L., through which the development of the 120 MW project in the region of Puglia was conducted.

870. *Blusun S.A., J.-P. Lecorcier AND M. Stein v. Italy*, ICSID Case No. ARB/14/3 Award, 27 December 2016, para. 55.

871. *Ibid.*, para. 53.

872. *Ibid.*, para. 310.

873. *Ibid.*

874. *Blusun S.A., J.-P. Lecorcier AND M. Stein v. Italy*, ICSID Case No. ARB/14/3 Award, 27 December 2016, para. 338.

875. *Ibid.*, para. 331. The Romani Decree provided that the feed-in tariffs will be applicable to plants commenced before 31 May 2011, thereby preponing the date of application that was previously 31 December 2013.

876. *Blusun S.A., J.-P. Lecorcier AND M. Stein v. Italy*, ICSID Case No. ARB/14/3 Award, 27 December 2016, paras 331-343.

877. *Ibid.*, para. 320 (legal instability claim).

878. *Ibid.*, para. 319.

879. *Ibid.*

880. *Ibid.*

impact was severe but not detrimental to the investors (the tribunal's assessment of the state's objective is addressed in section §7.02[B] of Chapter 7 below).[881]

In the renewable energy cases decided under the ECT, the question of finding a balance between a state's right to regulate and the stability of a regulatory framework that was relied upon by an investor constitutes the central issue. A further assessment of this issue is provided in section §6.05[D].

[E] Summary: Expectations Concerning the Stability of a General Regulatory Framework

Investment tribunals have provided that an investor investing in a host state should be able to rely on a certain degree of stability relating to its investment.[882] This does not, however, imply that investors should expect that the legal framework will not change at all. Tribunals have emphasised that a state's 'legal framework is by definition subject to change as it adapts to new circumstances day by day and a state has the sovereign right to exercise its powers which include legislative acts'.[883]

In assessing claims that are based on an investor's expectations concerning the stability of a general regulatory framework, tribunals have provided that such expectations can only be protected under certain limited conditions. The analysis of the case law demonstrates that these conditions include: (i) the transformation of a general regulatory framework that has had a large impact on the investor's investments; and (ii) the way in which the state has transformed the general regulatory framework, upon which the investor relied, was unfair and unreasonable towards the investor.[884]

With regard to the first-mentioned condition, i.e. the negative impact of the transformation of a general regulatory framework on the investor's investments, according to the tribunals it was key for their decision that the investor's legitimate expectations had been breached, that the changes had been drastic and/or discriminatory and had a severe financial impact on the investor.[885]

Regarding the second condition, i.e. the way in which the general framework has been transformed by a host state, it is noted that the key elements on the basis of which a tribunal can decide that the state has frustrated the investor's legitimate expectations are the extreme nature and the unpredictability of the transformation of the general regulatory framework. This has been explained by tribunals by using the term

881. *Blusun S.A., J.-P. Lecorcier AND M. Stein v. Italy*, ICSID Case No. ARB/14/3 Award, 27 December 2016, para. 342.
882. *See*: *Parkerings v. Lithuania*, ICSID Case No. ARB/05/8 Award (11 September 2007) para. 333. The tribunal provided that: 'in principle, an investor has a right to a certain stability and predictability of the legal environment of the investment'.
883. *AES Summit v. Hungary*, ICSID Case No. ARB/07/22 Award (23 September 2010) para. 9.3.29. Also *see*: *Parkerings v. Lithuania*, ICSID Case No. ARB/05/8 Award (11 September 2007) para. 333. *See also*: *Continental Casualty v. Argentina*, ICSID Case No. ARB/03/9 Award (5 September 2008) para. 258.
884. These conditions have not been applied cumulatively by the tribunals in the examined cases, satisfying one of the two mostly sufficed.
885. *Toto v. Lebanon*, ICSID Case No. ARB/07/12 Award (7 June 2012) para. 244; *El Paso v. Argentina*, ICSID Case No. ARB/03/15 Award (31 October 2011) para. 510.

'roller-coaster effect' of continuous legislative changes.[886] Tribunals have decided that the state can change its regulatory framework, but it has to respect 'basic features' entrenched in this legal framework which have been relied upon by an investor in making the investment in the first place.[887] To this end, several tribunals in the renewable energy cases underlined that an investor's legitimate expectations based on the stability of a regulatory framework will be undermined if a host state suddenly eliminates the essential features of such regulatory framework.[888] According to some tribunals, 'undermining' can be the case if a state's measures replace the existing regulatory framework by a 'wholly different regulatory approach', leading to a drastic adverse impact on the investor's investments.[889] In some decisions, the tribunals have justified an alteration to the regulatory framework on which the investors (had) relied when this alteration has been gradual, foreseeable and without implementing any contradictory norms or administrative processes, and in accordance with the long-term objectives of the state. Using the principle of proportionality as a yardstick, the tribunal in *Blusun v. Italy* emphasised that a state will violate the obligation of stability under the FET standard if the manner in which the changes have been conducted is 'disproportionate to the aim of the legislative amendment and has no due regard to the reasonable reliance interests of recipients who may commit substantial resources on the basis of the earlier regime.'[890]

§6.05 THE FACTOR OF SPECIAL ECONOMIC AND SOCIOPOLITICAL CIRCUMSTANCES IN A HOST STATE

[A] Introduction

In section §6.04, several cases were analysed in which an investor's expectations were frustrated because the general legal framework had been changed by the host state. In these cases, the tribunals stringently tested whether the negative impact on the investor which had been caused by such changes, or the manner in which the changes were implemented, led to a violation of legitimate expectations. In some cases, which are discussed in this section, the tribunals considered the economic or sociopolitical circumstances in the host states to be exceptional, thereby determining that the measures taken by the host state to address such circumstances were in the public

886. *PSEG v. Turkey*, ICSID Case No. ARB/02/5 Award (19 January 2007) para. 250.
887. *Total v. Argentina*, ICSID Case No. ARB/04/01 Decision on Liability (27 December 2010) para. 168. *Charanne Construction v. Spain*, SCC Case No. 062/2012 Award (21 January 2016) 539.
888. *Antin Infrastructure Services Luxembourg S.à.r.l. and Antin Energia Termosolar B.V. v. Kingdom of Spain*, ICSID Case No. ARB/13/31 Award (15 June 2018) para. 556; *Charanne Construction v. Spain*, SCC Case No. 062/2012 Award (21 January 2016) para. 539; *Eiser Infrastructure Ltd. and Energia Solar Luxembourg v. Spain*, ICSID Case No. ARB/13/36 Award (4 May 2017) para. 382.
889. *Eiser Infrastructure Ltd. and Energia Solar Luxembourg v. Spain*, ICSID Case No. ARB/13/36 Award (4 May 2017), paras 362 and 365.
890. *Blusun S.A., J.-P. Lecorcier AND M. Stein v. Italy*, ICSID Case No. ARB/14/3 Award, 27 December 2016, para. 319.

interest of the host state. In this section, it will be explored how tribunals deal with an investor's legitimate interests in such exceptional situations.

Special circumstances that relate to the economic and/or sociopolitical situation in a host state are specifically relevant in the context of legitimate expectations because such circumstances influence the general investment climate in the host state. In assessing an investor's expectations, tribunals assess the legitimacy of its expectations against the background of the general investment climate. For example, measures taken by a host state to address an economic crisis may frustrate an investor's expectations, especially with regard to the stability of a general regulatory framework. A reversal of a host state's specific representations, or a change in a general regulatory framework, is often a response by the host state to the external changes in economic or sociopolitical circumstances. In assessing whether an investor's expectations must still be protected in such a situation, tribunals have indicated that the expectations 'must rise to the level of legitimacy and reasonableness in light of the circumstances'.[891] Tribunals have stressed that 'legitimate expectations cannot be solely the subjective expectations of the investor, but have to correspond to the objective expectations' examined in the context of the circumstances that are present in the host state.[892]

In Chapter 7, measures in the public interest will also be discussed, but in a different context; i.e., in section §7.02, the legitimacy of a state's measure and the corresponding objective(s) will be analysed. The 'section §7.02 type' of public interests do not so much relate to the economic and sociopolitical situation in a host state, but rather represent key public interest areas, such as health, a clean environment and human rights, which any host state has a duty to protect. In section §7.02, the focus of the analysis of the FET standard is on the conditions, which apply to the lawful exercise of the right to regulate. Such an assessment, however, does not explicitly concern the weighing of the state's contested public interest measure against the legitimate expectations of an investor.

Economic and financial crises and a transition of the sociopolitical system as occurred in the former communist states are examples of relevant factors which tribunals consider when deciding on the protection of the legitimate expectations of an investor. Tribunals often determine that the responses of host states to address such circumstances are measures that are in the public interest because dramatic changes to the status quo in a state require adequate measures. In some of these cases, tribunals have also emphasised that the level of a state's economic development should be taken into account. In sections §6.05[B]-§6.05[D], examples are presented of cases in which economic and sociopolitical circumstances have been taken into consideration by tribunals. Several cases concern states that had to deal with a major economic and financial crisis, other cases concern former socialist states whose economy was in a state of transition before becoming a market economy, and the last category concerns cases in which a host state reduced the support schemes for producers in the field of renewable energy, because of the tariff deficit.

891. *Saluka Investments BV v. Czech Republic* [2006] UNCITRAL Arbitration Partial Award (17 March 2006) para. 304.

892. *El Paso v. Argentina*, ICSID Case No. ARB/03/15 Award (31 October 2011) para. 358.

[B] Economic and Financial Crisis in a Host State

In a series of disputes involving Argentina, it was noted that the economic and financial crisis had triggered a range of state emergency measures in the interest of stabilising the economy.[893] As noted by Bucheler, 'none of the Argentinian tribunals found that the emergency measures automatically violate the FET standard on the sole basis that they interfere with the interests of foreign investors.'[894] On the contrary, the particular circumstances of the financial crisis were taken into account by most of the Argentinian tribunals in assessing whether the expectations of an investor were legitimate and needed to be protected. However, the extent of this consideration varied among the tribunals.

The tribunal in *Total v. Argentina* emphasised that in reviewing the legitimate expectations of the investor, the state's right to regulate in the public interest should be taken into account. It argued that this involves considering the circumstances of the economic crisis:

> The circumstances and reasons (importance and urgency of the public need pursued) for carrying out a change impacting negatively on a foreign investor's operations on the one hand, and the seriousness of the prejudice caused on the other hand, compared in the light of a standard of reasonableness and proportionality are relevant.[895]

The tribunal underlined that the assessment of the fairness of a state's conduct towards an investor cannot be considered in isolation, i.e. only taking into account the bilateral relations between an investor and a host state. The assessment should include 'the context of the evolution of the host state's economy', as well as the 'reasonableness of the normative changes challenged and their appropriateness in the light of a criterion of proportionality also have to be taken into account.'[896]

The tribunal examined a series of state measures allegedly interfering with the investor's expectations. Some of these measures were adopted by Argentina as a response to the crisis before 2002, such as the 'pesification of the utility tariffs',[897] while

893. V. Beker, 'Argentina's Debt Crisis', in B. Moro, V. Beker (ed.) *Modern Financial Crises* (Springer, 2016) pp. 31-42; J. Alvarez, G. Topalian, 'The Paradoxical Argentina Cases' [2012] 6 *World Arbitration and Mediation Review*, pp. 491-544.

894. G. Bucheler, Proportionality in Investor-State Arbitration (Oxford University Press, 2015) 190. The analysis by the author focused on the Argentinian cases.

895. *Total v. Argentina*, Decision on Liability (27 December 2010) para. 123. The expectations are 'reasonable and hence legitimate' if they are based on 'principles of economic rationality, public interest (after having duly considered the need for and responsibility of governments to cope with unforeseen events and exceptional circumstances), reasonableness and proportionality'.

896. *Total v. Argentina*, ICSID Case No. ARB/04/01 Decision on Liability (27 December 2010) para. 123.

897. Pesification refers to the conversion of dollars into pesos. This measure entailed 'the elimination of the fixed link to the US dollar – necessarily also entailed the de-dollarisation of the public utilities' tariff regimes on the same terms, so that all tariff-related dollar denominated debt as well as future prices were converted into pesos at the previously fixed and official exchange rate of 1:1. Utilities were treated the same as all other holders of contractual rights, salary holders, etc. in Argentina.' (para. 123).

other measures were taken after 2002, e.g. the failure to renegotiate the tariffs, when Argentina 'emerged from the crisis'.[898] With regard to the 'pesification of the utility tariffs',[899] which was the emergency measure adopted by Argentina to remedy the consequences of the crisis, the tribunal provided that this measure was 'reasonable in the circumstances due to the crisis in Argentina and the general de-dollarisation of Argentina's economy'.[900] Hence, 'no expectations could reasonably be maintained (even less "legitimately") that only the tariffs would be excepted from such a pesification, especially as Total was not a beneficiary of any specific promise.'[901]

Another conclusion was reached with regard to the measure(s) entailing the 'freezing of tariffs since 2002'.[902] The *Total* tribunal concluded that the 'failure to promptly readjust the tariffs when the Emergency Law was enacted and during the height of the crisis could have been justified,' if Argentina had successfully renegotiated the tariffs to re-establish the basic principles of economic equilibrium.[903] After the adoption of the Emergency Law, Argentina's authorities delayed the renegotiation of the tariff regime in the public utility sector for a period of six years.[904] The tribunal found, as explained in section §6.04 that Argentina had failed to readjust the gas tariffs and had therefore violated the FET standard.[905]

The circumstances of an economic and financial crisis have also been taken into account in determining the protection of legitimate expectations in *National Grid v. Argentina*. This case concerned the investments of a UK company, National Grid (the investor), in Argentina's electrical power industry.[906] The investor claimed that the emergency measures had fundamentally changed the regulatory framework, thereby frustrating its legitimate expectations.

In its assessment, the tribunal noted that the FET standard protects 'reasonable and legitimate [expectations] in the context in which the investment was made'.[907] Therefore, the tribunal 'cannot ignore the context in which the Measures were taken. The determination of the Tribunal must take into account all the circumstances and in so doing cannot be oblivious to the crisis that the Argentine Republic endured at that time'.[908] The tribunal further explained 'what would be unfair and inequitable in

898. *Total v. Argentina*, ICSID Case No. ARB/04/01 Decision on Liability (27 December 2010) paras 171-172.
899. *Ibid.*, para. 163.
900. *Ibid.*, para. 167.
901. *Ibid.*
902. *Total v. Argentina*, ICSID Case No. ARB/04/01 Decision on Liability (27 December 2010) para. 166. The 'freezing of tariff' measure refers to the absence of any readjustment of the gas tariffs since 2002. This led to an inability on the part of investors to recover reasonable costs and to generate a reasonable rate of return, as was enshrined in the Gas Regulatory Framework for the tariffs of privatised gas utilities (para. 167).
903. *Total v. Argentina*, ICSID Case No. ARB/04/01 Decision on Liability (27 December 2010) para. 175.
904. *Ibid.*, para. 174.
905. *Ibid.*, para. 333.
906. *Ibid.*, para. 52.
907. *Ibid.*, para. 175.
908. *Ibid.*, para. 180.

normal circumstances may not be so in a situation of economic and social crisis.'[909] For this reason, the tribunal concluded that:

> The investor may not be totally insulated from situations such as the ones the Argentine Republic underwent in December 2001 and the months that followed. For these reasons, the Tribunal concludes that the breach of the fair and equitable treatment standard did not occur at the time the Measures were taken on January 6, 2002 but on June 25, 2002 when the Respondent required that companies such as the Claimant renounce the legal remedies they may have recourse to as a condition to re-negotiate the Concession.[910]

Ultimately, the tribunal came to the decision that Argentina had violated the FET standard because of (i) the adoption of the fundamental change to the legal framework relied upon by the investor; (ii) the absence of 'meaningful negotiations' between Argentina and the investor; and (iii) the requirement to renounce the investor's legal remedies imposed by Argentina on the investor as a condition to renegotiate the Concession.[911] However, the tribunal did take the economic crisis into consideration in deciding from which moment onwards the breach of the FET standard had occurred. The tribunal clarified that Argentina did not violate the FET standard when it had introduced the emergency measures in December 2001. However, Argentina had breached the FET standard when it had asked the investor on 25 June 2002 to abandon its rights to renegotiate the concession.[912]

In both *Total v. Argentina* and *National Grid v. Argentina*, the economic and financial crisis was a relevant consideration in the assessment of one of the emergency measures, i.e. the pesification of the utility tariffs, which was adopted by Argentina to address the crisis. The tribunals upheld this measure and concluded that foreign investors could not have legitimate expectations that the value of the peso would remain the same in the future (i.e., the Argentinian peso was fixed to the US dollar at the ratio of 1:1). However, several subsequent measures, and in particular the omission of Argentina to remedy the consequences of the emergency regulations for foreign investors, were found to be in violation of the FET standard. Hence, Argentina, notwithstanding the situation of a crisis and the post-crisis recovery, was expected by the tribunals in these cases to offer alternatives and solutions to the foreign investors in terms of renegotiating the utility tariffs/other financial agreements.

In other cases rendered against Argentina, initiated by investors because of the losses caused by the economic and financial crisis, the tribunals also acknowledged the severity of the crisis. However, this recognition only played a limited role in the assessment of the state's measures in the context of the FET standard.[913] In *CMS v. Argentina*, the case concerned a US company, CMS (the investor), which invested in the Argentinian gas transportation sector. The investor also challenged the state's measures, which had been adopted as a response to the economic and financial crisis.

909. *Ibid.*
910. *Ibid.*
911. *National Grid v. Argentina*, UNCITRAL, Award (3 November 2008), para. 179.
912. *Ibid.*, para. 180.
913. *Enron v. Argentina*, ICSID Case No. ARB/01/3(22 May 2017) paras 264-265; *CMS v. Argentina*, ICSID Case No. ARB/01/8 (12 May 2005), paras 354-356.

The measures included the termination of a possibility to calculate the tariffs in US dollars[914] and the suspension of an option to readjust the tariffs according to the inflation rate.[915] The tribunal found that Argentina had breached the FET standard because of the alteration of its regulatory framework resulting from the emergency measures.[916] In discussing the economic and financial crisis, the tribunal underlined that the 'Argentine crisis was severe but did not result in a total economic and social collapse.'[917] In this case, the tribunal considered that although the economic and financial crisis was indeed a relevant circumstance, it could not, however, serve as an excuse for the state to treat an investor in an unfair and inequitable manner.

[C] The Sociopolitical and Economic Transition of Former Socialist Countries

The role of certain 'circumstances' in the assessment of legitimate expectations has also featured in cases where the respondent states were former socialist Eastern European countries that were in the process of transitioning from a planned economy to a market economy.[918]

In *Parkerings v. Lithuania* (discussed above in sections §6.03[F] and §6.04[D]) and *Genin v. Estonia*, the tribunals took these sociopolitical circumstances into account in their analysis of the investors' expectations. In both cases, the tribunals considered the facts that both Estonia and Lithuania were undergoing a transformation of their economic and political institutions. For example, in *Genin v. Estonia*, the case concerned the revocation of the banking licence of a bank owned by several investors. This measure had been adopted by the state's authority for the purpose of regulating the Estonian banking sector.[919] In assessing the FET standard the tribunal emphasised that 'the circumstances of political and economic transitions prevailing in Estonia at the time, justified heightened scrutiny of the banking sector.'[920] As the tribunal put it, 'such regulation by a state reflects a clear and legitimate public purpose.'[921]

In *Parkerings v. Lithuania*, a similar assessment was made by the tribunal, in which it underlined that at the time of concluding the agreement between the state and the investor in 1998, 'the political environment in Lithuania was characteristic of a country in transition from its past being part of the Soviet Union to a candidate for EU membership.'[922] Consequently, the tribunal stressed that in Lithuania, the country in

914. *CMS v. Argentina*, ICSID Case No. ARB/01/8 (12 May 2005), para. 65.
915. *Ibid.*, para. 60.
916. *Ibid.*, para. 277.
917. *Ibid.*, para. 355.
918. D. Lane, 'Post-Communist States and the European Union' 23(4) *Journal of Communist Studies and Transition Politics*, 461-477; N. Bandelj, From Communists to Foreign Capitalists: The Social Foundations of Foreign Direct Investment in Postsocialist Europe, e-book (Princeton University Press, 2007).
919. *Genin v. Estonia*, ICSID Case No. ARB/99/2 Award (25 June 2001) para. 370.
920. *Ibid.*
921. *Ibid.*
922. *Parkerings v. Lithuania*, ICSID Case No. ARB/05/8 Award (11 September 2007) para. 335.

transition, 'legislative changes, far from being unpredictable, were in fact to be regarded as likely.'[923]

The tribunal in *Mamidoil v. Albania* (the facts have been discussed above in section §6.03[C]) expressly acknowledged the pivotal role of the hardship experienced by Albania that had 'just overcome a highly repressive and isolationist communist regime' and experienced a 'severe economic and financial crisis, which brought it to the brink of the complete collapse of its State structures'.[924] The tribunal explained that an investor could not expect that the legal framework at the time of the investment would remain stable, considering that the Albanian system was still rooted in communist traditions. This heritage of the host state and 'the overwhelming necessities of the present and future' were the key factors that had been considered in the tribunal's decision on the legitimate expectations.[925]

The tribunal underlined that 'these circumstances matter.'[926] It also pointed out that an investor investing in a country that was in a crisis was not entitled to expect the same level of stability as in countries such as Great Britain, the US or Japan.[927] Consequently, as was stressed in *Parkerings v. Lithuania* and *Genin v. Estonia*, the state's level of economic and political development has to be considered as a factor in assessing an investor's legitimate expectations.

In all three decisions, *Parkerings v. Lithuania*, *Genin v. Estonia* and *Mamidoil v. Albania*, the tribunals took into consideration the socio-economic conditions in the host states, pointing at the hardship of the transition period which each of these three host states had experienced. In all three cases, the tribunal did not find a violation of the FET standard.[928]

[D] The Economic Challenge of an Electricity Tariff Deficit in the Renewable Energy Sector

Investment cases in the renewable energy sector have been steadily increasing since a number of states have reduced their incentive schemes for renewable energy producers due to financial and economic difficulties.[929] Spain, Italy and the Czech Republic are

923. *Ibid.*
924. *Mamidoil Jetoil Greek Petroleum Products Société S.A. v. Republic of Albania*, ICSID Case No. ARB/11/24 Award (30 March 2015) para. 625.
925. *Ibid.*, para. 629.
926. *Mamidoil Jetoil Greek Petroleum Products Société S.A. v. Republic of Albania*, ICSID Case No. ARB/11/24 Award (30 March 2015) para. 626.
927. *Ibid.*
928. *Genin v. Estonia*, ICSID Case No. ARB/99/2 Award (25 June 2001) para. 371; *Mamidoil Jetoil Greek Petroleum Products Société S.A. v. Republic of Albania*, ICSID Case No. ARB/11/24 Award (30 March 2015) para. 771; *Parkerings v. Lithuania*, ICSID Case No. ARB/05/8 Award (11 September 2007) paras 320; 338, 346.
929. Y. Selivanova, 'Changes in Renewables Support Policy and Investment Protection under the Energy Charter Treaty: Analysis of Jurisprudence and Outlook for the Current Arbitration Cases' [2018] *ICSID Review, Volume 33 Issue 2*, 433-455; S. Matteotti, T. Payosova, 'The Role of Fair and Equitable Treatment Standard: Regulatory Coherence for Trade and Investment in Renewable Energy', in T. Cottier, I. Espa (eds) *International Trade in Sustainable Electricity* (Cambridge, 2017) 435.

among the respondent states that currently face investment claims because of alterations to their regulatory frameworks for renewable energy.[930] In cases rendered against Spain, i.e., *Charanne v. Spain, Eiser v. Spain, Isolux v. Spain* and *Antin v. Spain*, addressed in sections §6.03[D], §6.04[D] and §6.06, the host state's changes to the regulatory regime had been motivated by an increasing electricity tariff deficit. The deficit resulted from the difference between the subsidies in the form of feed-in tariffs granted by such host states to producers of renewable energy and the tariffs that had to be paid by consumers. The situation had even worsened because of the global economic crisis experienced by Spain between 2008 and 2014.[931] The combination of the tariff deficit and the crisis led to several regulatory measures being taken and implemented by the host state between 2010 and 2014. The measures had essentially transformed the regime of subsidies for renewable energy producers. These measures had an adverse impact on renewable energy investors because they had resulted in a substantial reduction of the profits gained by foreign investors and also cases of bankruptcies and forced financial renegotiations.[932] In the four aforementioned cases, the investors claimed a violation of the FET standard under the ECT referring to the changes implemented in the regulatory framework for renewable energy. The central issue in these investment cases was to what extent the host state can exercise its right to regulate by changing its laws without incurring liability under the FET standard.[933] The tribunals' answers to this question differed.

In *Charanne v. Spain, Eiser v. Spain, Isolux v. Spain* and *Antin v. Spain*, the tribunals did not dispute the legitimacy of the state's right to regulate with the purpose of remedying the tariff deficit problem. In all four cases, the tribunals emphasised that Spain had the right to regulate by changing its legislation in order to overcome the financial difficulties.[934] In weighing the economic circumstances concerning the tariff

930. *Antaris Solar GmbH and Dr. Michael Göde v. Czech Republic*, PCA Case No. 2014-01 Award (8 May 2018); *Natland and others v. Czech Republic*, PCA Case No. 2013-35, Notice of Arbitration 2013; *Masdar Solar & Wind Cooperatief U.A. v. Kingdom of Spain*, ICSID Case No. ARB/14/1 Award (16 May 2018); *CSP Equity Investment Sarl v. Kingdom of Spain*, SCC Case No. 094/2013, Notice of Arbitration, June 2013; *DCM Energy and others v. Kingdom of Spain*, ICSID Case No. ARB/17/41, Notice of Arbitration 2017; *Aharon Naftali Biram, and others v. Kingdom of Spain*, ICSID Case No. ARB/16/17, Notice of Arbitration 2016; *FREIF Eurowind v. Kingdom of Spain*, SCC Case No. 2017/060, Notice of Arbitration 2017; *Portigon AG v. Kingdom of Spain*, ICSID Case No. ARB/17/15, Notice of Arbitration 2017; *ESPF Beteiligungs GmbH and others v. Italian Republic*, ICSID Case No. ARB/16/5, Notice of Arbitration 2016; *Sun Reserve Luxco Holdings SRL v. Italy*, SCC Case No. 132/2016, *Eskosol S.p.A. in liquidazione v. Italian Republic*, ICSID Case No. ARB/15/50, Notice of Arbitration 2015; *Blusun S.A., J.-P. Lecorcier AND M. Stein v. Italy*, ICSID Case No. ARB/14/3 Award, 27 December 2016.
931. Bank of Spain, Report on the Financial and Banking Crisis in Spain, 2008-2014, Madrid, 2017, https://www.bde.es/f/webbde/Secciones/Publicaciones/OtrasPublicaciones/Fich/InformeCrisis_Completo_web_en.pdf accessed on 2 September 2018.
932. M. De Braekt, W. Geldhof, Mixed Results in Recent Arbitral Awards concerning Spain's Renewable Energy Policy, Stibbe Blog, Lexology, 19 July 2017; R. Power, P. Baker, The European Arbitration Review 2018 – Energy Arbitrations, Clyde&Co, 10 April 2018.
933. S. Matteoti, T. Payosova, 'The Role of Fair and Equitable Treatment Standard: Regulatory Coherence for Trade and Investment in Renewable Energy', in T. Cottier, I. Espa (eds) *International Trade in Sustainable Electricity* (Cambridge, 2017) 439.
934. *Antin Infrastructure Services Luxembourg S.à.r.l. and Antin Energia Termosolar B.V. v. Kingdom of Spain*, ICSID Case No. ARB/13/31 Award (15 June 2018) para. 555; *Charanne*

deficit challenge against the rights of investors under the FET standard, tribunals had adopted different views on the role of these circumstances in assessing the question of whether they could justify the disputed state's measures. In *Charanne v. Spain*, the tribunal, in evaluating whether the 2010 reforms were in the public interest or not, concluded that the measures of the Spanish authorities constituted legitimate public policies and had been adopted in order to 'limit the deficit and price increases'.[935] In this case, the special circumstances in the host state had been one of the main considerations to support the decision of the tribunal that the host state had not breached the FET standard. In *Antin v. Spain*, the tribunal had also considered the tariff deficit challenge faced by Spain in examining the transformation of a general regulatory framework. At first, the tribunal agreed with the host state's argument that the contested state's 2013 measures had been adopted with the purpose of remedying the tariff deficit. However, the tribunal referred to expert opinions which stated that 'the Tariff Deficit originated before Spain had any significant RE [renewable energy] capacity.'[936] This expert opinion contributed to the tribunal's conclusion that the special circumstance of the tariff deficit had not 'justified the elimination of the key features of the RD 661/2007 regime and its replacement by a wholly new regime, not based on any identifiable criteria'.[937] In *Eiser v. Spain*, the tribunal also acknowledged the tariff deficit as a legitimate public policy problem. However, the tribunal was of the view that Spain, in dealing with the tariff deficit challenge, should still be able to comply with the FET standard under the ECT.[938]

In the aforementioned cases, it was clear that the extent of the regulatory changes and the manner in which they were introduced were considered decisive factors in the weighing of the legitimate expectations of an investor concerning stability, on the one hand, and the state's right to regulate in the public interest, on the other (*see* section §6.04[D]). The tribunals indicated that the changes must be consistent with the public interest, economic reasonableness and the principle of proportionality.[939]

A central criterion in the tribunals' assessments on the question of maintaining regulatory stability was whether the change was disproportionate in view of the impact on the investors' investments. The tribunals specified that a state's regulatory measure would be considered disproportional when it amounts to a 'sudden and unpredictable

Construction v. Spain, SCC Case No. 062/2012 Award (21 January 2016) paras 500 and 536; *Eiser Infrastructure Ltd. and Energia Solar Luxembourg v. Spain*, ICSID Case No. ARB/13/36 Award (4 May 2017), para. 371.

935. *Charanne Construction v. Spain*, SCC Case No. 062/2012 Award (21 January 2016) para. 514; *Eiser Infrastructure Ltd. and Energia Solar Luxembourg v. Spain*, ICSID Case No. ARB/13/36 Award (4 May 2017), para. 536.
936. *Antin Infrastructure Services Luxembourg S.à.r.l. and Antin Energia Termosolar B.V. v. Kingdom of Spain*, ICSID Case No. ARB/13/31 Award (15 June 2018) para. 570 and para. 571.
937. *Antin Infrastructure Services Luxembourg S.à.r.l. and Antin Energia Termosolar B.V. v. Kingdom of Spain*, ICSID Case No. ARB/13/31 Award (15 June 2018) para. 572.
938. *Eiser Infrastructure Ltd. and Energia Solar Luxembourg v. Spain*, ICSID Case No. ARB/13/36 Award (4 May 2017), para. 371.
939. *Charanne Construction v. Spain*, SCC Case No. 062/2012 Award (21 January 2016) para. 514; *Eiser Infrastructure Ltd. and Energia Solar Luxembourg v. Spain*, ICSID Case No. ARB/13/36 Award (4 May 2017), para. 370.

elimination of the essential characteristics of the existing framework'.[940] Although the tribunals had different views on what constitutes such a sudden elimination, they had similar opinions concerning the conclusion that a disproportionate change is capable of breaching the FET standard under Article 10(1) of the ECT.

In *Eiser* and *Antin*, the tribunals adopted a broad interpretation of the stability requirement (i.e., broad from the investors' perspective), stressing that the 'obligation to accord fair and equitable treatment necessarily embraces the obligation to provide fundamental stability in the essential characteristics of the legal regime relied upon by investors in making long-term investments.'[941] Through this prism, these tribunals primarily focused on the impact of the regulatory change on the investors.[942]

For the *Charanne* and *Isolux* tribunals, however, the most important question to be addressed was whether the presence of the specific representations had led to legitimate expectations on the side of the investors regarding regulatory stability.[943] The state's duty to ensure the stability of the regulatory framework had been interpreted in a more restrictive fashion (again, viewed from the investors' perspective). In the same cases, the tribunals emphasised that the investors had a duty to conduct due diligence in order to be able to claim the protection of their (legitimate) expectations (*see* section §6.06).

The Spanish cases decided under the ECT demonstrate that the decision on the extent of the regulatory stability, which a host state is required to provide to an investor under the ECT's FET standard, depends on how tribunals balance the requirement of stability under the FET standard against the tariff deficit challenge, the due diligence duty of the investor and the presence of the specific representations that play a role in the specific case. Tribunals that adopted a broad interpretation of stability in relation to the ECT's FET standard (i.e., broad from the investors' perspective) tend to attach rather limited weight to the specific circumstances in the host state and primarily consider the impact of the change on the investor's investment. A narrow approach to stability (from the perspective of the investor) was adopted by other tribunals. In the

940. For example, *see*: *Charanne Construction v. Spain*, SCC Case No. 062/2012 Award (21 January 2016) para. 517.

941. *Eiser Infrastructure Ltd. and Energia Solar Luxembourg v. Spain*, ICSID Case No. ARB/13/36 Award (4 May 2017), para. 382. *Antin Infrastructure Services Luxembourg S.à.r.l. and Antin Energia Termosolar B.V. v. Kingdom of Spain*, ICSID Case No. ARB/13/31 Award (15 June 2018), para. 532. 'In sum, considering the context, object and purpose of the ECT, the Tribunal concludes that the obligation under Article 10(1) of the ECT to provide FET to protected investments comprises an obligation to afford fundamental stability in the essential characteristics of the legal regime relied upon by the investors in making long-term investments'.

942. *Eiser Infrastructure Ltd. and Energia Solar Luxembourg v. Spain*, ICSID Case No. ARB/13/36 Award (4 May 2017), para. 362 and para. 365; *Antin Infrastructure Services Luxembourg S.à.r.l. and Antin Energia Termosolar B.V. v. Kingdom of Spain*, ICSID Case No. ARB/13/31 Award (15 June 2018), para. 532.

943. *Charanne Construction v. Spain*, SCC Case No. 062/2012 Award (21 January 2016) paras 499 and 504; *Isolux Netherlands, BV v. Kingdom of Spain*, SCC Case V2013/153 Award (6 July 2016) paras 764 and 775. Also, the tribunal in Blusun placed emphasis on the presence of the specific representations. The tribunal emphasised that unless the state has not provided specific representations to an investor, there is 'no obligation to grant subsidies such as feed-in tariffs, or to maintain them unchanged once granted'. *Blusun S.A., J.-P. Lecorcier AND M. Stein v. Italy*, ICSID Case No. ARB/14/3 Award, 27 December 2016, para. 319.

latter cases, the tribunals limited the scope of the protection of legitimate expectations by placing emphasis on other elements that were pertinent to the assessment of legitimate expectations, e.g. the legitimacy of public policy objectives, the presence of specific representations and the due diligence exercised on the part of an investor (*see* section §6.06).

[E] Summary: The Economic and Socio-political Circumstances in a Host State

The economic and sociopolitical circumstances in a host state have been important factors in tribunals' assessments of the legitimacy of an investor's expectations. Tribunals have determined that in the situation of an economic and financial crisis or a sociopolitical transition, an investor could not expect that the state would act as in normal circumstances. Therefore, a tribunal's review of the investor's expectations involves – among other things – an assessment of whether the state has sufficient space to act in the public interest, e.g. by changing its laws in order to respond to the sociopolitical circumstances. In some of the cases presented above, the state's justification for a reversal of the state's representations to an investor, based on the need for the state to address, e.g., the consequences of a financial crisis or post-transition period, was upheld by the tribunals. Tribunals, to this end, found that solving the hardship experienced by such a state was reasonable and that therefore it sufficed as an explanation for interfering with an investor's expectations. To this end, several tribunals have clarified that an investor cannot have expectations that the state will not change or alter its laws and policies during the lifetime of its investment.[944] At the same time, a host state's response to difficult circumstances, such as an electricity tariff deficit, must be proportionate. In cases, in which the investors' legitimate expectations were based on the stability of a regulatory framework, the outcome depended on how much weight a tribunal put on (i) the urgency for the state to respond to the tariff deficit challenge, (ii) the fulfilment by the investor of his due diligence duty and (iii) the presence of any specific representations given by the state to the investor.

§6.06 INVESTOR'S CONDUCT

[A] Introduction

Another element that plays a role in establishing the existence of legitimate expectations on the part of the investor is the investor's own conduct.[945] As will be demonstrated in this section, some of the tribunals have underlined that they expect

944. *Saluka Investments BV v. Czech Republic* [2006] UNCITRAL Arbitration Partial Award (17 March 2006) para. 305. *See also*: *Continental Casualty v. Argentina*, ICSID Case No. ARB/03/9 Award (5 September 2008) para. 258. *AES Summit v. Hungary*, ICSID Case No. ARB/07/22 Award (23 September 2010) para. 9.3.29.

945. M. Potestà, 'Legitimate Expectations in Investment Treaty Law: Understanding the Roots and the Limits of a Controversial Concept' [2013] 28(1) *ICSID Review*, 38; M. Sornarajah, Resistance and Change in the International Law on Foreign Investments (Cambridge University Press, 2015) 278.

from an investor that it first assesses the possible risks and performs a due diligence investigation before deciding to invest in a host state. On the part of an investor, the performance of due diligence and risk assessment may include the collection of information about the rules and regulations that are pertinent to the proposed investment, as well as the economic situation in and the sociopolitical background of a host state.

[B] Due Diligence and Risk Assessment

In assessing the legitimacy of an investor's expectations, a number of tribunals have underlined the importance of the investor's own diligent conduct aimed at the preparation and protection of his (future) expectations.[946]

The tribunal in *Biwater v. Tanzania* underlined that 'countervailing factors such as the responsibility of foreign investors, both in terms of prior due diligence as well as subsequent conduct' should be considered in establishing a violation.[947] It also observed that the legitimate expectations of an investor might be reduced 'in circumstances where an investor itself takes on risks in entering a particular investment environment'.[948] This point was also made by the tribunal in *Parkerings v. Lithuania*, discussed in sections §6.03[F] and §6.04[D]. The tribunal stated that considering the sociopolitical and economic transition in Lithuania, the investor should have anticipated changes to the regulatory framework. The tribunal provided: 'As any businessman would, the Claimant was aware of the risk that changes of laws would probably occur after the conclusion of the Agreement.'[949]

Therefore, the investor is expected to consider business risks, which to a large extent depend on the country to be invested in.[950] This point has been illustrated by Vinuales who has stated that 'it would not be reasonable for an investor investing in a highly volatile political environment, whatever the assurances received, that the investment will no longer affected by further disruptions.'[951]

Several tribunals have clarified the extent of the due diligence by the investor. The tribunal in *Frontier v. Czech Republic* asserted that the investor should perform due diligence checks and make business decisions on the basis of the law and the factual situation at the time of investment.[952] Under this due diligence obligation, the investor has to consider not only the relevant regulations that are applicable to investment transactions, e.g. specific permit requirements, but also 'the entire legal framework

946. F. Dupuy, P.-M. Dupuy, 'What to Expect from Legitimate Expectations? A Critical Appraisal and Look Into the Future of the "Legitimate Expectations" Doctrine in International Investment Law', in M.A. Raouf, et al. (eds) *Festschrift Ahmed Sadek El- Kosheri: From the Arab World to the Globalization of International Law* (Kluwer, 2015) 297.
947. *Biwater v. Tanzania,* ICSID Case No. ARB/05/22 Final Award (24 July 2008) para. 601.
948. *Ibid.*
949. *Parkerings v. Lithuania,* ICSID Case No. ARB/05/8 Award (11 September 2007) para. 335.
950. A.R. Sureda, 'Legitimate Expectations, Risk and Due Diligence', in A.R. Sureda (ed.) *Investment Treaty Arbitration: Judging under Uncertainty* (Cambridge University Press, 2012) 79.
951. J. Vinuales [2017] p. 363.
952. *Frontier v. Czech Republic* [2010] UNCITRAL Arbitration, Award (12 November 2010) para. 287.

potentially applicable to the investment' and 'the potential changes of such framework that are foreseeable at the time the investment is made'.[953]

In *Mamidoil v. Albania*, the tribunal further stressed the importance of considering the investor's conduct:

> The investor is entitled to rely on the stability and transparency of the legal framework. However, the obligation of the State does not dispense the obligation of the investor to evaluate the circumstances. Reliance has at its prerequisite diligent inquiry and information. The investor has to understand the content and the context of the law and the administrative practice. Put differently, the standard is addressed to both the State and the investor. Fairness and equitableness cannot be established adequately without an adequate and balanced appraisal of both parties' conduct.[954]

A comparable requirement to exercise due diligence in order to obtain protection under the standard of legitimate expectations was articulated in *Charanne v. Spain*, *Isolux v. Spain* and *Masdar Solar v. Spain*. The *Charanne* tribunal came to the view that for an investor to be able to 'exercise the right of legitimate expectations', it should perform a 'diligent analysis of the legal framework for the investment'.[955] It follows that an investor can only claim protection under the notion of legitimate expectations in the situation that any regulatory measures were not 'reasonably foreseeable at the time of the investment'.[956] In this particular case, the tribunal was of the opinion that these changes were foreseeable and the claim therefore failed.

In *Isolux v. Spain*, the tribunal, while employing a similar test as in *Charanne*, clarified that in order for an investor to rely on legitimate expectations, he should have conducted a proper due diligence investigation into the regulatory framework before making an investment. An investor's legitimate expectations can only be considered violated if the new regulatory changes were not foreseeable by 'a prudent investor'.[957] In this case, the tribunal established that the investor had made his investments in a PV plant in 2012, at the time when Spain had already introduced significant modifications to the regime that regulates renewable energy. The investor could have foreseen that additional state reforms were coming.[958] The tribunal also noted that the investor possessed specific knowledge that the feed-in tariffs introduced by the Spanish authorities would not last for the entire lifetime of his investments.[959] On this basis, the tribunal rejected the investor's claim that his legitimate expectations arising out of the stability of a regulatory framework should have been protected.[960]

953. J. Vinuales, [2017] p. 362.
954. *Mamidoil Jetoil Greek Petroleum Products Société S.A. v. Republic of Albania*, ICSID Case No. ARB/11/24 Award (30 March 2015) para. 634.
955. *Charanne Construction v. Spain*, SCC Case No. 062/2012 Award (21 January 2016) para. 505.
956. *Ibid.*, para. 505.
957. *Isolux Netherlands, BV v. Kingdom of Spain*, SCC Case V2013/153 Award (17 July 2016) para. 781.
958. *Ibid.*, para. 787.
959. *Ibid.*
960. *Isolux Netherlands, BV v. Kingdom of Spain*, SCC Case V2013/153 Award (17 July 2016) para. 796. At the same time, the tribunal underlined that the investor could expect a reasonable return on his investment in view of the new regulatory framework.

In *Antin v. Spain*, the tribunal also considered the topic of due diligence performed on the part of the investor. In this case, as in *Isolux*, the investor made his investments when several legislative reforms regarding the renewable energy regime had already been made. However, the tribunal explained that the factual situation in the *Antin* case was different from the one in *Isolux v. Spain*. The state's regulatory changes that had been adopted prior to Isolux's investment mostly affected PV installations, which were the subject of Isolux's investments.[961] However, the CSP sector, in which Antin had invested, was impacted to a lesser extent and had continued to receive support from the state's authorities. To this end, the tribunal concluded that Antin – based on a legal report that confirmed that the regime for CSP installations was not likely to be modified in the near future – had carried out satisfactory due diligence.[962]

The tribunal in *Masdar Solar v. Spain* also determined that the investor had complied with the due diligence requirement (for a discussion of this case, *see*: section §6.03[C] of this Chapter). The tribunal explained this requirement as follows: 'the investor must demonstrate that it has exercised appropriate due diligence and that it had familiarized itself with the existing laws.'[963] In this case, the tribunal found that the investor had conducted a due diligence investigation, i.e. by commissioning reports from external experts; by having discussions with its co-venturer and the Spanish banks that provided the detailed knowledge of the regulatory framework; and by consulting law firms concerning the regulatory issues, e.g. the anticipated reforms in RD661/2007.[964]

The examples of these recent cases indicate the growing importance of cautiousness and proper preparation by the investor. This means that an investor should thoroughly assess beforehand 'the possibility of a change' specifically with regard to a general regulatory framework relied upon in its investment.[965] This implies that an investor has to be aware of, and must carefully examine and take into account in its decision to invest, all the pertinent regulations, policies and decisions and possible risks. Furthermore, the investor is expected to take into account the political, social, economic and social background prevailing in the host state at the time of the investment, in order to reasonably assess the possibility of a change in the host state. The threshold for violating legitimate expectations as outlined by *Isolux v. Spain*, is whether the new regulatory changes were not foreseeable by a prudent investor.[966] The foreseeability is judged by the efforts undertaken by the investor to assess the

961. *Antin Infrastructure Services Luxembourg S.à.r.l. and Antin Energia Termosolar B.V. v. Kingdom of Spain*, ICSID Case No. ARB/13/31 Award (15 June 2018) paras 126-127.
962. *Ibid.*, para. 123.
963. *Masdar Solar & Wind Cooperatief U.A. v. Kingdom of Spain*, ICSID Case No. ARB/14/1 Award (16 May 2018) para. 494.
964. *Ibid.*, para. 497.
965. F. Dupuy, P.-M. 'Dupuy, What to Expect from Legitimate Expectations? A Critical Appraisal and Look Into the Future of the "Legitimate Expectations" Doctrine in International Investment Law', in M.A. Raouf, et al. (eds) *Festschrift Ahmed Sadek El- Kosheri: From the Arab World to the Globalization of International Law* (Kluwer, 2015) 292.
966. *Isolux Netherlands, BV v. Kingdom of Spain*, SCC Case V2013/153 Award (17 July 2016) para. 781.

possibility of any chances. These recent awards demonstrate that such efforts by investors have to be supported by specific evidence in the form of reports, and communicating with state's bodies and organisations that can provide reliable information regarding the regulatory framework.

In evaluating an investor's legitimate expectations stemming either from the specific representations of the state towards an investor or from the expectation of the stability of the applicable general regulatory framework, tribunals have expressed that such expectations have to be assessed in the light of the circumstances in a host state and with due regard to the investor's conduct. The consideration of the specific circumstances in a host state is reinforced by the tribunals' view that an investor should make a due diligence and risk assessment by taking into account the laws and regulations that are relevant to its investment, as well as the broader sociopolitical and economic background prevailing in a host state. The lack of an investor's efforts to conduct a due diligence investigation can contribute to a tribunal's conclusion that its (legitimate) expectations cannot be protected under the FET standard.[967]

§6.07 SUMMARY OF THE CHAPTER AND INTERIM CONCLUSIONS

The tension between the state's right to regulate and the legitimate expectations of the investor tends to arise when the stability of an investor's investment is undermined by a state's measure. The state's measure can be taken in the public interest, aiming for instance to mitigate the circumstances of an economic crisis. The question is whether such a measure interferes with the investor's legitimate expectations as protected under the FET standard. Tribunals have tried to resolve this tension. The tribunals assess whether the investor may rely on his expectations in order for them to qualify as legitimate expectations protected by the FET standard. This evaluation includes a balancing of different interests; i.e., the legitimate expectations of the investor have to be weighed against the state's right to regulate in the public interest. To this end, the assessment of legitimate expectations does not involve merely the 'subjective' interests of the investor.[968] It also takes into account the 'reality, experience and context' in which the investor's expectations were created and allegedly frustrated by a host state.[969] Consequently, in order to determine whether the legitimate expectations of the

967. *Mamidoil Jetoil Greek Petroleum Products Société S.A. v. Republic of Albania*, ICSID Case No. ARB/11/24 Award (30 March 2015) para. 634; *Parkerings v. Lithuania*, ICSID Case No. ARB/05/8 Award (11 September 2007) para. 335; *Isolux Netherlands, BV v. Kingdom of Spain*, SCC Case V2013/153 Award (17 July 2016) para. 781; *Masdar Solar & Wind Cooperatief U.A. v. Kingdom of Spain*, ICSID Case No. ARB/14/1 Award (16 May 2018) para. 494.
968. *Saluka Investments BV v. Czech Republic* [2006] UNCITRAL Arbitration Partial Award (17 March 2006) para. 304; also *see*: *El Paso v. Argentina*, ICSID Case No. ARB/03/15 Award (31 October 2011) para. 358. The tribunal emphasised that 'legitimate expectations cannot be solely the subjective expectations of the investor ... investor's legitimate expectations must be grounded in reality, experience and context'.
969. UNCTAD 'Fair and Equitable Treatment: UNCTAD Series on International Investment Agreements II' (New York, 2012) 67. The report provides that 'in order to avoid an overbroad reading of the FET standard by reference to legitimate expectations, several awards have sought to identify factors that delimit the scope of such expectations ...'.

investor are subject to protection, four elements are important in the evaluation of the facts. These are: (1) the specific representations made to the investor; (2) the stability of a general regulatory framework; (3) the economic and sociopolitical circumstances in the host state; and (4) the investor's conduct, e.g. a proper and adequate due diligence and risk assessment. These four elements - including several sub-elements - are displayed in Table 1 and are further explained in this section.

Table 1 Elements That Play a Central Role in the Determination of Whether the Expectations of an Investor Should be Considered Legitimate

1. The specific representations made by the state to an investor 1.1 The competence of the state authority making the representation 1.2 The 'legal force' of the representation, which depends on its: (i) Legal form (ii) Content (iii) Wording 1.3 The distinctive designation of the investor in the state's representations
2. The stability of the general regulatory framework 2.1 The level of the impact on investments due to the transformation of a general regulatory framework 2.2 The manner of the transformation of a general regulatory framework
3. The economic and sociopolitical circumstances in the host state 3.1 An economic and/or financial crisis in the host state 3.2 The sociopolitical and economic transition of former socialist countries 3.3 The economic challenge of an electricity tariff deficit in the renewable energy sector
4. The investor's conduct 4.1 Due diligence and risk assessment

In section §6.03, legitimate expectations generated by a specific representation by the host state have been discussed (*see* Table 1: element 1). To determine whether the representations qualify as specific, tribunals address three questions, namely: (i) whether the representations are created by a competent state authority; (ii) what is the legal force of the specific representation in terms of its legal form, content and the wording?; and (iii) how has the investor been designated in the state's representations? On the basis of the case law analysis, it has been found that:

(i) in several decisions, the tribunals have clarified that the state's representations can only be regarded as specific if they were provided by a competent state authority that has the relevant decision-making power;[970]
(ii) furthermore, in analysing the legal form, content and wording of a representation, tribunals have emphasised that in order to qualify as specific, a representation should have a formal character, aimed at the purposeful and

970. *Metalclad v. Mexico*, ICSID Case No. ARB(AF)/97/1 Award (30 August 2000) para. 86; *Crystallex v. Venezuela*, ICSID Case No. ARB(AF)/11/2 Award (4 April 2016) paras 561-562; *Total v. Argentina*, ICSID Case No. ARB/04/01 Decision on Liability (27 December 2010) para. 121.

specific inducement of an investment.[971] In some decisions, it has been underlined that the specific promise should be expressed as an explicit commitment;[972]

(iii) moreover, tribunals have been consistent in ruling that the state's representations should be addressed directly to a particular investor and cannot be aimed at large or even small groups of potential investors.

In section §6.03[F], a special type of specific representation has been analysed, i.e. in contracts between a state and an investor. In some FET decisions, this category of representation has been classified as an example of a specific representation. Contracts between a host state and an investor usually satisfy the requirements for specificity addressed above. For contractual commitments, the issue is not so much whether the competent authority has made the representation but whether the state or the state agency has acted as a sovereign authority in the contractual relationship with the investor. Tribunals emphasise that in order to differentiate ordinary contractual rights from treaty rights, the test is to determine whether states or their agencies have acted as 'holders of sovereign power or as parties to a contract'.[973] To differentiate whether the state has acted as a sovereign power or just as a contractual party, tribunals assess whether the breaches involve, e.g., 'some forms of State interference with the operation of the contract'.[974] In the case of such interference, a breach of the contract may lead to a frustration of the legitimate expectations under the FET standard. Ordinary contractual breaches, however, are unlikely to give rise to the protection of legitimate expectations, as they generally belong to the domain of contractual relationships between commercial parties. Upon the fulfilment of the requirement that the state has acted in the capacity of a sovereign authority, tribunals are generally of the view that other treaty breaches, such as a violation of due process or discrimination, are required in order for the contractual expectations to give rise to the protection of legitimate expectations under the FET standard.[975]

In section §6.04, another ground, the stability of the general regulatory framework, which can lead to the protection of legitimate expectations, has been analysed. Investors often allege that state measures which change the general regulatory framework upon which the investor relied at the time of the investment have violated its (legitimate) expectations (*see* Table 1: element 2). Tribunals have asserted that an investor investing in a host state should be able to rely on a certain degree of stability

971. *Glamis v. US* [2009] NAFTA, ICSID 48 ILM 1039 Award (8 June 2009) para. 766.

972. *Mamidoil Jetoil Greek Petroleum Products Société S.A. v. Republic of Albania*, ICSID Case No. ARB/11/24 Award (30 March 2015) para. 648; *LG&E Energy Corp., LG&E Capital Corp. & LG&E International v. The Argentine Republic*, ICSID Case No. ARB/02/1 Decision on Liability (3 October 2006) para. 130.

973. *Impregilo S.p.A v. Argentina*, ICSID Case No. ARB/07/17 Award (21 June 2011) para. 296.

974. *Joy Mining Machinery v. Egypt*, ICSID Case No. ARB/03/11 Decision on Jurisdiction (6 August 2004) para. 72.

975. *Glamis v. US* [2009] NAFTA, ICSID 48 ILM 1039 Award (8 June 2009) para. 620; *Waste Management v. Mexico II* [2004] ICSID Case No. ARB(AF)/00/3 Award (30 April 2004), para. 115.

for its investment.[976] It does not imply that investors should expect that the legal framework will not change. Tribunals have been consistent in stating that only severe changes to a general regulatory framework may give rise to protection under the FET standard. In assessing the claims brought on the basis of changes to a general regulatory framework, the tribunals evaluate: (1) the level of the impact that the changes to the general regulatory framework may have on an investor and its investments, and (2) the manner in which the transformation of the general regulatory framework has been conducted. On the basis of the case law analysis, it has been found that:

(1) regarding the impact on investments, tribunals underline that the change to the regulatory framework has to be drastic and/or discriminatory and has a substantial financial impact on the investor in order to come to the conclusion that the investor's legitimate expectations have been breached;[977]
(2) most tribunals have emphasised the significance of the way in which the state has transformed the general regulatory framework that has been relied upon by the investor. Tribunals often emphasised that the transformation of a regulatory framework should be proportional. This implies that the changes must not lead to a 'sudden and unpredictable elimination of the essential characteristics of the existing framework'.[978] Tribunals have underlined that the state can change its regulatory framework, but it has to respect 'basic features' that are entrenched in the legal framework regulating the specific field or industry and which have been relied upon by an investor in making the investment in the first place.[979] The alteration of the regulatory framework upon which the investors had relied can be justified by tribunals if the alteration has been gradual and in accordance with the long-term objectives of the state.

In section §6.05, the role of sociopolitical and economic circumstances in the determination of the protection of legitimate expectations was analysed (*see* Table 1: element 3). In assessing the investor's expectations, tribunals consider the economic and sociopolitical circumstances that have affected the reversal of the state's representations interfering with the expectations of an investor. In claims on the protection of

976. *Parkerings v. Lithuania*, ICSID Case No. ARB/05/8 Award (11 September 2007) para. 333. The tribunal stated that 'In principle, an investor has a right to a certain stability and predictability of the legal environment of the investment'.
977. *Toto v. Lebanon*, ICSID Case No. ARB/07/12 Award (7 June 2012) para. 244. Also *see*: *El Paso v. Argentina*, ICSID Case No. ARB/03/15 Award (31 October 2011) para. 510.
978. *Charanne Construction v. Spain*, SCC Case No. 062/2012 Award (21 January 2016) para. 517; *Antin Infrastructure Services Luxembourg S.à.r.l. and Antin Energia Termosolar B.V. v. Kingdom of Spain*, ICSID Case No. ARB/13/31 Award (15 June 2018) para. 556; *Eiser Infrastructure Ltd. and Energia Solar Luxembourg v. Spain*, ICSID Case No. ARB/13/36 Award (4 May 2017), para. 370.
979. *Total v. Argentina*, ICSID Case No. ARB/04/01 Decision on Liability (27 December 2010) para. 168. *Charanne Construction v. Spain*, SCC Case No. 062/2012 Award (21 January 2016) 539.

an investor's legitimate expectations, tribunals have recognised that for these expectations to be protected, they 'must rise to the level of legitimacy and reasonableness in light of the circumstances'.[980] Three types of special economic and sociopolitical circumstances have been distinguished in this study: (1) an economic and/or financial crisis in the host state, (2) the sociopolitical transition of former socialist countries and (3) the economic deficit challenge in the renewable energy sector. These special circumstances are examples of the public interest often featuring as a relevant factor in deciding on the protection of the legitimate expectations of an investor. Tribunals have provided that in a situation of economic crisis or a sociopolitical transition, the investor cannot expect that the state will act as it would in normal circumstances. The reversal of some of the state's representations interfering with the expectations of an investor has been justified on the basis of a public interest measure adopted to remedy the consequences of the crisis or the post-transition period.

At the same time, a host state's response to the crisis cannot be justified if it is disproportionate to the impact of such measures on the investment.[981] In the case that (i) the key features of the state's regulatory framework relied upon by the investor are eliminated and (ii) the investor suffers serious financial losses, it will be more likely that a tribunal concludes that the FET standard has been violated.[982] The question of to what extent a state can regulate to respond to special circumstances without violating the FET standard depends on elements such as how severe the crisis is, whether the investor has performed a proper due diligence investigation and whether the state has provided specific representations to the investor. In the renewable energy decisions under the ECT, the tribunals, which emphasised the state's obligation to provide stability as a part of FET, directed their primary focus to the impact of the regulatory change on the investor.[983] Whereas, in decisions in which the stability of the regulatory framework had been interpreted restrictively (considered from the perspective of the investor), the tribunals imposed more requirements on investors to demonstrate that their legitimate expectations had not been fulfilled, thereby creating more policy space for a host state to regulate in the public interest.

In section §6.06, the role of the investor's conduct in the protection of legitimate expectations has been discussed (Table 1: element 4). Tribunals have underlined that an investor has the responsibility to appraise the reality and the context of the state where the investment is to be made by performing due diligence and risk assessments. It may be expected from the investor that it should 'evaluate the circumstances' and

980. *Saluka Investments BV v. Czech Republic* [2006] UNCITRAL Arbitration Partial Award (17 March 2006) para. 304.

981. *Antin Infrastructure Services Luxembourg S.à.r.l. and Antin Energia Termosolar B.V. v. Kingdom of Spain*, ICSID Case No. ARB/13/31 Award (15 June 2018) para. 556; *Blusun S.A., J.-P. Lecorcier AND M. Stein v. Italy*, ICSID Case No. ARB/14/3 Award (27 December 2016) para. 319.

982. *Eiser Infrastructure Ltd. and Energia Solar Luxembourg v. Spain*, ICSID Case No. ARB/13/36 Award (4 May 2017), para. 365.

983. *Ibid.*, para. 380; *Antin Infrastructure Services Luxembourg S.à.r.l. and Antin Energia Termosolar B.V. v. Kingdom of Spain*, ICSID Case No. ARB/13/31 Award (15 June 2018) para. 526.

'understand the content and the context of the law and the administrative practice'.[984] Before claiming protection under legitimate expectations, an investor has to be aware and take into account the relevant regulations, policies and decisions concerning its investment in order to anticipate the possible risks. The investor is also expected to take into account the political, social, economic and social background prevailing in the host state at the time of the investment, in order to reasonably assess the possibility of a change in a host state. It means that a prudent investor should be able to foresee the possibility of a change specifically with regard to a general regulatory framework which has been relied upon for its investment.[985] Some tribunals emphasised that legitimate expectations will not be protected in the case that the regulatory changes were foreseeable.[986] Some tribunals judged the investor's due diligence to be satisfactory if the investor had demonstrated clear efforts to properly collect information regarding the possibility of changes in a regulatory framework, e.g. by commissioning a due diligence investigation to experts.[987]

The analysis of the elements which are central to the protection of the legitimate expectations of the investor demonstrates that a tribunal's decision on the legitimacy of expectations relied upon by an investor is a complex exercise. It involves a legal analysis of the investor's claims concerning its reliance on specific representations made by the host state or on the stability of a general regulatory framework. At the same time, tribunals also pay attention to the special circumstances in the host state and the degree of the investor's preparation before taking the decision to invest in the host state.

What follows from the analysis of the legitimate expectations of an investor is that tribunals since the *Saluka* award in 2006 have developed certain criteria in deciding on tensions between the expectations of an investor and the state's right to regulate. These criteria help tribunals to assess the expectations of an investor and to decide whether they are legitimate. Tribunals, however, have not been consistent in applying these criteria in their analyses and decisions.

As explained in this Chapter, legitimate expectations can only be recognised if they are based on specific representations or, sometimes, on a general legal framework. Specific representations have to be made by the competent state authority of the host state, must have legal force and must be addressed to the designated investor. Legal force can be established based on the legal form, the content and the wording of the representation by the state to the investor. These criteria have not been consistently applied by tribunals and also not in a cumulative way. Tribunals rarely follow the

984. *Mamidoil Jetoil Greek Petroleum Products Société S.A. v. Republic of Albania*, ICSID Case No. ARB/11/24 Award (30 March 2015) para. 634.
985. *Isolux Netherlands, BV v. Kingdom of Spain*, SCC Case V2013/153 Award (17 July 2016) para. 781.
986. *Charanne Construction v. Spain*, SCC Case No. 062/2012 Award (21 January 2016) para. 505; *Isolux Netherlands, BV v. Kingdom of Spain*, SCC Case V2013/153 Award (17 July 2016) para. 787.
987. *Antin Infrastructure Services Luxembourg S.à.r.l. and Antin Energia Termosolar B.V. v. Kingdom of Spain*, ICSID Case No. ARB/13/31 Award (15 June 2018) para. 123; *Masdar Solar & Wind Cooperatief U.A. v. Kingdom of Spain*, ICSID Case No. ARB/14/1 Award (16 May 2018) para. 497.

step-by-step process developed in this Chapter in providing the legal foundation for their decision on the question of specific representations. Only in the *Total v. Argentina* case did the tribunal, first, review the origins and the use of legitimate expectations in multiple legal systems[988] and, second, articulate all three criteria that have to be satisfied for establishing that specific representations were provided to the investor. Other tribunals in assessing the specificity of representations – the central basis for the protection of legitimate expectations – do not provide a legal basis for their assessment.

The state's right to regulate has sometimes surfaced in the context of assessing the question of the legitimate expectations of an investor. That has occurred, e.g., when tribunals have taken into consideration special circumstances related to the economic or sociopolitical situation in a host state. The public interest, such as the resolution of a financial or economic crisis, the response to an electricity deficit and the realisation of the sociopolitical transition of the economy have been relevant in the assessment of legitimate expectations in the cases analysed. Tribunals have been consistent in providing that in a situation of economic and sociopolitical hardship, the investor cannot expect that its expectations will be honoured in the same way as in the normal circumstances. However, a discrepancy was noted in some decisions concerning the impact of the economic and financial crisis on the legitimate expectations of an investor, e.g. in the case of the state measure regarding the pesification of Argentinian utility tariffs, as well as in the cases concerning the Spanish renewable energy reform. This discrepancy suggests that the analysis concerning the role of the public interest vis-à-vis the legitimate expectations of an investor needs to be further refined. Also, the investor's due diligence, emphasised by recent jurisprudence, raises some questions regarding the extent of the application of this condition in assessing the protection of legitimate expectations. These questions are further addressed in Chapter 8, where the case law and the new generation of IIAs are compared.

988. *See*: Chapter 4, section §4.03[D] where this decision is analysed with regard to reliance on national law.

CHAPTER 7

Conditions for a State to Lawfully Exercise Its Right to Regulate

§7.01 INTRODUCTION

This Chapter focuses on an assessment of a state's measure that aims to protect public health, the environment or any other public interest which falls within its right to regulate, while at the same time the same measure might possibly violate the state's obligations pursuant to the FET standard. From the case law, it appears that tribunals employ several tests to assess whether a disputed state's measure is lawful (and falls within the ambit of the right to regulate), or whether it, as alleged by the investor, violates the FET standard. This Chapter presents and discusses these tests with the aim of defining the conditions that apply to lawfully exercising the right to regulate within the legal regime of the FET standard.

The first test will be addressed in section §7.02. This test focuses on whether the objective of the state's measure is legitimate. In particular, tribunals evaluate whether the objective of the state's measure serves a public interest and whether the said objective can be substantiated by the host state through records and other evidence.

The second test, explained in section §7.03, concerns the lawfulness of the contested state's measure itself and its implementation. First, the question of whether the measure relates to the state's objective will be addressed. Second, this test includes the question of how the measure has been implemented and which effects has it had as far as the investor is concerned. These two aspects are assessed by tribunals on the basis of several principles of international law, in particular the principles of reasonableness, proportionality, the prohibition of arbitrariness, non-discrimination and transparency.

The third test concerns the question of subject to which criteria does a host state's violation of its national law lead or contributes to a breach of the FET standard (section §7.05). In evaluating an investor's claim that a breach of national law by the host state violates the FET standard, tribunals have provided some clarity regarding the question of whether, and to what extent, a state's measure under national law can be reviewed. The circumstances under which a breach of national law results in a breach of the FET standard or can contribute thereto are analysed.

§7.02 THE OBJECTIVE OF THE STATE'S MEASURE

[A] Introduction

A review of a host state's measure, which is contested by a foreign investor, is at the core of the analysis of a claim based on the FET standard. To determine the lawfulness of the state's measure, the first test commonly applied by tribunals concerns an assessment of what is often termed the *legitimacy* of the objective of the state's measure.[989]

In section §7.02[B], the criteria used by tribunals in evaluating the legitimacy of the state's objectives are explained. In assessing whether a state's objective is legitimate or not, tribunals consider whether it has been pursued with the goal of regulating a public interest. Section §7.02[C] analyses several investment cases where the state's measures have been motivated by a specific public interest objective, such as an environmental, a human rights and/or a public health objective. As demonstrated in Chapter 2, under section §2.03[E], these types of policy objectives represent examples of recognised public interests that are most commonly included in the newest series of IIAs.[990] Consequently, the purpose of this section is to assess how tribunals treat these acknowledged public interest objectives. This will be contrasted in section §7.02[D], in which several cases will be discussed in which tribunals have decided that the states' objectives were illegitimate. In the latter cases, tribunals have found that such objectives were motivated primarily by the political considerations of the state authority.

[B] The Legitimacy of the State's Objectives

In evaluating a contested host state's measure, a significant number of tribunals have assessed whether the objective of the state's measure was legitimate. Two elements play a role in the tribunals' reviews. First, tribunals consider whether a state measure's objective was to serve a public interest. This concerns the significance and content of

989. J. Bonnitcha, (2014), e-book, section 4.7, p. 163: 'Many arbitral awards have held that the FET standard also allows tribunals to review government conduct on substantive grounds.' It involves an assessment of the state's objective. Also *see*: C. Henckels, Proportionality and Deference in Investor-State Arbitration (Cambridge University Press, 2015) 126. Henckels notes that different tribunals have attached different weight to the assessment of the objective of the state's measure.

990. *See* Chapter 2, section §2.03[E]. For examples of IIAs which include environmental, human rights and/or public health objectives, *see*: Article 8.9(1) of the CETA (signed on 30 October 2016), http://ec.europa.eu/trade/policy/in-focus/ceta/ accessed on 15 March 2017; Articles 12*bis* of the EU-Vietnam FTA, draft text (January 2016), European Commission, http://trade.ec.europa.eu/doclib/press/index.cfm?id=1437 accessed on 27 May 2017.

the objective of the state's measure. Second, the tribunals consider whether the objective that is claimed to be in the public interest can be substantiated by the host state through records and other evidence. The cases below provide an analysis of the tribunals' considerations in deciding whether the objective of a state's measure is legitimate.

The first case to be discussed is a landmark one, i.e. the case of *Saluka v. Czech Republic*, which concerned the privatisation of the Czech banking system.[991] Saluka, the Dutch subsidiary of the Japanese Nomura financial group (the investor), became the owner of Investiní a Potovní banka (IBP), a bank which had been fully privatised in 1998.[992] IBP was among the 'Big Four' banks in the Czech Republic. However, at that time, the other three banks had not been fully privatised and were still partly owned by the state.[993] By the end of the 1990s, all of the 'Big Four' banks experienced serious financial problems due to the country's 'bad debt problem'.[994] Despite this, only the three banks owned by the Czech Republic received financial assistance from the state.[995] Having not received this aid, IBP continued to struggle financially. In 2000, the regulatory authority, the Czech National Bank (CNB), 'put IPB into forced administration'.[996]

Saluka initiated investment arbitration proceedings against the Czech Republic under the Netherlands-Czech Republic BIT in 2001.[997] The investor claimed that the Czech Republic's measures with regard to IPB violated the FET standard under the said IIA.[998] These measures included: (i) adopting regulations concerning the provision of financial assistance to banking competitors; (ii) the failure to ensure a transparent and predictable framework for Saluka's investment; (iii) the failure of the state to negotiate with IBP in good faith, prior to the forced administration of the bank by the Czech Republic; and (iv) the lack of state assistance to IBP following its forced administration.[999]

In deciding whether the state had breached the FET standard, the *Saluka* tribunal stated that it had to balance 'the host State's legitimate right subsequently to regulate domestic matters in the public interest' against the rights of the investor, i.e. the protection of its legitimate expectations.[1000] The *Saluka* tribunal distinguished two elements that are relevant concerning the objective of the state's measure. First, the state measure should have the objective of addressing a public interest. Second, the

991. *Saluka Investments BV v. Czech Republic* [2006] UNCITRAL Arbitration Partial Award (17 March 2006) para. 32.
992. *Ibid.*, para. 42.
993. *Ibid.*, para. 33.
994. *Ibid.*, paras 36-38. The bad debt problem was primarily due to 'a large level of outstanding debt, much of which included non-performing loans granted to large State enterprises which were insolvent' (para. 36)
995. *Saluka Investments BV v. Czech Republic* [2006] UNCITRAL Arbitration Partial Award (17 March 2006) paras 77-80.
996. *Ibid.*, para. 136.
997. *Ibid.*, para. 26.
998. *Ibid.*, para. 310.
999. *Ibid.*
1000. *Saluka Investments BV v. Czech Republic* [2006] UNCITRAL Arbitration Partial Award (17 March 2006) para. 305.

state measure, which has been taken in the public interest has to be 'reasonably justifiable by public policies'.[1001] The tribunal assessed these two elements in order to evaluate the objective of the measures of the Czech Republic aimed at reforming the banking sector.

In appraising the state's decision to put the investor's bank into forced administration, the *Saluka* tribunal noted that 'in the absence of clear and compelling evidence that the CNB erred or acted otherwise improperly in reaching its decision ... the Tribunal must in the circumstances accept the justification given by the Czech banking regulator for its decision.'[1002] The objective of the Czech Republic in imposing the measure of involuntary administration on IBP was neither improper nor erroneous, according to the tribunal. This was because, first, the Czech Republic's objective to put the bank into state administration was taken in the public interest, i.e. with the aim of stabilising the banking sector.[1003] Second, the tribunal found that the objective of the state's measure to put the bank into forced administration had been sufficiently substantiated by the state authorities; e.g., it had been justified by a regulatory authority, the CNB.[1004]

In subsequent decisions, tribunals have adopted the *Saluka* reasoning in evaluating the objective of a state's measure, assessing the legitimacy thereof, and considering whether the objective was properly substantiated.

In *EDF v. Romania*, the tribunal also provided that the relevant criterion in assessing the objective of a state's measure is whether the measure has been taken 'in the public interest'.[1005] The dispute in this case arose as a result of several duty-free shops operated by a British company, EDF (the investor), having their licences revoked.[1006] The revocation occurred as a result of Government Emergency Ordinance No. 104 (GEO 104) adopted in 2002, which aimed to combat corruption by regulating duty-free shops at airports.[1007] The revocation of the licences led to the closure of three duty-free operations at several Romanian airports operated by the investor.[1008] The investor initiated investment arbitration proceedings against Romania under the UK-Romania BIT in 2005,[1009] claiming that Romania had failed to provide FET to it by applying GEO 104.[1010] In particular, the investor argued that the state's adoption of GEO 104 was just a pretext to eliminate EDF from airport services,[1011] as EDF was the only 'significant provider of duty-free business in Romanian airports'.[1012]

1001. *Ibid.*, para. 307.
1002. *Ibid.*, para. 273.
1003. *Ibid.*, para. 275 and para. 136.
1004. *Ibid.*, para. 271.
1005. *EDF Limited v. Romania*, ICSID Case No. ARB/05/13 Award (8 October 2009) para. 293.
1006. *Ibid.*, para. 45. EDF's investment involved participation in two joint venture companies with Romanian entities providing airport services.
1007. *EDF Limited v. Romania*, ICSID Case No. ARB/05/13 Award (8 October 2009) para. 57.
1008. *Ibid.*, para. 57.
1009. *Ibid.*, para. 64.
1010. *Ibid.*, para. 105.
1011. *Ibid.*, para. 85.
1012. *Ibid.*

In reviewing the Romanian objective to enact GEO 104, the tribunal provided that this Ordinance had a 'legitimate aim for the benefit of the public interest'.[1013] The tribunal also assessed the 'evidence on record regarding the various procedural steps which led to the adoption of GEO 104'.[1014] It explained the steps taken by Romania in order to adopt GEO 104, including the seeking of approval from various members of the government and state committees. The tribunal asserted that Romania had followed a 'complex procedure' in enacting the Ordinance.[1015] The procedural steps taken by Romania supported the tribunal's view that the objective of the measure taken by the state was legitimate and was not 'put in place merely for the purpose of enacting legal provisions directed against EDF', as argued by the investor.[1016] The tribunal came to the conclusion that the state's measure was motivated by the 'need to fight corruption' and that, consequently, the 'GEO 104 was ... a measure falling within the police power of the State, taken in the public interest.'[1017]

In *AES Summit v. Hungary*, the dispute concerned amended legislation, which applied to energy operators. The new legislation allowed Hungary to reintroduce regulatory prices for electricity.[1018] This measure, i.e. the reintroduction of regulatory prices, aimed to reduce the profitability of the energy operators, including the claimant AES, an English company (the investor). The investor contested the regulatory pricing system claiming that the measure was in breach of the APPAs, which the investor had concluded with the Hungarian state-owned company and that the measure impacted its profitability. AES initiated investment proceedings against Hungary under the ECT.[1019]

In assessing the legitimacy of the state's objective in reintroducing regulatory prices for electricity, the tribunal underlined that it should rely on a 'rational policy'.[1020] The tribunal explained how the 'existence of a rational policy' had to be established.[1021] A rational policy was defined by the tribunal as 'a policy taken by a state following a logical (good sense) explanation with the aim of addressing a public interest matter'.[1022] Two elements surface from the tribunal's definition. First, the goal of the policy must address a matter, which is within the public interest. Second, the policy should be properly justified by the state by means of the records relating to this reform, and an explanation thereof should be provided in the state's documents and discussions. In its assessment, the tribunal established that the state's measure had been motivated by the goal of combating 'luxury profits' in the public utility sector, thereby reducing costs

1013. *EDF Limited v. Romania*, ICSID Case No. ARB/05/13 Award (8 October 2009) para. 293.
1014. *Ibid.*, para. 290.
1015. *Ibid.*, para. 292.
1016. *Ibid.*
1017. *EDF Limited v. Romania*, ICSID Case No. ARB/05/13 Award (8 October 2009) para. 292.
1018. *AES Summit v. Hungary*, ICSID Case No. ARB/07/22 Award (23 September 2010) para. 4.20. Regulatory pricing had been cancelled in 2004 but was reintroduced with an Electricity Energy Law Amendment in 2006.
1019. *AES Summit v. Hungary*, ICSID Case No. ARB/07/22 Award (23 September 2010) para. 3.2. *See also* the facts of the case in Chapter 6, section §6.04[B].
1020. *AES Summit v. Hungary*, ICSID Case No. ARB/07/22 Award (23 September 2010) para. 10.3.7.
1021. *Ibid.*, para. 10.3.7.
1022. *Ibid.*, para. 10.3.8.

for consumers.[1023] The tribunal considered that this goal was a 'perfectly valid and rational policy objective'.[1024]

The tribunal further explained that although the regulation of the pricing system can be a burden for some, this is still a rational public policy, which can 'give rise to legitimate reasons for governments to regulate or re-regulate'.[1025] Furthermore, the tribunal explained that a rational policy should be properly justified by the state or followed by a 'logical (good sense) explanation'.[1026] Hungary, in the view of the tribunal, was able to demonstrate a proper justification for the reintroduction of regulatory pricing, as this matter became an important political concern. Furthermore, the reforms had been indirectly motivated by the pressure exerted by the European Commission, as the electricity pricing system contradicted the free market policies of the EU.[1027] The tribunal summarised that the introduction of regulatory pricing was a rational policy by the Hungarian government.[1028] The tribunal linked the state's policy objective to its measure and underlined that the latter was 'reasonable, proportionate and consistent with the public policy expressed by the parliament'.[1029]

In the *Electrabel v. Hungary* case,[1030] the dispute concerned a Belgian company, Electrabel (the investor), that challenged Hungary's decision to terminate a Power Purchase Agreement (PPA) between Hungary and the investor. The reason for terminating the agreement was to ensure compliance with a European Commission decision, which stated that these types of contracts constitute unlawful state aid.[1031] In assessing the 'rationality' of the Hungarian measure to pay partial compensation to the company (85% of its total eligible stranded costs), the tribunal provided that it was 'reasonably related to a legitimate policy objective'.[1032] In assessing Hungary's measure to pay partial compensation to the investor, the tribunal relied on the 'public interest' and 'logical sense explanation' criteria that were put forward in *AES Summit v. Hungary*.[1033] In *Electrabel v. Hungary*, the tribunal concluded that Hungary's policy objective to align its 'electricity sector with the EU market' and to eliminate 'distortions to competition within and without Hungary'[1034] was a legitimate government policy which had been taken in the public interest. The tribunal thereby rejected the argument

1023. *Ibid.*, para. 10.3.31.
1024. *Ibid.*, para. 10.3.34.
1025. *Ibid.*, para. 10.3.34.
1026. *Ibid.*, para. 10.3.8.
1027. *Ibid.*, para. 10.3.19. Reference was made to the European Commission Decision on State Aid awarded by Hungary through Power Purchase Agreements (Brussels, 2008.VI.04 C (2008) 2223 final) http://ec.europa.eu/competition/state_aid/cases/201965/201965_827719_388_1 .pdf accessed on 27 May 2017.
1028. *AES Summit v. Hungary*, ICSID Case No. ARB/07/22 Award (23 September 2010) para. 10.3.34.
1029. *Ibid.*, para. 10.3.36.
1030. *Electrabel v. Hungary*, ICSID Case No. ARB/07/1 Final Award (25 November 2015).
1031. *Ibid.*, para. 204. The tribunal referred to the Commission's Compensation Decision of 27 April 2010.
1032. *Electrabel v. Hungary*, ICSID Case No. ARB/07/1 Final Award (25 November 2015) para. 214.
1033. *Ibid.*, para. 179.
1034. *Ibid.*, para. 215.

of the investor that the goal of the Hungarian government was to protect the budget of the state and to 'keep the money'.[1035]

The *Mamidoil v. Albania* case, decided under the ECT, concerned a Greek company, Mamidoil (the investor), which had invested in Albania by undertaking the task of constructing and operating an oil terminal in the port of Durrës.[1036] The Albanian authorities wanted to relocate the project for environmental and socio-economic reasons. However, the investor claimed that, following its lease contract, it had the right to use the specific port facilities for tankers. To this end, the investor claimed that Albania had breached the FET standard under Article 10.1 of the ECT by failing (i) to provide a stable and transparent legal framework; (ii) to respect the legitimate expectations of the investor; and (iii) to abstain from exerting pressure and by denying justice to an investor.[1037]

In assessing the objectives of Albania in relocating the project, the tribunal underlined that the 'fair and equitable standard brings foreign investors into the normative sphere of rational policy in the general interest.'[1038] Any policy taken in the general interest should take into account a range of social and economic interests so that individuals can also pursue their interests.[1039] In this case, the tribunal stated that the disputed measures had been taken in the general interest as they involved the 'responsibility [of the state] to provide long-term physical and social infrastructure such as public transport, including sustainable port facilities ...'.[1040] By taking into account the inevitable changes in the social, economic and legal environment that affect regulations in the field of public infrastructure[1041] and the specific sociopolitical circumstances in Albania,[1042] the tribunal determined that the state's measures had 'a legitimate objective of public policy, [and] were carried out in a transparent way, were proportionate and not arbitrary, and did not lead to unreasonable instability ...'.[1043] The tribunal underlined that the state's objectives had been directed at the modernisation of the transport sector. To this end, Albania had taken some 'initial steps to provide an infrastructure that would allow private investors, national as well as international, to pursue structured and sustainable business activities'.[1044]

In *Blusun v. Italy*,[1045] the tribunal examined the objectives of the state's measures, i.e. the Romani Decree and the Fourth Energy Account, which significantly reduced the feed-in tariffs for the renewable energy producers (the facts of this case are discussed in section §6.04[D] of Chapter 6). The tribunal noted that the alteration of the

1035. *Ibid.*, para. 214.
1036. *See*: discussion on this case in Chapter 6, section §6.04.
1037. *Mamidoil Jetoil Greek Petroleum Products Société S.A. v. Republic of Albania*, ICSID Case No. ARB/11/24 Award (30 March 2015) para. 584.
1038. *Ibid.*, para. 614.
1039. *Ibid.*
1040. *Mamidoil Jetoil Greek Petroleum Products Société S.A. v. Republic of Albania*, ICSID Case No. ARB/11/24 Award (30 March 2015) para. 612.
1041. *Ibid.*, para. 617.
1042. *Ibid.*, paras 625, 658.
1043. *Ibid.*, para. 657.
1044. *Ibid.*, para. 625.
1045. *Blusun S.A., J.-P. Lecorcier AND M. Stein v. Italy*, ICSID Case No. ARB/14/3 Award (27 December 2016).

conditions for receiving feed-in tariffs was a measure that was proportionate to the state's public interest objective, i.e. 'response to a genuine fiscal need, given the large take-up under the earlier Energy Accounts'.[1046] Curiously, the tribunal underlined that the notion of 'public interest' is 'largely indeterminate and is, anyway, a judgment entrusted to the authorities of the host state'.[1047] The tribunal explained that for this reason the public interest is not the right criterion to establish whether the changes to a legal framework had frustrated the legitimate expectations of the investor. The tribunal nevertheless had assessed the legitimacy of the state's objective by evaluating whether it was taken in a public interest in order to judge the proportionality of the state's measure. To this end, the tribunal concluded that the Romani Decree as well as the Fourth Energy Account were in a public interest because they were adopted to implement the EU Directive on the promotion and the use of the renewable energy.[1048] Hence, Italy had to comply with the specific obligations under this Directive.[1049]

To summarise, the objective of the state's measure must be legitimate. The tribunals' assessment of whether the objective of the state's measure is legitimate is the initial step in determining the legality of the state's measure under the FET standard. To this end, tribunals distinguish between the legitimate objectives of the state's measure and those that are not legitimate. Two elements play a role in assessing whether the objective of the state's measure is legitimate. First, the state's measure should be taken in the public interest both in terms of the significance and content of the objective. Public interest objectives are diverse and, according to the tribunals, they may include the reformation of the banking sector, combating corruption, reducing the luxury profits of energy providers, the modernisation of the transport sector, the alignment of the electricity sector with the EU market, access to (clean) water and the protection of the environment, indigenous people and public health. At the same time, the *Blusun* tribunal underlined that the public interest is an indeterminate criterion in the assessment of an alleged breach of the FET standard and that the decision whether the state's measure was adopted in the public interest should be left to the state.[1050] Second, the legitimacy of a state's measure also requires substantiation by the host state. Any available records and official documents that can clarify the nature and purpose of the state's measure can be submitted to the tribunals for the purpose of substantiation.

[C] Protection of the Environment, Human Rights and Public Health

The goal of this section is to assess how tribunals deal with public interest objectives concerning the protection of the environment, human rights and public health. That is,

1046. *Ibid.*, para. 342.
1047. *Ibid.*, para. 318.
1048. Directive 2009/28/EC, of the European Parliament and of the Council on the Promotion of the Use of Energy from Renewable Sources and Amending and Subsequently Repealing Directives 2001/77/EC an 2003/30/EC, 2009 O.J. (L 140).
1049. *Blusun S.A., J.-P. Lecorcier AND M. Stein v. Italy*, ICSID Case No. ARB/14/3 Award, 27 December 2016, EU Directive 2009/28, para. 331.
1050. *Ibid.*, para. 318.

in some FET cases, states have argued that their measures had been adopted in the interest of protecting the environment, human rights and public health. Sometimes, states also have claimed that such objectives constitute public interest goals and that they had committed themselves in various international treaties to fulfil such goals.[1051]

In recent IIAs, such as the Comprehensive Economic Trade Agreement between Canada and the EU (CETA), the EU-Singapore FTA,[1052] the EU-Vietnam FTA[1053] and the Trans-Pacific Partnership Agreement (TPP), the public interest objectives acknowledged in these treaties include the protection of the environment, public health and human rights.[1054] In order to better understand the developments that led to a new generation of IIAs, in this section, cases in which the above-stated public interests play a role are reviewed. The analysis of the tribunals' assessments of the legitimacy of the state measures' objectives contributes to providing the answer to the main research question; i.e., how the host state's right to regulate is balanced against its obligations under the FET standard. Additionally, by comparing the outcome of this analysis with the public interests incorporated in recent IIAs, observations and predictions can be made regarding the question of how a host state pursuing such objectives will be dealt with by future FET tribunals.

(i) *Metalclad v. Mexico* (an environmental regulation concerning hazardous waste)[1055]

1051. *See*, e.g., *Chemtura v. Canada* [2010] NAFTA-UNCITRAL Arbitration, Award (2 August 2010) para. 131. In this case Canada had taken the contested regulatory measures to comply with its international environmental obligations under the Aarhus Protocol on the Long-Range Transboundary Air Pollution on Persistent Organic Pollutants (LRTAP) Convention. Also *see*: *Philip Morris v. Uruguay*, ICSID Case No. ARB/10/7 Award (8 July 2016) para. 401. In this case, Uruguay adopted the measures in the interest of public health, challenged by the investor, in order to comply with its international obligation under the Framework Convention on Tobacco Control (FCTC).

1052. *See*: EU-Singapore FTA (authentic text as of April 2018), Investment Protection Agreement, Article 2.2(1): 'The Parties reaffirm their right to regulate within their territories to achieve legitimate policy objectives, such as the protection of public health, social services, public education, safety, environment or public morals, social or consumer protection privacy and data protection and the promotion and protection of cultural diversity.' http://trade.ec.europa.eu/doclib/docs/2018/april/tradoc_156741.pdf accessed on 20 April 2018.

1053. *See*: EU-Vietnam FTA (text agreed as of January 2016), Chapter 8, Articles 13*bis*(1): 'The Parties reaffirm the right to regulate within their territories to achieve legitimate policy objectives, such as the protection of public health, safety, environment or public morals, social or consumer protection or promotion and protection of cultural diversity.' http://trade.ec.europa.eu/doclib/docs/2016/february/tradoc_154210.pdf accessed on 20 April 2018.

1054. *See*: Consolidated text of CETA, 30 October 2016, Article 8.9(1). 'For the purpose of this Chapter, the Parties reaffirm their right to regulate within their territories to achieve legitimate policy objectives, such as the protection of public health, safety, the environment or public morals, social or consumer protection or the promotion and protection of cultural diversity,' http://ec.europa.eu/trade/policy/in-focus/ceta/ceta-chapter-by-chapter/; also *see*: Trans-Pacific Partnership Agreement (TPP), 4 February 2016, Article 9.16. 'Nothing in this Chapter shall be construed to prevent a Party from adopting, maintaining or enforcing any measure otherwise consistent with this Chapter that it considers appropriate to ensure the investment activity in its territory is undertaken in a manner sensitive to environmental health, or other regulatory objectives,' https://ustr.gov/sites/default/files/TPP-Final-Text-Investment.pdf. Both websites accessed on 15 March 2018.

1055. *Metalclad v. Mexico*, ICSID Case No. ARB(AF)/97/1 Award (30 August 2000).

In *Metalclad v. Mexico*, a dispute arose as a result of the Mexican state's refusal to issue a construction permit to a US company, Metalclad (the investor), to operate a hazardous landfill. The case involved the following sequence of events.

In 1990, the federal Mexican government authorised the construction of a hazardous waste landfill, which was granted to Metalclad. The location of the landfill should have been in an area close to the city of Guadalcazar.[1056] Around 800 inhabitants lived within 10 km of the landfill.[1057] After Metalclad had obtained the federal permit, the construction of the site began. The local government, however, opposed the construction of this landfill and required the investor to obtain a municipal construction permit to build and to operate the site. Metalclad duly applied to the local government for this permit and, before obtaining it, Metalclad in the meanwhile had completed the construction of the site in 1995.[1058] Upon the opening of the landfill, Metalclad met resistance from demonstrators protesting against the site. Tensions between the local government and Metalclad resulted in lengthy negotiations that were ultimately unsuccessful. The negotiations were further undermined by the denial of the construction permit by the local government and the enactment of the Ecological decree by the local government on 23 September 1997.[1059] This decree declared that the landfill zone was a natural area for the protection of rare cacti, thereby preventing Metalclad from operating the landfill site.[1060] The investor filed an investment arbitration claim against Mexico under the NAFTA on 2 January 1997.[1061]

In its assessment of the FET standard, the tribunal examined the objectives of the local government in denying a construction permit to the foreign investor.[1062] Mexico, in justifying the conduct of the local government, referred to such factors as 'the opposition of the local population'[1063] to the site on environmental grounds, and 'the ecological concerns regarding the environmental effect and impact on the site and surrounding communities'.[1064]

The tribunal determined that although the local government had the authority to refuse to issue the permit, in fact, the 'federal authority was controlling' the process in that respect. The authority of the local government 'only extended to appropriate construction considerations'.[1065] Consequently, none of the reasons provided by the local government, among which was the negative environmental impact, were valid reasons for denying the permit. The tribunal decided that the local government's competence was restricted; it could only deny the permit if there were 'problems

1056. *Ibid.*, para. 28.
1057. *Ibid.*
1058. *Metalclad v. Mexico*, ICSID Case No. ARB(AF)/97/1 Award (30 August 2000) para. 45.
1059. *Ibid.*, para. 59.
1060. *Ibid.*
1061. *Metalclad v. Mexico*, ICSID Case No. ARB(AF)/97/1 Award (30 August 2000) para. 58.
1062. *See* C. Henckels, Proportionality and Deference in Investor-State Arbitration (Cambridge University Press, 2015) 115. In referring to *Metalclad*, the author emphasises that 'several tribunals have assessed the legitimacy of the state's regulatory objective as a means to determine whether the state had breached fair and equitable treatment ...'.
1063. *Metalclad v. Mexico*, ICSID Case No. ARB(AF)/97/1 Award (30 August 2000) paras 92-93.
1064. *Ibid.*
1065. *Metalclad v. Mexico*, ICSID Case No. ARB(AF)/97/1 Award (30 August 2000) para. 86.

associated with the physical construction of the landfill or to any physical defects therein'.[1066] This, according to the tribunal, would be the only possible justification for denying the permit.[1067]

Nevertheless, the tribunal briefly examined the arguments based on the environmental grounds invoked by Mexico. In addressing the environmental objectives behind the denial of the permit, the tribunal referred to Article 1114 of the NAFTA entitled 'Environmental Measures'. Article 1114, in its first paragraph, provides that:

> Nothing in this Chapter shall be construed to prevent a Party from adopting, maintaining or enforcing any measure ... that it considers appropriate to ensure that investment activity in its territory is undertaken in a manner sensitive to environmental concerns.[1068]

In its assessment, the tribunal concluded that the denial of the permit to the investor by the local government had nothing to do with the grounds mentioned in Article 1114 of the NAFTA.[1069] The tribunal underlined that according to Article 1114 of the NAFTA, a party is permitted to ensure that 'investment activity in its territory is undertaken in a manner sensitive to environmental concerns.'[1070] The tribunal concluded that in this case Mexico 'was satisfied that this project was consistent with, and sensitive to, its environmental concerns'.[1071] This conclusion was based on the tribunal's observation that Mexico had willingly entered into an agreement with Metalclad and issued the federal permits that had, in the first instance, approved the site.[1072] These factors, according to the tribunal, were sufficient to conclude that Mexico had first been satisfied with the environmental soundness of the project.[1073]

(ii) *Glamis v. US* (human rights of indigenous people)[1074]

In *Glamis v. US*, the dispute arose out of the US authorities' refusal to grant a mining permit to a Canadian gold mining company, Glamis (the investor). Glamis had invested in an area of the Californian desert conservation zone to explore and extract gold from mines. The investor was faced with problems in obtaining the necessary permits from the federal authorities as the project was located in a tribal area. The risk identified by the authorities was that the mining activities would 'destroy the historic resources in the project area. ...'.[1075] The situation for the investor worsened after the Californian government introduced new laws and regulations directed at the protection of the

1066. *Ibid.*, para. 93.
1067. *Ibid.*
1068. Article 1114(1) of NAFTA [1994] 'Environmental Concerns' http://www.sice.oas.org/trade/nafta/chap-111.asp accessed on 3 June 2017.
1069. *Metalclad v. Mexico*, ICSID Case No. ARB(AF)/97/1 Award (30 August 2000) para. 98.
1070. Article 1114(1) of NAFTA [1994] 'Environmental Concerns' http://www.sice.oas.org/trade/nafta/chap-111.asp accessed on 3 June 2017.
1071. *Metalclad v. Mexico*, ICSID Case No. ARB(AF)/97/1 Award (30 August 2000) para. 98.
1072. In 1995, Metalclad and Mexico had entered into an agreement that provided for and allowed the operation of the landfill (the name of the agreement was the *Convenio*). *Metalclad v. Mexico*, ICSID Case No. ARB(AF)/97/1 Award (30 August 2000) para. 47.
1073. *Metalclad v. Mexico*, ICSID Case No. ARB(AF)/97/1 Award (30 August 2000) para. 98.
1074. *Glamis v. US* [2009] NAFTA, ICSID 48 ILM 1039 Award (8 June 2009).
1075. *Ibid.*, para. 127.

cultural, religious and ecological practices of the Quechan tribal people. The regulatory measures adopted by the local authorities required mining operators to refill open-pit metal mines and to grade the mining activities in areas close to the sacred area of the Quechan tribal people, where cultural artefacts had been discovered.[1076] The investor argued if it would comply with these requirements, this would destroy the value of its investments because of the high costs required to implement these requirements. Glamis initiated the investment arbitration against the US under the NAFTA, arguing that the US authorities had violated the FET standard under Article 1105 of the NAFTA.[1077]

The tribunal assessed whether the objectives of the state's measures were legitimate by adopting a deferential approach. This approach referred to the restraint exercised by the tribunal in assessing the objectives of the state's measures.[1078] The 'threshold' that the tribunal articulated in evaluating the state's reasons was to establish whether there was a 'manifest lack of reasons for the legislation'.[1079] In applying the latter threshold, the tribunal concluded that the state's objective to protect cultural resources by introducing the legislation, as contested by the investor, was legitimate,[1080] because the legislation had been 'reasonably drafted to address its objectives'.[1081] The tribunal further provided that 'governments must compromise between the interests of competing parties and, if they were bound to please every constituent and address every harm with each piece of legislation, they would be bound and useless.'[1082]

(iii) *AWG v. Argentina*; *Impregilo v. Argentina*; *Azurix v. Argentina*; *Urbaser v. Argentina* (the right to have access to water)

The following cases will be discussed in this section: *AWG v. Argentina*,[1083] *Impregilo v. Argentina, and Azurix v. Argentina*, and *Urbaser v. Argentina*. They all arose out of water concession disputes between several foreign investors and Argentina. The

1076. *Ibid.*, para. 175.
1077. *Ibid.*, para. 11.
1078. The deferential approach by international investment tribunals in the assessment of states' measures is explained in Chapter 4, section §4.04[B]. Also *see*: C. Henckels, 'Proportionality and the Standard of Review in Fair and Equitable Treatment Claims: Balancing Stability and Consistency with the Public Interest' [2012] *Paper for Society of International Economic Law*, 11; J. Sharpe, 'The Minimum Standard of Treatment: Glamis Gold and Neer's Enduring Influence', in M. Kinnear et al. (eds) *Building International Investment Law: The First 50 Years of ICSID* (Kluwer Law International, 2015) 274.
1079. *Glamis v. US* [2009] NAFTA, ICSID 48 ILM 1039 Award (8 June 2009) para. 803.
1080. *Ibid.*
1081. *Ibid.*
1082. *Glamis v. US* [2009] NAFTA, ICSID 48 ILM 1039 Award (8 June 2009) para. 804.
1083. Note that *AWG v. Argentina* is one of three cases where the tribunal issued one consolidated decision on liability for three separate but procedurally consolidated cases in 2010. These three cases are: *Suez, Sociedad General de Aguas de Barcelona S.A., Vivendi Universal v. Argentina*, ICSID Case No. ARB/03/19 Decision on Liability (30 July 2010); *Suez, Sociedad General de Aguas de Barcelona S.A., and InterAguas Servicios Integrales del Agua S.A. v. Argentina*, ICSID Case No. ARB/03/17 Decision on Liability (30 July 2010); and *AWG Group v. Argentina* UNCITRAL Arbitration, Decision on Liability (30 July 2010). These three cases will hereinafter be referred to as '*AWG v. Argentina*' and the 'AWG tribunal'.

argument that Argentinian citizens have a right to have access to water was raised in all four cases. In *Impregilo v. Argentina*[1084] and *Azurix v. Argentina*,[1085] it was raised by Argentina, and in *AWG v. Argentina*, it was brought up in an amici curiae brief, which had been submitted in this case by five non-governmental organisations (NGOs) that supported Argentina.[1086] In *Urbaser v. Argentina*, Argentina as the host state filed a counterclaim against the investor for an alleged violation of the human right to water.[1087] The *Urbaser* tribunal assumed jurisdiction over Argentina's counterclaim and examined the alleged human rights violations by the investor under international human rights treaties. The facts of the aforementioned cases are very similar and are outlined below.

In *AWG v. Argentina*, the facts were as follows. After the privatisation of water and waste water services in 1991, Argentina awarded a thirty-year concession to operate water and waste services in the city of Buenos Aires and surrounding municipalities. By means of a bidding process, the concession was granted to a consortium of companies including certain foreign investors.[1088] In 1992, the consortium, according to the rules of the bidding process, formed an Argentinian company, Aguas Argentinas S.A. (AASA), to hold and to operate the concession.[1089] By 2000, Argentina began to experience a severe economic crisis that led to the adoption of various measures by the government.[1090] In 2002 an Emergency Law was enacted. This law abolished the currency board that had linked the Argentinian peso to the US dollar. The crisis and the measures taken resulted in a substantial depreciation of the Argentinian currency. The investors sought to renegotiate the terms of the concession and to receive adjustments to the tariffs from the government. AASA attempted to raise the tariffs for water distribution and waste water services, which were subsequently blocked by the state because of its public policy goal to ensure affordable water to its citizens. Unable to reach an agreement with the Argentinian authorities, the investors submitted the dispute to an arbitral tribunal in 2003. They claimed that the state's measures relating to the financial crisis had destroyed the value of their investment. In addition, the investors argued that the forceful renegotiations of the concession and the

1084. *Impregilo S.p.A v. Argentina*, ICSID Case No. ARB/07/17 Award (21 June 2011) para. 228.
1085. *Azurix Corp. v. The Argentine Republic*, ICSID Case No. ARB/01/12 Award (14 July 2006) para. 254.
1086. *See AWG v. Argentina* [2010] UNCITRAL Arbitration, Decision on Liability (30 July 2010) para. 256. These NGOs were: Asociación Civil por la Igualdad y la Justicia, Centro de Estudios Legales y Sociales, Center for International Environmental Law, Consumidores Libres Cooperativa Ltda. de Provisión de Servicios de Acción Comunitaria and Unión de Usuarios y Consumidores.
1087. *Urbaser S.A. and Consorcio de Aguas Bilbao Bizkaia, Bilbao Biskaia Ur Partzuergoa v. Argentina*, ICSID Case No. ARB/07/26 Award (8 December 2016).
1088. Suez, AGBAR, Vivendi and AWG, together with the Argentinian companies Banco de Galicia y Buenos Aires S.A., Sociedad Comercial del Plata S.A., and Meller S.A., formed a consortium in 1992 to participate in the bidding for the concession, *see Suez, Sociedad General de Aguas de Barcelona, S.A. and Vivendi Universal, S.A. v. Argentine Republic*, ICSID Case No. ARB/03/19 Decision on Liability (30 July 2010) para. 23.
1089. *AWG v. Argentina* [2010] UNCITRAL Arbitration, Decision on Liability (30 July 2010) para. 33.
1090. *Ibid.*, para. 41.

unwillingness of Argentina to raise the tariffs for water services undermined the FET of the investors.[1091]

In *Impregilo v. Argentina*, a consortium of international companies was awarded a concession for water and sewerage services for thirty years in seven municipalities of the Buenos Aires region.[1092] The consortium incorporated an Argentinian company, Aguas del Gran Buenos Aires (AGBA), which provided water services to consumers.[1093] AGBA, in which the Italian company Impregilo (the investor) had a dominant interest, presented a five-year plan that was approved by the Argentinian authorities.[1094] From the start, AGBA encountered difficulties in obtaining payments from its customers.[1095] The non-collection rate was 60%, and this had significantly affected the financial position of AGBA. This development made it impossible for the company to reach its planned five-year goals. The financial crisis and the unwillingness of the Argentinian authorities to raise the tariffs and to interrupt the water services of those customers who had not paid - because of the state's public policy goal to ensure access to water for its citizens - had escalated the dispute between the governmental authorities and AGBA. Argentina argued that it objected to the tariffs being increased because of its obligation to guarantee that its citizens have a right to affordable water.[1096] In 2006, AGBA was fined for various violations under the concession agreement and the concession was ultimately terminated by Argentina. The investor claimed that this termination was unlawful.[1097] In 2007, the investor initiated arbitral proceedings for violations of the treaty provisions, including the FET standard under the Argentina-Italy BIT.[1098]

In *Azurix v. Argentina*, a US-based water services company (the investor) obtained an exclusive thirty-year concession to run the water and sewage systems in the province of Buenos Aires in 1999.[1099] Winning the bid for the concession, the investor operated under the name Azurix Buenos Aires S.A. (ABA).[1100] The dispute between the state authorities and the investor occurred primarily due to a disagreement concerning an increase in water tariffs for consumers. The argument of the state was based upon its public policy goal to ensure affordable water for its citizens. The conflict had escalated after an algae outbreak in Bahia Blanca that led to the alleged contamination of the water supply. This had - as a result - provoked public outrage.[1101] The state authorities blamed the investor for the incident, thereby discouraging people from

1091. *Ibid.*, paras 44-57.
1092. *Impregilo S.p.A v. Argentina,* ICSID Case No. ARB/07/17 Award (21 June 2011).
1093. *Ibid.*, para. 14.
1094. *Ibid.*, para. 20.
1095. *Ibid.*, para. 21.
1096. *Ibid.*, para. 261.
1097. *Ibid.*, para. 67.
1098. *Ibid.*, para. 5.
1099. *Azurix Corp. v. The Argentine Republic,* ICSID Case No. ARB/01/12 Award (14 July 2006) para. 41.
1100. Indirect subsidiaries of Azurix - Azurix AGOSBA S.R.L. (AAS) and Operadora de Buenos Aires S.R.L. (OBA) - had incorporated Azurix Buenos Aires S.A. that acted as a concessionaire.
1101. *Azurix Corp. v. The Argentine Republic,* ICSID Case No. ARB/01/12 Award (14 July 2006) para. 124, 'Algae bloom in the reservoir on April 10-11, 2000 resulted in the water appearing cloudy and hazy and with earth-musty taste and odor'.

paying their water bills.[1102] The investor, however, argued that the state was responsible for failing to complete the infrastructural works and repairs that, according to ABA, led to the incident.[1103] ABA eventually terminated the concession contract in 2001.

In *Urbaser v. Argentina*, a Spanish company, Urbaser (the investor), was one of the main shareholders in a project company named AGBA SA, which held a concession to provide water services in Buenos Aires.[1104] The problems in relation to the concession had arisen when Argentina introduced the emergency measures. These measures impacted the financial position of the investment. The problems persisted as the investor and the state's authorities could not agree on a renewed assessment of the tariffs and a review of the concession.[1105] After several unsuccessful attempts to renegotiate the concession, the authorities of Buenos Aires terminated it in 2006. Urbaser and other claimants initiated arbitration proceedings under the Spain-Argentina BIT. The investor argued that Argentina had violated the FET standard under Article IV of the Spain-Argentina BIT by terminating the concession and denying the investors any 'possibility to restore the economic-financial equilibrium of the Concession'.[1106] Argentina filed a counterclaim against the investor for the alleged failure to provide the necessary financing to the concession, which failure - according to the state - resulted in the violations of the human right to water.[1107]

(iv) *The assessment of the state's objectives by the tribunals in the Argentinian water cases*

In the *AWG* case, the human rights objectives of Argentina's measures had been raised in an amici curiae brief submitted by five NGOs.[1108] In the amici curiae brief, it was argued that the contested state measures, namely its unwillingness to increase the tariffs, were motivated by the state's objective of ensuring that the local population has access to water.[1109] In the amici curiae brief, it was underlined that 'human rights law recognises the right to water and its close linkages with other human rights, including

1102. *Azurix Corp. v. The Argentine Republic*, ICSID Case No. ARB/01/12 Award (14 July 2006) para. 125.
1103. *Azurix Corp. v. The Argentine Republic*, ICSID Case No. ARB/01/12 Award (14 July 2006) para. 124.
1104. *Urbaser S.A. and Consorcio de Aguas Bilbao Bizkaia, Bilbao Biskaia Ur Partzuergoa v. Argentina*, ICSID Case No. ARB/07/26 Award (8 December 2016) para. 34. The water Concession was granted to 'Aguas Del Gran Buenos Aires S.A. (AGBA), a Company established by foreign investors and shareholders' that included Urbaser.
1105. *Urbaser S.A. and Consorcio de Aguas Bilbao Bizkaia, Bilbao Biskaia Ur Partzuergoa v. Argentina*, ICSID Case No. ARB/07/26 Award (8 December 2016) para. 34.
1106. *Ibid.*, para. 562.
1107. *Ibid.*, paras 36-37.
1108. In 2007, five NGOs submitted the amici curiae brief. These were Asociación Civil por la Igualdad y la Justicia, Centro de Estudios Legales y Sociales, Center for International Environmental Law, Consumidores Libres Cooperativa Ltda. de Provisión de Servicios de Acción Comunitaria and Unión de Usuarios y Consumidores. *See AWG v. Argentina* [2010] UNCITRAL Arbitration, Decision on Liability (30 July 2010) para. 256.
1109. *AWG v. Argentina* [2010] UNCITRAL Arbitration, Decision on Liability (30 July 2010) para. 256.

the right to life, health, housing, and an adequate standard of living.'[1110] According to the amici curiae brief, in interpreting BITs, the tribunal should take into account the rationale for the crisis measures based on human rights law.[1111]

The *AWG* tribunal admitted the legitimate nature of the state's objectives. It underlined the severity of the crisis experienced by Argentina.[1112] The *AWG* tribunal also agreed that the provision of water and sewage services was 'vital to the health and well-being of nearly ten million people' and was thereby an 'essential interest of the Argentine State'.[1113]

At the same time, the *AWG* tribunal was not convinced that the only way to secure this vital interest (i.e., the provision of water to the population) was by refusing to adjust the tariffs and by engaging in 'forceful' treatment of the company in the state's attempt to renegotiate the concession contract.[1114] With regard to the human rights argument raised in the amici curiae brief, the tribunal made a few important observations. The tribunal disagreed with the amici that there was a conflict between the human rights obligations and the investment obligations under the BIT. It stressed that Argentina is subject to its international human rights obligations, as well as to its obligations stemming from this international investment treaty and 'must respect both of them equally ...'.[1115] In this line of reasoning, the tribunal pointed out that Argentina's human rights obligations and its investment treaty obligations were 'not inconsistent, contradictory, or mutually exclusive ... [t]hus ... Argentina could have respected both types of obligations'.[1116]

In the *AWG* case, it can be observed that the tribunal recognised the legitimacy of the state's objectives motivated by the protection of the right to have access to water.[1117] The tribunal, however, declined to establish a hierarchy between the state's obligation to provide FET to the investors and the state's human rights obligation to provide access to water for its population.[1118] It implied, however, that Argentina should have looked at other solutions that could have fulfilled both the human rights obligations and the FET obligation.

In both *Impregilo v. Argentina* and *Azurix v. Argentina*, human rights arguments had been invoked by Argentina in order to justify its measures. In particular, in both cases, these human rights arguments were invoked in relation to Argentina's reluctance to increase water tariffs. In *Impregilo v. Argentina*, the state argued that its regulatory actions were proportionate and were 'particularly important to guarantee its

1110. *Ibid.*
1111. *Ibid.*
1112. *AWG v. Argentina* [2010] UNCITRAL Arbitration, Decision on Liability (30 July 2010) para. 257.
1113. *Ibid.*
1114. *Ibid.*
1115. *AWG v. Argentina* [2010] UNCITRAL Arbitration, Decision on Liability (30 July 2010) para. 262.
1116. *Ibid.*
1117. *AWG v. Argentina* [2010] UNCITRAL Arbitration, Decision on Liability (30 July 2010) para. 260.
1118. J. Viñuales, Foreign Investment and the Environment in International Law (Cambridge University Press, 2012) 180.

inhabitants the human right to water'.[1119] The state contended that its investment obligations:

> Do not prevail over the obligations assumed in treaties on human rights. Therefore, the obligations arising from the BIT must not be construed separately but in accordance with the rules on protection of human rights. Treaties on human rights providing for the human right to water must be especially taken into account in this case.[1120]

However, the tribunal did not respond to these arguments. The state, in this case, also argued that increasing the prices for water would harm the economically disadvantaged people of the region in particular.[1121] The tribunal had found this argument to be legitimate, by providing that: 'In the face of the acute crisis, the Argentine Republic and the Province took a series of measures that were fully justified by the need to reduce as much as possible its effects on the country in general and on investments in particular.'[1122] Nevertheless, it concluded that in this circumstance, Argentina could have chosen other measures to achieve this goal that would not result in the 'disturbance of the equilibrium between the rights and obligations in the concession'.[1123] This argument by the tribunal is explored in more detail in section §7.04[A][2] below, where the employment of alternative measures in assessing the reasonableness of a state's conduct is addressed.

In *Azurix v. Argentina*, the tribunal also examined arguments concerning the refusal of the state to raise its tariffs. Unlike in *Impregilo v. Argentina*, however, the tribunal came to the conclusion that the government of Argentina, by refusing to negotiate an increase in prices, was motivated primarily by the 'forthcoming elections' and not by a concern for its people.[1124] In its ruling on the FET standard, the tribunal found that the government of Argentina had politicised the concession.[1125] This argument is further explored in section §7.02[D] below. The tribunal also declined to explore the argument raised by the state's experts that the 'consumers' public interest must prevail over the private interest of the service provider.'[1126] The tribunal noted that, first, 'this matter has not been fully argued' by the government of Argentina.[1127] Second, it argued that 'the tribunal fails to understand the incompatibility in the specifics of the instant case.'[1128]

1119. *Impregilo S.p.A v. Argentina*, ICSID Case No. ARB/07/17 Award (21 June 2011) para. 228.
1120. *Ibid.*, para. 230.
1121. *Ibid.*, paras 328-329.
1122. *Ibid.*, para. 229.
1123. *Ibid.*, para. 330.
1124. J. Bonnitcha, (2014) section 4.7.4, p. 195. He underlines that in this case the measures adopted by the state were considered by the tribunal to be not 'related to a rational policy'.
1125. *Azurix Corp. v. The Argentine Republic*, ICSID Case No. ARB/01/12 Award (14 July 2006) para. 378. The tribunal used the term 'the politicization of the Concession'.
1126. *Azurix Corp. v. The Argentine Republic*, ICSID Case No. ARB/01/12 Award (14 July 2006) para. 254.
1127. This argument was raised in the expert opinion of Dr Solomoni. This opinion is not publicly available, which makes it problematic to judge whether this argument had been fully considered by the tribunal.
1128. *Azurix Corp. v. The Argentine Republic*, ICSID Case No. ARB/01/12 Award (14 July 2006) para. 254.

Urbaser v. Argentina contrasts with the water privatisation cases discussed above. In examining the FET claim, the tribunal in *Urbaser* upheld the legitimacy of the state's objectives to safeguard the human right to water. In the context of the state's counterclaim, the tribunal examined whether the investor had human rights' obligations concerning the right to water.

In assessing the FET standard, the tribunal noted that in privatising water resources, the important objective of the government was 'to ensure the population's health and access to water' according to its Constitution.[1129] The tribunal noted that a host state is 'bound by obligations under international and constitutional laws', i.e. the right to water.[1130] The tribunal emphasised:

> When measures had been taken that have as their purpose and effect to implement such fundamental rights protected under the Constitution, they cannot hurt the fair and equitable treatment standard because their occurrence must have been deemed to be accepted by the investor when entering into the investment and the Concession Contract. In short, they were expected to be part of the investment's legal framework.[1131]

In assessing the state's objective to provide water to its population, the tribunal underlined that the state's conduct should be compatible with the FET standard.[1132] At the same time, the investor cannot invoke 'the protection of its own interests as a prevailing objective, because these interests were part of a legal environment also covering core interests of the host State, as protected by sources of law prevailing over the Contract based on international or on constitutional law'.[1133] Therefore, the state's objective to provide water to its citizens constitutes a part of Argentina's regulatory framework in which the investor had made its investment.[1134] The tribunal concluded that the termination of the concession was in the legitimate public interest and not contrary to the FET standard. However, the tribunal found that the investor had violated the FET standard because of the non-transparent conduct of the state in the negotiation process concerning the concession.[1135]

The important part of the *Urbaser* decision concerns the state's counterclaim. The *Urbaser* tribunal assumed jurisdiction over Argentina's human rights counterclaim, by rejecting the investor's argument that the examination of its human rights obligations was outside the tribunal's jurisdiction.[1136] By assessing the state's arguments regarding the alleged human rights violations by an investor, the tribunal took a significant step

1129. *Urbaser S.A. and Consorcio de Aguas Bilbao Bizkaia, Bilbao Biskaia Ur Partzuergoa v. The Argentine Republic*, ICSID Case No. ARB/07/26 Award (8 December 2016) para. 622.
1130. *Ibid.*, para. 621.
1131. *Ibid.*, para. 622.
1132. *Ibid.*
1133. *Urbaser S.A. and Consorcio de Aguas Bilbao Bizkaia, Bilbao Biskaia Ur Partzuergoa v. The Argentine Republic*, ICSID Case No. ARB/07/26 Award (8 December 2016) para. 622.
1134. *Ibid.*, para. 624.
1135. *Ibid.*, para. 845.
1136. *Ibid.*, para. 1155.

in recognising the responsibility of an investor for possible human rights violations concerning the disputed investment.

In its decision on the merits of the counterclaim, the tribunal made several important observations regarding the obligation of foreign investors to respect human rights when operating in a host state. First, the tribunal rejected the claimant's argument that the 'human right to water is a duty that may be borne solely by the State, and never borne by private companies like the Claimants as well.'[1137] The tribunal explained that. First, international law considers CSR to be of crucial importance for companies operating in the field of international commerce. Second, CSR involves 'commitments to comply with human rights in the framework of those entities' operations conducted in countries other than the country of their seat or incorporation'.[1138] Third, the tribunal observed that it is no longer the case that 'companies operating internationally are immune from becoming subjects of international law.'[1139]

The tribunal proceeded with an examination of whether companies have obligations relating to the human right of having access to water. The tribunal found that the right to have access to water is a human right under international law and that private parties have an obligation to comply with this right. To this end, the tribunal referred to a number of international instruments, such as the Universal Declaration of Human Rights (UDHR), the International Covenant on Social Economic and Cultural Rights (ICSECR), the UN Guiding Principles on Business and Human Rights and the International Labour Office's Tripartite Declaration of Principles concerning Multilateral Enterprises and Social Policy. The tribunal applied Article 30 of the UDHR and Article 5(1) of the ICSECR to establish that companies can have human rights obligations under these instruments. In interpreting these provisions, however, the tribunal determined that in this case the counterclaim could not be awarded because of various arguments, which will not be discussed here as they extend beyond the context of this study concerning the right to regulate and the FET standard.

Nonetheless, the *Urbaser v. Argentina* counterclaim decision has important implications for companies. Through this decision, the *Urbaser* tribunal demonstrated that counterclaims filed by host states against investors based on human rights violations might fall within the jurisdiction of investment tribunals. The tribunal clearly emphasised that companies cannot escape liability because of the argument that they are not subjects of international law. The assessment of the human rights arguments as conducted by the *Urbaser* tribunal is clearly different from the assessments in *AWG v. Argentina*, *Imregilo v. Argentina* and *Azurix v. Argentina*. Whereas the latter tribunals primarily abstained from examining the human rights arguments relating to the right to water, the *Urbaser* tribunal thoroughly assessed these human rights arguments. By referring to human rights treaties, the *Urbaser* tribunal not only stressed the investor's responsibilities in that field but also emphasised that a state's right to regulate in providing adequate access to water may take precedence over the rights of investors under IIAs.

1137. *Ibid.*, para. 1193.
1138. *Ibid.*, para. 1195.
1139. *Ibid.*

(iv) *Chemtura v. Canada* (the protection of public health and the environment)[1140]

In *Chemtura v. Canada*, the dispute arose out of Canada's delay in reviewing and its subsequent refusal to register lindane (a pesticide), produced by the US chemical company Chemtura (the investor).[1141] The company argued that the Canadian Pest Management Regulatory Agency had undertaken a Special Review as the result of a trade irritant.[1142] It also argued that the review process was flawed and unfair.[1143] Canada asserted that reviewing the lindane-based pesticides was part of its mandate as a regulatory agency. Furthermore, the results of the Special Review were confirmed in the re-evaluation process. In the course of this review, it was established that the registration of these types of products should be terminated or suspended because of the threat to workers' health and certain adverse environmental effects.[1144] Also, the state asserted that it had acted according to its international obligations under the Aarhus Protocol concerning the Convention on Long-Range Transboundary Air Pollution and its Protocol on Persistent Organic Pollutants (LRTAP) (hereinafter 'the Protocol').[1145] The Protocol imposed restrictions on the use of lindane for six specific uses and required a reassessment of the use of lindane no later than two years after the Protocol entered into force.[1146] Consequently, Canada argued that the Special Review of lindane was motivated by its commitments under the Protocol.[1147]

In assessing the legitimacy of the state's objectives motivated by health and environmental concerns, the tribunal took a deferential approach towards the state's measures. As a starting point, the tribunal underlined that it is not appropriate for the tribunal to judge the decisions of the state's scientific agencies. It stated that it is not its task to determine whether 'certain uses of lindane are dangerous, whether in general or in the Canadian context.'[1148] However, the tribunal could not ignore the fact that lindane had raised serious concerns both in other countries and at the international level since the 1970s.[1149] The tribunal also noted that lindane was included in the list of chemicals designated for elimination in 2009 under the Stockholm Convention on Persistent Organic Pollutants (POPs).[1150] The tribunal also recognised Canada's international obligations under the Protocol, concurring with the host state on the legitimacy of its actions to conduct the review.[1151] The tribunal found that the state's

1140. *Chemtura v. Canada* [2010] NAFTA-UNCITRAL Arbitration, Award (2 August 2010).
1141. *Ibid.*, para. 93.
1142. *Ibid.*, para. 133.
1143. *Ibid.*, paras 126-130.
1144. *Ibid.*, paras 21-29.
1145. *Ibid.*, para. 131.
1146. *See* Annex II: Substances Scheduled for Restrictions on Use. Annex II provides that '[a]ll restricted uses of lindane shall be reassessed under the Protocol no later than two years after the date of entry into force.' *See*: The 1998 Aarhus Protocol on Persistent Organic Pollutants (POPs), entry into force 23 October 2003 available at http://www.unece.org/fileadmin/DAM/env/lrtap/full%20text/1998.POPs.e.pdf accessed on 28 May 2017.
1147. *Chemtura v. Canada* [2010] NAFTA-UNCITRAL Arbitration, Award (2 August 2010) para. 139.
1148. *Ibid.*, para. 134.
1149. *Ibid.*, para. 135.
1150. *Ibid.*, para. 136.
1151. *Ibid.*, para. 143.

measure concerning its refusal to register lindane was legitimate because it had been taken in the public interest in order to protect public health and this objective had been properly substantiated by Canada.

(v) *Apotex v. US* (the protection of public health)[1152]

In *Apotex v. US*, the Canadian pharmaceutical companies Apotex Holding Inc. and Apotex Inc. (the investors) disputed certain regulatory measures by the US that affected the import of drugs manufactured in the investors' facilities located in Canada.[1153] Specifically, the investors argued that their 'due process' rights had been violated by the imposition of an 'import alert measure' on their imported goods. An import alert is a notice communicated by the US Food and Drug Administration (FDA) to the US customs, which calls for the detention of a specific category of products. This measure had been created by the US, on the basis of the US Federal Food, Drug and Cosmetic Act. In practice, this measure meant that a specific category of products would not be permitted to pass at the US border.[1154] Referring to Article 1105 of the NAFTA, the investors disputed the import alert measure and the way in which it was imposed. In particular, they argued that there was a lack of basic procedural due process conducted by the FDA, i.e. the responsible administrative body.

In evaluating the state's objectives, the tribunal stressed the importance of tribunals to recognise the 'special roles and responsibilities of regulatory bodies charged with protecting public health and other important public interests'.[1155] It also recognised the necessity for tribunals to 'exercise caution in cases involving a state regulator's exercise of discretion, particularly in sensitive areas involving protection of public health and the well-being of patients'.[1156] Apparently, such regulatory bodies are recognised by tribunals as specialised institutions whose expert opinions are valued in assessing states' objectives and measures. The *Apotex* tribunal, in assessing the US objectives to introduce the regulatory measures that affected the importation of the investors' drugs, concluded that the US had pursued legitimate objectives in the public interest. These objectives were substantiated by the state's specialised institutions that were in charge of protecting public health.

(vi) *Philip Morris v. Uruguay* (the protection of public health in regulating tobacco control)[1157]

In *Philip Morris v. Uruguay*, a Swiss tobacco company - Philip Morris - challenged certain tobacco control measures implemented by Uruguay as a part of the country's

1152. *Apotex v. US*, ICSID Case No. ARB(AF)/12/1 Award (25 August 2014).
1153. Apotex US - the investor that indirectly owned and controlled Apotex-Holding, a Canadian investor in the generic pharmaceutical industry. Also, Apotex Inc, operating several facilities in Canada, is an investor under NAFTA that is indirectly owned by Apotex Holdings.
1154. *Apotex v. US*, ICSID Case No. ARB(AF)/12/1 Award (25 August 2014) para. 2.15.
1155. Specifically, the *Apotex* tribunal referred to the Thunderbird award and the Chemtura award.
1156. *Apotex v. US*, ICSID Case No. ARB(AF)/12/1 Award (25 August 2014) para. 9.37.
1157. *Philip Morris v. Uruguay*, ICSID Case No. ARB/10/7 Award (8 July 2016) (formerly *FTR Holding SA, Philip Morris Products S.A. and Abal Hermanos S.A. v. Oriental Republic of Uruguay*).

anti-smoking campaign. In particular, under the 1991 Uruguay-Swiss BIT, Philip Morris claimed a number of treaty violations, including a breach of the FET standard.[1158] The company challenged Uruguay's health legislation adopted in the form of Presidential Decree No. 287/009, Ordinance No. 466 and Ordinance No. 514 (hereinafter the 'tobacco laws'). The challenged measures included: (1) the introduction of anti-smoking warnings that covered up to 80% of the surface of cigarette packages (the 80/80 Regulation);[1159] and (2) the prohibition of multiple presentations of packages produced by the same brand. The latter rule, i.e. the Single Presentation Requirement (SPR), had the objective of prohibiting tobacco producers from marketing more than one variant of tobacco products under one single brand.[1160]

In assessing the state's objectives in the context of the alleged violation of the FET standard, the tribunal stressed the deference of states in regulating public health. The tribunal set the threshold for the illegitimacy of the state's objectives and, referring to *Glamis v. US* and *Electrabel v. Hungary*, it stated that only a 'manifest lack of reasons', 'bad faith' or 'irrationality' behind the state's conduct could undermine the legitimacy of the state's aims.[1161]

The tribunal took into consideration both the amici curiae briefs of the World Health Organisation and the Pan American Health Organisation in establishing the link between Uruguay's health objectives and the disputed measures.[1162] It concurred with both opinions that the challenged measures had been taken for the 'purpose of protecting public health'.[1163]

The tribunal investigated each of the state measures separately. It concluded that both measures – the SPR and the 80/80 Regulation – were reasonable measures taken in the interest of public health. With regard to the 80/80 Regulation, in particular, the tribunal emphasised that states addressing a 'major public health problem' should possess 'substantial deference'.[1164] The tribunal stressed that a state should have the discretion to decide the percentage by which a cigarette package should be covered with anti-smoking warnings. The tribunal stated:

> The fair and equitable treatment standard is not a justiciable standard of good government, and the tribunal is not a court of appeal. Article 3(2) [of the 1991 Uruguay-Swiss BIT] does not dictate, for example, that a 50% health warning requirement is fair whereas an 80% requirement is not ....[1165]

In this case, the tribunal relied on the doctrine of 'the margin of appreciation' in justifying the state's objectives in regulating the tobacco industry. Drawing on the

---

1158. *Philip Morris v. Uruguay*, ICSID Case No. ARB/10/7 Notice of Arbitration (19 February 2010).
1159. Presidential Decree 287/009 of 15 June 2009 (the 80/80 Regulation). The 80/80 Regulation was introduced with the purpose of increasing the size of graphic health warnings placed on cigarette packs from 50% to 80%.
1160. *Philip Morris v. Uruguay*, ICSID Case No. ARB/10/7 Award (8 July 2016) para. 9.
1161. *Ibid.*, para. 399.
1162. *Ibid.*, para. 391.
1163. *Ibid.*
1164. *Philip Morris v. Uruguay*, ICSID Case No. ARB/10/7 Award (8 July 2016) para. 418. *See*: Chapter 4, section §4.04[B], where the concepts of deference and the margin of appreciation are explained.
1165. *Philip Morris v. Uruguay*, ICSID Case No. ARB/10/7 Award (8 July 2016) para. 418.

ECtHR margin of appreciation doctrine, the tribunal underlined the need for investment tribunals to respect the states' choices and measures that have the objective of protecting public health.[1166]

[D] The Illegitimacy of State Objectives

In assessing the legitimacy of the state's objectives, several tribunals have indicated the circumstances in which the state's objectives may be found illegitimate. To this end, these tribunals have provided that the 'irrationality' behind the state's conduct could undermine the legitimacy of the state's aims.[1167] There are a number of decisions where the irrationality of a state's objective has been found primarily on the basis of political motives involved in state conduct.[1168] Following an analysis of the case law, Bonnitcha similarly asserts that in some cases a 'sufficiently irrational measure will breach the FET standard even if it is introduced and applied through a fair procedure and does not upset an investor's legitimate expectation.'[1169] The decisions based on 'political reasons' or 'one-sided arguments' are set against legitimate public interest objectives. In some decisions, the tribunals indicated distrust concerning the sincerity of a state's motives if it involved a political element. In these cases, there is a presumption that a 'politically motivated measure does not pursue a rational objective.'[1170] Several examples of such decisions are discussed below.

(i) *Tecmed v. Mexico*[1171]

In evaluating the objectives of Mexico in denying a permit to operate a hazardous waste disposal site and ultimately in closing the site in question, the tribunal in *Tecmed v. Mexico* focused on the political reasons behind this decision.[1172] The dispute concerned a Spanish company, Tecmed, that had the renewal of a permit to operate a hazardous landfill rejected.[1173] The Mexican government refused to renew the permit claiming that the site had not been properly maintained and its further development had negative effects on the environment and health.[1174] Community pressure against the landfill had also been a factor in the government refusing the final permit.[1175] The company claimed that the denial to renew the permit had an adverse effect on its investments and violated the FET standard under the Spain-Mexico BIT.[1176]

1166. *Ibid.*, para. 399.
1167. *Ibid*; *Electrabel v. Hungary*, ICSID Case No. ARB/07/1 Final Award (25 November 2015), para. 8.35.
1168. J. Bonnitcha, (2014), e-book, section 4.4.2. p. 43.
1169. *Ibid.*, e-book, section 4.7.2. p. 175.
1170. *Ibid.*, e-book, section 4.7.3. p. 177.
1171. *Tecmed v. Mexico*, ICSID Case No. ARB(AF)/00/2 Award (29 May 2003).
1172. *Ibid.*, para. 164.
1173. Tecmed is a subsidiary that bought a landfill of hazardous industrial waste and afterwards transferred the landfill to Cytrar, a company created by Tecmed to operate the landfill. *Tecmed v. Mexico*, ICSID Case No. ARB(AF)/00/2 Award (29 May 2003) para. 35.
1174. *Tecmed v. Mexico*, ICSID Case No. ARB(AF)/00/2 Award (29 May 2003) paras 97, 125.
1175. *Ibid.*, paras 105-112.
1176. *Ibid.*, paras 43, 98, 158.

In evaluating the objectives of Mexico in denying the renewal of a permit and ultimately its decision to close the site, the tribunal focused primarily on the political reasons behind these decisions. Adopting the position of the claimant, the tribunal underlined that the refusal to renew the permit had been taken because of the 'political reasons relating to the community's opposition expressed in a variety of forms, regardless of the company in charge of the operation and regardless of whether or not it was being properly operated'.[1177]

The tribunal referred to the company's arguments that the newly elected authorities encouraged citizens' opposition to the landfill and who wanted to see the withdrawal or non-renewal of the permit.[1178] This led to a confrontation with the community that eventually resulted in blocking access to the landfill.[1179] The negative attitude of the community towards the landfill had been justified by its close proximity to the urban centre and the dissatisfaction of the people with how the company had transported and confined the hazardous toxic waste.[1180] Mexico's argument was that the 'denial of the permit is a control measure in a highly regulated sector and which is very closely linked to public interests.'[1181] Mexico also added that the decision to deny the permit was issued in 'compliance with the State's police power within the highly regulated and extremely sensitive framework of environmental protection and public health'.[1182]

The tribunal disputed the true objectives of the state's conduct, stating that there was no real evidence of the damage caused by the operation of the waste facility to the environment and public health.[1183] The tribunal emphasised that the state had not provided a clear indication that the operation of the landfill by the company endangered 'public health, ecological balance or the environment'.[1184] The tribunal referred to the Resolution issued by the government informing the company that the permit had been denied. The Resolution had not mentioned specific environmental dangers; it focused on certain conditions that were not met by the company in operating the landfill. It becomes clear that the tribunal chose not to elaborate on the factors presented by Mexico, including the 'irregularities while operating the landfill ... that triggered strong community pressure' and that 'community pressure suggested that the operation of the landfill was not feasible due to its location.'[1185]

As Henckels points out, the tribunal assessed the community riots as a part of the political agenda of the state's authorities, without considering other possible motivations behind this opposition.[1186] In a similar vein, Pavoni emphasises that the tribunal

1177. *Ibid.*, para. 164.
1178. *Ibid.*, para. 42.
1179. *Ibid. See also* para. 108 '...around 200 people organised a demonstration, marching to the landfill and closing it down symbolically ...'.
1180. *Tecmed v. Mexico*, ICSID Case No. ARB(AF)/00/2 Award (29 May 2003) para. 49.
1181. *Ibid.*, para. 46.
1182. *Ibid.*, para. 97.
1183. *Ibid.*, paras 124; 127-128; 130-139; 145-147.
1184. *Ibid.*, para. 162.
1185. *Ibid.*, para. 105.
1186. *See* the analysis in C. Henckels, Proportionality and Deference in Investor-State Arbitration (Cambridge University Press, 2015) 109. She asserts that 'in its evaluation of the importance

had not made a connection between community pressure, on the one hand, and health and environmental issues, on the other.[1187]

(ii) *Azurix v. Argentina*

In *Azurix v. Argentina*, the tribunal found that the state's refusal to raise the water tariffs was motivated by political reasons relating to the upcoming elections and the fact that the concession had been awarded to the investor by the previous government.[1188] Furthermore, the tribunal considered that the encouragement of the governor and other officials not to pay the water bills 'verge[d] on bad faith' in the light of the Bahia Blanca poisoning incident.[1189] According to the tribunal, the governmental authorities were responsible for this incident. If the necessary repairs had been carried out by the state, the contamination of the water could have been avoided.[1190] Referring to the Bahia Blanca incident, the tribunal concluded that the actions of the government at the time of the water contamination were based on its wish not only to protect public health but also to gain political support. The tribunal emphasised that governments 'have to be vigilant and protect the public health of their citizens but the statements and actions of the provincial authorities contributed to the crisis rather than assisted in solving it'.[1191]

(iii) *Gold Reserve v. Venezuela*

The *Gold Reserve v. Venezuela* case concerned mine and copper investments in Venezuela. The dispute between Venezuela and the Venezuelan subsidiary of a US company, the Gold Reserve Corporation (the investor), arose as a result of the so-called Brisas Project.[1192] This project concerned near-surface gold resources situated on the Brisas property.[1193] The investor's investment included two mining concessions: the Brisas Concession and the Unicornio Concession that were a part of the Brisas Project. In the course of almost ten years of developing the Brisas Project, the investor had been

---

of the authorities' objective, the tribunal did not appear to seriously consider what might have motivated the community opposition; namely, the possibility of risks to health and the environment emerging over time given the landfill's urban location and the increasing population in the area'.

1187. R. Pavoni, 'Environmental Rights, Sustainable Development, and Investor-State Caw Law: A Critical Appraisal', in. P.-M. Dupuy, et al. (eds) *Human Rights in International Investment Law and Arbitration* (Oxford University Press, 2010) 554. In his analysis of *Tecmed*, he provides that '[t]he tribunal seemingly unaware of the human rights implications of public participation, labelled 'community pressure' as mere "socio-political circumstances" or "political problems"'.
1188. *Azurix Corp. v. The Argentine Republic*, ICSID Case No. ARB/01/12 Award (14 July 2006) para. 375.
1189. *Ibid.*, para. 376.
1190. *Ibid.*
1191. *Azurix Corp. v. The Argentine Republic*, ICSID Case No. ARB/01/12 Award (14 July 2006) para. 144.
1192. The Brisas Project included the Unicornio Concession and the Brisas Concession granted to the investor and together they are referred to as the Brisas Project.
1193. *Gold Reserve v. Venezuela*, ICSID Case No. ARB(AF)/09/1 Award (22 September 2014) para. 10.

involved in the exploration of mines. The investor obtained the necessary authorisations and permits from the authorities and received two concessions: the Brisas Concession and the Unicornio Concession.[1194] However, Venezuela blocked the start of the production process and terminated the concessions between 2009 and 2010.[1195]

Between 1993 and 2007, various Ministry departments had approved the feasibility plan and the environmental and impact assessment necessary for the project. The Initiation Act was the final stage before the investor could begin its exploitation activities. The Initiation Act is the approval that has to be provided by the Venezuelan Ministry of Environment (MinAmb) confirming that the investor has complied with the environmental requirements under the construction permit.[1196] However, in 2008, the MinAmb refused to sign the Initiation Act declaring the project an 'absolute nullity' and revoking the construction permit for reasons of public order.[1197] The authorities explained that the Brisas Project was located in the 'environmentally fragile Imataca Forest Reserve' and that raised serious environmental concerns.[1198] The affected area had to undergo a special management plan in order to avoid a deterioration of the environment and to preserve the rights of the indigenous people.[1199]

In assessing the legitimacy of the argument offered by the state to annul the construction permit, the tribunal indicated that the termination of the project had not only been motivated by official reasons presented by Venezuela, namely the environmental impact of the project.[1200] Rather, the tribunal provided that the changes in natural resources policies, initiated by the former President Chavez, was another reason for the termination of the concessions.[1201] The tribunal referred to statements and public announcements on the new policy relating to the state's natural resources. The new policy aimed to reclaim the privatised mining resources and to place them under state control. This led to a change in the procedure concerning decisions relating to the issuing of mining permits to the Gold Reserve Corporation, including the Brisas Project. Referring to public statements and the President's failure to reply to the letter sent by the Gold Reserve Corporation, the tribunal stated:

> The real reason for MinAmb's failure to sign the Initiation Act was not (or not only) the serious concern over the environmental impacts for the Brisas Project, as alleged by the Respondent during the proceedings. Clearly, the change of policy by Venezuela regarding the mineral exploitation, as evidenced by the numerous announcements and statements made during this period by the highest level of the Administration, including President Chávez, motivated Respondent's conduct.[1202]

1194. *Ibid.*, para. 13.
1195. *Ibid.*, paras 10-28.
1196. *Ibid.*, paras 10-12.
1197. *Ibid.*, para. 24.
1198. *Ibid.*, para. 283.
1199. *Ibid.*
1200. *Gold Reserve v. Venezuela*, ICSID Case No. ARB(AF)/09/1 Award (22 September 2014) para. 580.
1201. *Ibid.*
1202. *Gold Reserve v. Venezuela*, ICSID Case No. ARB(AF)/09/1 Award (22 September 2014) para. 590.

To this end, the tribunal concluded that Venezuela had violated the FET standard because the Initiation Act had been enacted 'without explaining the reasons for such inaction',[1203] thereby emphasising that the revocation of the investor's construction permit had not been sufficiently substantiated by the state.

The aforementioned examples, as well as other cases,[1204] indicate that the involvement of certain forms of political considerations may lead to the conclusion that tribunals consider certain state objectives to be irrational and therefore illegitimate in the context of the FET standard. Some tribunals qualify certain governmental objectives as being based on 'political opportunism', constituting serious threats to investors and their investments.[1205] For example, in *Tecmed v. Mexico* and *Metalclad v. Mexico*, community pressure had been primarily considered as a political tool of the governments of respondent states in escalating conflicts with investors.[1206] The latter tribunal did not consider the community opposition that had influenced the decision of the state's authorities to deny the permit to be a legitimate public concern that fell within the domain of the public interest.

In assessing whether the objective of the state's measure is legitimate, other tribunals have also questioned political actions and the motivation behind certain measures by state authorities, but with a different outcome. In *AES Summit v. Hungary*,

1203. *Gold Reserve v. Venezuela*, ICSID Case No. ARB(AF)/09/1 Award (22 September 2014) para. 591. 'Respondent's failure to sign the Initiation Act despite Claimant's repeated requests without explaining the reasons for such inaction, rather reinforcing Claimant's expectation that such signature would be forthcoming once the proposed alternative access road had been accepted, amount to conduct evidencing (through acts and omissions) a lack of transparency, consistency and good faith in dealing with an investor.'

1204. *See CME v. Czech Republic* [2001] UNCITRAL Arbitration, Partial Award (13 September 2001), where the tribunal found that the Media Council was motivated by political reasons and not by legitimate regulatory goals. In *Biwater v. Tanzania*, some of the actions of the Minister regarding water concessions pursued the political due to the upcoming elections. *Biwater v. Tanzania*, ICSID Case No. ARB/05/22 Final Award (24 July 2008) para. 500. In *Lemire v. Ukraine*, several factors contributing to violations of the FET standard were based on political interference by the President in one of the tenders that, according to the tribunal, resulted in two others being won by two radio stations for allocated frequencies. The tribunal also accepted the claimant's arguments, which were not proven, that in a number of instances the winning radio stations had political connections or were associated with the government. *Lemire v. Ukraine*, ICSID Case No. ARB/06/18 Decision on Jurisdiction and Liability (14 January 2010) para. 370. In *Eureko v. Poland*, the additional factor that contributed to the establishment of a breach of the FET standard was the tribunal's conclusion that the governmental body had acted 'for purely arbitrary reasons linked to the interplay of Polish politics and nationalistic reasons of a discriminatory character'. *Eureko BV v. Republic of Poland* [2005] UNCITRAL Arbitration, Partial Award (19 August 2005) para. 233.

1205. T. Wood, 'Political Risk or Political Right? Reconciling the International Legal Norms of Investment Protection and Political Participation' [2015] 30(3) *ICSID Review*, 11. In this article, the author analysed the human right to political participation, specifically in relation to investment obligations.

1206. C. Henckels, 'Proportionality and the Standard of Review in Fair and Equitable Treatment Claims: Balancing Stability and Consistency with the Public Interest' [2012] *Paper for Society of International Economic Law*, 15. 'These decisions may be criticized for failing to properly assess the legitimacy of authorities' regulatory objectives in responding to civil society concerns, which included opposition to the locations and the facilities and ecological impacts.' https://papers.ssrn.com/sol3/papers.cfm?abstract_id=2091474 accessed on 27 May 2018.

e.g., the tribunal emphasised that it is normal and common that a 'public policy matter [may] become a political issue; that is the arena where such matters are discussed and made public.'[1207] The tribunal in *Electrabel v. Hungary* found that a high level of profit by energy providers was a public and political matter, stating that 'politics is what democratic governments necessarily address; and it is not, ipso facto, evidence of irrational or arbitrary conduct for a government to take into account political or even populist controversies.'[1208]

In *AES Summit v. Hungary* and *Electrabel v. Hungary*, the tribunals concluded that a politically motivated measure is not necessarily illegitimate, because the goal of such a measure was to regulate for the benefit of a certain public interest. In these decisions, the political motivations of the state were weighed against the other arguments in assessing the objectives of the state's measures, e.g. consumer protection.[1209] In *AES Summit v. Hungary* and *Electrabel v. Hungary*, the tribunals adopted a deferential approach towards the state's choice of a certain measure, even if it involved some form of political gain for the state's authority pursuing it. What was important for the tribunals in deciding on whether the objectives of the state's measures were legitimate was that these measures were justified by the state's records or were 'followed by a logical good sense explanation'.[1210] The tribunals in *Tecmed v. Mexico, Metalclad v. Mexico, Azurix v. Argentina* and *Gold Reserve v. Venezuela* did not assess other aspects of the objectives of the states' measures that might have justified the governments' decision-making process. In *Tecmed v. Mexico*, the objective to deny the permit to the investor had been considered illegitimate, primarily because the opposition of the community was considered to be only part of the political agenda of the state's authorities and not a legitimate concern of the state. In the same vein, the *Azurix v. Argentina* tribunal, when determining that the state's objectives for refusing to increase water tariffs had formed part of the election campaign, had not properly investigated the other objectives raised by this state, which included providing its citizens with access to water.

§7.03 SUMMARY: THE HOST STATE'S OBJECTIVES

The determination that a state's measure or conduct serves a legitimate objective is one of the conditions for tribunals to accept a state's right to regulate in the context of the FET standard. Table 2 provides an overview of the elements considered in evaluating the legitimacy of a state's objective.

1207. *AES Summit v. Hungary*, ICSID Case No. ARB/07/22 Award (23 September 2010) para. 10.3.24.
1208. *Electrabel v. Hungary*, ICSID Case No. ARB/07/1 Final Award (25 November 2015) para. 8.23.
1209. *AES Summit v. Hungary*, ICSID Case No. ARB/07/22 Award (23 September 2010) para. 10.3.31.
1210. *AES Summit v. Hungary*, ICSID Case No. ARB/07/22 Award (23 September 2010) para. 10.3.8; *Electrabel v. Hungary*, ICSID Case No. ARB/07/1 Final Award (25 November 2015) para. 179.

Table 2 Elements That Are Pertinent to Assessing the Legitimacy of a State's Objective

<table>
<tr>
<td>1. A state's legitimate objectives</td>
<td>1. Recognised public interests:
– the protection of environmental concerns, e.g. safeguarding against toxic waste
– the protection of human rights
– the protection of the right to have access to (clean) water
– the protection of public health
– the protection of indigenous people
– the protection of cultural heritage
– the reformation of the banking sector
– the fight against corruption
– the modernisation of the transport sector
– the reduction of excessive profits by energy companies
– the alignment of the electricity sector with the EU market
2. Ways to substantiate a public interest by the host state:
– motivated decision
– state's records
– parliamentary debates
– compliance with the state's obligations under other international treaties (other than the applicable IIA)</td>
<td rowspan="2">The judicial point of departure in the assessment of the objective of the state's measure is the degree of deference</td>
</tr>
<tr>
<td>2. A state's illegitimate objectives</td>
<td>1. Manifest lack of reasons
2. Irrational, one-sided objectives and/or pursuing a political agenda as a reason for the state's measures, e.g.:
– the measure is fuelled by community opposition to the investor's plans
– the state authority's measure is motivated by an upcoming election
– a drastic change of the political course concerning the management policies for natural resources</td>
</tr>
</table>

The most important criteria to acknowledge a state's right to regulate in the context of the FET standard is the determination that such a state's measure or conduct serves (i) a public interest and (ii) this is supported by public records and other evidence. These two criteria are discussed below.

With regard to the first criterion, in assessing the legitimacy of a state's objective, tribunals have provided that such an objective should be taken in the public interest. From the presentation of the cases addressed in this Chapter, it became clear that tribunals have qualified a broad spectrum of public interests as legitimate state objectives. It includes measures addressing the banking crisis, measures taken with the objective of combating corruption and measures addressing the problem of excessive profits being made by energy providers, among others. In section §7.02[C], several cases were discussed in which the host states were able to justify their conduct, at least to some extent, by pointing at a public interest that they intended to serve, e.g. the protection of public health, the human right to water, other human rights or the protection of the environment. Moreover, the comparison of these specific types of public interests (section §7.02[C]) with the public interests which have been identified in the text of several modern IIAs (Chapter 3) revealed a great similarity. By assessing the cases involving these public interests, the objective was to find out to what extent they have been applied by tribunals. This helps to better understand the recent legal developments as a part of the main research question.[1211]

Regarding the second criterion, it has been analysed in this section §7.02[B] that a state has to substantiate its objective.[1212] Any available state records and official documents, which can clarify the nature and purpose of the state's measure, can be submitted to the tribunals for the purpose of justifying the states' motives. Compliance with international obligations under international treaties other than the applicable IIA has, in some cases, served as adequate justification. For example, in *Philip Morris v. Uruguay*, *Chemtura v. Canada*, *Blusun v. Italy* and *Urbaser v. Argentina*, the obligations of the state under international treaties and European treaties regulating public health, the right to water, renewable energy and other environmental issues had been taken into account. In *Chemtura*, the tribunal took into account the Aarhus Protocol and the obligation of Canada to reassess the use of lindane, as required by the Protocol.[1213] In the *Philip Morris* case, the tribunal accepted the argument of Uruguay that the challenged measures had been adopted in order to comply with the provisions of the Framework Convention on Tobacco Control (FCTC).[1214] In *Blusun v. Italy*, the tribunal determined that the contested state's measures were adopted in order to comply with the EU Directive on the promotion and the use of the renewable

1211. *See*: Section §7.02[C], where the choice for including public interest objectives is provided.
1212. *EDF Limited v. Romania*, ICSID Case No. ARB/05/13 Award (8 October 2009); *AES Summit v. Hungary*, ICSID Case No. ARB/07/22 Award (23 September 2010); *Electrabel v. Hungary*, ICSID Case No. ARB/07/1 Final Award (25 November 2015).
1213. *Chemtura v. Canada* [2010] NAFTA-UNCITRAL Arbitration, Award (2 August 2010) para. 138.
1214. *Philip Morris v. Uruguay*, ICSID Case No. ARB/10/7 Award (8 July 2016) para. 401. 'The first point to be made is that both measures were adopted in an effort to give effect to general obligations under the FCTC'.

energy.[1215] In *Urbaser v. Argentina*, the tribunal applied national and international law, providing that the state's objective to guarantee the human right to water constitutes part of the regulatory framework in Argentina, in which country the investor has made his investment.[1216]

Tribunals differentiate between the legitimate and illegitimate objectives of states' measures. In some cases, the illegitimacy of a state's objective was established, where the state's objectives were considered to be one-sided and primarily 'politically' motivated or based on the 'political agenda' of certain state authorities.[1217] In earlier decisions, such as *Tecmed* and *Metalclad*, the presence of illegitimate state objectives motivated by national politics had been a defining criterion in finding a breach of the FET standard.[1218] In the examples of cases where a 'political element' played a role, this led some tribunals to determine that the state's objectives had to be qualified as irrational, without further examining other goals underlying the state's measure, such as the protection of a public interest.[1219]

An important judicial point of departure in assessing the objective of the state's measure is, however, the degree of deference afforded by tribunals to the choice of a state's measure in achieving the desired goals. The deference approach plays a role in determining whether the state's objective will be found to be legitimate or not.[1220] In such cases, tribunals thus tend to exercise restraint in making a judgment regarding the content and significance of the objective of the state's measure. Generally, tribunals are likely to find that the state's objectives are indeed legitimate, unless the reasons for the state's measure are 'manifestly unfounded' or that the measure has been taken in 'bad faith', or when the state's authorities are unable to substantiate the objectives underlying their measure.[1221] In the cases concerning the protection of public health, the *Chemtura*, *Apotex* and *Philip Morris* tribunals seem to have displayed a higher degree of deference to the objectives of the states' measures, in contrast to other cases discussed in section §7.02. The reason for providing a significant degree of freedom for states' authorities when they make such decisions may relate to the fact that all three tribunals recognised that the states' public health organs have specialist expertise and

---

1215. *Blusun S.A., J.-P. Lecorcier AND M. Stein v. Italy*, ICSID Case No. ARB/14/3 Award, 27 December 2016, EU Directive 2009/28, para. 331.
1216. *Urbaser S.A. and Consorcio de Aguas Bilbao Bizkaia, Bilbao Biskaia Ur Partzuergoa v. The Argentine Republic*, ICSID Case No. ARB/07/26 Award (8 December 2016) para. 624.
1217. J. Bonnitcha, Substantive Protection under Investment Treaties: A Legal and Economic Analysis (Cambridge University Press, 2014), e-book, section 4.7.4. pp. 173-180.
1218. C. Henckels, Proportionality and Deference in Investor-State Arbitration (Cambridge University Press, 2015) 129.
1219. J. Bonnitcha, Substantive Protection under Investment Treaties: A Legal and Economic Analysis (Cambridge University Press, 2014), e-book, section 4.7.4, p. 185.
1220. A similar observation has been made by Henckels, who observes that 'the greater the degree of deference afforded by investment tribunals, the greater the degree of regulatory flexibility will be enjoyed by host states.' C. Henckels, 'Balancing Investment Protection and the Public Interest: The Role of the Standard of Review and the Importance of Deference' [March, 2013] 4(1) *Investor-State Arbitration Journal of International Dispute Settlement*, p. 200.
1221. *Glamis v. US* [2009] NAFTA, ICSID 48 ILM 1039 Award (8 June 2009) para. 805. *Philip Morris v. Uruguay*, ICSID Case No. ARB/10/7 Award (8 July 2016) para. 399.

are in a better position to make decisions concerning public health, in comparison to the arbitrators that do not possess such specific knowledge.[1222]

Among the cases analysed in this section, which has discussed the issue of a public interest, the decisions in *Philip Morris v. Uruguay* and *Urbaser v. Argentina* certainly stand out. The *Philip Morris* decision represents an example where the state's right to regulate in the interest of public health is explicitly recognised. The tribunal, operating on the basis of the *margin of appreciation doctrine*, acknowledged the state's discretion to address the objectives concerning the protection of public health through the tobacco control measures in question, i.e. the SPR and the 80/80 Regulation. This does not imply, however, that such recognition will guarantee that the state will be immediately relieved of its liability under the FET standard. In recognising the legitimacy of the state's objective to protect public health, the tribunal proceeded with a review of the substantive and procedural aspects of the contested state's measures. An analysis of the tribunal's assessment of the reasonableness of some of Uruguay's measures is discussed in the following section.

Urbaser v. Argentina is the first investment case that assessed the application of the human right to water.[1223] In this case, the state's constitutional obligation to guarantee the human right to water has been considered by the tribunal not only as an important state's objective but also as a part of the law applicable to the water concession. Furthermore, the tribunal in its examination of the state's counterclaim observed that companies are not immune from international law obligations, including obligations relating to the human right of access to water.[1224]

§7.04 ASSESSMENT OF THE STATE'S MEASURE

Following an assessment of whether the objectives of a state's measure(s) are legitimate, the next step for many tribunals is to consider the state's measure vis-à-vis an investor. Tribunals assess the contested state's measure under the FET standard according to the international law principles of (i) reasonableness, proportionality and the prohibition of arbitrariness; (ii) non-discrimination; and (iii) transparency. The tribunal's assessment of the state's measure according to these principles is analysed in this section.

1222. This conclusion corresponds with the argument made by Henckels in the chapter of her book where she conceptualises the concept of deference. She argues that 'where uncertainty remains after adjudicators have taken into account the evidence of the parties in relation to a particular matter, this rationale for deference suggests that a tribunal should afford a measure of deference to the state due to the state's greater expertise and institutional competence as a regulator.' C. Henckels, Proportionality and Deference in Investor-State Arbitration (Cambridge University Press, 2015) 40.

1223. E. Guntrip, Private Actors, Public Goods and Responsibility for the Right to Water in International Investment Law: An Analysis of Urbaser v. Argentina (Brill Open Law, 2018) p. 4.

1224. *Urbaser S.A. and Consorcio de Aguas Bilbao Bizkaia, Bilbao Biskaia Ur Partzuergoa v. The Argentine Republic*, ICSID Case No. ARB/07/26 Award (8 December 2016) para. 1195.

[A] The Principles of Reasonableness, Proportionality and the Prohibition of Arbitrariness in the Assessment of a State's Measure

Tribunals take several principles into consideration when assessing a state's measure, such as the principles of reasonableness and proportionality and the prohibition of arbitrariness. Tribunals have used some of these principles interchangeably in their assessment of FET cases.

Tribunals regularly refer to both reasonableness and proportionality in evaluating a state's measure.[1225] As noted by some scholars, tribunals often refer to these two principles without making any distinction between them.[1226] This comes as no surprise, considering that the 'overlap between reasonableness and proportionality is extensive.'[1227] As explained by Ortino, the steps followed by tribunals in applying reasonableness or proportionality are often the same.[1228] The first step includes a review of whether 'the public decision is effective in, or materially contributes to, achieving its purported objective, so whether the state's objective relates to the state's measure,' also known as the suitability test.[1229] The second step for both reasonableness and proportionality is to consider whether 'the public decision under review is necessary to achieve its purported aim,'[1230] thereby examining the necessity of the measure, also known as the necessity test.[1231] The third step can include an assessment of whether 'the public decision has an excessive impact on the applicant's interests

1225. Tribunals often refer to these terms in the same sentence. For example, the tribunal in *Total v. Argentina* provided that the principles of proportionality, reasonableness and non-discrimination are of importance in the evaluation of a state's measure, *Total v. Argentina*, ICSID Case No. ARB/04/01 Decision on Liability (27 December 2010), para. 162; in *Philip Morris v. Uruguay*, the tribunal mentioned that a reasonable measure should also not be 'arbitrary, grossly unfair, unjust, discriminatory, or disproportionate'. *Philip Morris v. Uruguay*, ICSID Case No. ARB/10/7 Award (8 July 2016), para. 410.
1226. The interchangeable use of the terms 'proportionality' and 'reasonableness' in investment decisions is highlighted in the analysis by Henckles who explains that 'proportionality and reasonableness may be understood as a specific manifestation of the concept of reasonableness: both proportionality and reasonableness suggest a balance of interests and a rational connection between a measure and its objective.' (p. 13). C. Henckles, Proportionality and the Standard of Review in Fair and Equitable Treatment Claims, Working Paper for SIEL No. 2012/27, June 2012, p. 13. Also *see*: F. Ortino, 'Investment Treaties, Sustainable Development and Reasonableness Review: A Case Against Strict Proportionality Balancing' [2017] *Leiden Journal of International Law Volume 30*, Issue 1, 87.
1227. F. Ortino, 'Investment Treaties, Sustainable Development and Reasonableness Review: A Case Against Strict Proportionality Balancing' [2017] *Leiden Journal of International Law*, 87.
1228. These three steps are also described in Chapter 4, section §4.04[A].
1229. F. Ortino, 'Investment Treaties, Sustainable Development and Reasonableness Review: A Case Against Strict Proportionality Balancing' [2017] *Leiden Journal of International Law*, 87. The suitability test is also referred to and is described in Chapter 4, section §4.04[A].
1230. F. Ortino, 'Investment Treaties, Sustainable Development and Reasonableness Review: A Case Against Strict Proportionality Balancing' [2017] *Leiden Journal of International Law*, 88. The second step is also referred to and is described in Chapter 4, section §4.04[A].
1231. Note that the necessity test in the context of reasonableness and proportionality is different from the necessity defence, i.e. the principle of international law codified in Article 25 of the International Law Commission's Articles on State Responsibility.

compared to the benefits to the chosen public policy,' also known as the proportionality *stricto sensu* test.[1232] This test is considered by some scholars to be highly intrusive for states, as in applying the proportionality *stricto sensu* test tribunals question whether the effects of a state's measure are disproportionate or excessive in relation to the interests affected.[1233] By applying the proportionality *stricto sensu* test, tribunals test whether the state's measure has been excessively burdensome for the investor compared with the benefits produced by the measure. Hence, tribunals may question and review the original choice of a state to address a certain public interest. Thus, by applying the proportionality *stricto sensu* test, the arbitrators may give priority to the prevention of financial and economic disadvantages for an investor as a result of the contested state's measure over a state's public interest that is pursued by the measure.

Tribunals apply varying degrees of intrusiveness in reviewing a state's measure. In assessing the FET standard, tribunals are commonly 'at the lower end of the intrusiveness spectrum,' thereby limiting their assessment of reasonableness or proportionality to suitability and necessity tests, and rarely relying on the third step, i.e., a review of the effectiveness of the state's measure (the proportionality *stricto sensu* test).[1234]

The principle of the prohibition of arbitrariness also plays a role in the assessment of the state's measure under the FET standard. In some cases, tribunals refer to the prohibition of arbitrariness alongside reasonableness and proportionality, in particular when discussing the relationship between the objective and the measure, i.e. the suitability test.[1235] As observed by Dumberry, in analysing FET cases, the state's measures are considered to be arbitrary if 'no rational relationship exists between a

1232. F. Ortino, 'Investment Treaties, Sustainable Development and Reasonableness Review: A Case Against Strict Proportionality Balancing' [2017] *Leiden Journal of International Law*, 88.
1233. C. Henckels, Proportionality and Deference in Investor-State Arbitration (Cambridge University Press, 2015) 62. She explains why the proportionality *stricto sensu* test is intrusive for the state's room for manoeuvre in its right to regulate. This 'highly intrusive technique' may result in a 'value judgment' that 'substitute[s] the judgment in relation to whether the importance of avoiding harm to the protected right or interest outweighs the importance of achieving the objective'. G. Bucheler, Proportionality in Investor-State Arbitration (Oxford University Press, 2015), pp. 63-65. Buchler cautioned against the 'dark sides' of proportionality, e.g. the *stricto sensu* test, that can result in unwanted side effects such as judicial lawmaking, arbitrariness and a threat to the rule of law. *See* F. Ortino, 'Investment Treaties, Sustainable Development and Reasonableness Review: A Case Against Strict Proportionality Balancing' [2017] *Leiden Journal of International Law*, 89. Ortino explains the difference between the proportionality *stricto sensu* test and the suitability and necessity steps. '"Suitability" and "necessity" differ from "proportionality *stricto sensu*" since the former take as given the policy objective(s) pursued by the public authority (say environmental protection) including the specific level(s) of protection chosen by that public authority (say zero pollution)'.
1234. F. Ortino, 'Investment Treaties, Sustainable Development and Reasonableness Review: A Case Against Strict Proportionality Balancing' [2017] *Leiden Journal of International Law*, 72.
1235. J. Bonnitcha, Substantive Protection under Investment Treaties: A Legal and Economic Analysis (Cambridge University Press, 2014), section: 4.4.1, p. 45 (e-book). P. Dumberry, 'The Prohibition against Arbitrary Conduct and the Fair and Equitable Treatment Standard under NAFTA Article 1105' [2014] 15 *The Journal of World and Investment*, p. 124.

measure adopted by the government and the alleged purpose or goal of that measure.'[1236] Several authors have noted that in analysing the state's measures under the FET, 'tribunals do not appear to attach significance to the differences in terminology in terms of arbitrariness or unreasonableness, instead of using these terms synonymously.'[1237]

As will be further demonstrated in this section, in assessing the FET standard and when judging the state's measure, tribunals sometimes follow the stage(s) identified by Ortino under the principles of reasonableness and proportionality. First, many FET tribunals examine the relationship between the state's measure and its objective, i.e. suitability test. In doing so, they assess the 'existence of meaningful relations' between the state's objective and its measure (section §7.04[A][1]).[1238] By conducting this assessment, tribunals have made a reference to reasonableness and proportionality and the prohibition of arbitrariness. Second, several tribunals have performed the necessity test by examining the possibility of employing alternative measures in order to achieve a certain objective (§7.04[A][2]). Third, some tribunals have also analysed the impact of the loss suffered by an investor as a consequence of a state's measure (§7.04[A][3]). This latter assessment relies on the third stage of the reasonableness and proportionally test, i.e. the proportionality *stricto sensu* test. Mostly, tribunals do not follow all three stages in assessing the state's measure, instead of applying some of the aforementioned steps under the principles of reasonableness, proportionality and the prohibition of arbitrariness.

[1] The Relationship Between a State's Measure and Its Objective

In *Glamis v. US*, the tribunal stated that the state's measure should be 'rationally relate[d] to its stated purpose and [be] reasonably drafted to address its objectives'.[1239] The tribunal did not consider the question of whether the state measures imposed, i.e. the requirement that the mining operators refill open-pit metal mines and grade the mining activities, had actually attained the desired objective. It even concurred with the investor that the imposed legislation's requirement to refill the mines may have a counterproductive effect and lead to some of the artefacts of the tribal people being damaged.[1240] Despite this, the tribunal concluded that the 'government had a sufficient good faith belief that there was a reasonable connection between the harm and the

1236. P. Dumberry, 'The Prohibition against Arbitrary Conduct and the Fair and Equitable Treatment Standard under NAFTA Article 1105' [2014] 15 *The Journal of World and Investment*, p. 122.
1237. C. Henckles, Proportionality and Deference in Investor-State Arbitration (Cambridge University Press, 2015) 71; Also *see*: R. Klager who makes the similar point. R. Klager, (2011) 289. Also *see*: U. Kriebaum, 'Arbitrary/Unreasonable or Discriminatory Measures', in M. Bungenberg et al. (eds.) *International Investment Law* (Nomos, 2015) 792. The author emphasises that in some investment decisions tribunals refer to the notions of 'arbitrary' and 'unreasonable' interchangeably, without making a distinction between these two concepts.
1238. F. Ortino, 'From "Non-discrimination" to "Reasonableness": A Paradigm Shift in International Economic Law?' (2005) Jean Monet Working Paper 01/05, p. 34.
1239. *Glamis v. US* [2009] NAFTA, ICSID 48 ILM 1039 Award (8 June 2009) para. 803.
1240. *Ibid.*, para. 805.

proposed remedy.'[1241] The tribunal provided that even though the state's measures did not mitigate all of the harmful effects, this 'does not mean that it is manifestly without reason or arbitrary; it more likely means that it is a compromise between the conflicting desires and needs of the various affected parties'.[1242]

In *AES Summit v. Hungary*, the tribunal also examined the reasonableness of the measure in question. The AES tribunal stressed that the existence of a rational policy was not sufficient 'to justify all the measures taken by a state in its name ... [t]he measure must be "reasonable"'.[1243] The *AES Summit* tribunal examined the 'reasonableness of the act of the state in relation to the policy'.[1244] According to the tribunal, this included an 'appropriate correlation between the state's public policy objective and the measure adopted to achieve it [and] this has to do with the nature of the measure and the way it is implemented'.[1245]

By establishing that the objective of combating 'luxury profits' in the utility sector was rational and legitimate,[1246] the *AES Summit* tribunal turned to an analysis of how the state's measure was related to its objective. In this regard, the tribunal emphasised that the state's authorities had communicated with the energy providers concerning their intention to reintroduce the regulatory pricing system. Before adopting the amendment to the law on the reintroduction of administrative pricing, the state's authorities approached the energy companies in an attempt to renegotiate the pricing agreements.[1247] However, an agreement had not been reached between the parties. Also, as the tribunal underlined, there was no concrete promise to the investor that the 'administrative pricing was never going to be reintroduced.'[1248] For these reasons, the Hungarian Parliament 'voted for the reintroduction of administrative pricing, which the parliament considered to be the best option at the moment'.[1249] Consequently, the tribunal concluded that both the '2006 Electricity Act and the implementing Price Decrees were reasonable, proportionate and consistent with the public policy expressed by the parliament.'[1250]

In assessing the arbitrariness of the state's actions, the tribunal in *Electrabel v. Hungary* noted that 'a measure will not be arbitrary if it is reasonably related to a rational policy.'[1251] In this award, the tribunal used the term arbitrariness as an umbrella term comprising 'references to "arbitrariness", "irrationality", "unreasonable", "inequitable" and "disproportionate" treatment'. It thereby concluded that all of

1241. *Ibid.*
1242. *Ibid.*
1243. *AES Summit v. Hungary*, ICSID Case No. ARB/07/22 Award (23 September 2010) para. 10.3.9.
1244. *Ibid.*, para. 10.3.7.
1245. *Ibid.*, paras 10.3.7-10.3.9.
1246. *Ibid.*, para. 10.3.31.
1247. *Ibid.*, para. 10.3.35.
1248. *Ibid.*
1249. *Ibid.*
1250. *AES Summit v. Hungary*, ICSID Case No. ARB/07/22 Award (23 September 2010) para. 10.3.36.
1251. *Electrabel v. Hungary*, ICSID Case No. ARB/07/1 Final Award (25 November 2015) para. 179.

these terms refer to the 'same concept under the ECT's FET standard, conveniently here collectively addressed as "arbitrariness"'.[1252]

The *Electrabel* tribunal found that the state's measure to pay partial compensation to an investor was reasonably related to a rational policy.[1253] The tribunal provided that the state's decision concerning the amount of compensation payable to the company was based on a 'balancing exercise between the interests of generators and those of tax-payers'.[1254] The tribunal further asserted that the state's measure could be reasonable even if 'others disagree with that decision.'[1255] This, however, required – once again – an 'appropriate correlation' to exist between the objective and the measure.[1256] In light of the circumstances involving the economic hardship experienced by Hungary at this time, the lack of discriminatory intentions, and the legitimacy of the state's objectives, the tribunal considered that the aforementioned appropriate correlation had been demonstrated by Hungary.[1257]

In *Mamidoil v. Albania*,[1258] the tribunal examined whether Albania's order to relocate the project was a reasonable measure. The tribunal found that the 'state's conduct bore a reasonable relationship to some rational policy.'[1259] The tribunal accepted Albania's arguments that the plan to relocate the port of Duress was a part of the 'general transport sector strategy'.[1260] It also provided that the state's intention to relocate investors to another port was not 'an expression of irrationality but fits into the overall rationality of that policy'.[1261] In this regard, the state's consistent plan to realise its long-term transport strategy convinced the tribunal of the reasonableness and rationality of its actions. In terms of the implementation of the state's measure, the tribunal found that it was not 'discriminatory and unreasonable',[1262] as the closure of the port was not intended to favour the local competing company but applied to all importers of petroleum products.[1263]

In *Philip Morris v. Uruguay*, the tribunal assessed the reasonableness of Uruguay's measure in examining the SPR,[1264] which obliged tobacco producers to put anti-smoking images and written warnings on cigarette packs. The SPR also forbade

1252. *Ibid.*, para. 167.
1253. *Ibid.*, para. 214.
1254. *Ibid.*, para. 215.
1255. *Ibid.*, para. 180.
1256. *Ibid.*
1257. *Electrabel v. Hungary*, ICSID Case No. ARB/07/1 Final Award (25 November 2015) para. 181. *See also* M. Levine, 'ICSID tribunal dismisses final claim for compensation in relation to Hungary's 2008 termination of power purchase agreement' (2016) *Investment Treaty News* https://www.iisd.org/itn/2016/02/29/icsid-tribunal-dismisses-final-claim-for-compensation-in-relation-to-hungarys-2008-termination-of-power-purchase-agreement-electrabel-sa-v-republic-of-hungary-icsid-case-no-arb-07-1/ accessed on 12 June 2018.
1258. *Mamidoil Jetoil Greek Petroleum Products Société S.A. v. Republic of Albania*, ICSID Case No. ARB/11/24 Award (30 March 2015).
1259. *Ibid.*, para. 791.
1260. *Ibid.*
1261. *Mamidoil Jetoil Greek Petroleum Products Société S.A. v. Republic of Albania*, ICSID Case No. ARB/11/24 Award (30 March 2015) para. 791.
1262. *Ibid.*, para. 792.
1263. *Ibid.*, para. 791.
1264. *Philip Morris v. Uruguay*, ICSID Case No. ARB/10/7 Award (8 July 2016) paras 9-10.

the display of different variants of cigarette brands. The tribunal asserted that it was not its task to evaluate whether the SPR had achieved the desired effect, but rather to consider whether it was 'reasonable when it was adopted'.[1265] The tribunal determined that the measure was reasonable because the SPR was designed to 'address a real public health concern', was 'not disproportionate to that concern' and had been 'adopted in good faith'.[1266] The tribunal concluded that Uruguay's SPR measure had not violated the FET standard because it was not 'arbitrary, grossly unfair, unjust, discriminatory or disproportionate' and that the measure had a 'relatively minor impact' on the investor's business.[1267]

Some tribunals have looked at whether states could have employed alternative measures that would have had a less harmful impact on the investors and their investments (section §7.04[A][2]). Several tribunals have also taken into account the impact of the loss suffered by an investor as a consequence of the state's measures (section §7.04[A][3]). Both elements are elaborated upon below.

[2] The Possibility of Employing Alternative Measures in Achieving an Objective

In assessing the FET standard under the principles of reasonableness and proportionality as explained in section §7.04[A], several tribunals have evaluated whether the state's measure was, in fact, necessary to achieve the desired objective, or whether the state concerned could have employed alternative measures to achieve the same result that would have had a less adverse effect on the investor compared to the contested measure. This assessment of possible alternatives has featured as a factor in several FET cases, where the reasonableness of a state's conduct was assessed.

A number of tribunals in the Argentinian cases evaluated the possibility of employing alternative measures.[1268] In assessing the goals of Argentina's new Regulatory Framework on Water Services, the tribunal underlined that the Regulatory Framework had an aggravating effect on the investments and the investors.[1269] In this regard, the tribunal asserted that other measures could have been taken by the state to address the needs of low-income groups. The tribunal pointed out that Argentina should have taken measures 'to restore an equilibrium on a new modified basis', since, due to the introduction of the new Regulatory Framework on Water Services, the 'equilibrium between rights and obligations in the concession' had been disturbed.[1270]

This reasoning is comparable with the assessment provided in *AWG v. Argentina*. In this case, the tribunal confirmed the legitimacy of the state's measures in securing the right of the local population to water, including low-income disadvantaged groups.

1265. *Ibid.*, para. 409.
1266. *Ibid.*
1267. *Philip Morris v. Uruguay*, ICSID Case No. ARB/10/7 Award (8 July 2016) para. 410.
1268. C. Henckels, Proportionality and Deference in Investor-State Arbitration (Cambridge University Press, 2015) 147.
1269. *Impregilo S.p.A v. Argentina*, ICSID Case No. ARB/07/17 Award (21 June 2011) paras 330-331.
1270. *Ibid.*, para. 330.

At the same time, the tribunal was not convinced that the only way to achieve this objective was by refusing to adjust the tariffs and by the 'forceful' treatment of the company in its attempt to renegotiate the concession contract.[1271]

In the view of the *AWG* tribunal, alternative measures could have been adopted without harming investors and their investments. The tribunal explained that if the Argentinian authorities were concerned about protecting the disadvantaged population from increasing water prices, 'it might have allowed tariff increases for other consumers while applying a social tariff or a subsidy to the poor, a solution clearly permitted by the regulatory framework.'[1272]

The *Chemtura v. Canada* and *Philip Morris v. Uruguay* tribunals also addressed the possibility of employing alternative measures. In *Chemtura v. Canada*, the tribunal indicated that the alternative measure (a phase-out rather than a ban) was proposed to the claimant by the state's authorities, but the company had refused this offer. In *Philip Morris v. Uruguay*, the claimant underlined that there were other possibilities in terms of labelling tobacco packages with a health warning. The company argued that a 50% size increase proposed by the company was a good alternative to an 80% size increase adopted by Uruguay. However, the tribunal took a deferential approach and did not engage in a discussion of whether the state could achieve the same objective by using another alternative.[1273] The tribunal emphasised that health risks, such as those generated by tobacco, are 'a matter of public policy, to be left to the appreciation of the regulatory authority'.[1274]

[3] Loss Suffered by an Investor as a Consequence of a State's Measure

In the assessment of the state's contested measure, the impact of the measure or the state's conduct on an investor and its investments has been a consideration for several tribunals. Consequently, in a number of investment cases tribunals have assessed whether the state's contested measure had an 'excessive or disproportionate impact on the applicant's interests'.[1275]

The *EDF v. Romania* tribunal did not establish a breach of the FET standard. It determined that the measures taken against corruption were in the public interest and had a relatively minor impact on a limited group of investors. The tribunal explained that in addition to the presence of a legitimate aim in the public interest, there must be a 'reasonable relationship of proportionality between the means employed and the aim sought to be realized'.[1276] It followed by stating that proportionality would be lacking

1271. *AWG v. Argentina* [2010] UNCITRAL Arbitration, Decision on Liability (30 July 2010) paras 232-238.
1272. *Ibid.*, para. 235.
1273. *Philip Morris v. Uruguay*, ICSID Case No. ARB/10/7 Award (8 July 2016) para. 419.
1274. *Ibid.*
1275. F. Ortino, 'From "Non-discrimination" to "Reasonableness": A Paradigm Shift in International Economic Law?' (2005) Jean Monet Working Paper 01/05, 35.
1276. *EDF Limited v. Romania*, ICSID Case No. ARB/05/13 Award (8 October 2009) para. 293.

if the person involved 'bears an individual and excessive burden'.[1277] Such an excessive burden was not established in this case.

In *Electrabel v. Hungary*, the tribunal stated that in reviewing a state's conduct, an assessment should be made of whether the 'impact of the measure on the investor [was] proportional to the policy objective sought.'[1278] The tribunal assessed the impact of the state's measure not to pay maximum compensation (all eligible stranded costs) to the investor after the termination of the PPA. The tribunal pointed out that the state had discretionary powers in deciding on the amount of compensation, and therefore Hungary's decision to pay 85% of the eligible stranded costs to the investor was reasonable and proportionate.[1279] In a similar vein, in *AES Summit v. Hungary*, the tribunal concluded that despite the effect of the regulatory pricing decree, *AES* and other energy providers were able to receive reasonable returns.[1280] Consequently, the financial impact on the investor could not be considered disproportionate to the implemented policy.

In the assessment of the state's contested measure under the FET standard according to the principles of reasonableness, proportionality and the prohibition of arbitrariness, the relevant criteria emphasised by tribunals are the existence of a reasonable relationship between a state's measure and its objective; the possibility to employ alternative measures in achieving the same objective; and the impact of the loss suffered by an investor as a consequence of a state's measure.

[B] The Principle of Non-discrimination in the Assessment of a State's Measure

Alongside the evaluation of the reasonableness of a state's measure, tribunals have highlighted that the state's measure should be non-discriminatory. Under the FET standard, the prohibition of discrimination is not limited to a specific form of discrimination; it may be based on nationality, race, religion and political affiliation.[1281] According to the FET case law, tribunals have primarily assessed discrimination by comparing the position of a foreign investor with that of a national

1277. *Ibid.*
1278. *Electrabel v. Hungary*, ICSID Case No. ARB/07/1 Final Award (25 November 2015) para. 179.
1279. *Ibid.*, para. 186.
1280. *AES Summit v. Hungary*, ICSID Case No. ARB/07/22 Award (23 September 2010) paras 10.3.37-10.3.53.
1281. U. Kriebaum, 'Arbitrary/Unreasonable or Discriminatory Measures', in M. Bungenberg et al. (eds.) *International Investment Law* (Nomos, 2015), 797. In a few decisions of NAFTA tribunals discrimination has been assessed in the context of the FET standard and not on the basis of nationality. In *Waste Management II v. Mexico*, in interpreting the international minimum standard the tribunal found that the conduct is discriminatory if it 'exposes the claimant to sectional or racial prejudice'. *Waste Management v. Mexico*, ('Number 2'), ICSID Case No. ARB(AF)/00/3 decided under NAFTA, para. 98. In the *Loewen v. US* award, in assessing the fairness of the trial of the investor, the tribunal emphasised that it is the 'responsibility of the courts of a State to ensure that litigation is free from discrimination against a foreign litigant and that the foreign litigant should not become the victim of sectional or local prejudice'. *Loewen Group, Inc. and Raymond L. Loewen v. United States of America*, ICSID Case No. ARB(AF)/98/3, para. 123.

investor.[1282] However, in contrast to the IIAs' NT standard, e.g., when assessing the alleged discriminatory treatment in relation to the FET standard, tribunals do 'not oblige a host state to treat national and foreign investors equally'.[1283] As explained by Diehl, under the FET standard the state's authorities can provide privileges to national investors if there is a reasonable explanation for this and if such differential treatment of a foreign investor compared to that of a national investor 'does not in itself raise the notion of unfairness'.[1284] Thus, tribunals, in assessing the non-discrimination principle under the FET standard, require that differentiation in treatment between a foreign investor and a national investor must be non-arbitrary and that there is a reasonable explanation for this.[1285] The principles of reasonableness and the prohibition of arbitrariness are closely connected to the principle of non-discrimination.[1286] In the words of Klager, the principle of non-discrimination in the context of the FET standard derives from a broader notion of arbitrariness that is generally defined as 'a duty to act reasonably without any precondition of a differential treatment'.[1287] In this regard, the principle of non-discrimination relates to the question of whether the state's measure is reasonable, i.e. whether the state can justify its discriminatory actions vis-à-vis an investor with a reasonable explanation.[1288]

The discriminatory treatment of a foreign investor, however, has rarely played a conclusive role in finding violations of the FET standard by international investment tribunals.[1289] The reason why the discriminatory treatment of an investor seldom constitutes the basis for liability under FET is the existence of separate, non-discrimination provisions in IIAs, which provide investors with the possibility to enforce their claim through these provisions in the case of clear discriminatory conduct.[1290]

1282. R. Klager, (2011) 193.
1283. R. Klager, (2011) 193. Also on p. 285, Klager, in examining the intersections of the national treatment with the FET, explains the difference between two standards, by stating that 'while national treatment obligations are dependent on the treatment accorded to domestic investments, fair and equitable treatment provisions try to ensure a basic level of protection irrespective of the host state's laws'.
1284. A. Diehl, (2012) 452.
1285. R. Klager, (2013) 193.
1286. U. Kriebaum, 'Arbitrary/Unreasonable or Discriminatory Measures', in M. Bungenberg et al. (eds.) *International Investment Law* (Nomos, 2015), 795. As underlined by Kriebaum, the prohibition of arbitrary/unreasonable and discriminatory measures is included in IIAs either as a separate clause or in the context of the FET standard. Tribunals have usually considered the prohibition of arbitrary/unreasonable and discriminatory measures as being 'closely related [and have] usually examined them consecutively'.
1287. R. Klager, (2013) 196-197.
1288. R. Klager, (2013) 196. F. Ortino, 'From "Non-discrimination" to "Reasonableness": A Paradigm Shift in International Economic Law?' (2005) Jean Monet Working Paper 01/05, 49.
1289. This assessment is supported by the conclusions of Bonnitcha who underlines that the 'assessment of whether the impugned treatment is discriminatory is seldom decisive in the application of the FET standard.' As Bonnitcha further explains, considering that IIAs contain a separate provision on non-discrimination, it is not surprising that the discriminatory conduct is not a decisive factor in the FET evaluation. J. Bonnitcha, Substantive Protection under Investment Treaties: A Legal and Economic Analysis (Cambridge University Press, 2014), e-book, section: 4.3.2, p. 32.
1290. A. Newcombe, L. Paradell, (2009) 289-290.

A notable exception where discriminatory conduct was a decisive factor in establishing liability under the FET standard is *Saluka v. Czech Republic*. In this case, the tribunal established that, in comparison to other banks still owned by the state (national investors),[1291] the IBP bank owned by a foreign investor had experienced differential treatment. This constituted the main ground for finding the liability of the Czech Republic under the FET standard.[1292] The tribunal pointed out that:

> Any differential treatment of a foreign investor must not be based on unreasonable distinctions and demands, and must be justified by showing that it bears a reasonable relationship to rational policies not motivated by a preference for other investments over the foreign-owned investment.[1293]

The tribunal made use of several elements in defining the discriminatory measure. State actions are discriminatory where '(i) similar cases are (ii) treated differently (iii) and without reasonable justification.'[1294]

Based on an analysis of the facts, the *Saluka* tribunal found the conduct of the state to be discriminatory. The Czech Republic provided financial assistance to three other big banks, with the exception of the bank owned by the investors. Based on the third requirement (i.e., 'without reasonable justification'), the tribunal clarified that discriminatory treatment would not necessarily constitute unfair treatment if the state could provide a reasonable justification for such differential treatment.[1295] In this case, the Czech Republic was not able to present such a justification. The tribunal noted that the government's communication with the investor lacked transparency and consistency. This contributed to the tribunal's conclusion that the treatment of the investor was unfair.[1296] The requirement of transparency is explained below.

In the *Electrabel v. Hungary* case, the investor also argued that it had experienced differential treatment because Hungary provided full compensation for the costs of market liberalisation to national energy providers but not to it.[1297] In comparing these two situations, the tribunal provided that:

> [s]howing of differential treatment is not sufficient to establish unlawful discrimination or, in this context, irrationality in breach of the ECT's FET standard. For discriminatory treatment, comparators must be materially similar; and there must then be no reasonable justification for differential treatment.[1298]

The *Electrabel* tribunal referred to *Saluka's* threefold approach in assessing the state's alleged discriminatory conduct.[1299] Albeit in different words, the *Electrabel*

1291. *Saluka Investments BV v. Czech Republic* [2006] UNCITRAL Arbitration Partial Award (17 March 2006) para. 33.
1292. *Ibid.*, para. 407.
1293. *Ibid.*, para. 307.
1294. *Ibid.*, para. 313.
1295. *Ibid.*, paras 312-313.
1296. *Ibid.*, paras 307 and 408.
1297. *Electrabel v. Hungary*, ICSID Case No. ARB/07/1 Final Award (25 November 2015) para. 175.
1298. *Ibid.*, para. 175.
1299. *Ibid.*, para. 175.

tribunal provided that differential treatment towards an investor should be demonstrated. In order to establish that, the tribunal compared the treatment of the investor to that of other national energy providers.[1300] According to the tribunal, the presence of differential treatment does not suffice to establish discriminatory treatment. In its assessment, the tribunal also emphasised that it did not require any evidence that the discriminatory treatment of the investor is based on nationality.[1301] The tribunal stated that the 'comparators must be materially similar,' thereby replicating the requirement of 'similar cases' as provided in *Saluka*. Furthermore, the absence of a 'reasonable justification' as outlined in *Saluka* is another criterion underlined by the *Electrabel* tribunal to determine discriminatory treatment. In the latter case, the claim on the basis of discriminatory conduct had not been satisfied as the investor was not able to show that the situation of the other companies was 'materially similar to that of Dunamenti or Electrabel itself',[1302] because, as the tribunal explained, 'all Generators were "asked" to adjust their prices in similar terms; and the difference in their adjusted capacity fees reflected only the differences in profit level amongst different Generators.'[1303] In the absence of similar cases, the tribunal had no further need to investigate whether there was a reasonable justification for the alleged difference in treatment.

To summarise, FET tribunals provide that a state's measures, if they are discriminatory towards an investor, may violate the FET standard.[1304] As follows from *Saluka v. Czech Republic* and *Electrabel v. Hungary*, the fact that a foreign investor is treated differently in comparison to a national investor is not sufficient to establish discriminatory treatment under the FET standard. The state measures may be found discriminatory if an investor is treated differently compared to similar cases and when the state's authorities do not have a reasonable justification for such differential treatment.

[C] The Principle of Transparency in the Assessment of a State's Measure

Several tribunals have stressed the requirement of transparency in communicating with, and providing information to, an investor. This requirement constitutes a significant factor in reviewing the regulatory authority exercised by state bodies under the FET standard.[1305]

In FET cases, the obligation of transparency has been interlinked with the legitimate expectations of the investor and stability.[1306] Dolzer and Schreuer have

1300. *Ibid.*, para. 7.152.
1301. *Ibid.*
1302. *Electrabel v. Hungary*, ICSID Case No. ARB/07/1 Final Award (25 November 2015) para. 175.
1303. *Ibid.*, para. 7.153.
1304. A. Newcombe, L. Paradell, (2009) 288.
1305. R. Dolzer, [2014] 30.
1306. R. Dolzer, C. Schreuer, 2nd edn., (2012) 171. Transparency is closely linked to legitimate expectations, as transparency means that the legal framework for the investor's operations is readily apparent and that any decisions affecting investments can be traced to that legal framework.

outlined that transparency, in the context of the FET standard, implies that the 'legal framework for the investment's operations is readily apparent and that any decisions affecting an investor can be traced to that legal framework.'[1307]

Several FET cases have referred to 'transparency' within the framework of openness and the availability of information on the status of laws, regulations, relevant policies and justifications for decisions.[1308] In the *Tecmed* decision, the requirement of transparency was defined as being fulfilled where the state acts:

> [t]otally transparently in its relations with the foreign investor, so that it may know beforehand any and all rules and regulations that will govern its investments, as well as the goals of the relevant policies and administrative practices or directives, to be able to plan its investment and comply with such regulations.[1309]

In *Saluka v. Czech Republic*, a lack of transparency was observed in the failure of the state to respond to the proposals of the investor in any 'constructive way'.[1310] The tribunal provided that:

> Saluka was entitled to expect that the Czech Republic took seriously the various proposals that may have had the potential of solving the bank's problem and that these proposals were dealt with in an objective, transparent, unbiased and even-handed way.[1311]

The treatment of the investor fell below the articulated threshold, as the state's conduct lacked 'even-handedness, consistency and transparency and the Czech Government has refused adequate communication with … [the investor]'.[1312]

In *Ioan Micula v. Romania*, the lack of transparency was one of the factors contributing to Romania's liability under the FET standard.[1313] The case concerned the financial incentives provided for the investor for the improvement of some underdeveloped regions in Romania. These incentives were withdrawn by the state in the course of preparing for accession to the EU. The tribunal had not disputed the legitimacy of the state's measure. It underlined that Romania's decision to revoke the incentives was reasonably tailored to the pursuit of a rational policy (specifically, EU accession), and there was an appropriate correlation between that objective and the measure adopted to achieve it.[1314]

The tribunal concluded, however, that Romania had breached the expectations of investors that had legitimately expected that the incentives would last. Furthermore,

1307. R. Dolzer, C. Schreuer, 2nd edn., (2012) 171.
1308. K.J. Vandevelde, 'A Unified Theory of Fair and Equitable Treatment' [2010] 43 *International Law and Politics*, 83-84. On the basis of the case law, Vandevelde points out that transparency applies not only to the host state's laws but also to the host state's policies. In some cases, not only the non-disclosure of relevant laws and regulations but also a lack of reasons for certain actions taken by the state leads to the claim of a lack of transparency.
1309. *Tecmed v. Mexico*, ICSID Case No. ARB(AF)/00/2 Award (29 May 2003) para. 154.
1310. *Saluka Investments BV v. Czech Republic* [2006] UNCITRAL Arbitration Partial Award (17 March 2006) para. 423.
1311. *Ibid.*, para. 499.
1312. *Ibid.*
1313. *Ioan Micula v. Romania*, ICSID Case No. ARB/05/20 Final Award (11 December 2013).
1314. *Ibid.*, para. 825.

the tribunal established that Romania had not provided sufficient information for investors concerning the withdrawal of the incentives. The tribunal concluded that Romania had breached the FET obligation 'by failing to inform PIC [Permanent Investor Certificate] holders in a timely manner that the EGO 24 regime [Emergency Governance Ordinance 24/1998] would be ended prior to its stated date of expiry'.[1315]

In *Parkerings v. Lithuania*, the obligation of transparency also played a role in the assessment of the FET standard. This case concerned the termination of the investor's agreement to build and to maintain parking facilities in the historical town of Vilnius. Changes to the national law of Lithuania prevented the execution of the investor's project, and the agreement between the investor and the state's authorities was terminated. The investor claimed as aspects of its FET complaint that it had been subjected to a lack of transparency, as the state authorities had not disclosed information on the feasibility of the parking fee project and its compliance with national law before the execution of the project agreement.[1316] The investor argued that the state's authorities had information provided to them in the law firm's memorandum regarding the conformity of national law with the parking fee and that the authorities failed to inform the company about this.[1317] The tribunal rejected the investor's claim on the grounds that the information discussed at the time of the drafting of the agreement had been 'accessible to the public or at least to any other qualified law firm'.[1318] The tribunal underlined that an investor could have obtained the same information through the opinion of another law firm,[1319] thereby rejecting the claim that the state had acted in a non-transparent manner. The tribunal pointed out that in making investments an investor should exercise due diligence that, in the present circumstances, included the gathering of legal information that was relevant for assessing the agreement between the investor and the state's authority.[1320]

To summarise, in assessing the transparency of a state's measures, tribunals refer to criteria such as adequate and open communication with the investor; the availability of sufficient information concerning any laws and policies that may potentially affect an investment; and the timely notification of an investor by the state's authorities regarding changes to the status of the investment.[1321]

1315. *Ibid.*, para. 870.
1316. *Parkerings v. Lithuania*, ICSID Case No. ARB/05/8 Award (11 September 2007) para. 295.
1317. *Ibid.*
1318. *Parkerings v. Lithuania*, ICSID Case No. ARB/05/8 Award (11 September 2007) para. 304.
1319. *Ibid.*
1320. *Parkerings v. Lithuania*, ICSID Case No. ARB/05/8 Award (11 September 2007) paras 307-308 and 333.
1321. *Ioan Micula v. Romania*, ICSID Case No. ARB/05/20 Final Award (11 December 2013) para. 870; *Saluka Investments BV v. Czech Republic* [2006] UNCITRAL Arbitration Partial Award (17 March 2006) para. 499.

[D] Summary: The Assessment of the State's Measure

In the analysis of the FET decisions outlined above, the tribunals evaluated the content of the state's measure vis-à-vis an investor according to the principles of (i) reasonableness, proportionality and the prohibition of arbitrariness; (ii) non-discrimination; and (iii) transparency (*see* Table 3).

Table 3 The Assessment of a State's Measure

Criteria tested by arbitral tribunals when assessing the state's measures[1322]	1. The principles of reasonableness, proportionality and the prohibition of arbitrariness 1.1. The relationship between a state's measure and its objective (taken in the public interest) 1.2. The options for the state to employ alternative measures in achieving its objective 1.3. The loss suffered by the investor
	2. The principle of non-discrimination in the assessment of the state's measure on the basis of nationality 2.1. Similar cases, i.e. between a foreign investor and national investor(s) 2.2. Different treatment of a foreign investor and national investor(s) 2.3. Reasonable justification for a differentiation in treatment
	3. The principle of transparency in communications with the investor concerning the state's measure 3.1. Open communication with an investor 3.2. Availability of sufficient information concerning any laws and policies that may potentially affect an investment 3.3. Timely notification of an investor by the state's authorities regarding changes to the status of the investment

Under the principles of reasonableness, proportionality and the prohibition of arbitrariness, tribunals have evaluated whether a state's measure bears a reasonable relationship to its objective.[1323] To assess the relationship between a state's measure and its objective, tribunals have reviewed whether the state's measure has the potential to contribute to the desired objectives. The tribunal in *Glamis v. US* noted that

1322. This test, proposed by the tribunal in *Philip Morris v. Uruguay*, assesses the state's measure and summarises the criteria applied to the evaluation of the measure. It addresses whether the measure was implemented in an 'arbitrary, grossly unfair, unjust, discriminatory, or disproportionate' way. This test indicates that only serious misconduct on the part of the state towards an investor may give rise to a violation of the FET. *See*: *Philip Morris v. Uruguay*, ICSID Case No. ARB/10/7 Award (8 July 2016) para. 410.

1323. *Saluka Investments BV v. Czech Republic* [2006] UNCITRAL Arbitration Partial Award (17 March 2006) para. 460.

it was sufficient to establish whether 'the government had a sufficient good faith belief that there was a reasonable connection between the harm and the proposed remedy.'[1324] Some tribunals review the reasonableness of the state's conduct in view of how the measure has been implemented in relation to the investor.[1325] In *Mamidoil v. Albania*, the tribunal explained that the state's measure to relocate the investor's project was part of Albania's consistent plan to realise its long-term transport strategy. In the view of the tribunal, the state's measure was implemented in a non-discriminatory and reasonable way that indicated a clear link between the state's measure and its objective. To this end, a reasonable measure is one which addresses the public interest and is not implemented in an 'arbitrary, grossly unfair, unjust, discriminatory, or disproportionate' manner.[1326]

In evaluating reasonableness and proportionality, several tribunals have taken into account whether the state had the possibility to employ alternative measures to achieve the same objective that would have had a less adverse effect on the investor, while some tribunals also considered the loss suffered by the investor. For example, in *AWG v. Argentina* the tribunal acknowledged that the state's objectives to provide water to a disadvantaged group of the population was legitimate. At the same time, however, the tribunal underlined that the adverse effect on the investor could be avoided by employing alternative measures to address the state's objective. In *AWG*, the tribunal discussed the alternative measures that the state could have taken in order to achieve its objectives, thereby avoiding the negative effect on the investor and its investment. The tribunals in *Philip Morris v. Uruguay*, *Chemtura v. Canada* and *Apotex v. US* underlined that it is not the task of the tribunal to discuss whether the alternative measures should have been taken.[1327] Along the same lines as these tribunals, Henckels noted 'a necessity test imposes greater restrictions on regulatory autonomy ..., because it narrows the pool of potential measures available to a state to achieve its objective.'[1328]

In evaluating the state's measure, the requirement of non-discrimination has been rarely underlined so as to satisfy the requirement of FET. *Saluka v. Czech Republic* was one of the rare cases where establishing discriminatory treatment in comparing the foreign investor with the national investors had been a crucial element in finding a violation of the FET standard. To assess the differential treatment, the tribunal tested whether there were '(i) similar cases, whether an investor was (ii) treated differently (iii) and whether there was a reasonable justification for discriminatory treatment'.[1329]

In several decisions, tribunals have assessed the state's measure in relation to how transparent it is in relation to the investor. In FET decisions, the obligation of

---

1324. *Glamis v. US* [2009] NAFTA, ICSID 48 ILM 1039 Award (8 June 2009) para. 805.
1325. *AES Summit v. Hungary*, ICSID Case No. ARB/07/22 Award (23 September 2010) paras 10.3.7-10.3.9.
1326. *Philip Morris v. Uruguay*, ICSID Case No. ARB/10/7 Award (8 July 2016) para. 410. The Single Presentation Requirement was the measure which was discussed.
1327. *Philip Morris v. Uruguay*, ICSID Case No. ARB/10/7 Award (8 July 2016) para. 419.
1328. C. Henckels, Proportionality and Deference in Investor-State Arbitration (Cambridge University Press, 2015) 154.
1329. *Saluka Investments BV v. Czech Republic* [2006] UNCITRAL Arbitration Partial Award (17 March 2006) para. 313.

transparency extends to the obligation to provide information to an investor that is considered important in making the investment or in proceeding and maintaining an investment. Tribunals have found a lack of transparency when the state's authorities failed to inform the investor in a timely manner of the change in policy, thereby adversely affecting the investor,[1330] or when the state's authorities failed to respond to the proposals of the investor in any 'constructive way'.[1331] The limitation on the transparency obligation towards an investor under the FET standard was articulated by the tribunal in *Parkerings v. Lithuania*. In this case, it was provided that even if information that was relevant to the investor's investment was not provided by the state's authorities, it would not violate the obligation of transparency if such information was in the public domain. By exercising due diligence, an investor could have obtained such information.[1332]

§7.05 THE LEGALITY OF THE STATE'S MEASURE UNDER NATIONAL LAW

[A] Tribunals' Assessment of the Legality of a State's Measure under National Law

In a series of cases, discussed in this section, the determination of the legality of a state's measure under national law or the way in which the measure has been implemented in national law has been part of the assessment of the FET standard and the right to regulate.[1333] Tribunals have attempted to clarify whether and under what circumstances a deviation from compliance with national laws by state authorities can constitute grounds for violating the FET standard. The case law and the literature demonstrate that in order for a violation of domestic law to qualify as a breach of the (international) FET standard, such violations should be a 'serious and material failure to comply with its own law'.[1334]

In assessing the legality of a state's conduct under national law, the central question is the extent of scrutiny that tribunals apply in assessing the states' conduct under national law.[1335] This enquiry into the extent of this scrutiny is relevant in establishing the state's right to regulate, because in assessing the FET standard, the 'requirement of lawfulness [may] constitute a constraint on the manner in which a

1330. *Ioan Micula v. Romania*, ICSID Case No. ARB/05/20 Final Award (11 December 2013) para. 870.
1331. *Saluka Investments BV v. Czech Republic* [2006] UNCITRAL Arbitration Partial Award (17 March 2006) para. 423.
1332. *Parkerings v. Lithuania*, ICSID Case No. ARB/05/8 Award (11 September 2007) paras 307-308 and 333. *See* discussion on the due diligence of an investor in Chapter 6, section §6.06.
1333. *ADF v. US* [2003] NAFTA, ICSID Case No. ARB(AF)/00/1 Award (9 January 2003); *International Thunderbird Gaming Corp. v. Mexico* [2006] NAFTA-UNCITRAL Arbitration, Award (26 January 2006).
1334. J. Bonnitcha, Substantive Protection under Investment Treaties: A Legal and Economic Analysis (Cambridge University Press, 2014), section 4.6.2, p. 142; S. Schill, (2010) 162.
1335. S. Montt, State Liability in Investment Arbitration (Hart Publishing, 2009) 326.

state may exercise its powers.'[1336] Furthermore, tribunals often have to review the conduct of a state's administrative agencies, with no prior interference by the domestic courts.[1337]

Tribunals have adopted different perspectives on the level of scrutiny required in reviewing a state's conduct under national law when examining the FET standard. In several investment cases, tribunals have argued that 'tribunals are not courts of appeal' to assess violations of national law.[1338] As the *ADF v. US* tribunal emphasised, it requires 'something more than simple illegality or lack of authority under the domestic law' to violate the FET standard. In the investment cases that will be addressed in section §7.05[B], the tribunals adopted a restrictive view when evaluating the compliance of the state's contested measures with national law with regard to the alleged violation of the FET standard.

However, in a few decisions, i.e. *Gami v. Mexico, Lemire v. Ukraine and Bilcon v. Canada*, the tribunals clarified 'something more' by providing concrete criteria as to when a qualified breach of the national law of the host state may lead or contribute to a violation of the FET standard. These criteria are addressed in section §7.05[C]. The concluding remarks are provided in section §7.05[D].

[B] Restrictive Assessment of National Law Violations in the Evaluation of the FET Standard

(i) *Saluka v. Czech Republic*[1339]

In *Saluka v. Czech Republic*, the investor argued that the financial assistance granted to its banking competitor was illegal under the state's legislation and the Europe Agreement.[1340] The tribunal found this specific claim of the investor to be without merit.[1341] The tribunal explained that 'the unlawfulness of the host State's measures under its own legislation ... is neither necessary, nor sufficient for a breach of Article 3.1 (fair and equitable treatment) of the Treaty.'[1342] It also added that the state should

1336. J. Bonnitcha, Substantive Protection under Investment Treaties: A Legal and Economic Analysis (Cambridge University Press, 2014), section 4.6.2, p. 144.
1337. S. Montt, State Liability in Investment Arbitration (Hart Publishing, 2009) 313.
1338. S. Montt, State Liability in Investment Arbitration (Hart Publishing, 2009) 324. R. Klager, (2013) 247. Klager explains that some tribunals underline the importance of not acting as courts of appeal. In these cases, tribunals limited their review to '"manifest errors" in the administration of domestic justice'. (p. 247).
1339. *Saluka Investments BV v. Czech Republic* [2006] UNCITRAL Arbitration Partial Award (17 March 2006).
1340. *Saluka Investments BV v. Czech Republic* [2006] UNCITRAL Arbitration Partial Award (17 March 2006) paras 433-438. Reference was made to the Europe Agreement, concluded between the European Communities and the Czech Republic on 4 October 1993, COM/99/0604 final, ACC 99/0247, available at http://eur-lex.europa.eu/legal-content/EN/TXT/?uri=CELEX%3A51999PC0604 accessed on 9 June 2017.
1341. *Saluka Investments BV v. Czech Republic* [2006] UNCITRAL Arbitration Partial Award (17 March 2006) para. 441.
1342. *Ibid.*, para. 442.

not be penalised by the tribunal for every breach of its own rules and regulations.[1343] For violations of domestic law, an investor can seek recourse before the local courts.[1344] The tribunal in this case had distinguished between the issue of the legality of providing financial assistance that was disputed by the claimant and the treatment of the investor. The tribunal emphasised that:

> The only relevant question is whether the Czech Government's provision of financial assistance to CSOB/IPB constituted unfair and inequitable treatment [under a BIT] of Saluka irrespective of whether it was in compliance with the Czech Public Assistance Act or the Europe Agreement.[1345]

Consequently, the assessment of the provision of financial assistance should not be tested on the basis of the obligations which exist under domestic and/or the Europe Agreement but according to the FET standard under the applicable BIT.[1346]

(ii) *ADF Group v. US*[1347]

Several NAFTA tribunals, which assessed a breach of the FET standard under Article 1105(1) of NAFTA, also elaborated on the issue of the legality of state measures under national law. One of the first cases to address this issue was *ADF Group v. US*. In this case, the tribunal examined the complaint of a Canadian company, ADF (the investor). ADF argued that it was forced by the US to adhere to the 'Buy America' laws that required the company to buy and to manufacture steel from the US. The tribunal disagreed with the investor and emphasised that these types of domestic requirements are common to all three NAFTA parties and many other states.[1348] In particular, the investor argued that the US agency – the Federal Highway Administration – acted 'in disregard' of 'Buy America' terms. In reviewing the conduct of the state's agency, the tribunal stated that 'it has no authority to review the legal validity and standing of the U.S. measures here in question under U.S. internal administrative law ... [w]e do not sit as a court with appellate jurisdiction with respect to the U.S. measures.'[1349] The tribunal further emphasised that:

> even if the U.S. measures were somehow shown or admitted to be *ultra vires* under the internal law of the United States, that by itself does not necessarily render the measures grossly unfair or inequitable under the customary international law standard of treatment embodied in Article 1105(1) .... But something more than simple illegality or lack of authority under the domestic law of a State is necessary

1343. *Ibid.*
1344. *Ibid.*
1345. *Saluka Investments BV v. Czech Republic* [2006] UNCITRAL Arbitration Partial Award (17 March 2006) para. 444.
1346. Europe Agreement, concluded between the European Communities and the Czech Republic on 4 October 1993, COM/99/0604 final, ACC 99/0247, available at http://eur-lex.europa.eu/legal-content/EN/TXT/?uri=CELEX%3A51999PC0604 accessed on 9 June 2017.
1347. *ADF v. US* [2003] NAFTA, ICSID Case No. ARB(AF)/00/1 Award (9 January 2003).
1348. *Ibid.*, para. 188.
1349. *Ibid.*, para. 190.

to render an act or measure inconsistent with the customary international law requirements of Article 1105(1).[1350]

The tribunal did not elaborate on what would constitute 'something more' in order to be considered a breach under Article 1105(1) of the NAFTA. It only provided that 'something more' had not been demonstrated by ADF.[1351] In this case, the tribunal took a restrictive view regarding its role in reviewing the legal validity of the national measures under national law.

(iii) *Thunderbird v. Mexico*[1352]

Another NAFTA case in which the tribunal adopted a cautious approach towards reviewing the lawfulness of a state's measures under national law is *Thunderbird v. Mexico* This case concerned the US gaming company, Thunderbird, that disputed the prohibition on installing its gaming machines by the Mexican authorities.[1353] The principal matter in this case was the legality of gaming machines under Mexican law. The Mexican law prohibited gambling and one of the crucial questions in this case was whether gaming machines qualified under the definition of gambling. To this end, the investor requested a legal opinion (*Oficio*) from the Director General de Gobierno de la Secreteria de Gobernacion (SEGOB) regarding the proposed gaming operations in Mexico.[1354] SEGOB is a state regulatory body that concerns itself with Mexico's internal affairs. SEGOB issued a formal response to the company's request, the *Oficio*, that provided that if the machines were not based on 'luck and gambling' they would be allowed under national law.[1355] The company explained that its machines relied on the 'skills and abilities' of the gamer and not on luck. However, a year after the *Oficio* had been sent to the company, the state's authorities initiated administrative hearings to determine whether Thunderbird's machines complied with national law.[1356] On the basis of these administrative hearings, SEGOB issued the administrative order prohibiting Thunderbird's gaming equipment and ordering the closure of gaming facilities on the basis that these gaming machines were not in compliance with national law.[1357]

For the purposes of the current discussion, the relevant aspect of the *Thunderbird v. Mexico* decision on the FET standard is the extent of the scrutiny that the tribunal applied in assessing the legitimacy of the state's measure in accordance with its laws. The tribunal asserted that it was not its role to establish whether the claimant's machines were forbidden under domestic legislation. It stated that '[i]t is not the Tribunal's function to act as a court of appeal or review in relation to the Mexican judicial system regarding the subject matter of the present claims, or in relation to the

1350. *Ibid.*
1351. *Ibid.*
1352. *International Thunderbird Gaming Corp. v. Mexico* [2006] NAFTA-UNCITRAL Arbitration, Award (26 January 2006).
1353. *Ibid.*, paras 8-23.
1354. *Ibid.*, para. 50.
1355. *Ibid.*, para. 55.
1356. *Ibid.*, para. 70.
1357. *Ibid.*, paras 73-80.

SEGOB administrative proceedings for that matter.'[1358] Similar to *Saluka*, the *Thunderbird* tribunal asserted that it was its task to weigh the Mexican conduct against the international obligations of Mexico as laid down by Chapter 11 of the NAFTA.[1359]

To summarise, in *Saluka v. Czech Republic*, *ADF v. US* and *Thunderbird v. Mexico* the tribunals underlined that if the investor's claim regarding a breach of the FET standard is brought under the IIA, the state conduct in question should be measured against the international legal standards under the applicable IIA and not according to an assessment of domestic laws. That being said, this does not imply that a violation of domestic law is irrelevant in FET claims. On the contrary, such violations may contribute to a state's liability under international law. This, however, requires 'something more than simple illegality or lack of authority under the domestic law of a State', as emphasised by the tribunal in *ADF v. US*.[1360]

In the cases discussed below, the tribunals reviewed the state's measures according to national law or administrative procedures, explaining the circumstances in which a breach of national law may result in or contribute to a violation of the FET standard.

[C] Criteria for a Violation of the FET Standard by Breaching National Law

In the *Gami v. Mexico*, *Bilcon v. Canada* and *Lemire v. Ukraine* decisions, outlined below, the tribunals reviewed the states' measures by examining the requirements of national laws. In these decisions, the tribunals considered a qualified violation of national law to be the relevant factor in assessing the FET standard. The facts and the relevant legal issues are discussed below.

(i) *GAMI v. Mexico*[1361]

GAMI v. Mexico discussed the compliance of the national authorities with national laws in the context of sugar mills. GAMI, a US company, complained that the Mexican authorities had not carried out the 'Mexican Sugar Program'[1362] in accordance with its

1358. *Ibid.*, para. 125.
1359. *Ibid.*, para. 126.
1360. *ADF v. US* [2003] NAFTA, ICSID Case No. ARB(AF)/00/1 Award (9 January 2003) para. 190.
1361. *Gami Investments, Inc. v. Mexico* [2004] NAFTA-UNCITRAL Arbitration, Final Award (15 November 2004).
1362. *Gami Investments, Inc. v. Mexico* [2004] NAFTA-UNCITRAL Arbitration, Final Award (15 November 2004) para. 52. In 1991, a legal framework was created for the sugar industry. The Sugarcane Decree was passed on 31 May 1991. 'This decree declared all phases of the sugarcane industry – from planting to refining – to be of public interest. It is specifically fixed new rules for the supply of sugarcane to the mills.' (para. 52). In para. 65, it is stated that GAMI claimed that 'Mexico "fragrantly and systematically failed to implement and to enforce the law." It used unrealistic estimates to inflate the reference price for sugarcane. The export requirements were simply never enforced. Production ceilings were not even set. The result was ruinous for GAM's mills. The domestic price of sugar declined. The cost of sugarcane increased. Finally, the cost of production exceeded the price of the sugar produced'.

terms.[1363] The Mexican Sugar Program was effectuated by the Sugarcane Decree of 1991, which introduced new rules for the supply of sugarcane to the mills.[1364] The Sugar Program was supplemented by additional decrees that 'establish[ed] the manner of determining a national reference price for sugarcane'[1365] and setting 'production ceilings for mills'.[1366] The company accused the authorities of the poor enforcement of the Sugar Program and, on several occasions, a failure to implement the Mexican Sugar Program that in the opinion of the company had both led to a number of NAFTA violations, including the breach of the FET standard.

The tribunal underlined that the 'government's failure to implement or abide by its own laws in a manner adversely affecting a foreign investor may, but will not necessarily, lead to a violation of Article 1105 [NAFTA].'[1367] The tribunal alleged that a host state is 'not to be excused on the grounds that governmental compliance with its own law may be difficult'.[1368] Furthermore, the tribunal provided that a host state should accept liability when its officials 'implement regulations in a discriminatory or arbitrary fashion'.[1369] The tribunal, in assessing when a violation of the national law may give rise to a breach of the FET standard, provided that a 'claim of maladministration would be likely to violate Article 1105 if it amounted to an "outright and unjustified repudiation" of the relevant regulations.'[1370]

The tribunal tested the actions of the Mexican government against the standard of an 'outright and unjustified repudiation' of the relevant regulations. In particular, the tribunal addressed whether the refusal of the Mexican authorities 'to hold feckless administrators to account for failure to carry out their assigned task' would constitute a breach of the FET standard.[1371] The tribunal, in assessing the conduct of the state, evaluated 'what efforts by a government to implement its regulatory program suffice to fulfill the international standards requirement of Article 1105?'[1372] The tribunal agreed with the investor that Mexico had, on a number of instances, failed to implement the Sugar Program in an effective manner.

At the same time, the tribunal pointed to two significant mitigating factors. First, GAMI '[had] not been able to show anything approaching "outright and unjustified repudiation" of the relevant regulations'.[1373] Second, implementation and enforcement were very complex matters, and there was no indication that Mexico would not have preferred that all participants in the industry would adhere to the Sugarcane Decree and the related measures. The Mexican government was not solely responsible for

1363. *Gami Investments, Inc. v. Mexico* [2004] NAFTA-UNCITRAL Arbitration, Final Award (15 November 2004) para. 86.
1364. *Ibid.*, para. 52.
1365. *Ibid.*, para. 59.
1366. *Ibid.*, para. 63.
1367. *Ibid.*, para. 91.
1368. *Ibid.*, para. 94.
1369. *Ibid.*
1370. *Gami Investments, Inc. v. Mexico* [2004] NAFTA-UNCITRAL Arbitration, Final Award (15 November 2004) para. 103.
1371. *Ibid.*, para. 105.
1372. *Ibid.*, para. 100.
1373. *Ibid.*, para. 104.

some of the failures of this programme. The regulatory regime in question was structured on the premise of broad consultation and cooperation, whereas the 'intervention of the private sector was explicitly called for.'[1374] The tribunal concluded that the investor was not able to demonstrate that the actions of the state amounted to maladministration resulting in 'outright and unjustified repudiation' of Mexico's regulations.[1375] Based on the latter conclusion and on the fact that Mexico had not committed any other specific violations in implementing the Sugar Program, the tribunal decided that Mexico had not violated the FET standard.[1376]

(ii) *Bilcon v. Canada*[1377]

In *Bilcon v. Canada*, the compliance of the state's authorities with national law had been a central issue. The dispute concerned the rejection of a mining project by the US company, Bilcon. In this dispute, Canada claimed that the company had not met the criteria under the environmental assessment conducted by the provincial state authority, the Joint Review Panel (JRP).[1378] In its analysis of the FET standard, the tribunal underlined that the JRP had erroneously interpreted Canadian law. The tribunal found that the additional requirements imposed on the investor during the environmental assessment (i.e., compliance with 'community values') had been inconsistent with the requirements under Canadian law.

In the initial phase of its analysis, the tribunal pointed to the complexity of the tasks faced by state authorities and noted that caution should be exercised in evaluating their decisions.[1379] The tribunal stated that:

> even when state officials are acting in good faith there will sometimes be not only controversial judgments, but clear-cut mistakes in following procedures, gathering and stating facts and identifying the applicable substantive rules. State authorities are faced with competing demands on their administrative resources and there can be delays or limited time, attention and expertise brought to bear in dealing with issues. The imprudent exercise of discretion or even outright mistakes does not, as a rule, lead to a breach of the international minimum standard.[1380]

It further maintained that the international 'minimum standard has evolved in the direction of increased investor protection'[1381] and that 'third-party adjudicators may have their own advantages including independence and detachment from domestic pressures in examining the state's conduct in question.'[1382]

1374. *Ibid.*, para. 110.
1375. *Ibid.*, para. 104.
1376. *Ibid.*, paras 108; 110.
1377. *William Ralph Clayton, William Richard Clayton, Douglas Clayton, Daniel Clayton and Bilcon of Delaware Inc. v. Government of Canada* [2015] UNCITRAL, NAFTA, PCA Case No. 2009-04 Award on Jurisdiction and Liability (17 March 2015).
1378. *Ibid.*, para. 5.
1379. *Ibid.*, para. 437.
1380. *Ibid.*
1381. *William Ralph Clayton, William Richard Clayton, Douglas Clayton, Daniel Clayton and Bilcon of Delaware Inc. v. Government of Canada* [2015] UNCITRAL, NAFTA, PCA Case No. 2009-04, Award on Jurisdiction and Liability (17 March 2015) para. 438.
1382. *Ibid.*, para. 439.

The tribunal analysed the application of the environmental assessment procedure by the Canadian authorities. The tribunal found that the environmental assessment body had used a distinctive approach in assessing the project that - according to the tribunal - fundamentally departed 'from the standard of evaluation required by the laws of Canada ...'.[1383] It thereby took into account the legitimate expectations of the investor and established that the state's authorities had acted in an arbitrary manner by imposing an unlawful requirement. Consequently, the tribunal found that 'the approach to the environmental assessment taken by the JRP and adopted by Canada resulted in a breach of Article 1105 [NAFTA].'[1384]

In this case, the tribunal found a violation of the FET standard on the basis of the arbitrary conduct of the state agency. The dissenting arbitrator, Donald McRae, expressed his doubts regarding the standard used by the majority to determine the arbitrariness of the state's measures. In the dissenting judgment it was underlined that:

> By treating this potential violation of Canadian law as itself a violation of NAFTA Article 1105 the majority has in effect introduced the potential for getting damages for what it is breach of Canadian law, where Canadian law does not provide a damages claim for such a breach. That is not what NAFTA was intended to do. You cannot get a remedy under NAFTA Chapter 11 for breach of Canadian law; you can only get a NAFTA remedy for a breach of NAFTA.[1385]

The US, Canada and Mexico - the NAFTA parties - were invited to make submissions on the *Bilcon* decision by the tribunal in the case of *Mesa Power Group, LLC v. Government of Canada.*[1386] In its submission, the US asserted that the *Bilcon* tribunal - despite recognising the 'deference owed to a NAFTA Party's interpretation of its domestic law' - had 'failed to afford Canada any such deference. Instead, the tribunal made its own de novo determination of the "standard of evaluation required by the laws of Canada"'.[1387] A similar conclusion was reached in the Mexican submission. Mexico emphasised that the *Bilcon* decision 'failed to engage in a proper analysis of customary international law when it apparently determined that a failure to comply with applicable domestic law amounted to a failure to meet the minimum standard of treatment of international law'.[1388]

In *Bilcon v. Canada*, according to the tribunal, the state's conduct was arbitrary due to, among other things, an erroneous interpretation of Canadian law. This formed

1383. *Ibid.*, para. 594.
1384. *Ibid.*, para. 604.
1385. *Ibid.*, Dissenting Opinion, para. 43.
1386. *See* the written submissions of the NAFTA parties that had been submitted in the course of the proceedings of another NAFTA case, *Mesa Power Group, LLC v. Government of Canada*, NAFTA-UNCITRAL, PCA Case No. 2012-17. The tribunal was invited to make the submission in the Tribunal Letter in Inviting Submissions on Bilcon Award, 4 May 2015. All of the parties made submissions, *see*: *Mexico Submission on the Bilcon Award*, 12 June 2015; *US Submission on the Bilcon Award*, 12 June 2015, *Canada Observations on the Bilcon Award*, 14 May 2015; Claimant Observations on the Bilcon Award, 14 May 2015. All documents can be retrieved from http://www.italaw.com/cases/1619 accessed on 29 January 2017.
1387. US Submission on the Bilcon Award, 12 June 2015, para. 21 available at http://www.italaw.com/cases/1619 accessed on 29 January 2017.
1388. Mexico Submission on the Bilcon Award, 12 June 2015, para. 11 available at http://www.italaw.com/cases/1619 accessed on 29 January 2017.

the basis for the state's liability under the FET standard. The behaviour of the state was considered arbitrary primarily due to the fact that the state's agency had imposed new requirements on the investor (due to their misinterpretation) and therefore violated the national law, which led to the tribunal establishing that there had been a breach of the FET standard.[1389]

(iii) *Lemire v. Ukraine*[1390]

The case of *Lemire v. Ukraine* concerned a US investor (Mr Lemire) investing in the Ukrainian radio broadcasting industry (namely in Gala Radio). The dispute was submitted under the US-Ukraine BIT.[1391] The claimant argued that the Ukrainian legal procedure for the allocation of frequencies was unfair, inequitable and arbitrary.[1392] The claimant referred to the six tenders for frequencies from 2002 to 2008 that included more than 200 applications for all types of frequencies for this period of time. These investors' attempts only resulted in one successful application for a radio frequency in a small village in Ukraine, whereas the competitors of Gala Radio were able to secure between thirty-eight and fifty-six frequencies.[1393]

The tribunal evaluated several elements, including the procedure for awarding licences in the broadcasting sector, Gala's application for additional frequencies and the tender procedures.[1394] Overall, the tribunal stressed its respect for Ukraine's sovereignty and its 'right to promulgate the laws, which its Parliament deems are best suited to further the Nation's public interest'.[1395] The tribunal proceeded with an analysis of the measures affecting the treatment of the investor. It specified its intention to evaluate the 'general legal framework within which specific conduct took place'.[1396]

The tribunal established that the administrative procedure for the issuing of radio frequencies had 'significant shortcomings'.[1397] First, the tribunal pointed to the shortcomings of the Ukrainian legislation in assessing the transparency of the procedure for awarding licences for frequencies in a tender procedure. The voting system in deciding the winning contender was evaluated by the tribunal. The national law at the time of the investment did not require that the decision on awarding frequencies during the tender process should be 'reasoned' or 'explained'.[1398] The tribunal was of the view, however, that 'the absence of reasoning of the decision represents a significant

1389. N. Bernasconi-Osterwalder, 'Giving Arbitrators Carte Blanche – Fair and Equitable Treatment in Investment Treaties', in C.L. Lim (ed), *Alternative Visions on International Law on Foreign Investment* (Cambridge University Press, 2016) 342. *See also* the submissions of the NAFTA parties above.
1390. *Lemire v. Ukraine*, ICSID Case No. ARB/06/18 Decision on Jurisdiction and Liability (14 January 2010).
1391. *Ibid.*, para. 33.
1392. *Ibid.*, para. 214.
1393. *Ibid.*, para. 321 (examples of competitors) and para. 420.
1394. *Ibid.*, paras 287-418.
1395. *Ibid.*, para. 315.
1396. *Ibid.*
1397. *Lemire v. Ukraine*, ICSID Case No. ARB/06/18 Decision on Jurisdiction and Liability (14 January 2010) para. 419.
1398. *Ibid.*, para. 308 and paras 304-305.

weakness in the administrative procedure for the issuance of the licenses.'[1399] Eventually, the state's failure to provide reasons had contributed to the finding of liability under the FET standard.[1400] Second, another shortcoming of the administrative process in awarding the licences, as analysed by the tribunal, was that the National Council did not require the bidders for the frequencies to disclose who were the ultimate owners of the companies that were bidding for the frequencies.[1401] According to the tribunal, this lack of transparency in the administrative process made the selection procedure unaccountable for public and judicial bodies.[1402] Overall, the tribunal concluded that the state had acted in an arbitrary manner.[1403] According to the tribunal, the fact that the National Council had not considered the information provided by a qualified applicant and engaged in favouritism violated 'essential notions of fairness'.[1404] The tribunal linked the violation of national law with the notion of arbitrariness, stating that:

> [A]lthough not every violation of domestic law necessarily translates into an arbitrary or discriminatory measure under international law and a violation of the FET standard, in the Tribunal's view a blatant disregard of applicable tender rules, distorting fair competition among tender participants, does.[1405]

In *Lemire v. Ukraine*, the tribunal examined the tender rules under national law. The arbitrary procedures, i.e. the failure to provide reasons for awarding frequencies, contributed to the breach of the FET standard.

To summarise, in the three FET cases discussed above, the tribunals indicated which qualified violations of national laws may constitute a relevant factor in finding liability under the FET standard. One of the criteria for a violation of the FET standard, as established in *Gami v. Mexico*, is when the state's maladministration amounted to an 'outright and unjustified repudiation' of the relevant regulations.[1406] In this case, the tribunal found that even though the Mexican authorities had made errors in the implementation of the 'Mexican Sugar Program', their actions did not amount to an 'outright and unjustified repudiation'.[1407] In both *Lemire* and *Bilcon*, the tribunals underlined that not all violations of domestic law would give rise to a breach of the FET standard. The threshold should be high. In both cases, the state's arbitrary conduct had met this threshold. In *Lemire*, the tribunal considered that the state's measures had been taken in 'blatant disregard of applicable tender rules' that led to the violation

1399. *Ibid.*, para. 309.
1400. J. Bonnitcha, Substantive Protection under Investment Treaties: A Legal and Economic Analysis (Cambridge University Press, 2014), section 4.6.2, p. 126. 'The licensing body's failure to state reasons for its decisions was central for the tribunal's decision that licensing authority's decision making procedures had breached the FET standard'.
1401. *Lemire v. Ukraine*, ICSID Case No. ARB/06/18 Decision on Jurisdiction and Liability (14 January 2010) paras 313-314.
1402. *Ibid.*, para. 314.
1403. *Ibid.*, paras 369, 372, 385.
1404. *Ibid.*, para. 283.
1405. *Ibid.*, para. 385.
1406. *Gami Investments, Inc. v. Mexico* [2004] NAFTA-UNCITRAL Arbitration, Final Award (15 November 2004) para. 104.
1407. *Ibid.*, para. 110.

under the FET standard.[1408] In *Bilcon v. Canada*, the erroneous interpretation of Canadian law formed the basis for the state's liability under the FET standard.

[D] Summary: The Legality of a State's Conduct under National Law

The tribunal's evaluation of the fairness of a state's conduct often intersects with the review of a state's decisions by state bodies under national law. As follows from the analysis undertaken in this section, and as is consistent with Schill's observation, not all violations of national law translate into a breach of the FET standard, but only a 'qualified violation of domestic law can constitute a violation of FET standard.'[1409] A qualified violation is the mistreatment of an investor that goes beyond 'simple' illegality under domestic law. *See* Table 4 for the criteria in assessing the legality of a state's measure/conduct under national law by arbitral tribunals.

A restrictive approach in testing the legality of state conduct under national law was demonstrated in *ADF v. US*, *Thunderbird v. Mexico* and *Saluka v. Czech Republic*. The tribunals in these international investment arbitration cases initiated under IIAs stressed that the contested state measures should be assessed solely according to international legal standards (under the applicable IIA) and not against the national law of the host state. The tribunals in the aforementioned cases had not reviewed the state measures according to national law; at the same time, these tribunals had not excluded the possibility that violations of national law can contribute to liability under the FET standard. However, this would require 'something more' than just the illegal conduct of the state under national law.[1410]

Other tribunals concretised the criteria under which the state's qualified violations under national law may result in or contribute to a breach of the FET standard. A state's grave arbitrary measures against an investor, resulting from violations of national law, may be the basis for liability under the FET standard. For example, in *GAMI v. Mexico*, the tribunal asserted that the poor enforcement of the 'Sugar Program' that resulted in maladministration and which amounted to an 'outright and unjustified repudiation' would likely violate Article 1105 of the NAFTA.[1411] In *Lemire v. Ukraine* and *Bilcon v. US*, the violations of national law were interpreted by the tribunals as arbitrary actions of the states in question. In *Lemire*, the tribunal indicated that the 'blatant disregard' of the rules by the authorities and the distortion of fair competition had breached the FET standard.[1412] The erroneous interpretation of Canadian law in *Bilcon v. Canada* that involved the invocation of an extra requirement by the state's organ had been found to constitute arbitrary conduct by the state and was therefore in violation of the FET standard.

1408. *Lemire v. Ukraine*, ICSID Case No. ARB/06/18 Decision on Jurisdiction and Liability (14 January 2010) para. 385.
1409. S. Schill, (2006) International Justice and Law Working Papers 2006/6 (NYU Law School) 13.
1410. *ADF v. US* [2003] NAFTA, ICSID Case No. ARB (AF)/00/1 Award (9 January 2003) para. 190.
1411. *Gami Investments, Inc. v. Mexico* [2004] NAFTA-UNCITRAL Arbitration, Final Award (15 November 2004) para. 103.
1412. *Lemire v. Ukraine*, ICSID Case No. ARB/06/18 Decision on Jurisdiction and Liability (14 January 2010) para. 385.

As some cases indicate, the legality of a state's measure under national law can be one of the conditions of the state's right to regulate. The tribunals vary in the extent of the scrutiny that they apply in assessing the legality of a state's measure. These tribunals that have adopted a restrictive approach towards the decisions of the state's competent authorities usually attach a high degree of deference to the choices made by these authorities, thereby avoiding an extensive review of national laws and procedures.

Table 4 Legality of a State's Measure/Conduct under National Law

Criteria	A qualified violation of national law might result in (or contribute to) finding a breach of the FET standard in the case of: The state's serious arbitrary conduct towards an investor, expressed in: - The state's outright and unjustified repudiation of the relevant domestic regulations. - A 'blatant disregard' of domestic rules by the state authorities. - A 'misinterpretation' of the legal requirements, e.g., the imposition of additional requirements on an investor for the environmental assessment, i.e., compliance with 'community values' that had been inconsistent with national law.

§7.06 SUMMARY OF THE CHAPTER AND INTERIM CONCLUSIONS

The objective of this Chapter was to identify the conditions under which the right to regulate can be exercised in a lawful manner (in the context of an applicable FET standard). In assessing the state's measure, tribunals make use of several tests. The first test concerns a consideration of whether the objective of the state's measure is legitimate. In this test, tribunals determine whether (i) the objective of the state's measure serves a public interest and whether (ii) this objective is sufficiently justified. The second test is about the state's measure itself. The state's measure is assessed according to the following principles: (i) reasonableness, proportionality, the prohibition of arbitrariness; (ii) non-discrimination; and (iii) transparency. Additionally, a third test concerns a determination of the legality of the state's measures under national law in relation to the violation of the FET standard. The application of all three tests is presented in the flow chart in Figure 1. Based on these tests, the three conditions that apply to a legitimate exercise of the host state's right to regulate are summarised and commented upon in this section.

Figure 1 Flow Chart: Conditions for Lawfully Exercising the State's Right to Regulate

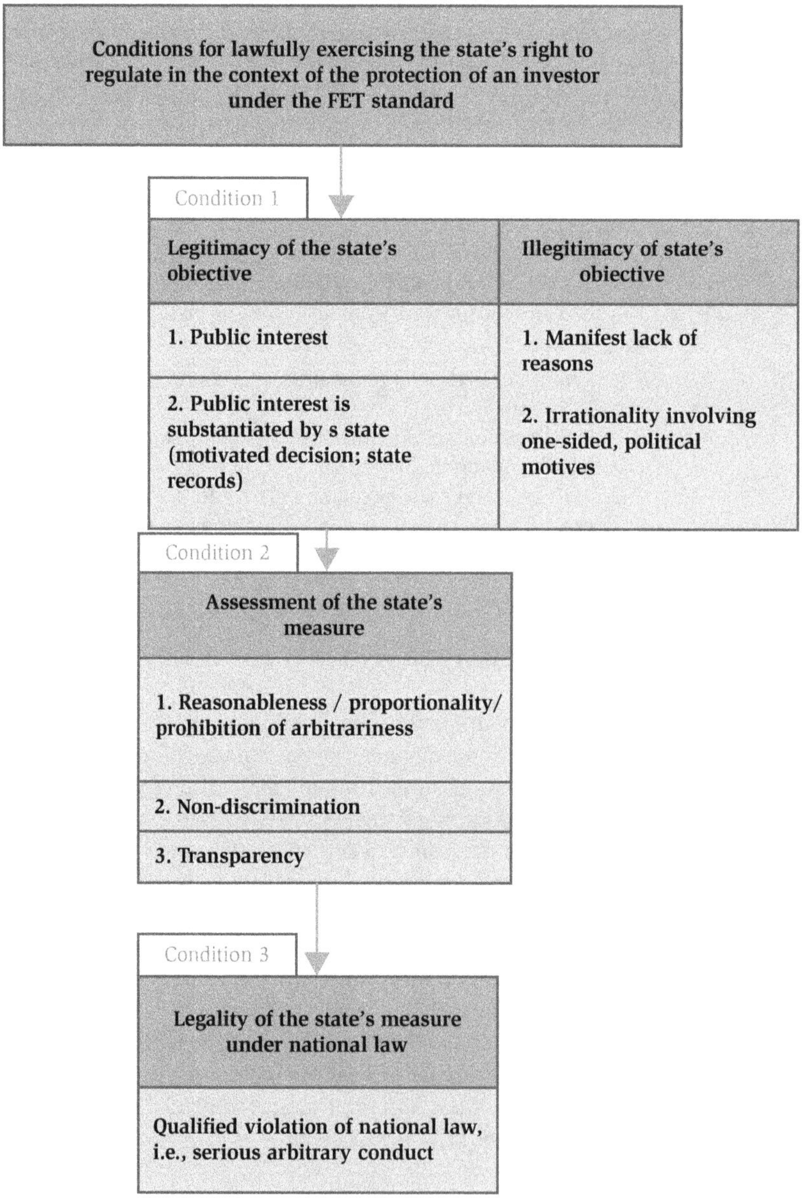

1. The condition concerning the right to regulate focusing on the legitimacy of the state's objective

The assessment of the legitimacy of a state's objective usually constitutes the first step in the determination of the legality of the state's measure, which is disputed by an investor. For tribunals, the review of a state's objective is an integral part in balancing the state's right to regulate against the rights of an investor under the FET standard. To assess how the state's right to regulate is weighed against the interests of an investor, the tribunal has to determine the goals that underlie the state's measure. The objective of the state's measure must be legitimate. To this end, two elements play a role in assessing whether the objective of the state's measure is legitimate.

First, tribunals have determined that the objective of the state's measure should be directed at addressing the public interest. This concerns the content and significance of the objective of the state's measure. The cases analysed in this section demonstrate that tribunals have accepted a broad spectrum of public interests to qualify a state's objectives as being legitimate. The public interest may include the protection of public health, the safeguarding of ecological and the environmental values, the protection of cultural rights and vulnerable groups of citizens, reforming the banking sector, combating corruption, the reduction of the excess profits of energy companies, the modernisation of the transport sector and the alignment of the electricity sector within the EU market.

Second, tribunals consider whether the objective of the state's measure that is claimed to be in the public interest can be substantiated by the host state through records and other evidence. To determine whether the objective of the state's measure has been sufficiently substantiated, tribunals assess whether the 'policy taken by a state [followed] a logical (good sense) explanation with the aim of addressing the public interest matter.'[1413] Among other things, the state's available records and official documents preceding the adoption of the contested measure are examples of the substantiation examined by tribunals to understand the nature and true purpose of the state's conduct. Furthermore, in some cases, compliance with international obligations under international treaties has served as one of the justifications in the assessment of a state's objectives. For example, in *Philip Morris v. Uruguay*, *Urbaser v. Argentina* and *Chemtura v. Canada*, the obligations of the state under national law and international treaties regulating human rights, public health and environmental issues were taken into account by tribunals in assessing the legitimacy of the state's objective.

As indicated in the flow chart, if both conditions for the assessment of the legitimacy of the state's objectives (a public interest and justification by the host state) are not fulfilled, the state's objectives are likely to be found illegitimate. In some cases, the illegitimacy of a state's objective was established where the state's objectives were one-sided and had been primarily politically motivated or based on the political agenda of the state's authorities.[1414]

1413. *AES Summit v. Hungary*, ICSID Case No. ARB/07/22 Award (23 September 2010) para. 10.3.8.
1414. *Gold Reserve v. Venezuela*, ICSID Case No. ARB(AF)/09/1 Award (22 September 2014) para. 590; *Eureko BV v. Republic of Poland* [2005] UNCITRAL Arbitration, Partial Award (19 August

A judicial point of departure in the assessment of the objective of the state's measure is the degree of deference afforded by tribunals to the choice of a state's measure in achieving the desired goals. This deference plays a role in determining whether or not the state's objective will be found to be legitimate. In the FET investment cases in which tribunals adopted a deferential approach, the tribunals accepted all types of objectives of the state's measure as legitimate, including political motives, unless the state's objectives were manifestly unreasonable.[1415] That implies that the state has to provide sufficient reasons for its measure, substantiated with records and other evidence.

Tribunals afforded a higher degree of deference to the state's measures in cases that addressed an important public concern, e.g. the protection of public health. Tribunals have emphasised, in deciding on measures directed at safeguarding public health in the context of the FET standard, that it is important to 'pay great deference' to the decisions of the state's authorities when deciding on the necessity of the measures to protect public health.[1416] The tribunals in the *Chemtura*, *Apotex* and *Philip Morris* cases displayed a higher degree of deference to the objectives of the states' measures, in contrast to other cases discussed in section §7.02. This might be explained by the fact that in all three cases the tribunals acknowledged that the states' public health organs possessed specialised expertise and were better equipped to make important decisions concerning public health, in comparison to the arbitrators who do not possess such specific knowledge.[1417]

2. The condition concerning the right to regulate focusing on the content of the state's measure

If the state's objectives are found to be legitimate, most tribunals proceed with an assessment of the state's measure according to the principles: (i) reasonableness, proportionality and the prohibition of arbitrariness; (ii) non-discrimination; and (iii) transparency (*see* the flow chart). These principles embody the key requirements for the state measure vis-à-vis an investor and constitute a condition that applies to a host state lawfully exercising the right to regulate.

2005) para. 233; *Azurix Corp. v. The Argentine Republic*, ICSID Case No. ARB/01/12 Award (14 July 2006) para. 375. *See also*: J. Bonnitcha, *Substantive Protection under Investment Treaties: A Legal and Economic Analysis* (Cambridge University Press, 2014), section 4.7.4. pp. 173-180.

1415. *Glamis v. US* [2009] NAFTA, ICSID 48 ILM 1039 Award (8 June 2009) para. 803; *Philip Morris v. Uruguay*, ICSID Case No. ARB/10/7 Award (8 July 2016) para. 399. *AES Summit v. Hungary*, ICSID Case No. ARB/07/22 Award (23 September 2010) para. 10.3.24.

1416. *Philip Morris v. Uruguay*, ICSID Case No. ARB/10/7 Award (8 July 2016) para. 399. *Chemtura v. Canada* [2010] NAFTA-UNCITRAL Arbitration, Award (2 August 2010) para. 134.

1417. This conclusion corresponds with the argument by Henckels that 'where uncertainty remains after adjudicators have taken into account the evidence of the parties in relation to a particular matter, this rationale for deference suggests that a tribunal should afford a measure of deference to the state due to the state's greater expertise and institutional competence as a regulator.' C. Henckels, *Proportionality and Deference in Investor-State Arbitration* (Cambridge University Press, 2015) 40.

In examining the reasonableness, proportionality and non-arbitrariness of the state's contested measure, tribunals assess the existence of a reasonable relationship between a state's measure and its objective, the possibility to employ alternative measures in achieving its objective and the impact of the loss suffered by an investor as a consequence of the state's measure.

To assess the relationship between a state's measure and its objective, tribunals have reviewed whether the state's measure has the potential to contribute to the realisation of the objective taken in the public interest. According to the cases analysed in section §7.04[A] tribunals have not questioned whether the state's measure was successful in achieving the desired objectives. Rather, the tribunals have focused on the question of whether the state's measure corresponded with the state's objective and was reasonable when it was adopted.[1418]

Under the principles of reasonableness and proportionality as discussed in section §7.04[A], some tribunals review the necessity of the state's measure by assessing the possibility to employ alternative measures in achieving the objective taken in the public interest. The tribunals vary in their approach towards assessing the possibility to adopt less restrictive measures concerning the investor's investment. For instance, in the public health case where the tribunal afforded a high degree of deference to the choices made by the state to achieve the objective to protect public health, the tribunal was reluctant to discuss any alternative measures.[1419] Some of the tribunals have thereby emphasised that the decisions regarding the appropriate means to achieve the goals related to public health should lie with the state's authorities.[1420] In the Argentinian cases concerning the privatisation of water, the tribunals discussed the use of the less aggravating measures vis-à-vis an investor.[1421] In these cases, the tribunals, by testing the necessity of the state's measures, primarily focused on the impact of the measure on the investor, and the deference afforded to the state was limited.[1422]

In assessing the reasonableness and proportionality of the state's measure, some tribunals also evaluated the impact of the loss suffered by an investor as a consequence of the state's measure. The relevant criterion in this regard has been the excessive financial burden experienced by the investor as a result of the state's measures.

Non-discrimination is another principle according to which tribunals assess the state's measure under the FET standard. This is understandable, as a discriminatory measure does not correspond to the notion of equity and fairness embedded into the

1418. *Philip Morris v. Uruguay*, ICSID Case No. ARB/10/7 Award (8 July 2016) para. 399. *Chemtura v. Canada* [2010] NAFTA-UNCITRAL Arbitration, Award (2 August 2010) para. 409; *Electrabel v. Hungary*, ICSID Case No. ARB/07/1 Final Award (25 November 2015) paras 179-181; *Mamidoil Jetoil Greek Petroleum Products Société S.A. v. Republic of Albania*, ICSID Case No. ARB/11/24 Award (30 March 2015) para. 792.

1419. *Philip Morris v. Uruguay*, ICSID Case No. ARB/10/7 Award (8 July 2016) para. 419.

1420. *Ibid.*, paras 399, 419; *Chemtura v. Canada* [2010] NAFTA-UNCITRAL Arbitration, Award (2 August 2010) para. 134.

1421. *Impregilo S.p.A v. Argentina*, ICSID Case No. ARB/07/17 Award (21 June 2011) para. 330; *AWG v. Argentina* [2010] UNCITRAL Arbitration, Decision on Liability (30 July 2010) para. 235.

1422. *Ibid.*

FET standard. Tribunals are consistent in requiring that the state's conduct be non-discriminatory towards an investor in order to be in compliance with the FET. In assessing discrimination in the context of the FET cases, tribunals compare the position of a foreign investor with that of a national investor(s). The criteria used by investment tribunals, in judging whether an investor was treated in a discriminatory manner is to assess whether there were '(i) similar cases, whether an investor was (ii) treated differently (iii) and whether there was a reasonable justification for discriminatory treatment'.[1423]

In appraising the state's measure, FET tribunals have stressed the relevance of the transparency principle. In assessing the transparency of a state's measures, tribunals refer to such criteria as adequate and open communication with the investor; the availability of sufficient information concerning any laws and policies that may potentially affect an investment; and the timely notification of an investor by the state's authorities regarding changes to the status of the investment.[1424]

A measure taken in the public interest, which has been found to be reasonable, proportionate, non-arbitrary, transparent and non-discriminatory is likely to be in compliance with the FET standard.

3. The condition concerning the right to regulate focusing on the legality of the state's measure under national law

The legality of a state's measure under national law has been part of the assessment of the FET standard and the right to regulate. Tribunals are consistent in their view that only a qualified, i.e. serious, violation of national law can result in a breach of the FET standard. A qualified violation constitutes something more than 'simple' illegality under domestic law. Tribunals have provided that a state's serious arbitrary conduct, resulting from breaches under national law, may violate the FET standard. Such arbitrary conduct may follow from the maladministration of the state's authority which has led to an 'outright and unjustified repudiation' of the relevant regulations,[1425] a 'blatant disregard' of the rules by the authorities[1426] or an erroneous interpretation of national law leading to the imposition of new requirements for the environmental assessment that had to be conducted by the investor.[1427]

1423. *Saluka Investments BV v. Czech Republic* [2006] UNCITRAL Arbitration Partial Award (17 March 2006) para. 313.

1424. *Ioan Micula v. Romania*, ICSID Case No. ARB/05/20 Final Award (11 December 2013) para. 870; *Saluka Investments BV v. Czech Republic* [2006] UNCITRAL Arbitration Partial Award (17 March 2006) para. 499.

1425. *Gami Investments, Inc. v. Mexico* [2004] NAFTA-UNCITRAL Arbitration, Final Award (15 November 2004) para. 103.

1426. *Lemire v. Ukraine*, ICSID Case No. ARB/06/18 Decision on Jurisdiction and Liability (14 January 2010) para. 385.

1427. *William Ralph Clayton, William Richard Clayton, Douglas Clayton, Daniel Clayton and Bilcon of Delaware Inc. v. Government of Canada* [2015] UNCITRAL, NAFTA, PCA Case No. 2009-04 Award on Jurisdiction and Liability (17 March 2015) para. 604.

CHAPTER 8

Towards a More Balanced Approach

§8.01 INTRODUCTION

This book had a goal to answer the question of *how can a host state's right to regulate concerning the protection of a public interest be balanced against a host state's obligation to provide fair and equitable treatment under international investment law?* The answer to this question has been provided on the basis of the findings discussed in Chapters 2-7. To this end, some of the key findings are reiterated.

In section §8.02, the meaning of the right to regulate under international investment law is explained, while building on the analysis is provided in Chapter 2. In section §8.03, the conclusions concerning the formulation of the FET standard in IIAs as presented in Chapter 3 are elaborated upon. Section §8.04 outlines how the FET standard has been developed and interpreted by arbitral tribunals. Here, the content of Chapter 4 is briefly summarised. In section §8.05, the legal conditions under which host states may regulate in the public interest are discussed and clarified. The identified conditions are based on the research results, which are presented in Chapters 6 and 7.

The second part of this Chapter (section §8.06) analyses the relationship between the FET standard and the state's right to regulate in the new generation of IIAs[1428] and investment jurisprudence in FET cases. To analyse this issue, first, it is discussed which elements that have emerged from the FET case law as being relevant in relation to the state's right to regulate have been incorporated into the new IIAs and which elements have not? The answer to this question is provided in section §8.06[B]. Second, the other issue that is addressed is whether and in which direction these new generations

1428. The new generation of IIAs discussed in this section are the three examples of IIAs in which the FET standard has been clarified with additional content. These treaties are: the CETA (signed on 30 October 2016) http://ec.europa.eu/trade/policy/in-focus/ceta/; the EU-Singapore FTA (April 2018), Investment Protection Agreement http://trade.ec.europa.eu/doclib/press/index.cfm?id=961; and the EU-Vietnam FTA draft text (January 2016) http://trade.ec.europa.eu/doclib/press/index.cfm?id=1437. All websites accessed on 12 June 2018.

of IIAs shift the balance between the protection of investors under the FET standard and the state's right to regulate. The answers to these two enquires that build on the findings revealed from the treaty and the case law analysis has the main contribution to providing the answer to the key question of this book.

§8.02 THE RIGHT TO REGULATE IN INTERNATIONAL INVESTMENT LAW

The state's right to regulate is the right that allows states to exercise its regulatory powers. The state has the right to 'prescribe the laws that set the boundaries of the public order of the state' in its territory.[1429] The right to regulate is also the right that gives the authority to and which imposes duties on a state to protect the public interest of its citizens, e.g. in relation to public health and safety.

The right to regulate has its legal basis in the international legal principle of state sovereignty. Sovereignty has both internal and external dimensions.[1430] The right to regulate is an expression of internal sovereignty. In this context, the state has the freedom to decide and implement its regulatory objectives, e.g. to enhance its economic prosperity, to promote sustainable development and to respect the fundamental rights of its citizens. The state also has the right to negotiate and to enter into international agreements, which is an expression of its external sovereignty. When states conclude IIAs, their right to regulate as a part of their internal sovereignty may be limited in line with the obligations under these agreements.

The right to regulate has been directly and indirectly referred to in the texts of IIAs, in the decisions of investment tribunals and in academic writings. Based on these sources, the right to regulate has the following characteristics.

First, the state's right to regulate is limited by IIAs. Hence, when states conclude IIAs, their right to regulate may be limited by their obligation to provide FET under these treaties. A host state must observe the rights of investors under the FET standard. At the same time, while complying with its FET obligations towards investors, a host state also seeks to retain sufficient policy space to regulate in the public interest so as to ensure public welfare for its population. The limitations on the state's right to regulate can be fairly substantial, considering the open nature of the FET standard. The extent of these limitations is examined by identifying the legal conditions for the state's right to regulate while providing protection to investors under the FET standard. These conditions are elaborated upon in Chapters 6 and 7.

Second, considering that the state's right to regulate is based on the international legal principle of state sovereignty, this right is always present in relation to the state's obligation under the FET standard. Therefore, the FET standard is ultimately all about balancing the rights and obligations of host states and investors. From the perspective of a host state, the FET standard is a tool for attracting investors and investments into

1429. C. Staker, (2014) 316.
1430. I. Brownlie, (2008); J. Crawford, Brownlie's Principles of Public International Law (8th edn., Oxford University Press, 2012); R. Brand, 'External Sovereignty and International Law' [1995] 18 *Fordham Journal of International Law*, 1685.

a host state by providing legal guarantees against the state's regulatory risks.[1431] Simultaneously, a host state also aims to preserve the policy space to regulate in the public interest while complying with the rights of investors under the FET standard. From an investor's perspective, FET is reflected in a state's consistent and stable conduct, which allows an investor to plan and operate its investment in a host state for the long term. The tension between the state's right to regulate and the rights of investors may arise when the host state exercises its right to regulate by, e.g., amending its legislation so that it adversely affects the position of the investor's investments, thereby leading to a claim for a breach of the FET standard by the investor. This tension can be resolved by tribunals by balancing the rights of states to regulate and the rights of investors under the FET standard.

Third, the right to regulate is regularly laid down in IIAs and investment decisions by the inclusion of the notion of public interest. Public interest implies that the measures of a state have been taken in the interest of the 'welfare of the general public'.[1432] The findings of this book demonstrate that the spectrum of recognised public interests is broad, including the protection of public health, the safeguarding of ecological and environmental values, the maintenance of basic labour standards, the protection of cultural rights and vulnerable groups of citizens, the reformation of the banking sector, the fight against corruption, the reduction of excessive profits made by energy companies, the modernisation of the transport sector and the alignment of the electricity sector within the EU market.[1433]

There are several ways to ensure the public interest in IIAs. By including an exception to the FET standard in an IIA, a host state can exclude specific public interest(s) from the scope of the particular FET provision.[1434] Such exceptions might be directed at a specific regulatory concern, e.g. the protection of human, animal or plant life.[1435] In some IIAs, states have included positive obligations concerning the regulation of specific public interests, e.g. labour standards. These provisions also apply to

1431. D. Gaukrodger, 'The Balance between Investor Protection and the Right to Regulate in Investment Treaties' (2017) OECD Working Papers on International Investment 2017/02, 5. According to the consultations with the governments, the report provides that states nevertheless give 'some priority' to 'protecting the right to regulate in most recent government action relating to treaties'; the 'value of reducing regulatory risk [e.g. by including the investment protection standards] is also underlined.' http://www.oecd-ilibrary.org/finance-and-investment/the-balance-between-investor-protection-and-the-right-to-regulate-in-investment-treaties_82786801-en accessed on 1 June 2018.

1432. Random House, Random House Webster's Unabridged Dictionary (2nd edn., Random House Books, 2014) 151.

1433. *See* Chapter 2, section §2.03[B] (on the right to regulate in IIAs) and Chapter 2, section §2.03[C] (on the right to regulate in investment cases), as well as section §7.02 (on the objective of the state's measure where examples of a public interest have been also identified).

1434. The inclusion of exceptions to FET standard provisions is extremely rare. An example of such provision: Article 3(d) of the Colombia-Model BIT (2008) http://investmentpolicyhub.unctad.org/Download/TreatyFile/2821 accessed on 1 June 2018.

1435. An example of such exceptions is included in: Canada-Peru BIT (2006) http://investmentpolicyhub.unctad.org/Download/TreatyFile/626 accessed on 1 June 2018.

the FET standard in such IIAs, hence reaffirming that the contracting states must regulate in the interest of this public interest.[1436]

Furthermore, in recent IIAs, the public interest is specifically referred to in the provisions on the state's right to regulate. For example, the state's legitimate policy objectives are explicitly laid down, e.g. safety, public morals, the environment and public health.[1437] In the same vein, tribunals have also recognised the significance of the public interest in FET cases by examining the legitimacy of the objective of the state's measure and by taking into account the sociopolitical and economic circumstances that are relevant in assessing the legitimate expectations of the investor.[1438]

§8.03 THE IIAs' FET STANDARD PROVISIONS IN CONNECTION WITH THE RIGHT TO REGULATE

The text of IIA FET standard provisions is the legal basis for the decisions of arbitrators in FET claims. In Chapter 3 of this study, eighty-nine selected IIAs, all concluded between the 1960s and 2016, were analysed and the FET standard provisions therein were categorised (*see* Annex A).

In Chapter 3, the following five categories of FET standard provisions were identified: (1) FET standard provisions formulated as unqualified treaty standards; (2) IIAs in which the FET standard provisions included a reference to a norm of unwritten international law, e.g. (a) the minimum standard of the treatment of aliens under customary international law, (b) general international law and/or (c) principles of international law (for (b) and (c); (3) IIAs in which the FET standard provisions were qualified with additional content; (4) IIAs in which the preamble provided a reference to the FET standard; and (5) IIAs with (a) a joint interpretative instrument clarifying the intent of the parties to the treaty and/or (b) one or more decisions by a treaty body on the interpretation of the FET standard. Figure 1 provides an overview thereof.

Some of the IIAs discussed above include a combined approach between category (2) and (3) in the sense that they have an FET standard provision that refers to international law but which also has additional content.

The findings of the research produced in Chapter 3 indicate that in the majority of IIAs – especially those negotiated from the early 1960s through to the end of the

1436. *See* Chapter 2, section §2.03[B] (on the right to regulate in IIAs) where the role of public interests mentioned in the exceptions to a treaty and/or the provisions of specific public interests are explained.

1437. EU-Singapore FTA (2018), Investment Protection Agreement, Article 2.2(1) http://trade.ec.europa.eu/doclib/press/index.cfm?id=961; EU-Vietnam FTA (2016), Chapter 8, Articles 13*bis*(1) http://trade.ec.europa.eu/doclib/press/index.cfm?id=1437; Consolidated text of CETA, 30 October 2016, Chapter 8, Article 8.9(1) http://ec.europa.eu/trade/policy/in-focus/ceta/ceta-chapter-by-chapter/; all websites were accessed on 1 June 2018.

1438. *See* Chapter 7, section §7.02 (on legitimate policy objectives) and Chapter 6, section §6.05 (on the economic and sociopolitical circumstances in a host state).

1990s (hereinafter referred to as 'the old generation of treaties')[1439] many of which still continue to be in force[1440] – the FET standard was concisely formulated as an unqualified treaty standard that provided that 'each contracting party shall at all times ensure fair and equitable treatment to investments.'[1441] This type of FET standard provision falls within category (1) indicated above. The unqualified FET standard provisions under category (1) are characterised by a minimalist and open language that does not contain any clarification of the content of the FET standard.

In the survey, it was demonstrated that in some IIAs, the FET provisions included a reference to general international law, principles of international law or customary international law (category (2) above). The FET standard, which was referred to in category (2)(a) above, i.e. the standard which is linked to the minimum standard of the treatment of aliens under customary international law, is a formulation which is still adopted by states in the new generation of IIAs (i.e., after 2010). The way in which states usually do this is by including formulations of the NAFTA FTC Notes in IIAs, thereby replicating the notion that the FET standard 'does not require treatment beyond the minimum standard of the treatment of aliens under customary international law'. With the inclusion of the international minimum standard provision in IIAs, states attempt to indicate the level of fair and equal treatment that will be afforded to investors. If a conflict between a state and an investor arises, the state will only be held liable if there has been gross misconduct on the part of the state.[1442] The inclusion of the international minimum standard provision in IIAs can be seen as a response by

1439. UNCTAD defines the old generation of IIAs as treaties that were concluded before 2010. *See* UNCTAD, 'Phase 2 of IIA Reform: Modernising the Existing Stock of Old Generation Treaties' (6 June 2017) http://investmentpolicyhub.unctad.org/Publications/Details/173 accessed on 1 May 2018.

1440. *See*: UNCTAD, 'IIA Mapping Project' (2016). Of 1,321 IIAs negotiated between 1960 and 1997, 1,121 IIAs continue to be in force http://investmentpolicyhub.unctad.org/IIA/mappedContent#iiaInnerMenu accessed on 21 June 2017.

1441. *See*, e.g., Article 4(1) of the Australia-Argentina BIT (1997). *See also* section §3.03[A]. These types of FET formulations have been adopted in 46 of 81 IIAs. This is in line with the UNCTAD research conclusions, which include a more representative sample of 1,456 IIAs, among which 1,132 IIAs included unqualified FET standard provisions in their treaties. UNCTAD, 'IIA Mapping Project' (2016) http://investmentpolicyhub.unctad.org/IIA/mappedContent accessed on 12 June 2018.

1442. UNCTAD, 'Fair and Equitable Treatment: UNCTAD Series on International Investment Agreements II' (New York, 2012) 28, http://unctad.org/en/Docs/unctaddiaeia2011d5_en.pdf accessed on 1 June 2018. The view that has sometimes been expressed by several tribunals and scholars, followed by some states, is that the international minimum standard covers only a 'relatively base level of conduct such as bad faith or a gross insufficiency of governmental action'. Also *see*: Y. Fortier, 'Expectations of Governments and Investors v. Practice: A View from the Bench ICSID Review' [2009] 24(2) *Foreign Investment Law Journal*, 353. Furthermore, as explained in section §3.03[B], in the interpretation of the FET standard with reference to the international minimum standard, reference is made to the *Neer* case, decided by the US-Mexico Claims Commission in 1926. In this case, the tribunal provided that the international minimum standard would be considered violated where the state's conduct amounts to an 'outrage, to bad faith, to wilful neglect of duty, or to an insufficiency of governmental action so far short of international standards that every reasonable and impartial man would readily recognize its insufficiency'. *L. F. H. Neer and P. Neer (USA) v. United Mexican States* [1926] United States-Mexico Claims Commission, Decision, (15 October 1926) Reports of International Arbitral Awards, Vol. IV (United Nations, 2006) para. 4, pp. 61-62.

states to situations in which IIAs with an unqualified FET standard (category (1) above) have been interpreted by arbitrators as covering a broader spectrum of state conduct.[1443] However, some tribunals take the position[1444] that the dissimilarities between the unqualified FET standard (i.e., category (1)) and the FET standard linked to the international MST (category (2)) in the context of the specific facts of the case 'may well be more apparent than real'.[1445] This position is also supported by several scholars.[1446]

Consequently, while noticing the generality of the unqualified FET standard and the FET standard linked to the international MST, in terms of their clarity on the meaning of FET, some states have chosen to clarify the FET standard with additional content. [1447] This is further explained below.

The research findings presented in Chapter 3 revealed that the emerging trend in treaty drafting is to specify the FET standard with additional content (category 3). Several states have chosen to adopt more elaborate language in the text of the treaty, especially concerning the question as to which state behaviour qualifies as a violation of the FET standard. They have included either an exhaustive or a non-exhaustive list of *unacceptable* state conduct, hence focusing on the obligations of the state towards investors. Such elaborate language is not explicitly linked to the right to regulate,

1443. For example, the frustration of the legitimate expectations of an investor or the arbitrary and discriminatory treatment of an investor. Reference is made to the analysis of cases conducted in Chapters 5 and 6.

1444. *Saluka v. Czech Republic* [2006] Permanent Court of Arbitration, IIC 210, Partial Award (17 March 2006) para. 295; *Azurix Corp. v. The Argentine Republic,* ICSID Case No. ARB/01/12 Award (14 July 2006) para. 365; *Siemens A.G. v. The Argentine Republic,* ICSID Case No. ARB/02/8 Award (17 January 2007) para. 293. Several tribunals, especially under the NAFTA, have primarily taken a 'historic-evolutionary approach', underlining the importance of the high threshold set by the *Neer* case and at the same time emphasising the evolutionary character of the minimum standard. Cases that have accepted the 'historic-evolutionary approach' include *Pope & Talbot Inc. v. The Government of Canada* [2001] UNCITRAL Arbitration, Final Merits Award (10 April 2001); *Mondev International Ltd. v. United States,* ICSID Case No. ARB (AF)/99/2 Award (11 October 2002); *Cargill, Inc. v. United Mexican States,* ICSID Case No. ARB/AF/05/2 Award (18 September 2009); *Merrill & Ring Forestry L.P. v. Canada* [2010] UNCITRAL Award (31 May 2010); and *Loewen Group, Inc. and Raymond L. Loewen v. United States,* ICSID Case No. ARB(AF)/98/3 Award (26 June 2003).

1445. *Saluka v. Czech Republic* [2006] Permanent Court of Arbitration, IIC 210, Partial Award (17 March 2006) para. 291.

1446. R. Klager, (2016) 72. The author observes that the inclusion of the minimum standard of the treatment of aliens under customary international law does not provide certainty for the states as to whether this would lead to a higher liability threshold (p. 72); P. Dumberry, The Formation and Identification of Rules of Customary International Law in International Investment Law (Cambridge University Press, 2016) 108-109; R. Dolzer, A. von Walter, 'Fair and Equitable Treatment – Lines of Jurisprudence on Customary Law', in F. Ortino and others (eds) *Investment Treaty Law: Current Issues, Volume II* (British Institute for Comparative Law, 2007) 113; J. Bonnitcha, Substantive Protection under Investment Treaties (Oxford University Press, 2014), section 4.2.3 (e-book) p. 46. *See also* UNCTAD, 'Investment Policy Framework for Sustainable Development (IPFSD)' (2015) 95 http://investmentpolicyhub.unctad.org/Upload/Documents/INVESTMENT%20POLICY%20FRAMEWORK%202015%20WEB_VERSION.pdf accessed on 12 June 2018. In discussing the option of inserting an FET standard provision with reference to the minimum standard of the treatment of aliens under customary international law, this framework provides that the 'exact contours of MCT/CIL remain elusive'.

1447. *See* Chapter 3, section §3.04.

although the reason for including this additional content in the FET standard provision is to mark, in a clearer manner, where the right to regulate ends. Section §8.06 contains further reflections on examples of recent IIAs that include provisions, which explicitly clarify the state's right to regulate, such as the CETA.

The findings contained in Chapter 3 regarding the FET standard provisions that have been categorised in the fourth category (4) reveal that several IIAs include a reference to the FET standard in their preamble, in addition to the FET provision. The goal of such a reference is to stress the desirability of applying the FET standard to investors and their investments. In some IIAs' preambles, references have also been made to a stable framework for investments. The preambles are not intended to create legal obligations beyond the substantive provisions. However, in interpreting the FET standard, tribunals have relied on the preamble to provide content to the FET standard in the context and the object of the investment treaty. This point is further addressed in section §8.04 of this Chapter.

It has also been revealed that some states specified the FET standard in their IIAs through including an additional clarification of its meaning. Some states included either a joint interpretative instrument or a binding interpretation mechanism in relation to the FET standard, both to be performed by (the governments of) the parties concerned (i.e., category (5) above). For example, in EU agreements, NAFTA and several BITs the treaty parties have found it useful to institutionalise their competence to interpret the FET standard through empowering a treaty body usually composed of treaty parties' own representatives. These treaty bodies can issue an interpretation of the FET standard or, as exemplified by CETA, can review the content of the FET standard.

§8.04 THE DEVELOPMENT AND INTERPRETATION OF THE FET STANDARD BY INTERNATIONAL ARBITRAL TRIBUNALS

The IIAs regularly form the legal basis for international arbitral proceedings. International arbitral tribunals have authority, delegated to them in the IIAs by the contracting states, to interpret and apply the FET standard in deciding investment cases initiated by investors under the said IIAs.[1448]

It has been revealed that in interpreting the FET standard, tribunals turn to (i) the general rules of treaty interpretation, as laid down in Article 31 of the Vienna Convention on the Law of Treaties (VCLT); (ii) general principles of law; and (iii) the supplementary means of treaty interpretation, as laid down in Article 32 VCLT, and subsidiary means of the determination of international law, in particular judicial decisions.[1449]

1448. A. Roberts, 'Power and Persuasion in Investment Treaty Interpretation: The Dual Role of States' [2010] 104(2) *American Journal of International Law*, 188.

1449. Article 38(1)(d) of the Statute of the International Court of Justice (signed on 26 June 1945, entered into force 24 October 1945) 1055, 33 UNTS 933.

The first category (the general rules of treaty interpretation):

In applying the VCLT general rules of treaty interpretation, tribunals have primarily searched for the meaning of the FET standard by interpreting it according to its (i) ordinary meaning, its (ii) context and in the light of its (iii) object and purpose within the applicable IIA.[1450] In interpreting the ordinary meaning of the literal wording of 'fair' and 'equitable', tribunals have only arrived at an identification of synonyms of these terms, such as 'just' and 'even-handed'.[1451] In searching for the meaning of the FET standard, some tribunals have had recourse to the interpretation of the context and the object and purpose of the treaty. In the preamble to an applicable IIA, the context of the FET standard provision has often assisted tribunals in defining the scope of the FET standard. Therefore, in some cases, tribunals have provided a broad interpretation of the FET standard by relying on the objectives of the treaty, i.e. investor promotion and protection, which are generally stated in the preamble to the applicable IIA. In several decisions, tribunals have referred to the preamble in finding that the stability of the legal and business framework constitutes an element of the FET standard.[1452] More recently, however, tribunals have opted for a more balanced assessment of the context, object and purpose of the treaty, by underlining that investor protection is not the 'sole aim of the Treaty'.[1453]

The second category (general principles of law):

In their decisions on the FET standard, tribunals have applied the principles of proportionality, reasonableness, deference and margin of appreciation. These principles are generally understood and have been identified as general principles of law under Article 38(1c) of the ICJ Statute. Tribunals have primarily applied the principles of reasonableness and/or proportionality in assessing the states' measures vis-à-vis the rights of investors under the FET standard, or in deciding on the legitimate expectations of an investor. Tribunals have often applied the tests to the principles of proportionality and reasonableness in weighing the interests of states and investors under the FET standard. In some investment cases, tribunals exercised restraint in assessing the legitimacy of the objective of the state's measure against the state's obligations under IIAs by referring to the principles of deference and margin

1450. Article 31(1) of the Vienna Convention on the Law of Treaties, 1155 UNTS 331 (23 May 1969). https://treaties.un.org/doc/Publication/UNTS/Volume%201155/volume-1155-I-18232-English.pdf accessed on 12 March 2018.

1451. *See*, e.g., *MTD v. Chile*, ICSID Case No. ARB/01/7 Award (25 May 2004) para. 113; *Azurix Corp. v. The Argentine Republic*, ICSID Case No. ARB/01/12 Award (14 July 2006) para. 360. Also *see*: Chapter 4, section §4.02[A].

1452. *See* Chapter 4.2.3. *Occidental v. Ecuador*, LCIA Case No. UN3467, Final Award (1 July 2004), para. 183; *CMS Gas Transmission Co. v. The Argentine Republic*, ICSID Case No. ARB/01/8 Award (12 May 2005) para. 274.

1453. *Saluka v. Czech Republic* [2006] Permanent Court of Arbitration, IIC 210, Partial Award (17 March 2006) para. 300.

of appreciation. The application of the principles of proportionality, reasonableness, deference and margin of appreciation by arbitral tribunals is further explained in sections §8.05 and §8.06 of this Chapter.

The third category (the supplementary and subsidiary means of treaty interpretation):

In some cases, tribunals have also relied upon supplementary and subsidiary means in providing interpretations of the FET standard, which include the preparatory work of the treaty and the circumstances of its conclusion, previous arbitral decisions, scholarly writings and national law.[1454] The study has revealed that in interpreting the FET standard, tribunals rely primarily on previous decisions of arbitral tribunals, in comparison to the other supplementary and subsidiary means of interpretation analysed in Chapter 4.

Previous decisions by investment tribunals are subsidiary means of interpretation in accordance with Article 38(1)(d) of the ICJ Statute.[1455] Tribunals differ in how they refer to previous jurisprudence. Early FET decisions have been frequently criticised for a lack of consensual interpretation of this standard, even in cases which are alike.[1456] The more recent FET cases have developed in a more predictable manner. Tribunals are mostly in consensus in formulating the FET standard as a list of elements. To be more specific, tribunals usually formulate the FET elements as a list of obligations that a state owes to an investor.[1457] These obligations are identified by tribunals on the basis of a 'recurring pattern of argumentation' applied to specific situations by previous tribunals.[1458]

1454. *See* Chapter 4, section §4.03.

1455. Article 38(1)(d) of the Statute of the International Court of Justice (signed on 26 June 1945, entered into force 24 October 1945) 1055, 33 UNTS 933.

1456. An illustration of the inconsistency of investment awards in the context of FET claims can be observed in two contradictory decisions on the FET standard based on the same facts. These cases are *CME v. Czech Republic* [2001] UNCITRAL Arbitration, Partial Award (13 September 2001) and *Ronald S. Lauder v. The Czech Republic* [2001] UNCITRAL Arbitration, Final Award (3 September 2001). These two awards resulted in two contrasting decisions regarding liability under the FET standard. Moreover, the tribunal in *Mamidoil v. Albania* emphasised the lack of consistency in the case law, stating that '[t]he Tribunal has looked for and found assistance in awards and decisions that the Parties have submitted. However, this assistance is not only limited by the fact that international arbitral tribunals are under no obligation to rely on precedents, but also by the lack of a jurisprudence constante.' *See Mamidoil Jetoil Greek Petroleum Products Societe S.A. v. Republic of Albania*, ICSID Case No. ARB/11/24 Award (30 March 2015) para. 603.

1457. M. Valenti, (2014) 33. In the words of Valenti, 'such elements can be viewed as more specific obligations in which the principle is deemed to materialise depending on the circumstances of the case'.

1458. R. Klager, (2011) 116.

§8.05 THE LEGAL CONDITIONS UNDER WHICH STATES MAY REGULATE IN THE PUBLIC INTEREST

[A] Introduction

The legal conditions for a state to regulate while providing protection to the investor under the FET standard as identified in this study are: (i) conditions for the lawful exercise of the state's right to regulate focusing on the legitimate expectations of an investor (Chapter 6); and (ii) conditions for the lawful exercise of the state's right focusing on the state's measure (Chapter 7).

[B] Conditions Focusing on the Legitimacy of an Investor's Expectations

There is tension between the legitimate expectations of an investor and the state's right to regulate. Tribunals resolve this tension by attempting to reconcile the subjective interests of the investor deriving from its legitimate expectations and the state's right to regulate in the public interest. On the basis of the case law analysis conducted in this dissertation, four elements have been identified that are considered in order to establish whether the expectations of an investor are legitimate and thus capable of limiting the state's right to regulate. These are: (i) the specific representations made by the host state to an investor; (ii) the investor's expectations based on the stability of a general regulatory framework; (iii) the economic and sociopolitical circumstances in the host state; and (iv) the investor's conduct. These elements are not always systematically considered by tribunals, and they are not applied in a cumulative way, but they emerged out of the research as important elements in the decision-making process of tribunals with regard to legitimate expectations.

(i) The element of the state's specific representations

As found in Chapter 6, in assessing a claim for the protection of the legitimate expectations of an investor, tribunals have differentiated between claims made on the basis of a state's specific representations towards an investor and claims made on the basis of the stability of the general regulatory framework. With regard to the former, most tribunals follow the line that a state's specific representation can create a legitimate expectation by an investor. The criteria under which tribunals determine the specific nature of a state's representation have been analysed in Chapter 6 (section §6.03[C]). In determining whether a state's representation is specific, tribunals commonly pose three questions: (1) are the representations generated by the competent state authority?; (2) what is the legal force of the specific representations?; and (3) how has the investor been designated in the state's representations?

Based on an analysis of the answers to these three questions in many cases, it can be concluded that a specific representation is one that: (1) is provided by a competent authority with a relevant decision-making power over the investment; (2) is aimed at the express and specific inducement of investment that should be crystallised in an agreement or licence or other assurance in writing and constitutes an explicit right (which depends on: (i) its legal form; (ii) its content; and (iii) the wording of the representation); and (3) is directed at the specific investor and is not aimed at a large or even small groups of potential investors.[1459]

For the contractual commitments that in some FET decisions qualified as specific representations under the concept of legitimate expectations, the issue is not so much that the competent authority provided a specific representation. It is whether the state or the state agency exercised its sovereign authority in its contractual relations with an investor.[1460] This type of authority involves the state's interference with the operation of a contract that is beyond an ordinary contractual breach. Besides the requirement that the state has acted in its capacity as a sovereign authority, tribunals have required, in some FET decisions, additional violations of the treaty, such as a breach of due process or discrimination, in order to be able to come to a decision that the contractual expectations of an investor are protected under the FET standard.[1461]

The three criteria, mentioned above, that are pertinent for a determination of specific representations, namely: (1) the competence of the state's authority; (2) legal force: (i) the legal form, (ii) the content and (iii) the wording of the representation; and (3) the designation of the investor have not always been applied by tribunals in a cumulative way. Tribunals rarely follow a step-by-step process in providing the legal foundation for their decision on specific representations.

(ii) The element of the stability of a general regulatory framework

Tribunals have also emphasised that a state has the obligation to provide a certain degree of stability as to the applicable national regulations which will apply to an investor and its investment.[1462] Tribunals have clarified that an investor can - to some extent - expect that a state's regulatory framework - on which an investor has relied in making its investment - will not be significantly changed by such a host state. Tribunals have emphasised that a mere change in the regulatory framework would not suffice for a finding that an investor's expectations have been frustrated.[1463] Tribunals are generally in consensus that a state's 'legal framework is by definition subject to change as it adapts to new circumstances day by day and a state has the sovereign right to exercise its powers which include legislative acts.'[1464] As part of its right to regulate, a host state can amend its laws. Only in a limited number of situations can an investor's claim based on the instability of a general regulatory framework be successful. That can be the case if: (1) the amended framework resulted in a severe negative impact on the investor and its investment and/or (2) the way in which the transformation of the regulatory framework was conducted was extraordinary.

With regard to the first situation, the central criteria for determining whether the transformation of the general regulatory framework constitutes a breach of the

1459. *See* Chapter 6, section §6.03.
1460. *Impregilo S.p.A v. Argentina*, ICSID Case No. ARB/07/17 Award (21 June 2011) para. 296.
1461. *See* Chapter 6 section §6.03[F].
1462. Chapter 6, section §6.04.
1463. *Ibid.*
1464. *AES Summit v. Hungary*, ICSID Case No. ARB/07/22 Award (23 September 2010) para. 9.3.29.

legitimate expectations of an investor, according to the tribunals, was whether the changes had been drastic and/or discriminatory and had a severe financial impact on the investor.[1465]

With regard to the second situation, i.e. the way in which the general framework has been transformed by a host state, the main components on the basis of which a tribunal can decide that the state has frustrated the investor's legitimate expectations are the extreme nature and the unpredictability of the transformation of the general regulatory framework.[1466] The transformation to the general regulatory framework will be contrary to the FET standard if the manner in which the changes were conducted is disproportionate.[1467] This according to tribunals can occur upon a 'sudden and unpredictable elimination of the essential characteristics of the existing framework',[1468] or when the regulatory change is 'disproportionate to the aim of the legislative amendment and has no due regard to the reasonable reliance interests of recipients who may commit substantial resources on the basis of the earlier regime'.[1469] A state can amend its laws and regulations, but the process should be gradual, foreseeable and without implementing any contradictory norms or administrative processes and in accordance with the long-term objectives of the state.[1470]

The state's obligation to provide stability for investments occupies a prominent role in the assessment of the FET standard. Based on the recent decisions, the threshold for breaching this obligation is relatively high, as the transformation must have a complete and drastic character, e.g. by replacing the original regulatory framework with a 'wholly different regulatory approach'.[1471]

In the assessment of the legitimate expectations of an investor, in many decisions tribunals have taken into account the special economic and/or sociopolitical circumstances in a host state and also the conduct of the investor itself. This is further explained below.

(iii) The element of special economic and/or sociopolitical circumstances in a host state

1465. *Toto v. Lebanon,* ICSID Case No. ARB/07/12 Award (7 June 2012) para. 244; *El Paso v. Argentina,* ICSID Case No. ARB/03/15 Award (31 October 2011) para. 510.

1466. *PSEG v. Turkey,* ICSID Case No. ARB/02/5 Award (19 January 2007) para. 250.

1467. *Charanne Construction v. Spain,* SCC Case No. 062/2012 Award (21 January 2016) para. 517. *Eiser Infrastructure Ltd. and Energia Solar Luxembourg v. Spain,* ICSID Case No. ARB/13/36 Award (4 May 2017), para. 370.

1468. *Charanne Construction v. Spain,* SCC Case No. 062/2012 Award (21 January 2016) para. 517; *Antin Infrastructure Services Luxembourg S.à.r.l. and Antin Energia Termosolar B.V. v. Kingdom of Spain,* ICSID Case No. ARB/13/31 Award (15 June 2018) para. 556; *Eiser Infrastructure Ltd. and Energia Solar Luxembourg v. Spain,* ICSID Case No. ARB/13/36 Award (4 May 2017), para. 370.

1469. *Blusun S.A., J.-P. Lecorcier AND M. Stein v. Italy,* ICSID Case No. ARB/14/3 Award, 27 December 2016, para. 319.

1470. *Mamidoil Jetoil Greek Petroleum Products Société S.A. v. Republic of Albania,* ICSID Case No. ARB/11/24 Award (30 March 2015) para. 660.

1471. *Eiser Infrastructure Ltd. and Energia Solar Luxembourg v. Spain,* ICSID Case No. ARB/13/36 Award (4 May 2017), para. 365.

As revealed in Chapter 6, section §6.05, the special economic and/or sociopolitical circumstances in a host state became an important factor in deciding on the protection of the legitimate expectations of an investor.

Tribunals stressed that the subjective interests of an investor are not the sole consideration in the assessment of legitimate expectations. The economic or sociopolitical circumstances in a host state that affected such a state's conduct leading to interference with the investor's expectations should also be taken into account.

Circumstances which have been taken into account by tribunals in their assessment of the legitimate expectations of an investor include: an economic and financial crisis;[1472] the political and economic transition in post-Soviet countries;[1473] the economic challenge of an electricity tariff deficit in the renewable energy sector; and - in some cases - the different levels of a state's development.[1474]

Tribunals have found that in a situation of economic and financial crisis or sociopolitical transition, the investor could not have expected that the host state would act as it would have acted in normal circumstances. Tribunals have found that when some of the host state's representations have not turned out to be true - which interfered with the expectations of the investor - this does not necessarily lead to a breach of the investor's legitimate expectations. In some instances, tribunals have accepted the justification put forward by the host state that the measure that had been adopted in order to protect the public interest was necessary to remedy the consequences of the economic crisis or the post-transition period in that country.[1475] In the renewable energy cases, the tribunals assessed whether the state had undermined the legitimate expectations of the investors by transforming the regulatory framework with the purpose to address the tariff deficit. The decisions in these cases demonstrate that the balance between the state's right to regulate and the protection of the legitimate expectations varies per case. It depends on how much weight the tribunal gave to the various elements as explained in the sections §6.03-§6.06. In the cases, in which the consideration of stability had occupied the central role, the tribunals tended to impose more limits on the state's right to regulate by directing their primary focus to the impact the regulatory change had on the investor.[1476] In the decisions, in which the stability of the regulatory framework had been interpreted more restrictively, the tribunals tend to impose more requirements on protecting legitimate expectations of an investor, e.g. the

1472. *El Paso v. Argentina*, ICSID Case No. ARB/03/15 Award (31 October 2011) para. 358; *Total v. Argentina*, ICSID Case No. ARB/04/01 Decision on Liability (27 December 2010) para. 168.
1473. *Genin v. Estonia*, ICSID Case No. ARB/99/2 Award (25 June 2001) para. 370.
1474. *Mamidoil Jetoil Greek Petroleum Products Société S.A. v. Republic of Albania*, ICSID Case No. ARB/11/24 Award (30 March 2015) para. 626.
1475. *See* Chapter 6. Examples of cases where some of the state's measures have been justified because of an economic crisis or a sociopolitical and economic transition include *Genin v. Estonia*, ICSID Case No. ARB/99/2 Award (25 June 2001) para. 370; *National Grid v. Argentina*, UNCITRAL, Award (3 November 2008), para. 180; *Total v. Argentina*, ICSID Case No. ARB/04/01 Decision on Liability (27 December 2010) para. 167.
1476. *Eiser Infrastructure Ltd. and Energia Solar Luxembourg v. Spain*, ICSID Case No. ARB/13/36 Award (4 May 2017) para. 382. *Antin Infrastructure Services Luxembourg S.à.r.l. and Antin Energia Termosolar B.V. v. Kingdom of Spain*, ICSID Case No. ARB/13/31 Award (15 June 2018) para. 532.

requirement of having performed a proper due diligence investigation, thereby providing more room for the state's regulatory flexibility.[1477]

(iv) The element of the conduct of an investor: due diligence and risk assessment

The investor's conduct is another relevant factor that has been emphasised by tribunals in determining whether the legitimate expectations of an investor give rise to protection under the FET standard. An investor is expected to exercise proper due diligence and to conduct a risk assessment when considering investing in a host state. Having applied due diligence and a proper risk assessment can play an important role in the argument of the investor that it relied upon its legitimate expectations.[1478] As follows from the analysis of the investment cases in Chapter 6, section §6.06, an investor, in claiming protection under the notion of legitimate expectations, has to be aware of and take into consideration the relevant host state's regulations, policies and decisions that are pertinent to its investment. The investor is also expected to take into account the political, economic and social background prevailing in the host state at the time of the investment, in order to reasonably assess the possibility of major changes in the host state.[1479] The threshold for the violation of the legitimate expectations is whether the state's contested regulatory changes were not foreseeable by a prudent investor. [1480] The foreseeability can be determined by the efforts undertaken by an investor to assess the risks of change. These efforts can be supported by reports and communication with the state's bodies and organisations that can provide reliable information regarding the regulatory framework.[1481] An investor's lack of efforts in conducting a due diligence investigation may contribute to a tribunal's conclusion that its (legitimate) expectations have not been breached under the FET standard.[1482]

1477. *Charanne Construction v. Spain*, SCC Case No. 062/2012 Award (21 January 2016) para. 499; *Blusun S.A., J.-P. Lecorcier AND M. Stein v. Italy*, ICSID Case No. ARB/14/3 Award, 27 December 2016, para. 319; *Isolux Netherlands, BV v. Kingdom of Spain*, SCC Case V2013/153 Award (17 July 2016) para. 781.
1478. M. Potestà, 'Legitimate Expectations in Investment Treaty Law: Understanding the Roots and the Limits of a Controversial Concept' [2013] 28(1) *ICSID Review*, 38; M. Sornarajah, Resistance and Change in the International Law on Foreign Investments (Cambridge University Press, 2015) 278.
1479. F. Dupuy and P.-M. Dupuy, 'What to Expect from Legitimate Expectations? A Critical Appraisal and Look Into the Future of the "Legitimate Expectations" Doctrine in International Investment Law', in M.A. Raouf, et al. (eds) *Festschrift Ahmed Sadek El- Kosheri: From the Arab World to the Globalization of International Law* (Kluwer, 2015) 292. *See also AES Summit v. Hungary*, ICSID Case No. ARB/07/22 Award (23 September 2010) para. 9.3.29. In assessing a claim that legitimate expectations had not been protected on the basis of the stability of the regulatory framework, the *AES* tribunal underlined that the 'legal framework is by definition subject to change as it adapts to new circumstances day by day and a state has the sovereign right to exercise its powers which include legislative acts'.
1480. *Isolux Netherlands, BV v. Kingdom of Spain*, SCC Case V2013/153 Award (17 July 2016) para. 781.
1481. *Masdar Solar & Wind Cooperatief U.A. v. Kingdom of Spain*, ICSID Case No. ARB/14/1 Award (16 May 2018) para. 497.
1482. *Mamidoil Jetoil Greek Petroleum Products Société S.A. v. Republic of Albania*, ICSID Case No. ARB/11/24 Award (30 March 2015) para. 634; *Parkerings v. Lithuania*, ICSID Case No. ARB/05/8 Award (11 September 2007) para. 335.

[C] Conditions Focusing on the Lawfulness of the State's Measure

The state's right to regulate in the public interest is central to the assessment of the lawfulness of the host state's measures under the FET standard. In deciding on the contested state's measures, tribunals assess three conditions: (1) the legitimacy of the objective of the state's measure; (2) the compliance of the state's measure with the principles of reasonableness, proportionality, the prohibition of arbitrariness, non-discrimination and transparency; and (3) the legality of the state's measure under national law in relation to the breach of the FET standard. These three conditions are not always systematically tested by tribunals, and they are not applied in a cumulative way, but they have appeared to be important conditions in the assessment of the contested state's measure by arbitral tribunals. The following conditions for the lawful exercise of the state's right to regulate stem from the tests which have been used by tribunals in assessing the state's measure.

(i) The legitimacy of the objective of the state's measure

In balancing the state's right to regulate and its obligations towards an investor, in many decisions tribunals have assessed whether a disputed state's measure pursued a legitimate objective. The criteria for determining the legitimacy of a state's objective are: (i) whether a state's measure was directed at a public interest; and (ii) whether it had been justified by the state through records and other evidence. These two criteria are of a different legal nature. The first deals with the content and significance of the objective of the state's measure. The second concerns the justification for the presence of the required objective.

Regarding the first criterion: from the investment jurisprudence discussed in Chapter 7, it follows that various state objectives can qualify as pursuing a public interest, i.e. the modernisation of the transport sector, the protection of ecological interests, the protection of human rights, the protection of the right of access to (clean) water, the protection of public health, the protection of indigenous peoples, the protection of cultural heritage, the reformation of the banking sector, the fight against corruption, the reduction of excessive profits of energy companies and the alignment of the electricity sector with the EU market.[1483]

Tribunals differentiate between legitimate and illegitimate objectives. The illegitimate objectives of a state's measure are those that are in bad faith or are manifestly without reason.[1484] Furthermore, as demonstrated in Chapter 7, section §7.02[D], some tribunals have found the objectives of the state's measure to be illegitimate because they were one-sided and primarily motivated by or based on the 'political agenda' of certain state authorities.[1485] In a number of investment decisions, the presence of

1483. Chapter 7, section §7.02 discusses cases that include a range of public interests assessed by tribunals.

1484. *Glamis v. US* [2009] NAFTA, ICSID 48 ILM 1039 Award (8 June 2009) para. 805. *Philip Morris v. Uruguay*, ICSID Case No. ARB/10/7 Award (8 July 2016) para. 399.

1485. J. Bonnitcha, Substantive Protection under Investment Treaties: A Legal and Economic Analysis (Cambridge University Press, 2014), e-book, section 4.7.4. pp. 189-198.

illegitimate state objectives motivated by national politics had been a defining criterion in finding a breach of the FET standard.[1486]

Regarding the second criterion: tribunals have emphasised the importance of a justification for the state's objective. They have thereby required that the objective of the state's measure must be logical and reflected in the state's records. In some cases, compliance with international obligations under national laws and international treaties has served as one of the justifications for introducing measures aimed at protecting public health or safeguarding the human right to water.[1487]

A judicial point of departure in assessing the objective of the state's measure taken in the public interest is the extent of deference applied by tribunals in judging the state's measure. Tribunals have referred to the concepts of deference and/or the margin of appreciation with regard to the choice of measures taken to achieve the public interest objective.[1488] In affording deference to the assessment of the state's measures, tribunals have exercised restraint in making judgments regarding the content and significance of the objective chosen to address a particular public concern.[1489] Several tribunals have underlined that the state has the right to regulate for the protection of public health and that they – the tribunals – should provide a higher degree of deference to public health objectives pursued by states.[1490] In these cases, tribunals did not question the choices of the states, acknowledging that states' specialised public health bodies had better expertise in making decisions concerning public health in those countries, in comparison to arbitrators who do not possess such specific knowledge.[1491]

(ii) Whether the state's measure complies with the principles of reasonableness, proportionality, the prohibition of arbitrariness, non-discrimination and transparency

1486. *Tecmed v. Mexico*, ICSID Case No. ARB(AF)/00/2 Award (29 May 2003) para. 164; *Gold Reserve v. Venezuela*, ICSID Case No. ARB(AF)/09/1 Award (22 September 2014) para. 590; *Azurix Corp. v. The Argentine Republic*, ICSID Case No. ARB/01/12 Award (14 July 2006) para. 375.

1487. *Philip Morris v. Uruguay*, ICSID Case No. ARB/10/7 Award (8 July 2016) para. 391; *Chemtura v. Canada* [2010] NAFTA-UNCITRAL Arbitration, Award (2 August 2010) para. 139; *Chemtura v. Canada* [2010] NAFTA-UNCITRAL Arbitration, Award (2 August 2010); *Urbaser S.A. and Consorcio de Aguas Bilbao Bizkaia, Bilbao Biskaia Ur Partzuergoa v. Argentina*, ICSID Case No. ARB/07/26 Award (8 December 2016).

1488. *See* section §7.04. *See also* section §4.04[B] on deference and a margin of appreciation.

1489. As underlined by Henckels, tribunals tend to adopt deference, specifically in cases concerning public interests that involve 'uncertainty as to what the "right" conclusion to an issue should be, by attaching weight to the primary decision-maker's view and refraining from making or from acting on the adjudicator's assessment of the matter'. (p. 311). C. Henckels, 'Balancing Investment Protection and Sustainable Development in Investor-State Arbitration: The Role of Deference', in A Bjorklund (ed.) *Yearbook on International Investment Law & Policy 2012-2013* (2013) 311. *See* Chapter 4, section §4.04[B].

1490. *Philip Morris v. Uruguay*, ICSID Case No. ARB/10/7 Award (8 July 2016) para. 399.

1491. This conclusion corresponds with the argument made by Henckels in the chapter of her book where she conceptualises the notion of deference. She argues that 'where uncertainty remains after adjudicators have taken into account the evidence of the parties in relation to a particular matter, this rationale for deference suggests that a tribunal should afford a measure of deference to the state due to the state's greater expertise and institutional competence as a regulator.' C. Henckels, Proportionality and Deference in Investor-State Arbitration (Cambridge University Press, 2015) 40.

Tribunals assess a host state's measure that is being contested under the FET standard according to the international law principles of: (i) reasonableness, proportionality and the prohibition of arbitrariness; (ii) non-discrimination; and (iii) transparency.

In most of the cases addressed in Chapter 7, tribunals refer to the principles of reasonableness, proportionality and the prohibition of arbitrariness in judging the state's measure. Following an analysis of the case law, and in consensus with a number of scholars, 'tribunals do not appear to attach significance to the differences in terminology.' [1492] As Ortino emphasised, the 'overlap between reasonableness and proportionality is extensive.'[1493] There are three steps in assessing reasonableness and proportionality.

The principles of reasonableness, proportionality and the prohibition of arbitrariness – The first step that is performed by most FET tribunals includes an assessment of whether there is a reasonable relationship between the state's measure and its objective (the suitability test). Under this test, tribunals evaluate whether the contested measure has contributed to the achievement of the desired objective. [1494] Several tribunals have stressed that the correlation between a state's measure and its objective can be assessed through the way in which the measure was implemented.[1495] If the state's measure was implemented in a reasonable, proportionate and non-arbitrary way and it corresponded with the stated objective, tribunals usually deem this to be sufficient for finding that the measure was reasonably related to its objective.[1496] As has been demonstrated in this study, the principle of the prohibition of arbitrariness, alongside reasonableness and proportionality, have often been applied by FET tribunals in discussing the relationship between the objective and the measure in question.[1497]

The second step that is undertaken by some tribunals in assessing the reasonableness and/or proportionality of the contested state measure is whether the measure was necessary for achieving the desired objective (the necessity test).[1498] Under this step, tribunals may examine the alternative options that a state could have employed and that would have had a less damaging effect on the investor, while achieving the

1492. C. Henckles, Proportionality and Deference in Investor-State Arbitration (Cambridge University Press, 2015) 71. *See also* R. Klager who makes a similar point. R. Klager (2013) 289. *See also* U. Kriebaum, 'Arbitrary/Unreasonable or Discriminatory Measures', in M. Bungenberg et al. (eds) *International Investment Law* (Nomos, 2015) 792. The author emphasises that in some investment decisions, tribunals refer to the notions of 'arbitrary' and 'unreasonable' interchangeably, without making any distinction between the two.

1493. F. Ortino, 'Investment Treaties, Sustainable Development and Reasonableness Review: A Case Against Strict Proportionality Balancing' [2017] *Leiden Journal of International Law*, 87.

1494. *Ibid.* The suitability test is also referred to and described in Chapter 4, in section §4.04[A].

1495. *AES Summit v. Hungary*, ICSID Case No. ARB/07/22 Award (23 September 2010) paras 10.3.7-10.3.9.

1496. These requirements are based on an analysis of the cases in Chapter 7, section §7.04[A][1].

1497. J. Bonnitcha, Substantive Protection under Investment Treaties: A Legal and Economic Analysis (Cambridge University Press, 2014), section: 4.4.1, p. 45 (e-book). P. Dumberry, 'The Prohibition Against Arbitrary Conduct and the Fair and Equitable Treatment Standard under NAFTA Article 1105' [2014] 15(1) *The Journal of World and Investment*, 124.

1498. Note that necessity test in the context of reasonableness and proportionality is different from the necessity defence, i.e. the principle of international law codified in Article 25 of the International Law Commission's Articles on State Responsibility.

same objective intended by the original measure. Tribunals differ in their approach towards assessing the possibility of adopting less-restrictive measures affecting the investor's investment. In cases in which tribunals afforded deference or a margin of appreciation for the states' measures taken in the public interest, the tribunals were reluctant to discuss alternative measures.[1499] In other cases, e.g. those concerning the privatisation of water in Argentina, the tribunals tested the necessity of the states' measures, focusing primarily on the impact of the measure on the investor. Here the deference afforded to the states was limited.[1500]

The third step, which is rarely undertaken by FET tribunals, focuses on the question of whether the contested state's conduct or measure that has been taken in the public interest has had an excessive effect on the investor, in comparison to the benefits of the addressed public interest (the proportionality *stricto sensu* test).[1501] In several cases, tribunals have assessed the impact of the loss suffered by an investor as a consequence of the state's measure. The relevant criterion in this regard has been the excessive financial burden experienced by the investor as a result of the state's measures. In the cases assessed in Chapter 7, in evaluating the public interest and the loss suffered by investors, the tribunals found that the financial consequences suffered by the investor had not been disproportionate to the state's policy regulating this public interest.[1502]

However, it should be noted that tribunals have not always followed all three steps in assessing the state's measure. They have often applied just one or two of the three aforementioned steps under the principles of reasonableness and proportionality and the prohibition of arbitrariness.

The principle of non-discrimination – The other principle according to which tribunals will judge the state's contested measure is the principle of non-discrimination. The discriminatory treatment of an investor does not correspond to the notion of equity and fairness embedded in the FET standard. Consequently, the prohibition of discriminatory treatment is considered to be an imperative component in the assessment of the FET standard. Tribunals do not limit discrimination to a specific form. However, in FET cases nationality-based discrimination is the most common contention in disputes. Therefore, in assessing discriminatory treatment under the FET standard, tribunals compare the position of a foreign investor with that of one or more national investors. Tribunals do not usually require that a foreign investor is treated in the same way as a national investor.[1503] The determining factor in assessing the non-discrimination principle under the FET standard is whether or not the difference in

1499. *Philip Morris v. Uruguay*, ICSID Case No. ARB/10/7 Award (8 July 2016) para. 419.
1500. *Impregilo S.p.A v. Argentina*, ICSID Case No. ARB/07/17 Award (21 June 2011) para. 330; *AWG v. Argentina* [2010] UNCITRAL Arbitration, Decision on Liability (30 July 2010) para. 235.
1501. F. Ortino, 'Investment Treaties, Sustainable Development and Reasonableness Review: A Case Against Strict Proportionality Balancing' [2017] *Leiden Journal of International Law*, 88.
1502. Chapter 7, section §7.04[A][3].
1503. R. Klager, (2011) 193 and 285.

treatment between the foreign investor and the national investor is non-arbitrary and has a reasonable explanation.[1504]

The principle of transparency – The principle of transparency also plays a role in the assessment of the contested state's measure by FET tribunals. The obligation of transparency in the context of the FET standard has been relevant in some decisions. Tribunals are consistent in stating that states must communicate with, and provide information to, an investor and should act transparently in doing so. In evaluating the obligation of transparency, tribunals have indicated that a host state has to have adequate and open communication with the investor and must share sufficient information concerning any changes to the status of the investment and/or laws and policies that may potentially affect the investment by an investor.[1505]

(iii) The legality of a state's measure under national law

The legality of a state's measure under national law has been part of the assessment of the FET standard and the right to regulate. In some cases, a state's violation of national law may contribute to a breach under the FET standard. The case law analysis is conducted in Chapter 7, section §7.05, and the literature indicates that in order for a violation of domestic law to qualify as a breach of the (international) FET standard, such a violation should be qualified and serious.[1506] As follows from several investment cases assessed in this study, a state's serious arbitrary conduct, e.g. blatant disregard of domestic rules, may be considered as a violation of the FET standard.[1507]

§8.06 THE REFLECTION OF FET JURISPRUDENCE IN THE NEW GENERATION OF IIAs

[A] Introduction

This section analyses how the investment jurisprudence in FET cases has been reflected in the new generation of IIAs in regard to the FET standard and the state's right to regulate. To evaluate this issue, two questions are addressed: *first*, which elements that have emerged from the FET case law as being relevant in relation to the state's right to regulate have been incorporated into the new IIAs, and which elements have not? *Second*, has the balance between the protection of investors under the FET standard and the state's right to regulate in these new IIAs shifted in comparison to FET decisions, and if so, in which direction?

1504. *Ibid.*, 196; F. Ortino, 'From "Non-discrimination" to "Reasonableness": A Paradigm Shift in International Economic Law?' (2005) Jean Monet Working Paper 01/05, 49.

1505. *Ioan Micula v. Romania*, ICSID Case No. ARB/05/20 Final Award (11 December 2013) para. 870; *Saluka Investments BV v. Czech Republic* [2006] UNCITRAL Arbitration Partial Award (17 March 2006) para. 499.

1506. J. Bonnitcha, Substantive Protection under Investment Treaties: A Legal and Economic Analysis (Cambridge University Press, 2014), e-book, section 4.6.2, p. 142; S. Schill, (2010) 162.

1507. *See* Chapter 7, section §7.05 on the legality of a state's measure under national law. *See also* Table 4 in Chapter 7, section §7.05[D].

[B] The Extent of Codification of FET Investment Jurisprudence in the New Generation of IIAs

The new generation of IIAs discussed in this section comprises of the Comprehensive Economic and Trade Agreement between the EU and Canada (CETA),[1508] the EU – Vietnam FTA[1509] and the EU – Singapore FTA.[1510] These agreements clarify what constitutes FET by, first, providing a list of state obligations owed towards an investor; second, the aforementioned IIAs contain references to the protection of the legitimate expectations of the investor; third, these agreements include provisions on the state's right to regulate in the public interest; fourth, in CETA, a provision is included on the assessment of the legality of the state's measure under national law. In the following paragraphs of this section, these provisions – all relevant for the application of the FET standard and the state's right to regulate – are compared with the elements identified in the investment jurisprudence analysed in this study.

(1) Specified state obligations towards an investor under the FET standard

In the IIAs concluded between the EU and Canada,[1511] the EU and Vietnam[1512] and the EU and Singapore,[1513] the obligation to provide FET has been clarified through an exhaustive, but expandable[1514] list of state obligations. The European Commission explains the approach towards the formulation of the FET standard in these IIAs by providing that 'the main objective of the EU is to clarify the [FET] standard, in particular by incorporating key lessons learned from case-law. This would eliminate uncertainty for both states and investors.'[1515] As the subsequent analysis of IIAs and the jurisprudence will demonstrate, the obligations formulated in the aforementioned IIAs correspond to those set out in the investment jurisprudence. However, the extent to which the obligations enumerated in the aforementioned IIAs and the FET investment jurisprudence converge and depart from each other is explained below.

1508. CETA, (signed on 30 October 2016) http://ec.europa.eu/trade/policy/in-focus/ceta/ accessed on 15 March 2017.
1509. The EU-Vietnam FTA, draft text (January 2016) http://trade.ec.europa.eu/doclib/press/index.cfm?id=1437 accessed on 15 June 2018.
1510. The EU-Singapore FTA, draft (April 2018), Investment Protection Agreement http://trade.ec.europa.eu/doclib/press/index.cfm?id=961 accessed on 12 June 2018.
1511. CETA, (signed on 30 October 2016) http://ec.europa.eu/trade/policy/in-focus/ceta/ accessed on 15 June 2018.
1512. The EU-Vietnam FTA, draft text (January 2016) http://trade.ec.europa.eu/doclib/press/index.cfm?id=1437 accessed on 15 June 2018.
1513. The EU-Singapore FTA, (April 2018), Investment Protection Agreement http://trade.ec.europa.eu/doclib/press/index.cfm?id=961 accessed on 12 June 2018.
1514. As explained in Chapter 3, section §3.03[E]: IIAs' additional agreement of the parties on the interpretation of the FET standard, CETA in Article 8.10(3) provides for possibility to review and to update the content of the FET standard by the contracting parties through a treaty organ. The same mechisms is contained in EU treaties with Vietnam and Singapore.
1515. European Commission, 'Online public consultation on investment protection and investor-to-state dispute settlement (ISDS) in the Transatlantic Trade and Investment Partnership Agreement' (European Commission Consultation, 13 January 2015) 55.

In the three aforementioned IIAs, the state obligations towards an investor have been formulated almost identically.[1516] To exemplify, the FET standard provision in Article 8.10(1) of the CETA provides that '[e]ach Party shall accord in its territory to covered investments of the other Party and to investors with respect to their covered investments fair and equitable treatment and full protection and security in accordance with paragraphs 2 through 6.'[1517] Article 8.10(2) of the CETA stipulates which type of state behaviour would violate the FET standard:

> (a) denial of justice in criminal, civil or administrative proceedings; (b) fundamental breach of due process, including a fundamental breach of transparency, in judicial and administrative proceedings; (c) manifest arbitrariness; (d) targeted discrimination on manifestly wrongful grounds, such as gender, race or religious belief; and (e) abusive treatment of investors, such as coercion, duress and harassment.[1518]

Some of these types of violations were also highlighted in the investment jurisprudence. In particular, tribunals found that state conduct violated the FET standard if a state did not comply with the principles of the prohibition of arbitrariness, non-discrimination and transparency (Chapter 7). This practice in case law is reflected in the analysed IIAs.[1519]

The following paragraphs will discuss how, and to what extent, such state obligations correspond to the FET investment jurisprudence. The order follows the structure of the case law analysis conducted in Chapter 7. First, the prohibition of arbitrariness is addressed. This principle - together with the principles of reasonableness and proportionality - is central to the assessment conducted by arbitral tribunals with regards to a state's contested measure.[1520] It is noted that the principles of reasonableness and proportionality are not included in the three analysed IIAs under the heading of 'state obligations'. In section §8.06[C], this will be elaborated. Second, the principle of non-discrimination is discussed, and third, the application of the principle of transparency in IIAs and the case law is explained.

1516. The lists of the state's obligations in the three IIAs are very similar. However, some variations exist. The variations in the EU-Vietnam FTA and the EU-Singapore FTA include: in Article 2.4(2)(b) of the EU-Singapore FTA, a reference is only made to a 'fundamental breach of due process'; in Article 14(2)(b) of the EU-Vietnam FTA, the obligation is phrased as 'fundamental breach of due process in judicial and administrative proceedings'. Further: in Article 2.4(2)(d) of the Singapore FTA, the obligation is formulated as 'harassment, coercion, abuse of power or similar bad faith conduct' and in Article 14(2)(e) of the Vietnam FTA, the obligation is formulated as 'abusive treatment such as coercion, abuse of power or similar bad faith conduct'.
1517. CETA, Article 8.10(1).
1518. CETA, Article 8.10(2)(a-e).
1519. In Article 2.4(2) of the EU-Singapore, reference is made to the prohibition of manifest arbitrariness, but not to transparency and discrimination. In Article 14(2) of the EU-Vietnam FTA, the reference is made to the prohibition of manifest arbitrariness, prohibition of discrimination but not to the principle of transparency.
1520. *See* Chapter 7, section §7.04[A].

The prohibition of arbitrariness

The prohibition of arbitrariness has been formulated in all three aforementioned IIAs. As cited, Article 8.10(2)(c) of the CETA provides that states should not treat an investor in a manifestly arbitrary way. Some scholars have underlined that by including the qualifier 'manifest' as a part of arbitrariness, the contracting states indicated that only serious arbitrary conduct would give rise to a violation of the FET standard.[1521] The concept of 'manifest arbitrariness' in relation to the FET standard has been mostly referred to by tribunals in NAFTA jurisprudence.[1522] In *Glamis v. US*, the tribunal explained that in order to violate the MST of aliens under customary international law laid down in Article 1105 of the NAFTA, the state's conduct 'should be sufficiently egregious and shocking, the example of which is manifest arbitrariness'.[1523] Following the case law analysis undertaken in Chapter 6, tribunals usually refer to the prohibition of arbitrariness alongside reasonableness and proportionality, in particular when discussing the relationship between the state policy objective and the content of the state measure, i.e. the suitability test.[1524] Tribunals emphasise that a measure can be considered arbitrary if it is not reasonably related to the state's legitimate objective.[1525] In comparing the case law and the provisions in IIAs, it is important to note that the prohibition of arbitrariness has been formulated more broadly, in comparison to the

1521. C. Tietje, K. Crow, The Reform of Investment Protection Rules in CETA, TTIP and other Recent EU-FTAs: Convincing? (December 13, 2016), 21. Article 8.10(2) (c) CETA requires 'manifest arbitrariness' which limits the scope of arbitrary discrimination that can fall under the FET provisions. Available at SSRN: https://papers.ssrn.com/sol3/papers.cfm?abstract_id =2884380. Also *see*: S. Schill et al, The Brave New (American) World of International Investment Law: Substantive Investment Protection Standards in Mega-Regionals in T. Rensmann, ed., *Mega-Regional Trade Agreements*, (Springer, 2017) 141. 'The provision's use of restrictive language such as ... "manifest arbitrariness" ... signifies a high threshold for a breach of fair and equitable treatment'.

1522. *See*: U. Kriebaum, 'FET and Expropriation in the Comprehensive Economic Trade Agreement between the European Union and Canada (CETA)' [2016] 13(1) *Transnational Dispute Management*, 19. Kriebaum refers to *Thunderbird v. Mexico*; *Glamis v. US*, *Gemplus v. Mexico*, where tribunals directly or indirectly refer to manifest arbitrariness (p. 20). *See also*: M. Paparinskins, Europe's Formulation of Fair and Equitable Treatment: Europe as an Investment Treaty Actor BIICL Investment Treaty Forum Meeting, Stockholm, 12 June 2015. The author elaborates that the CETA's FET standard list of obligations, including the manifest arbitrariness, has been primarily drawn from several NAFTA decisions.

1523. *Glamis v. US*, para. 616. Even though the concept of manifest arbitrariness is primarily referred to in NAFTA jurisprudence, it is also mentioned in decisions outside the NAFTA context, e.g. *Philip Morris v. Uruguay*.

1524. J. Bonnitcha, Substantive Protection under Investment Treaties: A Legal and Economic Analysis (Cambridge University Press, 2014), section: 4.4.1, p. 45 (e-book). P. Dumberry, 'The Prohibition Against Arbitrary Conduct and the Fair and Equitable Treatment Standard under NAFTA Article 1105' [2014] 15 *The Journal of World and Investment*, p. 124. The author states that FET 'tribunals do not appear to attach significance to the differences in terminology in terms of arbitrariness or unreasonableness, instead using these terms synonymously.' Also *see*: *Electrabel v. Hungary*, ICSID Case No. ARB/07/1 Final Award (25 November 2015) para. 167. In this award, the tribunal used the term arbitrariness as an umbrella term comprising of 'references to "arbitrariness," "irrationality," "unreasonable," "inequitable" and "disproportionate" treatment'.

1525. *Electrabel v. Hungary*, ICSID Case No. ARB/07/1 Final Award (25 November 2015) para. 179; *AES Summit v. Hungary*, ICSID Case No. ARB/07/22 Award (23 September 2010) paras 10.3.35-10.3.37.

application of this principle by tribunals in the assessment of the contested state's measure.

The principle of non-discrimination

Article 8.10(2)(d) of the CETA refers to the prohibition of 'targeted discrimination on manifestly wrongful grounds, such as gender, race or religious belief'.[1526] Such a formulation provides for extensive grounds under which the claim of an investor concerning the state's discriminatory treatment can give rise to a violation of the FET standard. There are a number of decisions of NAFTA tribunals where discrimination was assessed in the context of the FET standard. For example, in *Waste Management II v. Mexico*, the tribunal – in interpreting the international minimum standard – stated that the conduct would be discriminatory if it 'exposes the claimant to sectional or racial prejudice'.[1527]

Discrimination on the basis of *nationality* has explicitly not been included as one of the grounds in the CETA FET provision, nor has it been included in the EU-Singapore nor the EU-Vietnam FTAs. In FET cases, even though tribunals have assessed discrimination on the basis of nationality, such assessments have been conducted only to a limited extent.[1528] This is because the grounds for nationality-based discrimination are included in, and determined under, other provisions of IIAs. In the same vein, in all three IIAs, nationality-based discrimination has been included in separate clauses, i.e. the NT and MFN treatment clauses.

The principle of transparency

The principle of transparency has also been included in the CETA. Article 8.10(2)(b) refers to a 'fundamental breach of due process', with the 'fundamental breach of transparency in judicial and administrative proceedings' as an example of a breach of due process.[1529] The reference to transparency in the framework of due process in Article 8.10(2)(b) of the CETA does not, however, necessarily restrict the application of this principle under the FET standard only to a 'fundamental breach of transparency in judicial and administrative proceedings'. The examined case law on the FET standard demonstrates that tribunals referred to a broader notion of transparency in the state's conduct dealing with an investor. In judging a state's conduct against the rights of investors, tribunals referred to the obligation of transparency in a variety of situations,

1526. CETA, Article 8.10(2)(d).

1527. *Waste Management v. Mexico*, ('Number 2'), ICSID Case No. ARB(AF)/00/3 decided under NAFTA, para. 98. In the *Loewen v. US* award, in assessing the fairness of the trial of the investor, the tribunal has emphasised that 'responsibility of the courts of a State to ensure that litigation is free from discrimination against a foreign litigant and that the foreign litigant should not become the victim of sectional or local prejudice.' *Loewen Group, Inc. and Raymond L. Loewen v. United States of America*, ICSID Case No. ARB(AF)/98/3, para. 123.

1528. R. Klager, Fair and Equitable Treatment in International Investment Law (Cambridge University Press, 2011) 193.

1529. CETA, Article 8.10(2)(b).

i.e. requiring states to act transparently in relation to an investor by, e.g., communicating openly and by providing and disclosing relevant information.[1530] Reference is made to section §7.04[C] of Chapter 7.

Reflections

From the perspective of balancing the state's right to regulate, on the one hand, and affording FET treatment to an investor, on the other, the following conclusions can be drawn. By including a closed list of state obligations into IIAs, a step has been made towards better protecting the state's right to regulate and clarifying the extent to which investors can expect their investments to be protected under the FET standard. The formulation of the FET standard's obligation in the discussed IIAs demonstrates that only serious state violations directed at the investor will give rise to a breach of the FET standard.[1531] This is primarily achieved through the use of qualifiers, such as 'fundamental' breach of transparency and 'manifest' arbitrariness. The state obligations are defined in such a way so as to provide guidance to arbitrators. According to these IIAs, only if the state conduct reaches a certain threshold of gravity, it can be considered as violating the FET standard.[1532] It is noted that the principles of reasonableness and proportionality that play a role in tribunals' assessment of the contested measure have not been included in the provisions clarifying the obligation of a state towards an investor in these IIAs.

(2) The role of the legitimate expectations of an investor

Reference to the protection of legitimate expectations did not appear explicitly in the FET standard provisions of IIAs until recently. However, each of the new IIAs between the EU and Canada, the EU and Singapore and the EU and Vietnam includes a provision that refers to the legitimate expectations of an investor as part of the FET standard. The extent to which the scope of legitimate expectations included in these IIAs corresponds to the investment jurisprudence, and the points on which the application of this element diverges from the case law is analysed further below.

1530. *See* Chapter 7, section §7.04[C]. Also *see*: K.J. Vandevelde, 'A Unified Theory of Fair and Equitable Treatment' [2010] 43 *International Law and Politics*, 83-84. On the basis of the case law, Vandevelde points out that transparency applies not only to host state laws but also to host state policies. In some cases, not only the disclosure of relevant laws and regulations but also a lack of reasons for certain actions taken by the state led to the claim of a lack of transparency.

1531. N.-B. Osterwalder, H. Mann, A Response to the European Commission's December 2013 Document Investment Provisions in the EU-Canada Free Trade Agreement (CETA), February 2014, p. 6. 'This closed list seems very reasonable and also useful to provide the investor with clear protection from unacceptable treatment by the state'.

1532. The European Commission has clarified its goal in regard to the FET standard, providing: 'the standard of "fair and equitable treatment" in CETA is a clear, closed text which defines precisely the standard of treatment, without leaving unwelcome discretion to the Members of the Tribunal.' European Commission, Investment provisions in the EU-Canada Free Trade Agreement (CETA), Factsheet on investor-to-state dispute settlement (ISDS) in CETA, November 2013, http://trade.ec.europa.eu/doclib/docs/2013/november/tradoc_151918.pdf accessed on 12 June 2018.

In investment jurisprudence, the concept of legitimate expectations that is directed at the protection of an investor's legal rights has been recognised as a key element of the FET standard.[1533] In comparison to the case law, the role of the concept of legitimate expectations in the discussed IIAs appears to be reduced. This conclusion is based on (1) the place of legitimate expectations in the IIAs; (2) the formulation of the scope of legitimate expectations; and (3) the role of the stability of the general regulatory framework in the context of legitimate expectations. These points are addressed below.

The place of legitimate expectations

In the treaties, and as discussed above, the protection of the legitimate expectations of an investor has been placed outside of the list of state obligations.[1534] Admittedly, all three IIAs provide that a tribunal 'may take into account' the element of legitimate expectations in deciding on whether there has been a violation of the FET standard.[1535] However, in comparison to the other state obligations addressed above, which are included in the list under the FET standard, it appears that the protection of the legitimate expectations of an investor is more of a complementary element that a

1533. It can be observed in FET investment decisions (*see* Chapter 5). *See*: *Suez, Sociedad General de Aguas de Barcelona, S.A. and Vivendi Universal, S.A. v. Argentine Republic*, ICSID Case No. ARB/03/19 Decision on Liability (30 July 2010) para. 222. The tribunal stated that '[i]n an effort to develop an operational method for determining the existence or nonexistence of fair and equitable treatment, arbitral tribunals have increasingly taken into account the legitimate expectations that a host country has created in the investor and the extent to which conduct by the host government subsequent to the investment has frustrated those expectations.' For further analysis of the role of the legitimate expectations in the FET jurisprudence, *see*: Chapter 5. Also *see* in literature: J. Bonnitcha, Substantive Protection under Investment Treaties: A Legal and Economic Analysis (Cambridge University Press, 2014) 161-162. 'Since 2006, protection of the investor's legitimate expectations has emerged as the most significant element of the FET standard'; I. Laird and others, 'International Investment Law and Arbitration: 2014 in Review', in A.J. Bjorklund (ed.) *Yearbook on International Investment Law and Policy 2013-2014* (Oxford University Press, 2015) 105. Reviewing the decisions on the FET standard rendered in 2013, the authors emphasised that 'tribunals in 2013 recognized that the protection of the claimant's legitimate or reasonable expectations is a well-accepted component of the FET standard'.

1534. In all three IIAs, the legitimate expectations are included in the separate paragraph, where it is indicated that when applying the fair and equitable treatment obligation the tribunal may take into account the legitimate expectations of an investor. *See*: Article 8.10(4) CETA; Article 2.4(3) of the EU-Singapore FTA; Article 14(6) of the EU-Vietnam FTA.

1535. European Parliament, 'Study: The Investment Chapters of the EU's International Trade and Investment Agreements: In a Comparative Perspective' 2015, p. 141. Analysing CETA authors provide that 'a breach of legitimate expectations is not an independent category within the FET standard. Rather, it seems to been additional factor to be taken into account when determining a breach of any such category in the closed list.' *see*: http://www.europarl.europa.eu/RegData/etudes/STUD/2015/534998/EXPO_STU(2015)534998_EN.pdf accessed on 10 June 2018; Also *see*: U. Kriebaum, 'FET and Expropriation in the Comprehensive Economic Trade Agreement between the European Union and Canada (CETA)' [2016] 13(1) *Transnational Dispute Management*, 20. The author provides that the formulation of the legitimate expectations suggests that tribunals possess a 'margin of appreciation with regard to the relevance of the legitimate expectations' and they therefore may also decide not to take them into the account.

tribunal may take into account in determining whether the host state has breached the FET standard under the specific grounds laid down in the treaty.[1536]

The formulation of the scope of legitimate expectations

In the three recent IIAs, the formulation of the scope of the application of the concept of legitimate expectations appears to be more restrictive than in the FET jurisprudence. Under the three IIAs, a tribunal may take into account the legitimate expectations of an investor only if they are based on the state's specific representations. To exemplify, Article 8.10(4) of the CETA states that:

> when applying the above fair and equitable treatment obligation, the Tribunal may take into account whether a Party made a specific representation to an investor to induce a covered investment, that created a legitimate expectation, and upon which the investor relied in deciding to make or maintain the covered investment, but that the Party subsequently frustrated.[1537]

The EU-Singapore FTA and the EU-Vietnam FTA provide a more precise definition of the notion of specific representations. Article 2.4(3) of the EU-Singapore FTA states that 'the tribunal may take into account, where applicable, whether a Party made specific or unambiguous representations to an investor so as to induce the investment, that created legitimate expectations of a covered investor and which were reasonably relied upon by the covered investor, but that the Party subsequently frustrate.'[1538]

The inclusion of a 'specific representation' as a condition for taking into consideration the protection of the legitimate expectations of an investor in all three IIAs corresponds with the case law on the FET standard. According to arbitral tribunals, the presence of specific representations provided by a host state to an investor is the strongest factor in forming the legitimate expectations of an investor that can give rise to their protection under the FET standard.[1539]

The scope of specific representations under the concept of legitimate expectations included in the CETA, the EU-Singapore FTA and the EU-Vietnam FTA, replicate some of the criteria indicated by FET tribunals in their assessment of specific representations, and which are highlighted in Chapter 6 of this study.[1540] Tribunals judge the specificity of a state's representation on the basis of three criteria: (1) the competence of the state's authority; (2) the legal force of the specific representation, thereby taking into

1536. This conclusion is consistent with the clarification provided in the footnote to Article 2.4(3) of the EU-Singapore FTA which reads that 'for greater certainty, the frustration of legitimate expectations as described in this paragraph does not, by itself, amount to a breach of paragraph 2, and such frustration of legitimate expectations must arise out of the same events or circumstances that give rise to the breach of paragraph 2 [list of state's obligations]'.
1537. CETA, Article 8.10(4).
1538. The EU-Singapore FTA, Article 2.4(3). *See also*: the EU-Vietnam FTA, Article 14(6) in which it is provided that: 'When applying the above fair and equitable provisions, a Tribunal will take into account whether a Party made a specific representation to an investor to induce an investment referred to in Article 13. 1 (i) [Scope of section II Investment Protection], that created a legitimate expectation, and upon which the investor relied in deciding to make or maintain that investment, but that Party subsequently frustrated'.
1539. *See*: Chapter 6, section §6.03. Also *see*: R. Dolzer, C. Schreuer, (2nd edn., 2012) 371.
1540. *See* Chapter 6, sections §6.03[B] -§6.03[D].

consideration (i) the legal form, (ii) the content and (iii) the wording; and (3) the designation of the investor in the state's representation.

In the aforementioned treaties, a specific representation of an investor has been defined according to its *legal force*, i.e. the second criterion that emerged from the case law for establishing that a state representation is indeed a specific representation. In the treaties, reference is thereby made to the legal form and the content of the representation.[1541] Article 2.4(3) of the EU-Singapore FTA provides that in terms of its legal form, a representation should be 'specific' or 'unambiguous'.[1542] The EU-Singapore FTA and the EU-Vietnam FTA further define specific representations according to their content. For example, in Article 14(6) of the EU-Vietnam FTA and in Article 2.4(3) of the EU-Singapore FTA, it is provided that a specific representation should be made 'to induce an investment'.[1543] Furthermore, the footnote to Article 2.4(3) of the EU-Singapore FTA clarifies the meaning of inducement, providing that the state's representations should be 'made in order to convince the investor to continue with, not to liquidate or to make subsequent investments'.[1544] The description of the content provided in the EU-Singapore FTA and the EU-Vietnam FTA are in line with the case law. In testing the legal force of state representations, tribunals have often stressed that in order to qualify as 'specific representations', the content of such representations should be aimed at purposeful and specific inducement of an investment. Hence, all three elements that emerged from the examined case law as being relevant for deciding on the legal force of a representation, i.e. (i) the legal form, (ii) the content and (iii) the wording, have returned in the definitions concerning the specific representations offered in the three analysed IIAs.

With regards to the other two criteria concerning the determination of specific representations, i.e. *the competence of the state's authority* (first criterion) and *the designation of the investor* in the state's representations (third criterion), it is noted that the language in these IIAs seems to include these criteria as well. In all three IIAs, the formulation of the specific representations implies that the representation should originate from the state's authority and be directed at the concrete investor.

In establishing the specificity of the state's representations, the treaties appear to be stricter than the tribunals in the examined case law, requiring compliance with all three criteria. In comparison, tribunals do not apply the three criteria in a cumulative manner.

The role of the stability of the general regulatory framework in the context of legitimate expectations

The role of legitimate expectations appears to be further diminished through the provisions included in the three IIAs that stipulate that the investor's legitimate

1541. The EU-Singapore FTA refers not only to the specific representations but also to 'unambiguous representations'. In this respect, these two terms appear to be similar as they refer to specific state representations that are addressed to a specific investor.
1542. The EU-Singapore FTA, Article 2.4(3).
1543. The EU-Vietnam FTA, Article 14(7); The EU-Singapore FTA, Article 2.4(3).
1544. The EU-Singapore FTA, Article 2.4(3), footnote 10.

expectations will not be protected merely on the basis of the change to a general regulatory framework of a host state.[1545] For example, in the CETA, in the operational part of its Investment Chapter, Article 8.9(2) provides:

> [f]or greater certainty, the mere fact that a Party regulates, including through a modification to its laws, in a manner which negatively affects an investment or interferes with an investor's expectations, including its expectations of profits, does not amount to a breach of an obligation under this Section.[1546]

By including this provision, the CETA contracting states have attempted to reduce the possibility that tribunals will interpret the FET standard by focusing primarily on the interests of investors, without taking into account the state's right to change its laws and policies.[1547] In comparison to the CETA, the EU-Singapore FTA and the EU-Vietnam FTA note that investment jurisprudence has, in a limited number of circumstances, recognised that the changes in a general regulatory framework might give rise to the protection of an investor under the concept of legitimate expectations.[1548] This being said, tribunals have emphasised that the state's regulatory framework is not static and that a state should be able to change its laws in order to respond to external circumstances.[1549] In this regard, the IIAs' formulation that the 'mere fact' of a change to the regulatory framework will not amount to a breach of the FET standard is in line with the general position of tribunals.[1550] The IIAs' formulation does not, however, exclude the possibility that in combination with other facts, e.g. manifest arbitrariness, a change to a regulatory framework can certainly play a role in

1545. CETA, Article 8.9(2); EU-Singapore FTA, Article 2.2(2); EU-Vietnam FTA, Articles 13*bis*(2). The formulation in the EU-Vietnam FTA is slightly different than in CETA and the EU-Singapore FTA. In Articles 13*bis*(2) it provides: '2. For greater certainty, the provisions of this section shall not be interpreted as a commitment from a Party that it will not change the legal and regulatory framework, including in a manner that may negatively affect the operation of covered investments or the investor's expectations of profits'.
1546. CETA, Article 8(9)(2).
1547. *See*: European Commission, 'Online public consultation on investment protection and investor-to-state dispute settlement (ISDS) in the Transatlantic Trade and Investment Partnership Agreement' (European Commission Consultation, 13 January 2015) 56. In this document, the objective and approach towards the investment protection in EU agreements are explained. In this document, it is stated that by limiting the concept of legitimate expectations and excluding the obligation to provide stability of the regulatory framework 'the intention is to make it clear that an investor cannot legitimately expect that the general regulatory and legal regime will not change. Thus the EU intends to ensure that the standard is not understood to be a "stabilisation obligation," in other words a guarantee that the legislation of the host state will not change in a way that might negatively affect investors.' (p. 56) http://trade.ec.europa.eu/doclib/docs/2015/january/tradoc_153044.pdf. *See also*: European Commission, 'Investment provisions in the EU-Canada Free Trade Agreement (CETA)' (2016) 2. In this document it is explained that the objective of Article 8.9(2) is to ensure that states have the possibility to change their legislation even if this does, in some cases, impact the legitimate expectations for profit of an investor. The document provides: 'it is also explicitly foreseen that Governments can change their laws, including in a way that affects investors' expectations of profit and that the application of EU's state aid law does not constitute a breach of investment protection standards.' http://trade.ec.europa.eu/doclib/docs/2013/november/tradoc_151918.pdf. All websites accessed on 12 June 2018.
1548. Chapter 6, section §6.04. These changes have to be of a fundamental nature.
1549. Chapter 6, section §6.04[B].
1550. CETA, Article 8.9(2); EU-Singapore FTA, Article 2.2(2); EU-Vietnam FTA, Articles 13*bis*(2).

a tribunal's assessment of the question whether the expectations of an investor were legitimate.

It should be noted that some elements that emerged from the examined case law have not been included in the text of the IIA provisions that relate to the protection of legitimate expectations (*see* Chapter 6, sections §6.05-§6.06). This concerns the question of whether there were any special economic and sociopolitical circumstances in a host state and the question of whether the investor conducted proper due diligence and a risk assessment.[1551] The only indirect reference to these elements can be found in Article 2.4(3) of the EU-Singapore FTA, as this provision stipulates that legitimate expectations should be 'reasonably relied upon by the covered investor'.[1552] This reference to the principle of reasonableness in Article 2.4(3) of the EU-Singapore FTA does not contain any further clarification of its application in the context of the protection of the legitimate expectations of an investor. In this respect, the analysis of the case law revealed that the legitimacy and/or reasonableness[1553] of an investor's expectations depends on the question as to whether there were special circumstances in the host state and the question as to whether the investor has demonstrated diligent conduct.[1554]

Reflections

As had been demonstrated in the paragraphs above, the role of legitimate expectations as stated in the three IIAs appears to be diminished in comparison with the role of this concept in the examined case law. Accordingly, this development seems to shift the balance in the direction of the preservation of a state's policy space to regulate in the public interest. Particularly important for this conclusion are provisions such as the one included in the CETA that provides that a host state's change to a regulatory framework alone 'does not amount to a breach of an obligation under this Section'.[1555] This shift reduces, to some extent, the host state's risk of incurring liability under the FET standard when it decides to transform its regulatory framework.

1551. These elements are addressed in Chapter 6, sections §6.05-§6.06.
1552. The EU-Singapore FTA, Article 2.4(3).
1553. Tribunals in their assessment of the legitimate expectations refer to legitimacy and/or reasonableness of investor's expectations in judging whether the invoked expectations deserve the protection under the FET standard. It should be noted, however, that tribunals have not been consistent in their terminology. Sometimes using the term 'legitimate' and 'reasonable' as synonyms. In *Total v. Argentina*, tribunal refers to 'reasonable and hence legitimate expectations'. *Total v. Argentina*, ICSID Case No. ARB/04/01 Decision on Liability (27 December 2010) para. 333; In *El Paso v. Argentina*, the tribunal provided that 'the touchstone of fair and equitable treatment to be found in the legitimate and reasonable expectations.' *El Paso v. Argentina*, ICSID Case No. ARB/03/15 Award (31 October 2011) para. 348; In *National Grid v. Argentina*, tribunal provides that these expectations are protected which are 'reasonable and legitimate in the context of which the investment was made'. *National Grid v. Argentina*, UNCITRAL. Award (3 November 2008) para. 175. The lack of consistency in tribunal's terminology has been pointed by M. Potestà, 'Legitimate Expectations in Investment Treaty Law: Understanding the Roots and the Limits of a Controversial Concept' [2013] 28(1) *ICSID Review*, 118.
1554. Chapter 6, sections §6.05-§6.06.
1555. CETA, Article 8(9)(2).

Furthermore, it is reiterated that the recent IIAs explicitly state that only specific representations of a host state towards an investor may be taken into account by tribunals in their assessment of an alleged violation of the FET standard. In the discussed IIAs, three criteria[1556] for the determination of the specific representations identified from the case law analysis have been included. It appears from the text of these IIAs that compliance with all three criteria is required.

It has been observed in this study that several tribunals emphasised the role of special circumstances and the due diligence undertaken by the investor, elements which are not included in the aforementioned IIAs. Their possible role in the treaty frameworks is further discussed in section §8.06[C].

(3) Right to regulate and the public interest

The three discussed EU IIAs have all included provisions on the state's right to regulate in the public interest.[1557] They are formulated in the three IIAs in an almost identical manner.[1558] As explained in Chapter 2, IIA provisions on the state's right to regulate are still rare. Where these provisions are present, the position of the state's right to regulate is reinforced. For example, Article 8.9(1) of the CETA, entitled 'investment and regulatory measures', stipulates that:

> Parties reaffirm their right to regulate within their territories to achieve legitimate policy objectives, such as the protection of public health, safety, the environment or public morals, social or consumer protection or the promotion and protection of cultural diversity.[1559]

The objectives mentioned in this provision give an indication of the 'public interests' that are particularly relevant to the contracting parties. As provided in Chapter 7, section §7.02[C], in assessing the FET standard, several tribunals also tested the legitimacy of the policy objectives in judging the lawfulness of a host state's measures. They acknowledged public interests such as the protection of the environment, human rights and public health. The public interests which were found in the examined case law correspond to the legitimate policy objectives which are highlighted in the CETA, as well as in the EU-Vietnam FTA and the EU-Singapore FTA.

It is noted that the examined treaty provisions do not, however, elaborate on the criteria that need to be fulfilled for the policy objectives to be legitimate. In this respect, the jurisprudence provides relevant guidance. The condition considered important for legitimacy, underlined by tribunals, is whether the objective can be substantiated by the host state through records and other evidence. In several cases, compliance with

1556. These criteria are: (1) the competence of the state's authority; (2) the legal force of the specific representation, thereby taking into consideration: (i) the legal form, (ii) the content and (iii) the wording; and (3) the designation of the investor in the state's representation.

1557. CETA, Article 8.9(1); the EU-Singapore FTA, Article 2.2(1); and the EU-Vietnam FTA, Articles 13*bis*(1).

1558. In Article 2.2(1) of the EU-Singapore FTA, the additional legitimate policy objective – privacy and data protection – has been added to the list of the policy objectives in comparison to these laid down in Article 8.9(1) of CETA and Articles 13*bis*(1) of the EU-Vietnam FTA.

1559. CETA, Article 8.9(1).

national law or international obligations under international treaties other than the applicable IIA has also served as adequate justification.[1560] The assessment of the substantiation of the policy objectives of the state's measure assists tribunals in their determination of the question as to whether the state's conduct is, in fact, serving the public interest in the way the state claims.

Reflections

The finding that these three IIAs include an open list of legitimate policy objectives that may be considered to be in the public interest is in line with the findings of Chapter 7. In the examined cases, most tribunals recognised a diversity in the state objectives taken in the public interest. The criteria for establishing the legitimacy of policy objectives have not been reflected in the discussed IIAs.

(4) The legality of the state's measure under national law

In the CETA, the reference to the element of the legality of the state's measure under national law has found its place in the text of the treaty. Alongside the provision on the state's right to regulate, the CETA excludes the option of tribunals to challenge the state's measures under national law. This aims to further reinforce the policy space of the host state to regulate. Article 8.10(7) of the CETA provides for 'greater certainty, the fact that a measure breaches domestic law does not, in and of itself, establish a breach of this Article, the Tribunal must consider whether a Party has acted inconsistently with the obligations in paragraph 1'.[1561] In a press statement on the CETA, the European Commission clarified that the purpose of this paragraph is to ensure that tribunals only apply this agreement on the basis of 'the principles of international law' and that such an approach also 'puts in black and white that determining whether a measure of a Party is legal under domestic law remains the monopoly of the Party's competent authorities'.[1562]

The role of the legality of the state's measure under national law as phrased in Article 8.10(7) of the CETA corresponds to the manner in which tribunals deal with the question of the assessment of legality under national law in relation to the FET standard. As analysed in section §7.05[C] of Chapter 7, the tribunals in the examined cases did not find that a breach of national law, on its own, constitutes a ground of violation of the FET standard. Only a state's serious arbitrary conduct, e.g. a 'blatant disregard' of domestic rules by state authorities, may usually give rise to a violation of the FET standard.[1563]

1560. *Chemtura v. Canada* [2010] NAFTA-UNCITRAL Arbitration, Award (2 August 2010) para. 138; *Philip Morris v. Uruguay*, ICSID Case No. ARB/10/7 Award (8 July 2016) para. 401; *Urbaser S.A. and Consorcio de Aguas Bilbao Bizkaia, Bilbao Biskaia Ur Partzuergoa v. Argentina*, ICSID Case No. ARB/07/26 Award (8 December 2016) para. 622.
1561. CETA, Article 8.10(7).
1562. European Commission, Press release: CETA: EU and Canada agree on new approach on investment in trade agreement, Brussels, 29 February 2016, *see*: http://europa.eu/rapid/press-release_IP-16-399_en.htm accessed on 20 April 2018.
1563. *See*: Chapter 7, section §7.05, and Table 4 in section §7.05[D].

Reflections

The exclusion of the assessment of the legality of the state's measure under national law is rather categorical and strongly encouraged in the CETA and in the press statement of the European Commission.[1564] The breach of national law by a state may, however, be taken into consideration by tribunals, for instance, if the state's conduct was found to be 'manifestly arbitrary'.

[C] The Balance Between the State's Right to Regulate and Investor Protection under the FET Standard in Recent IIAs and Investment Jurisprudence

In the first part of this section §8.06[C], the question of whether and in which direction the new generation of IIAs shift the balance between the state's right to regulate and the FET standard will be discussed. The second part of this section explores whether other elements or parts of these elements found to be relevant for the FET standard and the right to regulate could be included in IIAs and whether such codification will contribute to the balance between investor protection under the FET standard and the host states' right to regulate.

(1) The direction in which the balance between the state's right to regulate and the FET standard has shifted

In the last two decades, the character of the FET standard has transformed from a legal provision that for a long time had a presence in most IIAs, but which had no important role in investment cases, to a substantive investment provision with an elaborated meaning.[1565] This transformation has happened primarily through the interpretation of the FET standard by international investment tribunals.[1566]

In early investment decisions, the FET standard was interpreted and applied by investment tribunals as an umbrella clause, which covered various state misconduct that did not qualify for protection under other investment standards such as the expropriation provision.[1567] Over time, in interpreting and applying the FET standard, tribunals identified concrete elements, e.g., the prohibition of discriminatory treatment of investors and the protection of an investor's legitimate expectations, that gradually

1564. European Commission, Press release: CETA: EU and Canada agree on new approach on investment in trade agreement, Brussels, 29 February 2016, *see*: http://europa.eu/rapid/press-release_IP-16-399_en.htm accessed on 20 April 2018.

1565. C. Schreuer, R. Dolzer, 1st edn., (2008) 119. 'It is only since 2000, the first significant cases being *Metalclad* and *Maffenzi*, that investment tribunals haven given content to the meaning of the standard and have applied it to a broad range of circumstances.' *Metalclad Corporation v. The United Mexican States*, ICSID Case No. ARB(AF)/97/1, NAFTA, Award 30 August 2000; *Emilio Agustín Maffezini v. The Kingdom of Spain*, ICSID Case No. ARB/97/7 Award 13 November 2000.

1566. Also *see*: F.M. Palombino, Fair and Equitable Treatment and the Fabric of General Principles (Springer, 2018) 157.

1567. D. Collins, An Introduction to International Investment Law (Cambridge University Press, 2016) 127.

embodied the meaning of what FET has become today. In parallel to this development, as of 2006, tribunals have begun recognising the state's right to regulate in the public interest, while assessing the investor's rights under the FET standard. To this end, tribunals have acknowledged the state's ability to modify its laws as a part of the right to regulate.[1568] Also, in a growing number of decisions, tribunals have stressed the significance of a state's measures adopted in the state's legitimate public interest, e.g. the protection of public health or to remedy the negative consequences of a financial and/or economic crisis. Tribunals indicated that such arguments clearly have to be taken into consideration when judging the fairness of a host state's conduct towards an investor.[1569]

The meaning provided by tribunals to FET has assisted the treaty parties to the new generation IIAs in formulating their FET standard. The FET standard provision is no longer a single line in the text of the IIA; it has become a detailed clause comprising of different elements, such as the obligation of states towards an investor; the protection of the legitimate expectations of an investor; the state's right to regulate in the public interest; and the legality of a state measure under national law.

As has been demonstrated in section §8.06[B], the balance between investor protection under the FET standard and the state's right to regulate in the case law and in the new generation of IIAs has gradually shifted towards the direction of the state's right to regulate. There are, however, variations between the three recent IIAs and investment jurisprudence on the FET standard in regard to certain subjects. These variations are explained below.

In the new generation of IIAs, this shift is achieved through a clarification of the obligations of the contracting states towards their foreign investors. As explained in section §8.06[B] of this Chapter, the state's obligations included in the IIAs between the EU and Canada, the EU and Singapore and the EU and Vietnam largely correspond to the investment jurisprudence. In these IIAs, the closed list of state obligations is formulated in a way that raises the threshold of a state's conduct that can lead to a breach of the FET standard to more qualified and serious violations. Despite this, not all obligations that were identified in the analysed jurisprudence are reflected in these IIAs. However, the case law on the FET standard corresponds to the application of the FET standard in treaties, mostly providing that the state's conduct should be sufficiently serious in order to give rise to a violation of the FET standard.[1570]

1568. *See* Chapter 2, section §2.03[C] on the right to regulate in FET investment cases. In this section, the examples are provided where tribunals have reaffirmed that states have the right to change and modify their laws as an integral part of their right to regulate. This point is also addressed and illustrated by examples in Chapter 6, section §6.04.

1569. *See* Chapter 2, section §2.03[C] on the right to regulate in FET investment cases. The decisions that stress the significance of a public interest are discussed. Also *see*: Chapter 6, section §6.05 that addresses the relevant public interests in tribunals' assessments of the legitimate expectations of an investor. *See* Chapter 7, section §7.02 on the objective of the state's measure, where the various public interests are exemplified.

1570. *See*, e.g., *Philip Morris v. Uruguay*, ICSID Case No. ARB/10/7 Award (8 July 2016), para. 410. The violation under the FET standard may occur when the measure was implemented in an 'arbitrary, grossly unfair, unjust, discriminatory, or disproportionate' way. For further examples, *see*: Chapter 7, section §7.04[D]. Also *see*: Table 3 in Chapter 7, section §7.04[D].

With regards to the protection of the legitimate expectations of an investor as a part of the FET standard, the new generation of IIAs and investment jurisprudence somewhat diverges. In IIAs, the role of legitimate expectations seems to be reduced in contrast to the case law in which the application of the legitimate expectations still occupies an important role in the assessment of the FET standard.[1571]

In IIAs, the perspective of the state has been explicitly recognised in the provision on the state's right to regulate, which is now included in the CETA, the EU-Singapore FTA and the EU-Vietnam FTA.[1572] Some commentators, however, question the legal significance of such a provision.[1573] Tietje and Crow argue that 'it is already well established in arbitral practice that investment treatment standards that favour the investor must be balanced against the legitimate regulatory interests of the host state.'[1574] However, as the analysis in Chapter 6 and 7 demonstrates, such a statement somewhat exaggerates the notion that it is well established in investment jurisprudence on the FET standard that the state's right to regulate is balanced against the rights of investors. Indeed, in contrast to earlier decisions, in assessing the legitimate expectations of an investor and/or the contested state's measures under the FET standard, tribunals are more sensitive to the concerns of a host state to regulate in the public interest. Nevertheless, tribunals are still far from consistent in considering legitimate public interest policy objectives in judging the fairness of the state's conduct.[1575] Consequently, what carries legal significance is the explicit wording in the recent IIAs that a state can exercise its right to regulate. The provisions on the right to regulate in the three IIAs clarify the intentions of the contracting states that tribunals must acknowledge that a state has the right to take measures to protect or otherwise regulate a public interest. The function of the aforementioned provision is not to exempt the state from liability under the FET standard. Rather, it requires tribunals to balance the state's public interests and the interests of the investor, while interpreting and applying the FET standard.

(2) Further elements of the FET standard for codification in the new generation of IIAs?

As analysed above, the codification of some investment jurisprudence elements in the new generation IIAs contributes to a balance between a host state's right to regulate and the protection of the rights of investors under the FET standard. However, some of the elements that were identified in the jurisprudence were not reflected in the IIAs. These are (1) the principles of reasonableness and proportionality which form part of

1571. *See* the concluding remarks of Chapter 6, in section §6.07. Also *see* Chapter 4, section §4.05 on the introduction to the legal conditions on the right to regulate, where the position of legitimate expectations in the assessment of the FET standard is highlighted.
1572. CETA, Article 8.9(1); the EU-Singapore FTA, Article 2.2(1) and the EU-Vietnam FTA, Articles 13*bis*(1).
1573. C. Tietje, K. Crow, The Reform of Investment Protection Rules in CETA, TTIP and other Recent EU-FTAs: Convincing? (13 December 2016), 12.
1574. *Ibid.*, 12 https://ssrn.com/abstract=2885279 accessed on 12 June 2018.
1575. *See* Chapter 7, section §7.02. See the assessment of the state's measures concerning the protection of public health in comparison to the cases where the measures pertinent to the right to access to water have been analysed.

the tribunals' assessment of the state's obligations under the FET standard; and (2) two criteria often discussed in the context of assessing whether an investor's expectations were legitimate, namely the special circumstances in a host state and the investor's conduct, both discussed in sections §6.05 and §6.06 of Chapter 6. The question emerges whether the codification of these principles and criteria in IIAs could change the balance between the state's right to regulate and the protection of investors under the FET standard. This question is addressed in the following paragraphs.

The principles of reasonableness and proportionality

In the examined case law, the principles of reasonableness and proportionality often play a role in weighing the rights of states and investors in the assessment of the FET standard. The investment jurisprudence provides useful insights on how the principles of reasonableness and proportionality are applied by tribunals in relation to the FET standard. What is central to the assessment of the principles of proportionality and reasonableness by FET tribunals is the legitimacy of the state's objective and its reasonable relationship with the state's measure. If the reasonable relationship between the state's measure and its objectives has been established, the next step, as articulated by the tribunal in *Philip Morris v. Uruguay*, is whether the measure was implemented in an 'arbitrary, grossly unfair, unjust, discriminatory, or disproportionate' way.[1576] The approach pursued by the tribunal in *Philip Morris* and in other decisions[1577] indicates that the misconduct of the state towards an investor should be sufficiently serious in order to give rise to a violation of the FET standard.

In the study on the comparison of the EU IIAs conducted following a request made by the European Parliament in 2015, the Committee on International Trade proposed to include the principle of proportionality into the text of the new IIA FET standard provisions.[1578] The argument for including proportionality in the text of the FET provisions was that this test 'would serve as a confining element for the tribunals' interpretations and add structure to the sometimes non-transparent process of appreciation of the facts undertaken by tribunals'.[1579] The authors of the study emphasise that in applying the principle of proportionality, states should also be provided with 'a wide margin of appreciation in determining the legitimacy of a measure's objective, the

1576. *Philip Morris v. Uruguay*, ICSID Case No. ARB/10/7 Award (8 July 2016), para. 410. Chapter 7, section §7.03[D]. Also *see*: Table 3 in Chapter 7, section §7.04[D].

1577. *Saluka Investments BV v. Czech Republic* [2006] UNCITRAL Arbitration Partial Award (17 March 2006) para. 307. 'A foreign investor protected by the Treaty may in any case properly expect that the Czech Republic implements its policies bona fide by conduct that is, as far as it affects the investors' investment, reasonably justifiable by public policies and that such conduct does not manifestly violate the requirements of consistency, transparency, even-handedness and nondiscrimination'; *AES Summit v. Hungary*, ICSID Case No. ARB/07/22 Award (23 September 2010) para. 10.3.36. The state's measure should be: 'reasonable, proportionate and consistent with the public policy expressed by the parliament'.

1578. European Parliament, Director-General for External Policies, The Investment Chapters of the EU's International Trade and Investment Agreements: In a Comparative Perspective, 2015, p. 142.

1579. *Ibid.*

appropriateness and the necessity of a measure to achieve this objective'.[1580] The author of this study takes the view that the inclusion of a reference to the principle of proportionality does not significantly contribute to achieving a balance between the host state's right to regulate and the investor's rights under the FET standard. Proportionality is a general principle of law, and therefore its inclusion in IIAs is not necessary for its application by tribunals. Even if such a reference in IIAs was made, tribunals could still decide on the manner in which the proportionality test is applied, which determines whether the balance shifts more towards the state's right to regulate or towards the FET standard. In this regard, a reference to the proportionality principle is unlikely to change the balance between the state's right to regulate and the FET standard.

Criteria for the assessment of legitimacy of an investor's expectations

In the new generation of IIAs, the recognition of the protection of the legitimate expectations is based on the presence of specific representations. The specificity of the state's representations, which is defined in IIAs according to the three cumulative criteria,[1581] is critical for determining the legitimacy of an investor's expectations. However, such an approach appears to be incomplete. As the case law demonstrates, in establishing the legitimacy of an investor's expectations, other criteria that can be of importance are the special circumstances in the host state and the investor's due diligence. The presence of a specific representation by the host state cannot justify protection under the FET standard in all circumstances. Consequently, tribunals have stressed that the reversal of the state's specific representations towards an investor may involve a response to special circumstances in the host state, e.g. an economic crisis. Also, a lack of due diligence on the part of an investor may weaken the claim for the protection of legitimate expectations on the basis of the specific representations.[1582] The analysed jurisprudence offers some insights into the application of the criteria for the assessment of the legitimacy of an investor's expectations that can be helpful for the future applicability of treaty frameworks.

In terms of special circumstances, this book identified the economic circumstances (e.g., financial and economic crises and the economic deficit challenge in the renewable energy sector) and the sociopolitical circumstances (e.g., the transition of

1580. In the study, the authors refer to the example of how such provision could be formulated. It reads: 'In assessing a breach of the obligation of fair and equitable treatment and full protection and security, a tribunal shall take into account whether the measure is appropriate for attaining the legitimate policy objectives pursued by that measure and must not go beyond what is necessary to achieve them. Each Party enjoys a wide margin of appreciation in determining the legitimacy of a measure's objective, the appropriateness and the necessity of a measure to achieve this objective.' S. Hindelang, S. Wernicke (eds) Grundzüge eines modernen Investitionsschutzes (Harnack-Haus Reflections, 2015) p. 5 http://tinyurl.com/ofzq7k3 accessed on 22 May 2018.

1581. The criteria are: competence of the state's authority; the legal force of the specific representation(s): legal form, content and wording; and designation of the investor.

1582. *Charanne Construction v. Spain*, SCC Case No. 062/2012 Award (21 January 2016) para. 505. Tribunal provided that in order for an investor to 'exercise the right of legitimate expectations', it should perform a 'diligent analysis of the legal framework for the investment'.

the former Soviet states) that were relevant in judging the legitimacy of the investor's expectations. However, as new cases arise, other types of circumstance are becoming relevant in assessments conducted by tribunals.[1583] Consequently, the inclusion of a list of special circumstances in IIAs may limit the assessment of tribunals to only those circumstances identified in the IIAs. This could potentially impose constraints on the state's right to regulate in the public interest. Incorporating a broad reference to circumstances that should be taken into account in IIAs will not add much in terms of the already existing recognition of the circumstances in host state that are taken into consideration by investment tribunals in weighing the investor's legitimate expectations. Furthermore, the provisions on the state's right to regulate in the new generation of IIAs, which recognise a diverse range of legitimate public interests, are also applicable in the assessment of the protection of legitimate expectations on the basis of specific representations.

A reference to an investor's conduct in IIAs may, however, change the balance between the state's right to regulate and the investor's protection under the FET standard.

First, the goals of the new generation of IIAs - as they are stated in these IIAs - will be better assisted by integrating a specific reference to the duties of investors in the preamble of an IIA and in text of an IIA, pursuant to the developments and regulations in the field of CSR. Reference is made to the OECD Guidelines on Multinational Enterprises,[1584] the Ten Principles of the UN Global Compact[1585] and the 2011 UN Guiding Principles on Business and Human Rights.[1586] Also, the IPFSD[1587] developed by the UNCTAD provides the relevant guidance for states on how to 'balanc[e] State commitments with investor obligations and promoting responsible investment'.[1588]

Second, the incorporation of other conditions referring to the investor's conduct, e.g. including an obligation that the investor undertake due diligence and risk assessments (this could be included under the umbrella of the legitimate expectations), may improve the balance between the rights and obligations of states and investors. These two suggestions are addressed below.

Until recently, IIAs have not imposed any obligations and responsibilities on investors.[1589] However, in the last five years, a reference to investor obligations and responsibilities has appeared in the arbitral awards and several recent agreements,

1583. The environmental policies in the renewable energy sector and climate change that affect the state's representations to investors.
1584. OECD, 'OECD Guidelines for Multinational Enterprises' (2011) http://mneguidelines.oecd.org/guidelines/ accessed on 12 June 2018.
1585. United Nations, 'UN Global Compact: The Ten Principles' (2005) https://www.unglobalcompact.org/what-is-gc/mission/principles accessed on 12 June 2018.
1586. UNHRC, 'Guiding Principles on Business and Human Rights', UN Doc. HR/PUB/11/04 (2011) http://www.ohchr.org/Documents/Publications/GuidingPrinciplesBusinessHR_EN.pdf accessed on 12 June 2018.
1587. UNCTAD, 'Investment Policy Framework for Sustainable Development' (2012) (updated in 2015).
1588. *Ibid.*, p. 8.
1589. G. Bottini, 'Extending Responsibilities in International Investment Law', in *The E15 Initiative: Strengthening the Global Trade and Investment System for Sustainable Development* (2015) p. 1.

primarily through the incorporation of provisions concerning CSR.[1590] In the decision *Urbaser v. Argentina* (*see* section §7.02 of Chapter 7), the tribunal asserted that companies are not immune from international law obligations, including obligations relating to the human right of access to water.[1591]

In IIAs, a reference to the responsibilities of investors pursuant to recognised CSR codes is found in the preamble of the CETA.[1592] It states that 'enterprises operating within their territory or subject to their jurisdiction [are encouraged] to respect internationally recognised guidelines and principles of corporate social responsibility, including the OECD Guidelines for Multinational Enterprises, and to pursue best practices of responsible business conduct.'[1593] This reference emphasises that investors should adhere to the OECD Guidelines for Multinational Enterprises and signals the growing role of the responsibility of investors in observing international human rights, labour and environmental standards while operating in a host state. Although the preamble of a treaty does not necessarily impose legally binding obligations on the investors, it can and has been taken into account by tribunals in interpreting and applying the FET standard. As the book demonstrates, tribunals refer to the preamble of IIAs in revealing the object and the purpose of the treaty and in identifying the meaning of the openly formulated FET standard.[1594] Some tribunals have interpreted the FET standard widely by emphasising the perspective of the investor through making reference to the investor promotion and protection objectives included in most IIAs. Consequently, the inclusion of preambular statements in IIAs that highlight the responsibilities of investors signals that in interpreting and applying the FET standard, tribunals have to take the obligations and responsibilities of investors towards a host state into account.

The inclusion of the investor's obligations in IIAs, e.g. the duty of conducting due diligence, as a condition for the protection of the legitimate expectations of an investor, could help to create a balance between the rights and obligations of states and investors under the FET standard. Some tribunals have underlined that an investor bears the responsibility of appraising the reality and the context of the state where the investment is being made by performing due diligence and risk assessments.[1595] The investor has to be aware and take into account the relevant regulations, policies and decisions concerning its investment in order to anticipate the possible risks.[1596] This is especially

---

1590. Examples of such reference to CSR provisions in IIAs are provided in section §2.03[C]. The UNCTAD IIAs Mapping Project states that of 1,958 IIAs, 28 included CSR provisions. Most of these IIAs were concluded after 2000. *See* UNCTAD 'IIA Mapping Project 2016' (2016) http://investmentpolicyhub.unctad.org/IIA/mappedContent#iiaInnerMenu accessed on 12 January 2018.
1591. *Urbaser S.A. and Consorcio de Aguas Bilbao Bizkaia, Bilbao Biskaia Ur Partzuergoa v. The Argentine Republic*, ICSID Case No. ARB/07/26 Award (8 December 2016) para. 1195.
1592. The EU-Singapore FTA and the EU-Vietnam FTA have not included such reference in their preambles.
1593. CETA, preamble, http://ec.europa.eu/trade/policy/in-focus/ceta/ceta-chapter-by-chapter/. The reference to CSR has been also made in CETA in Chapter 22 'trade and sustainable development'.
1594. *See* Chapter 4, section §4.03[E].
1595. *See* Chapter 6, section §6.06.
1596. *Charanne Construction v. Spain*, SCC Case No. 062/2012 Award (21 January 2016) para. 505.

relevant for the cases, where the claim of an investor for the protection of his legitimate expectations is based on the changes to a general regulatory framework. The extent of an investor's due diligence investigation can operate as a yardstick in judging whether the contested changes could have been predicted by an investor. Only if the changes were not foreseeable by a prudent investor,[1597] despite visible efforts to collect the information about the future of the regulatory framework, the legitimate expectations of the investor might rise to the protection under the applicable IIA.

By including provisions in IIAs that require an investor to undertake due diligence in order for them to benefit from the protection of legitimate expectations, the contracting states clarify that only a diligent investor, performing a proper assessment of the laws and regulations in a host state, may rely on the specific representations under the FET standard. From the perspective of balancing the rights of the investor and the state's right to regulate, such a reference not only accounts for both the interests of states and investors under the FET standard but also strengthens the importance of investors' responsibilities in international investment law.

1597. This threshold is indicated in *Isolux Netherlands, BV v. Kingdom of Spain*, SCC Case V2013/153 Award (17 July 2016) para. 781.

ANNEX A

Selected Bilateral Investment Treaties

OECD/Russia and China[1598]	Selected Host States										
	Mexico	Argentina	Venezuela	Ecuador	Egypt	India	Colombia	Trinidad & Tobago	The Czech Republic	Ukraine	Uruguay
Australia	T	Yes, 1995	No	No	Yes, 2001	Yes, 1999	No	No	Yes, 1993	No	Yes, 2001
Canada	No	Yes, 1991	Yes, 1996	T	Yes, 1996	No	No	Yes, 1995	Yes, 2009	Yes, 1995	Yes, 1997
Russia	No	Yes, 1998	Yes, 2008	Yes, 1996	Yes, 1997	T	No	No	Yes, 1994	Yes, 1998	No
China	Yes, 2008	Yes, 1992	No	T	Yes, 1994	T	Yes, 2008	Yes, 2002	Yes, 2005	Yes, 1992	Yes, 1993
Japan	No	No	No	No	Yes, 1977	No	Yes, 2011	No	No	Yes, 2015	Yes, 2015
US	No	Yes, 1991	No	T	Yes, 1986	No	No	Yes, 1994	Yes, 1991	Yes, 1994	Yes, 2005
UK	Yes, 2006	Yes, 1990	Yes, 1995	T	Yes, 1975	T	Yes, 2010	Yes, 1993	Yes, 1990	Yes, 1993	Yes, 1991
Germany	Yes, 1998	Yes, 1991	Yes, 1996	T	Yes, 2005	T	No	Yes, 2006	Yes, 1990	Yes, 1993	Yes, 1987
The Netherlands	Yes, 1998	Yes, 1992	T	Yes, 1999	Yes, 1996	T	No	No	Yes, 1991	Yes, 1994	Yes, 1988
France	Yes, 1998	Yes, 1991	Yes, 2001	T	Yes, 1974	T	Yes, 2014	Yes, 1993	Yes, 1990	Yes, 1994	Yes, 1993

1598. Please note that Russia and China are not the OECD Member States. Their inclusion into the selection is explained in Chapter 1, section §1.03.

T = Terminated

The dates indicated in Annex A are the dates when the treaties were signed. The last update of the table was on 3 April 2019. Please note that due to recent terminations of BITs by Ecuador and India, the number of analysed BITs in the book does not coincide with the number in this table on the moment of the final update.

Annex B

Regional Treaties

Regional Investment Treaties or Trade Treaties with an Investment Chapter	*FET Formulations*
1. Canada-EU Comprehensive Economic Trade Agreement (2016)	A comprehensive list approach of unacceptable state conduct, also ref. to legitimate expectations - linked with 'and' to FPS
2. NAFTA (1994)	A customary law approach, clarified in the Notes of Interpretation
3. US-EU Transatlantic Trade and Partnership Agreement (draft, 2015)	A comprehensive list approach of unacceptable state conduct, also ref. to legitimate expectations - linked with 'and' to FPS
4. Trans-Pacific Partnership Agreement (draft, 2016)	A customary law approach including a denial of justice element - linked with 'and' to FPS
5. Agreement establishing the ASEAN-Australia-New Zealand Free Trade Area (2010)	A customary law approach including a denial of justice element - linked with 'and' to FPS
6. CAFTA-DR (Dominican Republic-Central America FTA) (2009)	A customary law approach including a denial of justice element - linked with 'and' to FPS
7. Energy Charter Treaty (1991)	In accordance with international law
8. EU-Vietnam FTA (draft, 2016)	A comprehensive list approach of unacceptable state conduct
9. EU-Singapore FTA (draft, 2018)	A comprehensive list approach of unacceptable state conduct

ANNEX C
Categories of the IIAs' FET Standard Formulations

Categories of the FET standard's formulation	*IIAs*
1. FET as an unqualified, autonomous treaty standard (46 IIAs)	Australia-Argentina BIT, 1997; Australia-Czech Republic, 1994; Australia-Egypt, 2002; Australia-India, 2000; Australia-Uruguay, 2002; Netherlands-Uruguay, 1991; Netherlands-Czech Republic, 1992; Netherlands-Ecuador, 2001; Netherlands-Egypt, 1998; Netherlands-Argentina, 1994; Netherlands-India, 1996; Netherlands-Mexico, 1999; Netherlands-Ukraine, 1997; Germany-Trinidad and Tobago, 2010; Germany-Czech Republic, 1992; Germany-Ecuador, 1999; Germany-Argentina, 1993; Germany-Mexico, 2001; Germany-Egypt, 2008; Germany-India, 1998; Germany-Uruguay, 1990; Germany-Ukraine, 1996; Argentina-Russia, 2000; Russia-India, 1996; Russia-Egypt, 2000; Russia-Venezuela, 2009; Russia-Czech Republic, 1996; Russia-Ecuador, 1996; China-Argentine Republic, 1994; China- Czech Republic, 2006; China-Ecuador, 1997; China-Trinidad and Tobago, 2004; China-Egypt, 1996; China-India, 2007; China-Uruguay, 1997; UK-Egypt, 1976; Czech Republic-Slovak Republic-UK, 1992; Ecuador-UK, 1995; UK-Trinidad and Tobago, 1993; UK-Argentina BIT, 1993; UK-Venezuela, 1996; UK-India, 1995; UK-Ukraine, 1993; UK-Uruguay, 1997; France-Egypt, 1975; France-Uruguay, 1997

Categories of the FET standard's formulation	*IIAs*
2.a. FET linked to customary international law (13 IIAs)	Australia-Mexico BIT, 2007 (in Protocol: clarification of minimum standard); Canada-Czech Republic, 2012; Japan-Uruguay, 2015 (with a reference to customary international law with a prohibition of a denial of justice); Japan-Colombia BIT, signed in 2011 (a reference to customary international law with a prohibition of a denial of justice and access to courts); China-Colombia, 2013 (with a reference to customary international law with a prohibition of a denial of justice); Mexico-China BIT, 2009; UK-Colombia BIT, 2014 (with a reference to international law with a prohibition of a denial of justice); Mexico-UK, 2007; US-Uruguay 2006; Trans-Pacific Partnership Agreement; Agreement establishing the ASEAN-Australia-New Zealand Free Trade Area; NAFTA FTC Note; CAFTA-DR
2.b. FET linked to international law or general principles of law (21 IIAs)	Canada-Argentina, 1993; Canada-Ecuador, 1997; Canada-Egypt, 1997; Canada-Trinidad and Tobago, 1996; Canada-Ukraine, 1995; Canada-Uruguay, 1999; US-Argentina 1994 (less than that required by IL); US-Ukraine, 1996 (less than that required by IL); US-Ecuador, 1997 (less than that required by IL); US-Czech Republic, 1992 (less than that required by IL); US-Trinidad-Tobago, 1996 (less than that required by IL; clarify its position in the letter of submittal); Germany-Venezuela, 1998; Japan-Ukraine, 2015 (according to int. law); France-Mexico, 2000 (in accordance with the principles of int. law); France-Trinidad and Tobago BIT, 1993 (in accordance with the principles of int. law); France-Argentina, 1993 (in accordance with the principles of int. law and it is not impeded either de jure or de facto); France-Venezuela, 2004 (in accordance with the principles of int. law and it is not impeded either de jure or de facto); France-Ecuador, 1996 (in accordance with the principles of int. law and it is not impeded either de jure or de facto); France-India, 2000 (in accordance with internationally established principles); France-Czech Republic, 1991 (in accordance with the principles of int. law); Energy Charter Treaty

Categories of the FET standard's formulation	*IIAs*
3. FET standard provision is qualified with additional content (11 IIAs)	France-Colombia BIT, 2014; Canada-EU Comprehensive Economic Trade Agreement, 2016; US-EU Transatlantic Trade and Partnership Agreement, 2015; Japan-Colombia, 2011; China-Colombia, 2013; UK-Colombia, 2014; US-Uruguay 2006; Trans-Pacific Partnership Agreement; the Dominican Republic-Central America FTA (CAFTA-DR); EU-Singapore FTA, 2018; EU-Vietnam FTA, 2016.
4. IIAs in which the preamble provides a reference to the FET standard (12 IIAs)	Netherlands-Egypt BIT, 1998; Netherlands-Ecuador, 1999; Netherlands-Argentina, 1992; the Netherlands-Mexico, 1998; the Netherlands-Czech Republic, 1992; Netherlands-Ukraine, 1997; Netherlands-Uruguay, 1991; US-Argentina, 1994; US-Czech Republic, 1992; US-Ukraine, 1996; US-Ecuador, 1997; US-Uruguay, 2006
5. IIA's additional agreement of the parties on the interpretation of the FET standard (11 IIAs)	Canada-EU Comprehensive Economic Trade Agreement, 2016; NAFTA FTC Note; the Dominican Republic-Central America FTA (CAFTA-DR); China-Canada BIT, 2014; Trans-Pacific Partnership Agreement; US-EU Transatlantic Trade and Partnership Agreement; Colombia-Japan BIT, 2011; Japan-Ukraine BIT, 2015; Japan-Uruguay, 2015; EU-Singapore FTA, 2015; EU-Vietnam FTA, 2016

Annex D

Investment Cases

Please note that the table displays the entry into force dates.

Investment FET case	*IIA*
1. ADC v. Hungary	Cyprus – Hungary BIT
2. ADF Group Inc. v. United States of America	NAFTA
3. AES Summit v. Hungary	Energy Charter Treaty
4. Apotex v. US	NAFTA
5. AWG v. Argentina	Argentina-United Kingdom BIT
6. Antin v. Spain	ECT
7. Azurix Corp. v. The Argentine Republic	Argentina-United States BIT
8. Bayindir Insaat Turizm Ticaret Ve Sanayi A.S. v. Islamic Republic of Pakistan	Pakistan-Turkey BIT
9. Biwater Gauff (Tanzania) Ltd. v. United Republic of Tanzania	Tanzanian-United Kingdom BIT
10. Burlington Resources Inc. v. Republic of Ecuador	Ecuador-United States BIT
11. Blusun v. Italy	ECT
12. Cargill, Inc. v. United Mexican States	NAFTA
13. CMS Gas Transmission Co. v. The Argentine Republic	Argentina-United States BIT
14. CME v. Czech Republic	Czech Republic – the Netherlands BIT
15. Continental Casualty v. Argentina	Argentina-United States BIT
16. Crystallex International Corporation v. the Republic of Venezuela	Canada-Venezuela BIT
17. Charanne Construction v. Spain	Energy Charter Treaty
18. Chemtura v. Canada	NAFTA
19. Duke Energy v. Ecuador	Ecuador v. Unites States BIT

Investment FET case	*IIA*
20. EDF (Services) Limited v. Romania	Romania-United Kingdom BIT
21. Eureko BV v. Republic of Poland	Netherlands-Poland BIT
22. Eiser v. Spain	ECT
23. El Paso v. Argentina	Argentina-United States BIT
24. Electrabel v. Hungary	ECT
25. Emilio Agustín Maffezini v. The Kingdom of Spain	Argentina-Spain BIT
26. Enron v. Argentina	Argentina-United States BIT
27. Frontier v. Czech Republic	Canada-Czech Republic BIT
28. Gami Investments, Inc. v. The Government of the United Mexican States	NAFTA
29. Genin, Eastern Credit Limited, Inc. and A.S. Baltoil v. The Republic of Estonia	Estonia - United States BIT
30. Gold Reserve v. Venezuela	Canada-Venezuela BIT
31. Impregilo S.p.A v. Argentina	Argentina-Italy BIT
32. Impreglio S.p.A v. Islamic Republic of Pakistan	Italy-Pakistan BIT
33. International Thunderbird Gaming Corp. v. Mexico	NAFTA
34. Ioan Micula v. Romania	Romania-Sweden BIT
35. Isolux v. Spain	ECT
36. Joy Mining Machinery v. Egypt	Egypt-United Kingdom BIT
37. Lemire v. Ukraine	Ukraine-United States BIT
38. LG&E Energy Corp., LG&E Capital Corp. & LG&E International v. The Argentine Republic	Argentina-United States BIT
39. Loewen Group, Inc. and Raymond L. Loewen v. United States	NAFTA
40. Mamidoil Jetoil Greek Petroleum Products Societe S.A. v. Republic of Albania	Albania-Greece BIT, ECT
41. Masdar v. Spain	ECT
42. Metalclad v. Mexico	NAFTA
43. Merrill & Ring Forestry L.P. v. Canada	NAFTA
44. Mondev International Ltd. v. United States	NAFTA
45. Mr. Franck Charles Arif v. Republic of Moldova	France-Moldova BIT
46. MTD Equity Sdn. Bhd. and MTD Chile S.A. v. Republic of Chile	Chile - Malaysia BIT
47. Noble Ventures, Inc. v. Romania	Romania-United States BIT
48. National Grid plc v. The Argentine Republic	Argentina-United Kingdom BIT
49. Occidental v. Ecuador	Ecuador-United States BIT
50. Parkerings v. Lithuania	Lithuania-Norway BIT

Investment FET case	*IIA*
51. Pope & Talbot Inc. v. The Government of Canada	NAFTA
52. Philip Morris v. Uruguay	Switzerland-Uruguay BIT
53. PSEG v. Turkey	Turkey - United States BIT
54. Ronald S. Lauder v. The Czech Republic	Czech Republic-United States BIT
55. Saluka Investments B.V. v. Czech Republic	Czech Republic- the Netherlands BIT
56. Sempra Energy International v. The Argentine Republic	Argentina-United States BIT
57. Siemens A.G. v. The Argentine Republic	Argentina-Germany BIT
58. Suez, Sociedad General de Aguas de Barcelona, S.A. and Vivendi Universal, S.A. v. Argentine Republic	Argentina-France BIT; Argentina-Spain BIT
59. S.D. Myers v. Canada	NAFTA
60. Tecmed v. Mexico	Spain-Mexico BIT
61. Total S.A. v. Argentina	Argentina-France BIT
62. Toto v. Lebanon	Italy-Lebanon BIT
63. Venezuela Holdings B.V. et al v. Venezuela	Netherlands-Venezuela BIT
64. Waste Management v. Mexico	NAFTA
65. William Ralph Clayton, William Richard Clayton, Douglas Clayton, Daniel Clayton and Bilcon of Delaware Inc. v. Government of Canada	NAFTA
66. Urbaser v. Argentina	Argentina-Spain BIT

Index

A

Abs/Shawcross Draft Convention on Investment Abroad (1959), 46
AES Summit
  reasonableness test, 101–102
Amended Power Purchase Agreements (APPAs), 141
Assessment of state's measure, 204
  AES Summit v. Hungary, 208
  alternative measures in achieving an objective, 210–211
  Electrabel v. Hungary, 208–209
  Glamis v. US, 207–208
  loss suffered by investor, 211–212
  Mamidoil v. Albania, 209
  non-discrimination principle, 212–213, 254–255
    discriminatory conduct, 214
    discriminatory treatment of foreign investor, 213
    Electrabel v. Hungary case, 214–215
    elements in defining discriminatory measure, 214
    foreign investor *vs.* national investor, 213
    liability of Czech Republic under FET standard, 214
  Philip Morris v. Uruguay, 209–210
  reasonableness, proportionality and prohibition of arbitrariness principles, 205–212, 218–220, 253–254
    alternative measures in achieving an objective, 210–211
    loss suffered by investor, 211–212
    state's measure and its objective, relationship between, 207–210
  transparency principle, 219–220, 255
    FET cases, 215–216
    Ioan Micula v. Romania, 216–217
    Parkerings v. Lithuania, 217
    Saluka v. Czech Republic, 216
Association Agreement, 128–129

B

Bilateral Investment Treaty (BIT)
  arbitration, 22
  goals, 20–21
  ICSID Convention, 21–22
  operative part, 21
  procedural rights of investors, 21–22
  scope of application, 21
BIT. *See* Bilateral Investment Treaty (BIT)

C

CETA. *See* Comprehensive Economic and Trade Agreement between Canada and the EU (CETA)
CETA Joint Committee, 71
CETA's joint interpretative instrument, 66
Committee on Services and Investment, 71
Comprehensive Economic and Trade Agreement between Canada and the EU (CETA)
  Article 8.10(1), 61
  Article 8.10(2), 61
  Article 8.10(3), 69–70
  Article 8.10(4), 62
Corporate Social Responsibility (CSR), 29, 42, 191, 273–274
CSR. *See* Corporate Social Responsibility (CSR)

D

Due diligence
  investor's conduct, 250
    Antin v. Spain, 165
    Biwater v. Tanzania, 163
    countervailing factors, 163
    Frontier v. Czech Republic, 163–164
    Isolux v. Spain, 164
    legitimate expectations, 166
    Mamidoil v. Albania, 164

E

Economic and sociopolitical circumstances in host state, 162, 169–170, 248–250
  economic and financial crisis
    Argentina, 154–157
    circumstances of, 154, 155
    CMS v. Argentina, 156–157
    Emergency Law, 155
    FET standard, 155–156
    freezing of tariffs since 2002, 155
    pesification of the utility tariffs, 154–155
  electricity tariff deficit in renewable energy sector, economic challenge of, 158–162
  transition of former socialist countries, 157–158
ECT. *See* Energy Charter Treaty (ECT)
Energy Charter Treaty (ECT), 19–20
  Article 10(1), 131, 146, 148–150, 161
  FET standard, 161–162
  Mamidoil v. Albania case, 179
  renewable energy decisions under, 170
EU-Singapore FTA
  fundamental breach of due process, 62
EU-Vietnam FTA, 62

F

Fair and equitable treatment (FET)
  deference, 102–103
  development and interpretation of standard by international arbitral tribunals, 243–245
    general principles of law (*see* subhead: general principles of law)
    general rules of treaty interpretation (*see* subhead: general rules of treaty interpretation)
    supplementary and subsidiary means of interpretation (*see* subhead: supplementary and subsidiary means of interpretation)
  elements of FET standard for codification in new generation of IIAs, 270–271
    criteria for assessment of legitimacy of investor's expectations, 272–275

reasonableness and proportionality, principles of, 271-272
embodiment of concept of justice and rule of law, 8–9
general principles of law, 98–99, 244
deference and margin of appreciation, 102-103
proportionality and reasonableness, 99–102
general rule of treaty interpretation, standard interpretation under, 244
context of treaty, 78–81
object and purpose of treaty, 81–84
ordinary meaning of treaty, 78
subsequent agreement and subsequent practice, 84–86
VCLT, 75–77
growth of investment decisions, 75
interpretation and application of FET standard
Article 31 of VCLT, 96
Article 32 of VCLT, 96–97
jurisprudence in new generation of IIAs
balance between state's right to regulate and investor protection, 268–270
codification of FET investment, 256–268
legal research on
approaches in analysis of the FET standard, 6–7
case law approach, 9–10
embodiment of concept of justice and rule of law, 8–9
right to regulate and investment treaties, 11–12
state's right to regulate, 7
synthesis of literature, 12–16
legitimacy, issue of, 68
margin of appreciation doctrine, 103
methodology, 16–18
proportionality test
function of, 99
stages, 99–100
reasonableness test
AES Summit, 101–102
reasonableness test in international investment law, 101
legitimate expectations, 102
reasonable measure defined, 102
state obligations towards investor under FET standard, 256–257, 260
non-discrimination, principle of, 259
prohibition of arbitrariness, 258–259
transparency principle, 259–260
state's right to regulate, and, 1–5
complexities surrounding FET standard, 5
FET standard provisions, 2–4
IIA, 4
legal literature, in, 6–16
state's right to regulate and investor protection, balance between
investment decisions, 268–269
legitimate expectations of investor, protection of, 270
supplementary and subsidiary means of interpretation
interpretation and application of FET standard, 96–98, 245
legitimate expectations concept, 94–96, 98
national law, reliance on, 94–96
FET. *See* Fair and equitable treatment (FET)
Framework of Conditions of the Association Agreement. *See* Association Agreement
FTC Notes, 68–69

G

General regulatory framework, 168–169
claims based on expectation of stability
AES Summit v. Hungary, 141–142
investment process, 140–142
Occidental v. Ecuador, 142
Saluka v. Czech Republic, 142
element of stability of, 247–248
FET standard, 248
investor's claim based on the instability, 247–248
expectations concerning stability of, 151–152
investments due to transformation, impact level on
breach of legitimate expectations, 143
foreign investor, 143–144
notion of creeping expropriation, 144
transformation manner by host state
Blusun v. Italy, 147, 149–150
Charanne v. Spain, 147
Eiser v. Spain and *Antin Infrastructure v. Spain,* 148–149
financial and economic principles, 145
incentives for investors, 146–147
investors' claim of legal instability, assessment of, 150–151
Isolux v. Spain, 149
Parkerings v. Lithuania, 144
PSEG v. Turkey, 145–146
renewable energy sector cases, 146–151
Total v. Argentina, 144–145
Government Emergency Ordinance No. 104 (GEO 104), 176

H

Havana Charter for the Establishment of an International Trade Organization (1948), 46

I

IIAs. *See* International investment agreements (IIAs)
International Covenant on Economic, Social and Cultural Rights (ICESCR), 39
International economic law, 1 84, 2, 14, 25, 26, 40, 95, 98, 100, 103, 199, 207, 211, 213, 255
International investment agreements (IIAs)
additional agreement of parties on interpretation of FET standard
decisions of a treaty organ, 67–71
joint interpretative instrument clarifying intent of the treaty parties, 66–67
BITs and regional treaties, 59–60
categories of FET standard provision, 48–51
additional agreement of parties on interpretation of FET standard, 66–71
preamble providing reference to FET standard, 64–66
qualified with additional content, 59–64
unqualified treaty standard, as, 51–52
unwritten international law, reference to norm of, 52–59
CETA, 61–63
denial of justice principle, 60

ECT, 19–20
EU agreements, 62–64
France-Colombia BIT (2014), 63–64
Havana Charter, 46
ISDS, 23–24
OECD Draft Convention, 46–47
TTIP, 62
International investment law
right to regulate, 238–240
characteristics of right to regulate, 238–239
public interest in IIAs, 239–240
sovereignty, 238
right to regulate defined, 37
International minimum standard
treatment of aliens under customary international law
Article 3 of the UK-Mexico BIT, 56
NAFTA FTC Notes, 54–55
Neer standard, 53–54
Investment Policy Framework for Sustainable Development (IPFSD), 27
Investor's conduct
due diligence and risk assessment, 250
Antin v. Spain, 165
Biwater v. Tanzania, 163
countervailing factors, 163
Frontier v. Czech Republic, 163–164
Isolux v. Spain, 164
legitimate expectations, 166
Mamidoil v. Albania, 164
Investor-state dispute settlement (ISDS), 21, 23–24, 44, 50
IPFSD, 27
ISDS, 21, 23–24, 44, 50

L

Legitimacy
legitimate expectations of investor (*see* Legitimate expectations of investor)
state's objectives, of, 174, 232–234, 251–253
AES Summit v. Hungary, 177–178
Blusun v. Italy, 179–180
duty-free shops at airports, 176
EDF v. Romania, 176
Electrabel v. Hungary case, 178–179
feed-in tariffs for renewable energy producers, 179–180
Mamidoil v. Albania case, 179
PPA, termination of, 178–179
privatisation of the Czech banking system, 175–176
project relocation for environmental and socio-economic reasons, 179
regulatory prices for electricity, 177–178
Saluka v. Czech Republic, 175–176
Legitimate expectations of investor
Association Agreement, 128–129
breach of legitimate expectations, 131
competence of state authority
Crystallex v. Venezuela, 125–126
Metalclad v. Mexico, 124–125
content of state's representation
Glamis v. United States, 128
Mamidoil v. Albania, 129–130
Masdar Solar v. Spain, 130–131
Venezuela Holding v. Venezuela, 128–129
contractual commitments, specific representations from
breaches of agreement, 134–135
domestic law of host state, 134–135
Duke Energy v. Ecuador, 136
Glamis v. US, 137–138
host state and investor, contract between, 134
investment jurisprudence, 135
ordinary contractual breaches, 134
Parkerings v. Lithuania, 136–137
violation of contract under customary international law, 134

designation of investor in state's representations
- *Charanne v. Spain*, 133
- *El Paso v. Argentina*, 132–133
- *Philip Morris v. Uruguay*, 133–134
- *Total v. Argentina*, 133

FET investment decisions, in
- *CME v. Czech Republic* (2001), 116, 118–119
- *Tecmed v. Mexico* (2003), 116–117, 119–123

formulation of scope of, 262–263

general regulatory framework, 140–142
- claims based on expectation of stability, 140–142
- expectations concerning stability of, 151–152
- investments due to transformation, impact level on, 143–144
- role of stability of, 263–265
- transformation manner by host state, 144–151

legal force
- content, 128–131
- legal form, 126–128
- wording, 131–132

legal form
- *Continental v. Argentina* case, 127
- *Glamis v. United States*, 127
- *PSEG v. Turkey*, 126–127
- *Venezuela Holding v. Venezuela*, 127–128

reasonableness test, 102

specific representations made by host state, 123–124, 167–168
- competence of state authority, 124–126
- contractual commitments, specific representations from, 134–138
- definition of specific representations, 138–139
- designation of investor in state's representations, 132–134
- legal force, 126–132

state's right to regulate and, 113–116
- *CME v. Czech Republic* (2001), 116, 118–119
- general regulatory framework, 140–152
- host state, economic and sociopolitical circumstances in, 152–162
- investor's conduct (*see* Investor's conduct)
- representations made by host state, 123–139
- *Tecmed v. Mexico* (2003), 116–117, 119–123

tribunals' assessment of, 115–116

wording of representations
- *Crystallex v. Venezuela*, 131–132
- *Glamis v. US*, 131
- *Mamidoil v. Albania*, 132

M

Margin of appreciation doctrine, 103

Model BIT
- preparatory work of the treaty and the circumstances of its conclusion, 87–88

N

NAFTA
- Article 1131(2), 86
- CETA, and, 71

National law
- *ADF Group v. US*, 222–223
- criteria for violation of FET standard by breaching national law
  - *Bilcon v. Canada*, 226–228
  - *GAMI v. Mexico*, 224–226
  - *Lemire v. Ukraine*, 228–230
- legality of a state's conduct, 230–231, 236
- legality of state's measure l, 255, 267–268
- *Saluka v. Czech Republic*, 221–222

Thunderbird v. Mexico, 223–224
tribunals' assessment of legality of state's measure, 220–221

O

OECD Draft Convention on the Protection of Foreign Property (1967), 46

P

Power Purchase Agreement (PPA), 178–179
Proportionality *stricto sensu* test, 206
Public interest
legal conditions under which states may regulate in
lawfulness of state's measure, conditions focusing, 251–255
legitimacy of investor's expectations, 246–250
right to regulate and, 266–267

R

Right to regulate, 24–25
academic literature, in
applications and implications of right to regulate, 38–39
human rights, 39
legal research, 39
public interest, 38
The Right to Regulate in International Investment Law, right to regulate defined under, 37
sources, 38
Article 20(2) of SADC Model BIT, 41
conditions for lawfully exercising the state's right to regulate, 173–174, 232
assessment of state's measure, 205–212
host state's objectives, 200–204
national law, legality of state's measure under, 220–231
objective of state's measure, 174–200
consequences resulting from exercise of right to regulate, 42–43
definitions
Mouyal, by, 40
FET and State's right to regulate, 1-5
FET investment cases, 34–36
public health, 36–37
IIAS' FET standard provisions in connection with
categories of FET standard provisions, 240, 243
minimum standard of treatment of aliens under customary international law, 241–242
old generation of treaties, 240–241
treaty drafting, emerging trend in, 242–243
IIAs, in, 26–27
BIT between the US and Uruguay, 29–30
Canada-Peru BIT (2006), 27
CETA, 32–34
CSR provision, 29
exceptions, 27–28
foreign direct investment, 31–32
indirect expropriation clause, 28–29
SADC Model BIT, 30–31
international investment law, in, 238–240
characteristics of right to regulate, 238–239
public interest in IIAs, 239–240
sovereignty, 238
legal basis, 25–26
legal conditions identified by tribunals
arbitral interpretations on FET standard, 108–109
content of state's measure, 110
FET claims, 108

legality of measure under national law, 110–111
state's measure, objective of, 110
state's right to regulate *vs.* investor's right to receive FET, 108
legitimate expectations of investor (*see* Legitimate expectations of investor)
objective of state's measure
environment, human rights and public health, protection of, 180–195
illegitimacy, 195–200
legitimacy, 174–180
obligation to pay compensation, 43
public interest, and, 266–267
public interest/legitimate policy objectives in IIAs, 41–42
state's obligations under international law, 41

S

South African Development Community (SADC) Model Bilateral Investment Treaty Template of 2012, 30–31
State objectives, 234–236
environment, human rights and public health, protection of, 180–181
Apotex v. US (protection of public health), 193
assessment of state's objectives by tribunals in Argentinian water cases, 187–191
AWG v. Argentina; Impregilo v. Argentina, Azurix v. Argentina; Urbaser v. Argentina (right to have access to water), 184–187
Chemtura v. Canada (protection of public health and environment), 192–193
Glamis v. US (human rights of indigenous people), 183–184
Metalclad v. Mexico (an environmental regulation concerning hazardous waste), 181–183
Philip Morris v. Uruguay (protection of public health in regulating tobacco control), 193–195
host state's objectives
legitimacy of state's objective, elements pertinent to assess, 201–202
Philip Morris case, 202, 204
Urbaser v. Argentina (application of human right to water), 203–204
illegitimacy
Azurix v. Argentina (refusal to raise water tariffs), 197
*Gold Reserve v. Venezuela (*mine and copper investments in Venezuela*)*, 197–200
Tecmed v. Mexico, 195–197
legitimacy (*see* Legitimacy)
Subsequent agreement
defined, 84–85
Subsequent practice
defined, 84–85
Suitability test, 205

U

UK-Argentina BIT
Promotion and Protection of Investment (Article 2), 80
United Nations Commission for International Trade Law (UNCITRAL), 22
Unwritten international law
IIAs in which FET standard provisions include reference to

international minimum standard of treatment of aliens under customary international law, 52–57
principles of international law, 58–59

V

VCLT. *See* Vienna Convention of the Law of the Treaties (VCLT)
Vienna Convention of the Law of the Treaties (VCLT), 66
Article 31, 96
Article 31(3), 84
Article 32, 76, 96–97
preparatory work of the treaty and the circumstances of its conclusion, 87–88
rules of treaty interpretation in
object and purpose of agreement, 75–76
objective approach, 75
subjective approach, 75

W

World Bank
IIAs, 23

1. Moshe Hirsch, *The Arbitration Mechanism of the International Center for the Settlement of Investment Disputes,* 1993 (ISBN 07-923-1993-1).
2. Aida B. Avanessian, *Iran-United States Claims Tribunal in Action,* 1993 (ISBN 18-533-3902-4).
3. Isaak I. Dore, *The UNCITRAL Framework for Arbitration in Contemporary Perspective,* 1993 (ISBN 18-533-3573-8).
4. Vesna Lazić, *Insolvency Proceedings and Commercial Arbitration,* 1998 (ISBN 90-411-1115-8).
5. Joachim Frick, *Arbitration in Complex International Contracts,* 2001 (ISBN 90-411-1662-1).
6. Katherine Lynch, *The Forces of Economic Globalization: Challenges to the Regime of International Commercial Arbitration,* 2003 (ISBN 90-411-1994-9).
7. Christoph Liebscher, *The Healthy Award: Challenge in International Commercial Arbitration,* 2003 (ISBN 90-411-2011-4).
8. Hamid G. Gharavi, *The International Effectiveness of the Annulment of an Arbitral Award,* 2003 (ISBN 90-411-1717-2).
9. Abdulhay Sayed, *Corruption in International Trade and Commercial Arbitration,* 2004 (ISBN 90-411-2236-2).
10. Gabrielle Kaufmann-Kohler & Thomas Schultz, *Online Dispute Resolution: Challenges for Contemporary Justice,* 2004 (ISBN 90-411-2318-0).
11. Christopher R. Drahozal & Richard W. Naimark (eds), *Towards a Science of International Arbitration: Collected Empirical Research,* 2005 (ISBN 90-411-2322-9).
12. Ali Yeşilirmak, *Provisional Measures in International Commercial Arbitration,* 2005 (ISBN 90-411-2353-9).
13. Christian Bühring-Uhle, *Arbitration and Mediation in International Business,* second revised edition, 2006 (ISBN 978-9-041-12256-8).
14. Bernard Hanotiau, *Complex Arbitrations: Multiparty, Multicontract, Multiissue and Class Actions,* 2006 (ISBN 978-9-041-12442-5).
15. Loukas A. Mistelis & Julian D.M. Lew (eds), *Pervasive Problems in International Arbitration,* 2006 (ISBN 978-9-041-12450-0).
16. Julian D.M. Lew & Loukas A. Mistelis (eds), *Arbitration Insights – Twenty Years of the Annual Lecture of the School of International Arbitration, Sponsored by Freshfields Bruckhaus Deringer,* 2006 (ISBN 978-9-041-12606-1).
17. Mark Kantor, *Valuation for Arbitration: Compensation Standards, Valuation Methods and Expert Evidence,* 2008 (ISBN 978-9-041-12735-8).
18. Christoph Brunner, *Force Majeure and Hardship under General Contract Principles: Exemption for Non-Performance in International Arbitration,* 2009 (ISBN 978-90-411-2792-1).

19. Loukas A. Mistelis & Stavros L. Brekoulakis (eds), *Arbitrability: International & Comparative Perspectives*, 2009 (ISBN 978-90-411-2730-3).
20. Sam Luttrell, *Bias Challenges in International Commercial Arbitration: The Need for a 'Real Danger' Test*, 2009 (ISBN 978-90-411-3191-1).
21. Monique Sasson, *Substantive Law in Investment Treaty Arbitration: The Unsettled Relationship Between International Law and Municipal Law*, Second Edition, 2017 (ISBN 978-90-411-6103-1).
22. Ileana M. Smeureanu, *Confidentiality in International Commercial Arbitration*, 2011 (ISBN 978-90-411-3226-0).
23. Won Kidane, *China-Africa Dispute Settlement: The Law, Economics and Culture of Arbitration*, 2011 (ISBN 978-90-411-3674-9).
24. Karel Daele, *Challenge and Disqualification of Arbitrators in International Arbitration*, 2012 (ISBN 978-90-411-3799-9).
25. Crina Baltag, *The Energy Charter Treaty: The Notion of Investor*, 2012 (ISBN 978-90-411-3428-8).
26. Alexandra Diehl, *The Core Standard of International Investment Protection: Fair and Equitable Treatment*, 2012 (ISBN 978-90-411-3869-9).
27. Manuel Indlekofer, *International Arbitration and the Permanent Court of Arbitration*, 2013 (ISBN 978-90-411-4766-0).
28. Günther J. Horvath & Stephan Wilske (eds), *Guerrilla Tactics in International Arbitration*, 2013 (ISBN 978-90-411-4002-9).
29. Albert Badia, *Piercing the Veil of State Enterprises in International Arbitration*, 2014 (ISBN 978-90-411-5162-9).
30. Nadja Erk, *Parallel Proceedings in International Arbitration: A Comparative European Perspective*, 2014 (ISBN 978-90-411-5264-0).
31. Simon Vorburger, *International Arbitration and Cross-Border Insolvency: Comparative Perspectives*, 2014 (ISBN 978-90-411-5419-4).
32. Ahmad Ali Ghouri, *Interaction and Conflict of Treaties in Investment Arbitration*, 2015 (ISBN 978-90-411-5417-0).
33. Reto Marghitola, *Document Production in International Arbitration*, 2015 (ISBN 978-90-411-5159-9).
34. Alfonso Gómez-Acebo, *Party-Appointed Arbitrators in International Commercial Arbitration*, 2016 (ISBN 978-90-411-6671-5).
35. Jonas von Goeler, *Third-Party Funding in International Arbitration and Its Impact on Procedure*, 2016 (ISBN 978-90-411-5015-8).
36. Dean Lewis, *The Interpretation and Uniformity of the UNCITRAL Model Law on International Commercial Arbitration: Focusing on Australia, Hong Kong and Singapore*, 2016 (ISBN 978-90-411-6700-2).
37. Stavros Brekoulakis, Julian D.M. Lew & Loukas Mistelis (eds), *The Evolution and Future of International Arbitration*, 2016 (ISBN 978-90-411-7004-0).
38. Rémy Gerbay, *The Functions of Arbitral Institutions*, 2016 (ISBN 978-90-411-6217-5).

39. Maximilian Clasmeier, *Arbitral Awards as Investments: Treaty Interpretation and the Dynamics of International Investment Law*, 2017 (ISBN 978-90-411-8357-6).
40. Tony Cole (ed.), *The Roles of Psychology in International Arbitration*, 2017 (ISBN 978-90-411-5921-2).
41. Pietro Ferrario, *The Adaptation of Long-Term Gas Sale Agreements by Arbitrators*, 2017 (ISBN 978-90-411-8232-6).
42. Jacob B. van de Velden, *Finality in Litigation: The Law and Practice of Preclusion – Res Judicata (Merger and Estoppel), Abuse of Process and Recognition of Foreign Judgments*, 2017 (ISBN 978-90-411-8342-2).
43. Dolores Bentolila, *Arbitrators as Lawmakers*, 2017 (ISBN 978-90-411-8354-5).
44. Giacomo Marchisio, *The Notion of Award in International Commercial Arbitration: A Comparative Analysis of French Law, English Law, and the UNCITRAL Model Law*, 2017 (ISBN 978-90-411-8391-0).
45. Csaba Kovács, *Attribution in International Investment Law*, 2018 (ISBN 978-90-411-9675-0).
46. Mary Mitsi, *The Decision-Making Process of Investor-State Arbitration Tribunals*, 2019 (ISBN 978-90-411-9600-2).
47. Ahmet Cemil Yıldırım, *Interpretation of Contracts in Comparative and Uniform Law*, 2019 (ISBN 978-94-035-1130-6).
48. Beata Gessel-Kalinowska vel Kalisz, *The Legal, Real and Converged Interest in Declaratory Relief*, 2019 (ISBN 978-94-035-1244-0).
49. Maximilian Pika, *Third-Party Effects of Arbitral Awards: Res Judicata Against Privies, Non-mutual Preclusion and Factual Effects*, 2019 (ISBN 978-94-035-1273-0).
50. Yulia Levashova, *The Right of States to Regulate in International Investment Law: The Search for Balance Between Public Interest and Fair and Equitable Treatment*, 2019 (ISBN 978-94-035-0931-0).

www.ingramcontent.com/pod-product-compliance
Lightning Source LLC
LaVergne TN
LVHW020001031026
849161LV00023B/793